MARJORIE HOPE NICOLSON was Dean of Smith College from 1929 to 1941, and from then until her retirement in 1962, she was chairman of the Graduate English Department at Columbia University. She holds many degrees, among them a Ph.D. from Yale University, a D.Litt. from Mount Holyoke, and an LL.D. from Goucher College. A former vice-president and president of the united chapters of Phi Beta Kappa, she was also editor of *The American Scholar* and of the *Journal of the History of Ideas.*

Besides the present volume, Professor Nicolson's published works include: *The Conway Letters* (1930); *The Microscope and the English Imagination* (1935); *Newton Demands the Muse* (1946), which was awarded the Crawshay Prize for English Literature by the British Academy in 1947; *Voyages to the Moon* (1948), and *The Breaking of the Circle* (1950).

Mountain Gloom and Mountain Glory:

The Development of the Aesthetics of the Infinite

By MARJORIE HOPE NICOLSON

The Norton Library
W · W · NORTON & COMPANY · INC ·
NEW YORK

To

AILEEN WARD

and

To the Memory of

VICTORIA SCHRAGER

Preface

IN a way this volume had its inception as long ago as the academic year 1939-1940. I had become interested in the passages in *The Sacred Theory of the Earth* in which Thomas Burnet implied an apparently paradoxical attitude toward mountains, combining violent disparagement of the ugliest objects in Nature with an almost lyrical rhapsody on the exalted emotions he had experienced among the Alps. Basil Willey's *Eighteenth Century Background*, which called the attention of literary students to the importance of the "Burnet controversy," had not yet appeared. I had first met Burnet in Cecil Moore's early article "The Return to Nature in English Poetry of the Eighteenth Century." I knew Katharine Brownell Collier's *Cosmogonies of Our Fathers*, which treated some of Burnet's theological and scientific ideas, and had seen the brief but illuminating article "Grottoes, Geology, and the Gothic Revival," which Robert A. Aubin developed in his *Topographical Poetry in XVIII-Century England*. Important and interesting though these various studies were, they did not explain what seemed to me a basic problem in the history of taste: Why did mountain attitudes change so spectacularly in England?

When seventeenth-century poets described mountains—the majority did not—they vacillated between lip service to classical epithets such as "heaven-kissing" or "star-touching" and condemnation of the "warts, wens, blisters, imposthumes" that mar the face of Nature. On the other hand, eighteenth-century poets went out of their way to include mountains in their descriptive poetry, introducing long and exhaustive passages showing that mountain description had become an important part of landscape poetry. In the Romantic period, as anyone knows, mountains were not only central to descriptive poetry but almost as sacred as Sinai to the patriarchs. Burnet's ambivalence in the 1680's seemed symptomatic of a change in English taste. But how and why?

This was the question that I put to Aileen Ward, a senior at Smith College, when I suggested that she use as a point of departure for her Special Honors thesis the Burnet passages. Neither of us realized what a profound and difficult problem it was to prove to both of us for several years. When I remember that Special Honors theses at Smith College were written in six weeks, I am still amazed that any undergraduate—even so excellent and original a student as Aileen Ward—could have accomplished what she did. Her essay was called "The Lord's Controversy: A Study of the Changing Attitudes toward Mountains in the Seventeenth Century as a Phase in Pre-Romantic Thought." Deposited in the Smith College Library, it became and has remained a standard reference used by members of the faculty and succeeding generations of Smith students. In an essay of 127 pages Miss Ward surveyed previous scholarship and criticism on the subject (as I have done somewhat more fully in the Introduction to this volume), analyzed several of the theological problems I have treated in my second chapter (for which I have borrowed her title, "The Lord's Controversy"), dealt with some of the materials I treat in Chapter Four, "The Geological Dilemma," and both in text and in an Appendix provided a much more complete summary of the replies to Burnet than was available in any book at that time. I am sure that many of her phrases and sentences recur in my own chapters. I know that she was the source of many of my ideas.

So illuminating did I find her study that I suggested that she and I collaborate on a more exhaustive treatment of this problem in the dynamics of taste—the phrase is hers—that interested us so much. When Miss Ward and I found ourselves together in New York in 1942, we started on such a collaboration. Since we were both persuaded that long-established theological positions must have been basic to the change in mountain attitudes, we spent hours and days with the *Patrologia Latina*, studying the exegeses of the Fathers on the first chapters of Genesis. Unfortunately for me, Miss Ward left New York for Cambridge. Her studies for the Ph.D. at Radcliffe led her into other fields than those we had plowed together—led her, indeed, back to her real love, Romanticism, from which I had temporarily diverted her. A member of the Vassar College faculty, she is at present using a well-deserved fellowship to complete a book on Keats.

Although I still continued my interest in the problem of the change in English taste toward mountains—and developed certain aspects of the present volume in my graduate courses at Columbia —I did not make any real attempt to complete the study Miss Ward and I had begun together. Yet, in a way, all my publications since 1940, with one exception, have been offshoots of this underlying interest. As I studied the descriptive poetry of the eighteenth century, I became increasingly aware of a decided difference in the handling of light and color by seventeenth- and eighteenth-century poets, with the result that I interrupted myself to write *Newton Demands the Muse*, because it seemed clear to me that an important aspect of the difference went back to the interest of eighteenth-century poets in Newton's *Opticks*.

In 1945 when President Edmund Ezra Day invited me to deliver the Messenger Lectures at Cornell University in 1948, I promised myself that I would finish the study of mountains upon which I had been working in a more or less desultory fashion. The Messenger Lectures, delivered at Cornell in April and May, 1948, were entitled "The Sublime in External Nature." On that occasion I used material now expanded in the first five chapters of the present work. But even at that time, I was aware that, although I had found answers to some of my questions, I had not found them all, nor had I gone far enough with various aspects of those I had treated.

Once more my study of changing mountain attitudes was laid aside—this time because of the tremendous pressure experienced by many graduate schools as an aftermath of the Second World War and the "G.I. Bill," which sent so many veterans, hungry and thirsty for reading, into graduate schools. Since Columbia believed—rightly, I am persuaded—that men and women who had spent several years in the armed forces had the right to the best graduate training we could give them, we set no arbitrary limits upon the number of veterans, with the result that for nearly ten years we have spent our time and energies upon the dissertations of our graduate students, rather than upon our own books and articles. It has been a rewarding period for them and for us. If it has delayed our own work, perhaps this lack has been repaid by what our students may contribute to the advancement of learning.

When I had an opportunity to return to the problems raised in this volume, I began to realize more fully than before that my attempt to discuss attitudes of two centuries of English literature toward "Nature" had led me to problems in intellectual history that could not and should not be treated in a single volume. Again, as in the case of the "Newton" material, I decided to isolate some aspects, which, while having an integral connection, might be treated separately. The result was the series of essays which I delivered as the Norman Wait Harris Lectures at Northwestern University, published in 1950 under the auspices of that University as *The Breaking of the Circle*. Because the problems I treat in these two works—different though they may seem—are integral parts of a single whole, there is inevitable overlapping between that volume and this, chiefly between *The Breaking of the Circle* and Chapter Three of the present study, dealing with the "New Philosophy."

The scope of my study has greatly widened since those days at Smith College when I easily suggested to Miss Ward that she solve a problem of the "dynamics of taste" in six weeks. Neither she nor I had foreknowledge that this subject would prove "A gulf profound as that Serbonian bog . . . Where armies whole have sunk." I am much more acutely aware than any of my critics can be of the serious limitations I have gradually imposed upon myself. At one time I had planned to do much more with landscape painting, in part because such critics as Elizabeth Manwaring in *Italian Landscape in Eighteenth Century England* and Christopher Hussey in *The Picturesque* found in Italian landscape painting the origin of the "new" attitude in England and in part because, if the change in literary taste was as fundamental as I have made it, the same "climate of opinion" should have affected the plastic arts. When I discovered, however, that Mr. and Mrs. Henry V. S. Ogden were engaged upon an extensive study of landscape painting in England, since published in 1955 as *English Taste in Landscape in the Seventeenth Century* (which they were good enough to allow me to read in a more expanded earlier version), I deliberately restricted myself to literary attitudes.

So far as limiting the subject to England is concerned, I am, of course, aware that changes in taste are seldom bounded by countries. Winds of doctrine blow across the English Channel in either direction. I have pointed out occasionally that the phenomena in England were not paralleled in France, though they may have been in Germany. Something of the sort that occurred in England occurred also in America, though whether as a result of parallel causes or of "influence" I must leave others to decide. Because life is short and knowledge (at least my own knowledge) finite, I have set myself artificial geographical limitations.

When this study was first begun, I planned to consider equally attitudes toward mountains and toward ocean—the two "grandest" phenomena of Nature known to man. I found, however, that there is comparatively little "ocean literature" in comparison with "mountain literature," for reasons that are obvious enough. Insofar as "ocean" attitudes can be isolated, there are parallels, though the English—an island people and a seafaring race—never seem to feel the same distaste for the sea as for the "hook-shouldered" hills. During the eighteenth century ocean came to share with mountains the "sublime." A majority of poets and prose writers would have agreed with Addison who wrote in *Spectator* 489:

Of all objects that I have ever seen, there is none which affects my imagination so much as the sea or ocean. I cannot see the heavings of this prodigious bulk of waters, even in a calm, without a very pleasing astonishment; but when it is worked up in a tempest, so that the horizon on every side is nothing but foaming billows and floating mountains, it is impossible to describe the agreeable horror that arises from such a prospect. A troubled ocean, to a man who sails upon it, is, I think, the biggest object that he can see in motion, and consequently gives the imagination one of the highest kinds of pleasure that can arise from greatness. . . . Such an object naturally raises in my thoughts the idea of an Almighty Being, and convinces me of his existence as much as a metaphysical demonstration.

I shall bring my *apologiae* to an end with one final remark: If it occurs to a critic, as it well may, to quote the Horatian phrase that the mountains labored only to bring forth a mouse, may I say that I thought of it first—and often!

I can mention here only a few of the many who have helped me at various stages of this work. To my former student, Ernest Lee Tuveson, I owe a debt of gratitude for his generosity in giving up this subject, upon which he had made more than a beginning.

I like to remember that as a result of that sacrifice he produced his distinguished book, *Millennium and Utopia*. I thank him also for the phrase "the Aesthetics of the Infinite," which was his before it was mine. Three of my Columbia colleagues, Professors James L. Clifford, Jerome H. Buckley, and Gilbert Highet, have read some sections of my manuscript and made suggestions. My former colleague, Professor Pierre Garai, assisted me greatly in matters of research. I remember with pleasure the aid and courtesy I found in various libraries, particularly the Huntington Library, the New York Public Library, and those of the Union Theological Seminary and the Jewish Theological Seminary.

As this study really began at Smith College, it is fitting that it should have been completed there. In the spring of 1957, I was invited to give the Vanderbilt Lectures, which were entitled "Mountain Gloom and Mountain Glory." During my period of residence in Northampton, I experienced many courtesies, none more than those on the part of Miss Margaret Johnson, Librarian, and Miss Dorothy King, Curator of Rare Books. I was particularly delighted by Miss King's collection of Burnetiana, which I am sure has no duplicate in any other library. My greatest debt of all, however, as I have intended to indicate, is to Aileen Ward, who needs no explanation for my dual dedication.

M. H. N.

Columbia University
November 1958

Contents

Introduction

"Short Views We Take"

"TO me," said Byron's Childe Harold, "high mountains are a feeling." We comfortably agree, believing that the emotions we feel—or are supposed to feel—in the presence of grand Nature are universal and have been shared by men at all times. But high mountains were not "a feeling" to Virgil or Horace, to Dante, to Shakespeare or Milton. Today as the lordliest peaks are conquered and the ascent of Everest is front-page news, we take for granted that men have always climbed mountains for pleasure or triumph. Today when tours (by luxury train, private car, or auto bus) have become synonymous in thousands of minds with Mount Washington or Mount Hood, the Rockies, the High Sierras, Mont Blanc, the Jungfrau, the Alps or the Pyrenees, we assume that our feelings are the perennial ones of human beings. We do not ask whether they are sincere or to what extent they have been derived from poetry and novels we have read, landscape art we have seen, ways of thinking we have inherited. Like men of every age, we see in Nature what we have been taught to look for, we feel what we have been prepared to feel.

A century and a half ago, mountains became "temples of Nature built by the Almighty" and "natural cathedrals, or natural altars . . . with their clouds resting on them as the smoke of a continual sacrifice." A century and a half earlier, however, they had been "Nature's Shames and Ills" and "Warts, Wens, Blisters, Imposthumes" upon the otherwise fair face of Nature. For hundreds of years most men who climbed mountains had climbed them fearfully, grimly, resenting the necessity, only on rare occasions suggesting the slightest aesthetic gratification. Something has happened in human thinking to make Byron's phrase a literary commonplace.

Early in the nineteenth century Wordsworth wrote verses to a young lady who had made her first ascent of a mountain in the Lake District:

> Inmate of a mountain-dwelling,
> Thou hast clomb aloft, and gazed
> From the watch-tower of Helvellyn;
> Awed, delighted, and amazed! [1]

He described the sensations of the amateur climber, the "pantings of dismay" as the ascent became more precipitous, and the new emotions of the girl as she stood on the summit, looking down at the most extensive prospect she had ever seen, with "dwindled woods and meadows" and "a vast abyss" of clouds and shadows. Wordsworth concluded:

> Maiden! now take flight;—inherit
> Alps or Andes, they are thine. . . .
> For the power of hills is on thee,
> As was witnessed by thine eye
> Then, when old Helvellyn won thee
> To confess their majesty!

It is a slight poem, of no particular literary merit, yet the situation and emotions would not have occurred to a classical, me-

[1] "To —— on Her First Ascent to the Summit of Helvellyn." The lines were written at Rydal Mount and inscribed to a Miss Blackett who was visiting in the district.

dieval, or Renaissance [2] poet. In comparison with the Alps or Andes, Helvellyn is only a small mountain, but someone had climbed it, to feel as she had never felt before. As she stands on the summit, she is a symbol of something new that has entered into poetry and into human experience only in modern times—the power of hills.

During the first seventeen centuries of the Christian era, "Mountain Gloom" so clouded human eyes that never for a moment did poets see mountains in the full radiance to which our eyes have become accustomed. Within a century—indeed, within fifty years—all this was changed. The "Mountain Glory" dawned, then shone full splendor. Why? It was not merely a matter of literary language and conventions, though that played some part. It was a result of one of the most profound revolutions in thought that has ever occurred. Our search for an answer must sometimes lead us far from literature, with which we begin and to which we shall return. The change in human attitudes about mountains involved a reversal of many basic attitudes. What men see in Nature is a result of what they have been taught too see—lessons they have learned in school, doctrines they have heard in church, books they have read. They are conditioned most of all by what they mean by *Nature*, a word that has gathered around itself paradox and ambiguity ever since the fifth century B.C. Human response to mountains has been influenced by inherited conventions of literature and theology, but even more profoundly it has been motivated by man's conception of the world which he inhabits. Before the "Mountain Glory" could shine, men were forced to change radically their ideas of the structure of the earth on which they lived and the structure of the universe of which that earth is only a part. Theology, philosophy, geology, astronomy—basic and radical changes in all these occurred before the "Mountain Gloom" gave way to "Mountain Glory." The ascent of Hel-

[2] Throughout the Introduction, I use the term "Renaissance" loosely, applying it to English poetry down to Milton.

vellyn seemed arduous to Wordsworth's young novice. Our journey will lead us on a series of ascents of mountains that are part of a long range, each one of them a "Hill Difficulty." More than once we shall remember the lines in which Pope paraphrased Lucretius (lines that have been used as epigraphs for several of the chapters in this volume). Commonplace as the phrases had become before Pope gave them new brilliance, they were commonplaces only because, like many clichés, they were basically true:

> In fearless youth we tempt the heights of Art,
> While from the bounded level of our mind
> Short views we take, nor see the lengths behind;
> But more advanced, behold with strange surprise
> New distant scenes of endless science rise!
> So pleas'd at first the tow'ring Alps we try,
> Mount o'er the vales, and seem to tread the sky,
> Th' eternal snows appear already past,
> And the first clouds and mountains seem the last;
> But, those attained, we tremble to survey
> The growing labours of the lengthened way,
> Th' increasing prospect tires our wand'ring eyes,
> Hills peep o'er hills, and Alps on Alps arise.

I

In *Modern Painters* Ruskin imagined an intelligent contemporary, quite unfamiliar with modern art, entering a picture gallery for the first time.[3] Surprised at the number of landscapes showing mountains, lakes, clouds, and ruined castles or cathedrals, he might well say to himself: "There is something strange in the minds of these modern people! Nobody ever cared about blue mountains before, or tried to paint the broken stones of old walls." His mind went back to classical art: "Mountains!

[3] "Of the Novelty of Landscape," in *Modern Painters* (New York, 1856), vol. III, pt. IV, ch. xi, pp. 149–150. I am not treating in the Introduction the interest of Romantic poets in ruins, though I shall return to it later.

I remember none. The Greeks did not seem, as artists, to know that such things were in the world. They carved, or variously represented, men, and horses, and beasts, and birds, and all kinds of living creatures,—yes, even down to cuttle-fish; and trees, in a sort of way; but not so much as the outline of a mountain." He thought of medieval art: "Mountains! I remember none. Some careless and jagged arrangements of blue spires or spikes on the horizon, and, here and there, an attempt at representing an overhanging rock . . . but merely in order to divide the light behind some human figure. . . . Broken-down buildings! No; for the most part very complete and well-appointed buildings, if any; and never buildings at all, but to give place or explanation to some circumstance of human conduct." Human interest had all but disappeared from the pictures he saw on the walls of the gallery. Landscape had become engrossing to painters, and mountains, ravines, forests, and ruins the "exclusive subjects of reverent contemplation."

Whatever the limitations of Ruskin's treatment of classical and medieval art, there is little question that his imaginary observer, unfamiliar with the painting of Ruskin's period, would have agreed that there was indeed "something strange" in the contemporary obsession of artists with mountains and ruins. Ruskin himself devoted nearly half of *Modern Painters* to discussion of mountain attitudes in art and literature, past and present. Born in the flowering period of Romanticism, he had felt even in childhood the response of the Romanticists to the vast, the grand, the majestic in Nature. To him high mountains *were* a feeling. He wrote:

The first thing which I remember as an event in life, was being taken by my nurse to the brow of Friar's Crag on Derwentwater; the intense joy, mingled with awe, that I had in looking through the hollows in the mossy roots, over the crag, into the dark lake, has associated itself more or less with all twining roots of trees ever since. . . . In such journeyings, whenever they brought me near hills, and in all mountain ground and scenery, I had a pleasure, as early as I can remember, and continuing until I was eighteen or twenty, infinitely greater than any which has been since possible to me in anything . . . no more explicable or definable than that feeling of love itself. . . .

Although there was no definite religious sentiment mingled with it, there was a continual perception of Sanctity in the whole of nature, from the slightest thing to the vastest;—an instinctive awe, mixed with delight. . . . It would often make me shiver from head to foot with the joy and fear of it, when after being some time away from the hills, I first got to the shore of a mountain river.[4]

Indeed, mountains became Ruskin's "touchstones of taste," the measuring rod of excellence in art.[5] Many of the limitations in his treatment of classical and medieval art go back to what seemed to him an almost perverse refusal on the part of earlier artists to see the grandeur of the world about them. It is curious that he never used his own phrases, "Mountain Gloom" and "Mountain Glory," [6] chronologically to express the difference he felt between older painting and that of his century, since he constantly implied that "Mountain Gloom" had darkened the eyes of classical, medieval, and Renaissance artists, whereas "Mountain Glory" shone full splendor for the first time in the nineteenth century. The blindness of the painters had been shared, Ruskin felt, by poets, to whom he turned for proof as much as he turned to earlier artists.

[4] *Ibid.*, ch. xvii, pp. 295–298.

[5] He said (*ibid.*, ch. xvi, p. 263): "Connected with this love of liberty we find a singular manifestation of love of mountains, and see our painters traversing the wildest places of the globe in order to obtain subjects with craggy foregrounds and purple distances. Some few of them remain content with pollards and flat land; but these are always men of third-rate order; and the leading masters, while they do not reject the beauty of the low grounds, reserve their highest powers to paint Alpine peaks or Italian promontories."

[6] These are the heads of chapters xix and xx of book V, in which Ruskin was dealing with modern art. "Mountain Gloom" and "Mountain Glory" might exist at the same time in the same country. They were determined by social and economic factors.

Let us imagine another contemporary of Ruskin's, an intelligent man, familiar with classical, medieval, and Renaissance literature, but entirely unfamiliar with that of his own century, reading for the first time the longer descriptive poems of Byron, Shelley, Wordsworth.[7] His experience would have been similar to that of Ruskin's visitor to the art gallery, even though his discovery could not have been made at a glance. As he read *Childe Harold's Pilgrimage* and *Manfred*, *Prometheus Unbound* and *Alastor*, *The Prelude* and *The Excursion*, he too might go back to Greek literature. In spite of familiar allusions to Pelion, Ossa, Ida, and Olympus or an occasional lovely epithet for the "wine dark sea," he would recall few extended descriptions of mountains and ocean. If the reader were more familiar with Latin literature, he might recall such mountain adjectives as "inhospitable, barren, inaccessible, insolent." Virgil and Horace would give him little in the way of extended description of the wild, the rugged, and the grand in Nature. Medieval literature would afford him little more. Dante's Mountain of Purgatory, he would have realized, was as allegorical as Bunyan's Hill Difficulty and the Delectable Mountains in *Pilgrim's Progress*.

He might have been surprised to realize that Shakespeare, the idol of the Romanticists, did not share their interest in grand scenery. There was feeling for wild and elemental Nature in *King Lear*, but the mountain passages that would come to his mind were couched in old classical clichés:

LAERTES: Now pile your dust upon the quick and dead,
Till of this flat a mountain you have made
To o'ertop old Pelion or the skyish head
Of blue Olympus. . .
HAMLET: And if you prate of mountains, let them throw
Millions of acres on us, till our ground,

[7] In this brief survey I have confined myself to these three poets, because all of them wrote long descriptive poems in the eighteenth-century "excursion" tradition, all three described Alpine scenery, and all were self-conscious in their reactions toward such scenery.

> Singeing his pate against the burning zone,
> Make Ossa like a wart!

Our nineteenth-century reader would probably not have known well several of the seventeenth-century poets who are most familiar today. He would have remembered the "Mountains on whose barren breast The laboring clouds do often rest" of "L'Allegro" and known that this was not a realistic description of the country around Milton's Horton, but like many of his contemporaries, he probably felt that the characteristic Nature poetry of the seventeenth century was Milton's "Meadows trim with daisies pied, Shallow brooks and rivers wide." [8]

When he turned to the pages of the Romantic poets, he would have agreed with Ruskin's visitor that, so far as landscape was concerned, "there is something strange in the minds of these modern people." Even the most "classical" of them (all the poets he was reading were classically trained) were not classical at all when it came to landscape. *Prometheus Unbound* had a Greek source, but Aeschylus had not been obsessed by the vastness and wildness of Nature as was his modern descendant. The Greek drama had been laid in the Caucasus, but there was nothing in the original to correspond to the reiterated insistence of Shelley's settings: "A Ravine of icy Rocks in the Indian Caucasus. . . . A Forest, intermingled with Rocks and Caverns. . . . A Pinnacle of Rocks among Mountains. . . . The Cave of Demogorgon. . . . The top of a snowy Mountain. . . . The mouth of a great River. . . . A Forest. In the Background a Cave." The Greek dramatist had only implied what the Romantic poet developed in detail. In a single speech of Asia's, as she and Panthea look down from the mountains, Shelley included much that seemed "new" in the Romantic description of grand scenery:

---

[8] I am purposely generalizing in this section. These earlier attitudes will be discussed in more detail in Chapter One.

Fit throne for such a Power! Magnificent!
How glorious art thou, Earth! . . .
Beneath is a wide plain of billowy mist . . .
         Behold it, rolling on
Under the curdling winds, and islanding
The peak whereon we stand, midway around,
Encinctured by the dark and blooming forests
And wind-enchanted shapes of wandering mist;
And far on high the keen sky-cleaving mountains
From icy spires of sunlike radiance fling
The dawn, as lifted Ocean's dazzling spray
From some Atlantic islet scatter'd up,
Spangles the wind with lamp-like water-drops.
The vale is girdled with their walls, a howl
Of Cataracts from their thaw-cloven ravines
Satiates the listening wind, continuous, vast,
Awful as silence.[9]

Not only the descriptive details would have surprised our reader, but even more the characters—if characters they can be called: Voices of thunderbolts, earthquakes, whirlwinds, tempests, "the tongueless Caverns of the craggy hills," the "sound of whirlwind underground, Earthquakes and fire and mountains cloven,"

         from their loud abysses howling throng
         The genii of the storm, urging the rage
         Of whirlwind.

Shelley at least had classical precedent for placing his drama in the Caucasus, as unknown to him as it had been to Aeschylus. But Byron was not following a Greek dramatist in the settings of *Manfred:* "The Scene of the Drama is amongst the Higher Alps . . . The Mountains of the Jungfrau. Manfred alone upon

[9] *Prometheus Unbound*, II, iii, 11–36. In *Alastor* Shelley imagined

         At midnight
         The moon arose; and lo! the ethereal cliffs
         Of Caucasus, whose icy summits shone
         Among the stars like sunlight.

the cliffs. . . . A lower Valley in the Alps. A Cataract. . . .
The Summit of the Jungfrau." Here too are spirits of earth and
air and the voices of elemental forces: avalanche and glacier,
ocean and mountains, hurricane and lightning. The spirits sang
to Arimanes:

> Hail to our Master!—Prince of Earth and Air!
> Who walks the clouds and waters—in his hand
> The sceptre of the elements which tear
> Themselves to chaos at his high command!
> He breatheth—and a tempest shakes the sea;
> He speaketh—and the clouds reply in thunder;
> He gazeth—from his glance the sunbeams flee;
> He moveth—earthquakes rend the world asunder.
> Beneath his footsteps the volcanoes rise;
> His shadow is the Pestilence.

Whether in the Caucasus or the Alps, we feel the vastness of
Nature, its wild inaccessibility. On the summit of the Jungfrau,
the First Destiny speaks:

> The moon is rising broad, and round, and bright;
> And here on snows, where never human foot
> Of common mortal trod, we nightly tread
> And leave no traces; o'er the savage sea,
> The glassy ocean of the mountain ice,
> We skim its rugged breakers, which put on
> The aspect of a tumbling tempest's foam,
> Frozen in a moment—a dead whirlpool's image.
> And this most steep fantastic pinnacle,
> The fretwork of some earthquake—where the clouds
> Pause to repose themselves in passing by—
> Is sacred to our revels, or our vigils.[10]

The Alps of *Manfred* seem as remote and strange as the Caucasus of *Prometheus Unbound*, yet the Alps were real enough

[10] *Manfred*, II, iv, 371–380; II, iii, 299–310.

to the Romantic poets. Byron knew as well the mountains of
Greece, which were not the Pelion and Ossa long conventional
in English poetry:

> Once more upon the woody Apennine,
> The infant Alps, which—had I not before
> Gazed on their mightier parents, where the pine
> Sits on more shaggy summits, and where roar
> The thundering lauwine—might be worshipp'd more;
> But I have seen the soaring Jungfrau rear
> Her never-trodden snow, and seen the hoar
> Glaciers of bleak Mont Blanc both far and near,
> And in Chimari heard the thunder-hills of fear,
>
> Th' Acroceraunian mountains of old name;
> And on Parnassus seen the eagles fly
> Like spirits of the spot, as 'twere for fame,
> For still they soar'd unutterably high:
> I've looked on Ida with a Trojan's eye;
> Athos, Olympus, Aetna, Atlas made
> These hills seem things of lesser dignity.[11]

Shelley described Mont Blanc in "Lines Written in the Vale
of Chamouni":

> Far, far above, piercing the infinite sky,
> Mont Blanc appears, still, snowy and serene—
> Its subject mountains their unearthly forms
> Pile around it, ice and rock; broad vales between
> Of frozen floods, unfathomable deeps,
> Blue as the overhanging heavens that spread
> And wind among the accumulated steeps,
> A desert peopled by the storms alone,
> Save where the eagle brings some hunter's bone,
> And the wolf tracks her there. How hideously
> Its shapes are heap'd around! rude, bare, and high,

[11] *Childe Harold's Pilgrimage*, canto IV, stanzas lxxiii–lxxiv.

> Ghastly, and scarred, and riven.—Is this the scene
> Where the old Earthquake-demon taught her young
> Ruin? Were these their toys? or did a sea
> Of fire envelop once this silent snow?
> None can reply—all seems eternal now.[12]

Wordsworth, who called himself "an Islander by birth, a Mountaineer by habit," described this district, beginning with Mont Blanc—"From a bare ridge we also first beheld Unveiled the summit of Mont Blanc"—and continuing

> The wondrous Vale
> Of Chamouny stretched far below, and soon
> With its dumb cataracts and streams of ice,
> A motionless array of mighty waves,
> Five rivers broad and vast, made rich amends,
> And reconciled us to realities.[13]

Mountain climbers still read reminiscently the passage that follows, describing the separation of the young travelers from their companions, their belief that the highest ascent of all was still to come—"still we had hopes that pointed to the clouds"—and their emotions when, following directions of a peasant, they found that their "future course, all plain to sight, was downwards, with the current of the stream," and

> every word that from the peasant's lips
> Came in reply, translated by our feelings
> Ended in this—*that we had crossed the Alps.*

When our hypothetical reader turned to other passages of the three Romanticists, describing British rather than continental scenes, he would have found the same interest in grand Nature. Whether real or fancied, whether at home or abroad, such scenes, he would find, had produced an effect upon poetic imagination for which he had no parallel in his literary memories. One

---

[12] "Mount Blanc: Lines Written in the Vale of Chamouni," stanza iii.
[13] *The Prelude*, bk. VI, ll. 524 ff.

thing would have particularly surprised him: the insistence of many Romantic poets upon the influence of such scenery in childhood and youth,[14] a period in which earlier poets had shown almost no interest. Byron could treat the experience lightly in songs such as "Lochin Y Gair" or "When I Roved a Young Highlander," but in *Manfred* he developed seriously the effect of wild Nature upon a youthful personality:

> From my youth upwards
> My spirit walk'd not with the souls of men; . . .
> My joy was in the Wilderness, to breathe
> The difficult air of the iced mountain's top,
> Where the birds dare not build, nor insect's wing
> Flit o'er the herbless granite; or to plunge
> Into the torrent, and to roll along
> On the swift whirl of the new breaking wave
> Or river-stream, or ocean, in their flow.
> In these my early strength exulted.[15]

This, our reader would have found, was a persistent motif in Wordsworth, the subject of the early books of *The Prelude*, with many reminiscences of the experience in the later books and in shorter poems:

> And so I dare to hope,
> Though changed, no doubt, from what I was when first
> I came among these hills; when like a roe
> I bounded o'er the mountains, by the sides
> Of the deep rivers, and the lonely streams,
> Whenever Nature led; more like a man
> Flying from something that he dreads, than one
> Who sought the thing he loved. . . .

[14] Shelley differs in this respect from Byron, Wordsworth, and many of the Romanticists since, as Alfred North Whitehead said (*Science and the Modern World* [New York, 1926], p. 123): "What the hills were to the youth of Wordsworth, a chemical laboratory was to Shelley."

[15] *Manfred*, II, ii, 144 ff.

>   I cannot paint
> What then I was. The sounding cataract
> Haunted me like a passion; the tall rock,
> The mountain, and the deep and gloomy wood,
> Their colors and their forms, were then to me
> An appetite; a feeling and a love,
> That had no need of a remoter charm,
> By thought supplied, nor any interest
> Unborrowed from the eye.[16]

Whether discovered in childhood or maturity, mountains, crags, cataracts, lakes, rivers, and ocean had affected imagination to an extent never known among the classical, medieval, and Renaissance poets, none of whom had said, as in effect did nearly all the Romanticists:

> Are not the mountains, waves, and skies, a part
> Of me and of my soul, as I of them?
> Is not the love of these deep in my heart
> With a pure passion?
>
>   . . .
>
> Where rose the mountains, there to him were friends;
> Where roll'd the ocean, thereon was his home;
> Where a blue sky, and glowing clime, extends,
> He had the passion and the power to roam;
> The desert, forest, cavern, breaker's foam,
> Were unto him companionship; they spake
> A mutual language.[17]

What were the qualities of landscape that would have seemed "strange" to Ruskin's contemporary? They are all before us, even in these few passages dealing chiefly with Alpine scenery, and might be paralleled many times in Wordsworth, Shelley, Byron, and their contemporaries. Let us look more closely at a description in Shelley's *Alastor*, part of an extended passage in which the Poet travels through Nature:

[16] "Lines Composed a Few Miles above Tintern Abbey," ll. 65–83.
[17] *Childe Harold's Pilgrimage*, canto III, stanzas lxxv and xiii.

> On every side now rose
> Rocks, which, in unimaginable forms,
> Lifted their black and barren pinnacles
> In the light of evening, and, its precipice
> Obscuring the ravine, disclosed above,
> 'Mid toppling stones, black gulfs and yawning caves,
> Whose windings gave ten thousand various tongues
> To the loud stream. Lo! where the pass expands
> Its stony jaws, the abrupt mountain breaks
> And seems with its accumulated crags,
> To overhang the world; for wide expand
> Beneath the wan stars and descending moon
> Islanded seas, blue mountains, mighty streams,
> Dim tracts and vast, robed in the lustrous gloom
> Of leaden-colored even, and fiery hills
> Mingling their flames with twilight, on the verge
> Of the remote horizon.[18]

It is a vast and extensive canvas, in the foreground the abrupt mountain with its rocks, crags, and precipices, other mountains and hills stretching out to a background that includes streams and ocean until the eye reaches the verge of a remote horizon. One aspect of the foreground would immediately impress a classically trained reader—the interest, indeed the fierce pleasure, these poets felt in the irregularity of Nature, an asymmetry that violated all classical canons of regularity, symmetry, proportion. Here and elsewhere we are conscious of toppling rocks, black gulfs, yawning caves, crags "closed round with black and jagged arms," caverns, and rocks "rude and bare and high, ghastly, scarred and riven." The rough, jagged, monstrous stones that had once seemed the rubbish of the world have become an integral part of a savage or solemn Nature whose majesty is enhanced rather than marred by their presence and who seems to take as much delight in asymmetry and irregularity as she once felt in the limited, the restrained, the patterned.

[18] *Alastor*, ll. 543–559.

Especially striking is the magnitude of the new Nature, as the canvas stretches indefinitely, almost to infinity. It includes vast mountains and vaster mountain ranges; "islanded seas, blue mountains, mighty streams, dim tracts and vast"; "old woods and haunted springs, prophetic caves"; crawling glaciers, cataracts, waterfalls, whirlpools. All these may shine in sunlit radiance, or be lost in the obscurity of gloom. The landscape may be wild and savage; it may be magnificent and glorious. Sometimes we are conscious of elemental Nature, filled with sound and motion, with howls of thunder and earthquake, turbulent, fearful, exciting. Sometimes motion seems only to emphasize the essential stillness of Nature:

> the brook itself,
> Old as the hills that feed it from afar,
> Doth rather deepen than disturb the calm
> Where all things else are still and motionless.[19]

Immediately after the deafening roar of a Nature elemental in chaos and confusion, we may be suddenly aware of "a continuous vast, awful as silence." Always we are conscious of vastness. It seems natural to find such a statement as Shelley's in the Preface to *Prometheus Unbound:* "The poem was chiefly written upon the mountainous ruins of the Baths of Caracalla . . . upon its immense platforms and dizzy arches suspended in the air."

"Something strange" indeed has come into the minds of these modern people, something that has broken down idols of pattern, regularity, symmetry, restraint, proportion, and replaced them by ideals of diversity, variety, irregularity, most of all by ideals of indefiniteness and vastness, something that made these lines of Byron's characteristic of a modern taste in landscape scenery:

> Above me are the Alps,
> The palaces of Nature, whose vast walls

---

[19] Wordsworth, "Airey-Force Valley."

> Have pinnacled in clouds their snowy scalps,
> And throned Eternity in icy halls
> Of cold sublimity, where forms and falls
> The avalanche—the thunderbolt of snow!
> *All that expands the spirit, yet appals*
> Gather around these summits.[20]

II

It is surprising that critics have made so little effort to account for one of the most curious paradoxes in the history of literature: that mountains, upon which modern poets have lavished their most extravagant rhetoric, were for centuries described—when they were described at all—at best in coventional and unexciting imagery, at worst in terms of distaste and repulsion. During the last century, various theories have been offered to account for a general shift in taste that occurred sometime during the eighteenth century, but there has been little attempt to explain this particular phenomenon.

One of the first critics to discuss the change in any detail was William Wordsworth in a long letter [21] addressed to the editor of the *Morning Post* in 1844 on the subject of a proposed Kendal and Windermere Railway, which would have cut through the Lake District. The *Morning Post* had published a sonnet of Wordsworth's written on October 12, 1844:

> Is there no nook of English ground secure
> From rash assault? . . .
> Plead for thy peace, thou beautiful romance
> Of nature; and, if human hearts be dead,
> Speak, passing winds; ye torrents, with your strong
> And constant voice, protest against the wrong.

In his letter Wordsworth discussed the taste of his own times for landscape. As he looked back over preceeding centuries,

[20] *Childe Harold's Pilgrimage*, canto III, stanza lxii. The italics are mine.
[21] The sonnet and letter are included as Appendix II in the fifth edition of Wordsworth's *Guide to the Lakes* (London, 1906), pp. 146 ff.

he could find little to correspond to what he and his generation took for granted. He wrote:

Elaborate gardening, with topiary works, were in high request, even among our remote ancestors, but the relish for choice and pictur- esque *scenery* . . . is quite of recent origin. Our earlier travellers— Ray, the naturalist, one of the first men of his age—Bishop Burnet, and others who had crossed the Alps, or lived some time in Switzer- land, are silent upon the sublimity and beauty of those regions; . . . The accomplished Evelyn, giving an account of his journey from Italy through the Alps, dilates upon the terrible, the melancholy, and the uncomfortable; but till he comes to the fruitful country in the neighborhood of Geneva, not a syllable of delight or praise. In the *Sacra Telluris Theoria* of the other Burnet there is a passage— omitted, however, in his own English translation of the work—in which he gives utterance to his sensations, when, from a particular spot he beheld a tract of the Alps rising before him on the one hand, and on the other the Mediterranean Sea spread beneath him. Noth- ing can be worthier of the magnificent appearances he describes than his language. In a noble strain also does the Poet Gray address, in a Latin Ode, the *Religio loci* at the Grande Chartreuse. But before his time, with the exception of the passage from Thomas Burnet just alluded to, there is not, I believe, a single English traveller whose published writings would disprove the assertion, that, where precipi- tous rocks and mountains are mentioned at all, they are spoken of as objects of dislike and fear, and not of admiration.

Wordsworth quoted "a shrewd and sensible woman" under whose roof he had lived for a time in his Keswick youth, who used to exclaim: "Bless me! folk are always talking about pros- pects; when I was young there was never sic a thing neamed." But although Wordsworth was quite aware of what had hap- pened, he offered no explanation for the radical change in taste that he found among his contemporaries.

Nor do we find much help by turning back to the literary historians of the late nineteenth century, in spite of the fact that they wrote so many volumes dealing with Nature and

Romanticism. This does not mean that they showed no interest in the problem of changing taste. Myra Reynolds devoted pages of *The Treatment of Nature in English Poetry* to the general subject, only to conclude that "the persistent ignoring of the grand and terrible is the most convincing proof for the prevailing distaste for wild scenery." [22] In spite of her real appreciation of James Thomson (in which she was in advance of most of her contemporaries), she made short work of him as a mountain poet. In so far as any of these critics found an explanation for the change in attitude toward grand scenery that culminated in Romanticism, they were content with a simple one: in 1739 Thomas Gray crossed the Alps, kept a journal, and wrote letters in which he used the adjectives "romantic" and "poetic." Edmund Gosse contrasted Horace Walpole's Alpine terror with Gray's ecstasy, expressed in a letter "that shows him to have been the first of the romantic lovers of Nature." [23] Thomas Perry insisted that Gray "was nearly a half a century in advance of most of his contemporaries" and included Addison among the many who disliked mountains.[24] William Lyon Phelps declared that Gray "was one of the first men in Europe who had any appreciation of wild and romantic scenery." [25] If there was dissent, it was not with the idea that change in taste is the result of the experience and influence of one man, but merely with the priority of one individual over another. Alfred Biese, J. C. Shairp, and Leslie Stephen nominated as other candidates

[22] Myra Reynolds, *The Treatment of Nature in English Poetry* (Chicago, 1907), p. 27; the first edition appeared in 1896.

[23] Edmund Gosse, *Gray* (New York, 1882), p. 32.

[24] Thomas Sergeant Perry, *English Literature of the Eighteenth Century* (New York, 1883), p. 393.

[25] William Lyon Phelps, *The Beginnings of English Romanticism in the Eighteenth Century* (Boston, 1893), pp. 166, 169. More recent scholars repeat the old tradition, for example, Cornelis De Haas, *Nature and the Country in English Poetry* (Amsterdam, 1928), p. 244, and Emile Legouis and Louis Cazamian, *A History of English Literature* (London, 1933), p. 866.

Rousseau, Collins, and Thomson.[26] The pioneer theory continued for many years, but no early critic raised a problem of the dynamics of taste: *why* did Gray or Collins or Thomson feel the grandeur of mountain scenery and earlier writers not?

These nineteenth-century historians, as one leafs them over today, seem to have been almost perverse in their refusal to appreciate the many Nature passages they aided so much in collecting. Yet they were all conscious of a new feeling for Nature which they believed had come about during their own century. "How abhorrent this sort of stuff is to the modern feeling about Nature," wrote J. C. Shairp,[27] as he turned away from Gray's descriptions. Henry A. Beers' distaste for what he considered the "coldness and spiritual deadness" of the earlier eighteenth century made him incapable of appreciating either the Nature attitudes or the religious thought of the period.[28] Myra Reynolds, after quoting dozens of appreciative passages about Nature from Addison, Parnell, Shenstone, Thomson, and others, concluded that the dominant characteristic of neoclassical poetry was "a lack of interest in Nature." "Nature" was inevitably associated in their minds with Romanticism. Landscape was somehow the private possession of the Lake Poets, as their clichés show. Wordsworth's Nature descriptions were written with the eye on the object. Pope's "Nature tame

[26] Alfred Biese, *The Development of the Feeling for Nature in the Middle Ages and Modern Times* (London, 1906), p. 261; J. C. Shairp, *On Poetic Interpretation of Nature* (Boston and New York, 1885), pp. 206–207; Leslie Stephen, *English Literature and Society in the Eighteenth Century* (London, 1904), p. 133.

[27] Shairp, *Poetic Interpretation*, p. 210.

[28] Henry A. Beers, *History of English Romanticism in the Eighteenth Century* (New York, 1898), p. 31. In justice to these nineteenth-century critics, it should be said that they occasionally referred in passing to a few of the other arts. Biese (pp. 230–231) mentioned English gardens and the vogue of Chinese art in a brief discussion of Shaftesbury. Discussing Gray's appreciation of natural scenery, Beers (p. 178) mentioned Gothic architecture. Leslie Stephen (p. 123) made passing reference to English appreciation of Italian painting, particularly that of Salvator Rosa.

and Nature methodized" was culled from books. The critics did not seem to notice that the pattern of such poems as *The Excursion, Alastor,* and *Childe Harold's Pilgrimage* had been established in the "excursion" poems of Mallet, Savage, and Thomson, that the details of the Romantic mise-en-scène—mountains, caverns, cataracts, ruins, hurricanes, storms, volcanoes, earthquakes—had been the stock in trade of eighteenth-century descriptive poets, or that the characteristic adjectives and epithets of the Romantic poets had long been familiar: dark, gloomy, still, awful, unfathomable, ghastly, rude; magnificent, majestic, grand; glorious; terror and delight, joy and exultation. If there was "something strange" in Romantic Nature description, it lay elsewhere than in pattern, scene, vocabulary.

At about the time of the First World War, a different approach began, based upon a broader interpretation of the difficult word *Nature*. Raymond Havens' "Romantic Aspects of the Age of Pope," [29] published in 1912, may seem old-fashioned to younger scholars today, but it was radical in its own time. Mr. Havens insisted that sincere affection for Nature was not the private possession of the Romanticists but had been a continuous factor in the tradition of English poetry. He dealt specifically with the mountain problem, showing that Gray's enthusiasm was not unique and quoting passages from Addison and Lady Mary Wortley Montagu, who had anticipated Gray by thirty years. Professor Cecil Moore's "Return to Nature in English Poetry of the Eighteenth Century," [30] published in 1917, remains classic, the first significant treatment of the mountain problem and a fundamental contribution to the study of the whole naturalistic movement in eighteenth-century literature.

From this time on, various implications entered into pre-

[29] In *Publications of the Modern Language Association*, XXVII (1912), 297–324.

[30] Originally published in *Studies in Philology*, XIV (1917), 243–291. The essay has been reprinted in a collected edition of Professor Moore's essays, *Backgrounds of English Literature, 1700–1760* (Minneapolis, 1953).

Romantic criticism that had been absent from earlier histories of literature. "Nature" ceased to be something vaguely thought of as landscape. Appreciation of natural scenery could not be dissociated from other aesthetic considerations, which in turn must be considered in the light of nonaesthetic problems. Changes in taste in one field accompany or influence changes in others. The modern critic has become increasingly aware of the complexity of his problem. Before he can discuss the treatment of "Nature" by a poet or painter, he must determine what he means by "Nature."

Older scholars remember the immediate effect of Arthur O. Lovejoy's articles [31] of the 1920's, discriminating among "the Romanticisms" and untangling the snarls that had enmeshed the concept of Nature as aesthetic norm. "Follow Nature" had been the watchword of the neoclassicists a century before it became the clarion call of the Romanticists, as it had been a rule of life to men hundreds of years before either of them. What did "Nature" mean to neoclassicists on the one hand, Romanticists on the other, that they were able to deduce from it an ethics and an aesthetics in radical opposition to each other and sometimes to themselves? Professor Lovejoy pointed out that three distinct literary movements—all called "Romantic"—had been based upon three radically different aesthetic attitudes in which three concepts of *Nature* operated. Basically, adherents agreed only insofar as each group employed the familiar antithesis of *Nature* versus *art*. In his essay "Nature as Aesthetic Norm," Professor Lovejoy showed how complicated the confusion had become by discriminating among more than twenty different, often antag-

[31] Arthur O. Lovejoy, "On the Discrimination of the Romanticisms," *P.M.L.A.*, XXXIX (1924), 229–253; "Nature as Aesthetic Norm," *Modern Language Notes*, XLII (1927), 444–450. Both articles have been republished in *Essays in the History of Ideas* (Baltimore, 1948). The concept of Nature was further developed in Lovejoy and Boas, *Primitivism and Related Ideas in Antiquity* (Baltimore, 1935), and by implication at least in *The Great Chain of Being* (Cambridge, Mass., 1936).

onistic, meanings of *Nature* current in aesthetics alone. When he later added sixty-six normative uses of *Nature* in politics, ethics, and metaphysics, he laid a new basis for critical analyses of a "return to Nature" in any field. Professor Lovejoy made us conscious of the danger of using loosely such words as *Nature* and *Romanticism*. He also made us realize the extent to which, ever since the fifth century B.C., the "appeal to Nature for standards" has been a process of man's reading into Nature what he wished to find—and reading it out again. *Nature* is a hard word today, but one whose complex implications we cannot avoid in any study of the dynamics of taste.

Even though all the important critics who have dealt with any aspect of the subject since the 1920's are aware that aesthetic changes are part of a larger whole, I shall isolate a group of essays and books that have treated specifically aesthetic aspects of the change in taste occurring sometime between 1660 and 1800 and resulting in the "something strange" Ruskin's visitor found in the interest of painters in external Nature.

Professor Lovejoy himself dealt with the problem in two essays, "The Gothic Revival and the Return to Nature" and "The Chinese Origin of a Romanticism." [32] In the first he considered the vogue for Gothic architecture first in connection with the growing primitivistic interest of the eighteenth century and then in connection with one of the new concepts of Nature as aesthetic norm, when men, revolting against the long "classical" emphasis upon regularity, proportion and restraint as criteria, began to justify irregularity over symmetry as an aesthetic principle. Interest in asymmetry, Professor Lovejoy believed, began with landscape gardening, when the "natural" garden began to triumph over the "artificial." It was later extended to literature. Professor Lovejoy continued to discuss the prin-

---

[32] The first appeared in *Modern Language Notes*, XLVIII (1932), 419–446, the second in *Journal of English and Germanic Philology*, XXXII (1933), 1–20. They are also republished in *Essays in the History of Ideas*.

ciple of irregularity in his article on *chinoiserie*, in which he dealt, among other matters, with Addison's interest in the supposed Chinese principle of asymmetry—"sharawagi"—and with Sir William Temple's praise of the picturesque irregularity of Chinese art in *The Gardens of Epicurus*, published in 1695, the first protest in England against classical symmetry.

The idea that one of the most striking differences between the neoclassical and the Romantic aesthetic lay in this growing feeling for the asymmetrical was developed more extensively by B. Sprague Allen in *Tides in English Taste*. Although the book was published later than Professor Lovejoy's articles, Mr. Allen had apparently reached his conclusions independently.[33] He wrote:

The history of art constitutes a most vivid, enlightening commentary on the history of literature. . . . As the forces, intellectual and emotional, that mold art also influence literature, they have in each period of culture imparted a common characteristic quality to such apparently divergent manifestations of the sense of beauty as poetry, textile design, ceramic decoration, and garden and house planning.

Mr. Allen illustrated his thesis with a wide variety of examples drawn from every phase of seventeenth- and eighteenth-century art. He discussed the divergence from a neoclassical aesthetic in *chinoiserie*, the English garden, the grotto fad, the picturesque, rococo, sentimentalism, Italian painting. The "reaction against classicism," he believed, "began, not in the first half of the eighteenth century, but in the seventeenth century upon the gradual establishment of Indian chintz and Chinese lacquer, porcelain, and wallpaper in popular favor. . . . Is it too much to say that Orientalism prepared the way for romanticism?" [34]

[33] B. Sprague Allen, *Tides in English Taste* (Cambridge, Mass., 1937), I, vii. The book was published posthumously. Since the Preface is dated 1932, Mr. Allen had not seen Professor Lovejoy's articles on the Gothic and *chinoiserie*.

[34] *Ibid.*, I, 256.

In the meantime Elizabeth Manwaring and Christopher Hussey[35] considered the increased pictorial quality in eighteenth-century poetry, a growing emphasis upon "the picturesque." Miss Manwaring may have taken her point of departure from Horace Walpole's Alpine letter: "Precipices, mountains, torrents, wolves, rumblings, Salvator Rosa!" The new attitude, Miss Manwaring felt, was the result of the growing vogue for Italian landscape painting among cultivated Englishmen who journeyed to Italy and the consequent importation into England of many examples of Italian art. Christopher Hussey developed some of the same arguments upon a broader basis:

The relation of all the arts to one another, through the pictorial appreciation of nature, was so close that poetry, painting, gardening, architecture and the art of travel may be said to have been fused into a single "art of landscape." The combination might be termed "The Picturesque." The picturesque phase through which each art passed, roughly between 1730 and 1830, was in each case a prelude to Romanticism. It appeared at a point when an art shifted its appeal from reason to the imagination.

An interregnum was necessary between neoclassicism and Romanticism, a period when men were learning to see. Visual qualities were emphasized. Imagination was learning to "feel through the eyes." So far as grand scenery was concerned, Mr. Hussey did not agree with Miss Manwaring that it was primarily the painted landscapes of Italy that produced the English interest in the picturesque, though he did feel that "the awakening of England to an appreciation of landscape was a direct result of the Grand Tour fashionable with the aristocracy after the isolation of the country from the rest of Europe, during the greater part of the seventeenth century," and that a new appraisal of mountains "was a test of how far the relish of grand

[35] Elizabeth Manwaring, *Italian Landscape in Eighteenth Century England* (New York, 1925); Christopher Hussey, *The Picturesque* (London and New York, 1927; the quotation will be found on p. 4).

landscape had overcome the natural distaste of danger and discomfort."

All these theories were important, and each of them contributed to a better understanding of modern attitudes toward external Nature. Yet neither individually nor as a group did these critics go far enough in attempting to solve basic problems of the dynamics of taste. The contention that after the Restoration more gentlemen crossed the Alps and saw Italian landscape painting is an advance over the pioneer theory, though some of the difficulties remain. Elizabethan and seventeenth-century gentlemen had traveled to the continent and crossed the Alps long before 1660, yet none had shown such stirring of the imagination before grand Nature as we find in the eighteenth century. Critics later than Mr. Hussey imply that the relish for mountain scenery was a result of the fact that, as the dangers of travel lessened, fear gave way to pleasure. But no matter how much roadways were improved in nonmountainous districts, how many more inns were built, mountain travel, as Gray's letters show,[36] was no safer in 1739, when Gray and Walpole crossed the Alps, than it had been when Thomas Coryat made the same journey in 1610. Walpole's terror, indeed, was very similar to Coryat's. There is, of course, a personal equation here, as true today as it was in the seventeenth century—the natural fear of a person who suffers from acrophobia, who, as we say in ordinary language, "has no head for heights." Yet "terror," in the eighteenth-century sense of the word, was an integral part of the new aesthetic experience of men who sought a new language to express their mingled feelings of joy and awe.

[36] Gray was as conscious of the dangers as was Walpole. He wrote to Richard West (Thomas Gray, *Works*, ed. by Edmund Gosse [New York, 1885], I, 43–46): "You have Death perpetually before your eyes. . . . The horrors were accompanied with too much danger to give one time to reflect upon their beauties." Gray's reactions to the Alps will be discussed later, as well as the question of the growing "safety" of mountain travel.

These critics made a marked advance over the nineteenth-century historians of literature, but they concerned themselves, in these particular books and articles, primarily with Nature as *aesthetic* norm. Although they considered more fully than earlier writers the interrelationship of the arts, they limited themselves to *arts*, insisting that changes in literary taste are results of changes in some other art—painting, landscape gardening, architecture. But why the change in the other arts?

The emphasis of these writers upon asymmetry is very important. As we have seen, delight in irregularity is one of the obvious elements in the descriptions of Byron, Shelley, and Wordsworth. Asymmetry was not, however, the quality of the "new" Nature that particularly roused the poets to rapture for "all that expands the spirit, yet appals." These emotional responses, they themselves declared, were to the mighty, the majestic, the mysterious aspects of Nature, to a sense of vastness and spaciousness never expressed—and apparently never felt—before the closing years of the seventeenth century. The discovery that makes the most profound difference between older and "modern" landscape was of what we now call the "Sublime" in Nature.

III

"When you are criticising the philosophy of an epoch," wrote Alfred North Whitehead, "do not chiefly direct your attention to those intellectual positions which its exponents feel it necessary explicity to defend. There will be some fundamental assumptions which adherents of all the variant systems within the epoch unconsciously presuppose. Such assumptions appear so obvious that people do not know what they are assuming because no other way of putting things has ever occurred to them." [37] We shall remember Whitehead's words as we seek the causes of the change in mountain attitudes that began to take place sometime in the late seventeenth century in England.

[37] Whitehead, *Science and the Modern World*, p. 71.

Various fundamental assumptions, accepted for generations, had to be broken down before new attitudes appeared. In 1611 John Donne, lamenting the corruption of microcosm, geocosm, and macrocosm, wrote:

> But keeps the earth her round proportion still?
> Doth not a Tenarif, or higher Hill
> Rise so high like a Rocke, that one might thinke
> The floating Moone would shipwrack there, and sinke? . . .
> Are these but warts, and pock-holes in the face
> Of th' earth? Thinke so: but yet confesse, in this
> The worlds proportion disfigured is.[38]

Involved in this passage are various "unconscious presuppositions" strange to us but familiar to Donne's contemporaries. The language of Donne's passage echoes literary conventions inherited from the classics and the Bible. The idea that mountains are a blemish to the earth goes back to theological positions long argued by Christian and Jewish Fathers. The basic conception of the "round proportion" of the earth, now disfigured by Teneriffe and other hills, implies an aesthetic accepted by classical and medieval philosophers. In addition to these literary, theological, and philosophical conventions and traditions— all of which must disappear before the attitudes we take for granted can emerge—there are scientific problems which did not occur to Donne, problems which we call geological. Even after we have gone back to the classics and the Fathers to determine "unconscious presuppositions" that led Donne and others to think and speak of mountains as they did, we shall be at less than mid-point of our search, "as one who on his journey baits at noon."

While one group of fundamental assumptions and unconscious presuppositions die, others are born, as in a redwood

---

[38] John Donne, "An Anatomy of the World: The First Anniversary," in *Complete Poetry and Selected Prose*, ed. by John Hayward (Bloomsbury, 1929), pp. 204–205, ll. 284–301.

forest young trees rise, perhaps to guard, perhaps to supplant the dying giant of a thousand years. At the moment men find themselves between the two worlds, one dead, one struggling to be born, we shall find a clash and conflict between various "intellectual positions which its exponents feel it necessary explicitly to defend"—one of the important battles in the long warfare of science versus religion, another Titanomachy with mountains becoming missiles hurled by either side. As the battle subsided, the mountains we see today began to appear to men who looked at them with new eyes, seeing them no longer as "warts, and pock-holes in the face Of th' earth," but as the grandest, most majestic objects on the terrestrial globe, discovering in them the "Sublime."

Historians and critics have done little justice to English genius and originality, so far as the Sublime is concerned. Almost unanimously they have insisted that the conception of sublimity as it developed in the eighteenth century had its origin in a rhetorical treatise, that it was the result of ideas expressed in the *Peri Hupsous* of the pseudo-Longinus, as translated and interpreted by Boileau in 1674. Here again we find the tendency to attribute changes in one art to development in another. When the critics who have considered the problem distinguish between two "Sublimes," they give priority, chronologically and qualitatively, to a rhetorical Sublime, which, as Ronald Crane has said, "is that quality, difficult to determine, but easily detectable to sensitive minds . . . which gives distinction to works of literature and plastic art." [39] If they consider the natural Sublime

[39] I quote from a review of Samuel Monk's *The Sublime* written by Ronald Crane in *Philological Quarterly*, XV (1936), 165–167. I am willing to agree with Mr. Crane that many of the exponents of the "natural Sublime" were "psychologists inquiring about the emotions, not critics investigating the sources of high excellence in art," and more than willing to grant that there was debasement of the Sublime among third-rate eighteenth-century poets. But I feel that Professors Crane and Monk and various others have their cart before their horse. In England, as I

(the Sublime in external Nature), they tend to classify it as "a degraded form of Longinianism," following upon the rhetorical theory, but debasing it, "showing itself in an excessive emotion for natural objects in the external world." Insofar as they find a Longinian source for this, they discover it in one passing remark in the *Peri Hupsous*, in which Longinus said that men do not admire "the little streams, transparent though they be, and useful too, but Nile, or Tiber, or Rhine, and far more than all, Ocean."

Let us consider the evidence offered by scholars for the effect in England of the rhetorical Sublime. The fragmentary work of Longinus had been available in England throughout the seventeenth century, both in the original and in translation. Between the first edition of 1554 and John Hall's English translation of 1652, at least five editions appeared. Yet Samuel Monk, who has most exhaustively traced the Longinian tradition in England, can find no real interest in Longinus before 1674. He says:

One might reasonably hope to find a noticeable increase in references to Longinus from this time on [1652]. Ninety-eight years had passed since the *editio princeps* had been printed, and both a Latin and an English translation were in existence. But the time had not yet come for Longinus to gain the ear of the critical world, and we find his name mentioned seldom. Milton himself, with all of his interest in the ancients, seems not to have felt Longinus's charm. In his essay "Of Education," he mentions Longinus as one of the teachers of "a graceful and ornate rhetoric," but that is all. It is a strange paradox that the most sublime of English poets should not have caught from Longinus the suggestion of the sublime as the expression of ultimate values in art, beyond the reach of rhetoric and her handmaidens, the rules. He did not; and it was left to the propounders of

---

shall attempt to show, the "natural Sublime" was earlier than the "rhetorical Sublime" and, far from being merely a "debased" Longinianism, was deeply sincere and religious in origin. Longinus did little else for the "natural Sublime" than to offer some assistance in vocabulary.

an adolescent aesthetic in the next century to find in John Milton's poems, not a "graceful and ornate rhetoric," but the supreme illustration of whatever particular type of the sublime they advocated.[40]

"The time had not come for Longinus to gain the ear of the critical world." Before 1674, when in a single year Boileau published his *L'Art Poétique* and his *Traité du Sublime ou du Merveilleux traduit du grec du Longin*, there seems no evidence that any important English writer was interested in the Greek rhetorical treatise. When the influence of the Longinian rhetoric began to appear, it was less that of Longinus himself than of Longinus-according-to-Boileau, who had somewhat clipped the wings of Pegasus. Radical in its science, more responsive than the continent to the "new philosophy," neoclassical England tended to remain conservative and derivative in its literary criticism. But if the rhetorical Sublime, its roots set down in France, was largely a transplantation, the natural Sublime was flowering in England well before the turn of the century, and travelers to the Alps were "ravished" and "rapt" by greatness, appalled and enthralled by the vast, the grand, the Sublime in external Nature.

In this study I am speaking only of what happened in England. The same phenomenon did not occur in France, where adulation of grand Nature appears later than in England and is possibly as derivative from England as the rhetorical Sublime in England was derivative from France. There are important differences in cultural outlook here, implied in "A Dissertation upon the Word Vast" which Saint-Evremond read to the French Academy, warning his countrymen:

Great is a perfection of Minds; Vast always a *Defect*. A just and regulated Extent makes the Great; an immoderate Greatness the *Vast*. *Vast* signifies an excessive Greatness. Vast Things differ

[40] Samuel Monk, *The Sublime: A Study of Critical Theories in XVIII-Century England* (New York, 1935), p. 20.

mightily from those which make an agreeable Impression upon us. *Vasta Solitudo* . . . 'tis a wild Solitude, where we are frighted with being alone. . . . Vast Forest put us into a Fright; the Sight loses it self in looking over Vast Plains. . . . Rivers too large, Overflowings and Inundations displease us by the Noise and Violence of their Billows, and our Eyes cannot with any Pleasure behold their Vast Extent.[41]

Boileau was thinking of rhetorical style rather than of natural scenery, when he wrote in *L'Art Poétique:*

> J'aime mieux un ruisseau qui sur la molle arène
> Dans un pré plein de fleurs lentement se promène,
> Qu'un torrent débordé qui, d'un cours orageux,
> Roule, plein de gravier, sur un terrain fangeux.[42]

Yet the implication is the same. In the mid-century Montesquieu lamented what he called "the destruction of the Sublime" among his countrymen, attributing it to the effect of the "new philosophy," by which he meant the Cartesian philosophy with its emphasis upon clear and distinct laws.[43] But England had caught other implications from a "new philosophy," as we shall see, and even the vastness that seemed excessive to Saint-Evremond was not vast enough for English taste, rivers never too large, inundations—even volcanoes and earthquakes—never too mighty for their imaginations.

Sometime during the eighteenth century the English discovered a new world. In a way, they were like the imaginary cosmic voyagers who, from Lucian to writers of modern science-fiction, have traveled to the moon or planets to find worlds that puzzle, amaze, astound, enthrall by their very differences from our world. Perhaps the experience of eighteenth-century Eng-

[41] *The Works of Mr. de St. Evermont* (London, 1700), I, 364–389.

[42] *L'Art Poétique*, I, 165–170, in Nicolas Boileau-Despréaux, *Œuvres Complètes* (Paris, 1873), II, 304.

[43] C. de S. Montesquieu, *Pensées et Fragmentes inédits* (Bordeaux, 1899–1901), I, 221–222.

lishmen was in some ways like that of C. S. Lewis' Ransom in *Out of the Silent Planet* [44] who after a voyage through space reached the new world of Malacandra. His foreboding imagination had peopled the new world with monsters, had led him to expect either rocky desolation or a network of nightmare machines. "But something he learned. Before anything else he learned that Malacandra was beautiful; and he even reflected how odd it was that this possibility had never entered into his speculations about it." For a time he could not analyze or define that beauty; he could indeed only feel rather than comprehend what made it beautiful:

A mass of something purple, so huge that he took it for a heather-covered mountain, was his first impression; on the other side, beyond the larger water, there was something of the same kind. But there, he could see over top of it. Beyond were strange upright shapes of whitish green: too jagged and irregular for buildings, too thin and steep for mountains. Beyond and above these again was the rose-coloured cloud-like mass.

"He gazed about him, and the very intensity of his desire to take in the new world at a glance defeated him." He could not describe what he was seeing. Indeed he did not know what he saw, for there was no parallel in his terrestrial experience. As Mr. Lewis says, "Moreover, he knew nothing yet well enough to see it: you cannot see things till you know roughly what they are."

Such—to a great extent—was the experience of many eighteenth-century Englishmen who discovered the Sublime in the external world. Perhaps they may be forgiven for their exaggerations, for their insistence that "the bigger, the better," for the fact that they spoke a language of extravagant hyperbole. To express their experience, new in the history of the human race, there was neither speech nor language.

[44] C. S. Lewis, *Out of the Silent Planet* (New York, 1946), pp. 40-42.

Chapter One

The Literary Heritage

"Hills Peep o'er Hills"

I

Here learn ye Mountains more unjust,
Which to abrupter greatness thrust,
That do with your hook-shoulder'd height
The Earth deform and Heaven fright,
For whose excrescence ill design'd,
Nature must a new Center find,
Learn here those humble steps to tread,
Which to securer Glory lead.[1]

IN one stanza Andrew Marvell suggested a half-dozen attitudes
toward mountains conventional in seventeenth-century literature. Mountains were "unjust"; "hook-shoulder'd," they were
deformities of the earth; their peaks frightened the heavens.
They were excrescences, swellings, protuberances, which by
their monstrous weight threatened the balance of the earth. They
were also symbols of warning to ambitious man who aspired

[1] "Upon the Hill and Grove at Bill-borow," in Andrew Marvell, *Poems
and Letters*, ed. by H. M. Margoliouth (Oxford, 1927), I, 56.

too high. No poet crowded more contemporary epithets of disparagement into one stanza.

Joshua Poole's *English Parnassus; or, A Help to English Poesie*,[2] one of many volumes of "readie and easie ways," offers a clue to accepted mountain attitudes in the mid-century. Of the threescore adjectives suggested by Poole to aspiring poets, some are neutral: "rocky, craggy, climbing." A few indicate only passing feeling for the grand and magnificent: "aspiring, stately, lovely, cloud-touching, star-brushing." Yet these are more than counterbalanced by adjectives of distaste: "insolent, surly, ambitious, barren, sky-threatening, supercilious, desert, uncouth, inhospitable, freezing, infruitful, crump-shouldered, unfrequented, forsaken, melancholy, pathless." We find, too, such epithets as "Earth's Dugs, Risings, Tumors, Blisters . . . Earth's Warts." Although this was an "English Parnassus," the long list of hills to which a poet might refer included no name of an English mountain. Olympus, Helicon, Ida, Parnassus, Pelion, Ossa were the stuff of conventional mountain poetry in 1657.

Marvell was obviously following an accepted literary pattern when he wrote the stanza about mountains. But his lyric poetry as a whole disproves the charge that seventeenth-century poets felt little response to Nature. Whatever the symbolism of the "Mower" poems, they were written by a man who knew the English countryside with its new-mown hay and glowworms. If his "melon" combined Sappho's apple and Eve's, his nectarine and curious peach grew against English walls in English gardens. Garden lovers as they have always been, English poets never

---

[2] References are to the edition of 1677, pp. 129, 387, 451. In 1600 Robert Allott had published a somewhat similar volume: *Englands Parnassus; or, The Choysest Flowers of our Modern Poets, with Their Poetical Comparisons; Descriptions of Bewties, Personages, Castles, Pallaces, Mountaines, Groves, Seas, Springs, Rivers* (ed. from the original text by Charles Crawford [Oxford, 1913]). To Allott mountains seem to have served only as convenient sites for castles, in which he was obviously more interested.

wrote more charmingly of flowers than during the late Renaissance. Wordsworth's daffodils were not more English than Shakespeare's "that come before the swallow dares," or Herrick's truants, fleeing before high noon, or even Milton's "daffydillies" that, growing side by side with the Greek amaranthus, filled their cups with tears for Lycidas. "Fields with flowers deckt in every hue" were familiar settings of seventeenth-century poets who wrote about the "yellow king-cup" and the "orange-tawny marigold," but also about the "thistle all with prickles." Birds were as familiar to these poets as blossoms. The nightingale might be merely a literary heritage like Milton's Philomela, singing of her "sweetest saddest plight," but she was often a real bird to whom poets listened, not with Midas' ears. And the poets were no less responsive to the English lark and swallow—even to the screech owl.

> I sing of brooks, of blossoms, birds, and bowers,
> Of April, May, of June, and July flowers,

said Herrick in the "Argument of His Book." We must not be misled by the self-conscious artistry of the seventeenth-century poets, their derivative vocabulary, to believe that the Nature of the seventeenth-century poets was really embodied in "L'Allegro" and "Il Penseroso." The youthful Milton's Nature was the product of his lamp at midnight hour. Many of his contemporaries described more realistically than he, "meadows trim with daisies pied, Shallow brooks and rivers wide." They too wrote in pastoral strain, yet more than one English shepherd localized his song.[3] To be sure, their pictures were often idyllic;

---

[3] Cf. Phineas Fletcher, *Purple Island*, in Alexander Chalmers, *Works of the English Poets* (London, 1810), VI, 85:

> But ah! let me, under some Kentish hill,
> Near rolling Medway, 'mong my shepherd peers,
> With fearless merry-make, and piping still,
> Securely pass my few and slow-pac'd years.

"such sights as youthful poets dream On summer eves, by haunted stream":

> The damasked meadows and the pebbly streams
>   Sweeten and make soft your dreams;
> The purling streams, groves, birds, and well weav'd bowers
>   With fields enamell'd with flowers,
> Present their shapes, while fantasy discloses
>   Millions of Lillies mixt with Roses.[4]

Although Herrick could write "Idyllica" and sing "of balm, of oil, of spice, and ambergris," we remember him better for his orchard and garden, his "blushing apple, bashful pear, And shame-fac'd plum, all simp'ring there," his "pea, or bean, or wort, or beet," his hen "which creaking day by day tells when she goes her long white egg to lay."

Yet, with all their affection for Nature, the poets of the earlier seventeenth century, with few exceptions, responded to her smaller rather than her grander aspects. They loved her best when she was beautiful rather than sublime. Their favorite landscape was serene, charming, lovely, rather than majestic, wild, and irregular. They were fond of the "little hills of England":

> Here and there two hilly crests
> Amidst them hug a pleasant green
> And these are like two swelling breasts
> That close a tender fall between.[5]

The vogue of "Cooper's Hill" was due in large part to its political occasionalism, yet some of its appeal lay in the fact that it celebrated hills familiar to Londoners. Although poets said they loved "those rich and glorious things, The rivers, mountains, woods, and springs," it is difficult to find extended descriptions

[4] Robert Herrick, "Idyllica," in *Lyrical Poems*, ed. by F. T. Palgrave (London, 1892), p. 59.

[5] William Strode, "On Westwell Downs," in *Seventeenth Century Lyrics*, ed. by Norman Ault (London and New York, 1928), p. 172.

of mountains in their poetry. Their occasional tributes were usually as conventional as Marvell's epithets of disparagement. Many English poets neither liked nor disliked mountains. They were merely uninterested in them. One reason is obvious: many English poets had never seen mountains. Some knew Wales or Scotland, a few had crossed the Alps. But for one Welsh Henry Vaughan or Scottish William Drummond, there were a dozen urban writers who drew their Nature from books alone. Their chief sources were classical poetry and Scripture, in each of which we shall find an implicit dualism subconsciously reflected in attitudes of seventeenth-century writers.

II

The early Greeks had shown some of the awe and aversion of many primitive peoples in the face of a Nature they did not understand, which must be propitiated by sacrifice.[6] According to etymologists, some of the names given by the Greeks in antiquity to peaks and mountains reflected this feeling, for there were "tempestuous," "wild," "terrifying" mountains and the "thunder range." Yet a people whose life was spent among mountains could hardly have continued this dread indefinitely. In time the earlier attitude gave way to a subconscious feeling of sympathy and kinship. Since mountains were their daily neighbors, they did not often pause to describe them at length, but accepted them as an integral part of life, as do other mountain peoples. Ruskin read too much "Mountain Gloom" into them when he said that the Greeks "shrank with dread from all the ruggedness of lower nature—from the wrinkled forest bank and the jagged hill-crest, and irregular, inorganic storms of sky." This could hardly have been the attitude of a people who worshiped their gods on Mount Olympus and invoked the Muses on Helicon. Gilbert Murray was closer to the truth when he

[6] Cf. Walter Woodburn Hyde, "The Ancient Appreciation of Mountain Scenery," *Classical Journal*, XI (1915), 70–85.

wrote: "They did not describe forests and mountains; they worshipped them, and built temples in them. Their love for nature was that of the mountaineer and the seaman, who does not talk much about the sea and mountains, but who sickens and pines if he is taken away from them." [7]

"Lord of every crest and mountain peak and rocky path," Pan with his companions ranged "over the high white hills . . . faring through the lofty crags." The Greek, like his god, was a part of elemental nature, so much a part that he seldom considered it objectively as something external to himself. He was involved in it. Although Greek poets rarely expressed the rapture, astonishment, amazement, and horror of the eighteenth-century English poets, some of them had a feeling for the "sublime" in our modern sense. Aeschylus felt the mingled majesty and terror of earthquake and storm, of "sky-piercing rocks" and "star-neighbored peaks," of the distant Caucasus. Alcman's "mountain summits . . . glens, cliffs and caves," like his "dark ocean's waves," were both beautiful and dangerous, associated with "black earth's reptile brood" and the "wild beasts of the mountain wood." The lowland English poets were to develop only in maturity what Greeks had always known—a feeling for the vast, the wild, the dangerous in elemental nature.

The Latin attitude toward mountains, however, at least among classical writers, remained almost consistently adverse. [8] Whether because the Alps were ultimate barriers against the barbarian or for some other reason, the Romans felt mountains aloof, inhospitable, desolate, and hostile. The Latin spirit found little refuge in the everlasting hills, to describe which its poets chose such adjectives as *ocris, arduus, asperus, horridus*. There were *montes inaccessi, Alpes gelidae, saeuae Alpes*, fastnesses inhos-

[7] John Ruskin, *Modern Painters*, vol. III, pt. XIII, ch. XV; Gilbert Murray, Introduction to *Greek and English Tragedy: A Contrast* (Oxford, 1912).

[8] Cf. Katherine Allen, *The Treatment of Nature in the Poetry of the Roman Republic* (Madison, 1899), pp. 117 ff.; Sir Archibald Geikie, *Love of Nature among the Romans* (London, 1912), pp. 283 ff.

pitable in their solitude. Catullus, who lived in full view of the Alps, seldom mentioned them as scenery. Virgil never really praised mountains, which he knew well enough. Horace, who loved the pastoral country, only occasionally described mountains with approval. To be sure, poets paused over the progress of sunlight or the succession of light and shadow on a hill, but on the whole mountains remained a background. Lucretius alone among major Latin poets seemed to feel sublimity in wild scenery, though, ironically enough, as a philosopher he insisted that mountains were the waste places of the world. Yet Lucretius made more than one ascent to see a prospect from a summit; he described clouds as they floated above mountains; he exulted in the violence of thunderstorms. Mountains and storms, volcanoes and earthquakes—no matter how Lucretius the philosopher explained their origin, Lucretius the poet experienced some of the "rapture" of the eighteenth-century poets, many of whom prided themselves upon being "anti-Lucretians."

Seventeenth-century poets in England tended to repeat adjectives and epithets of their classical ancestors when they mentioned mountains at all. The "mountains on whose barren breast The labouring clouds do often rest" were not native to Cambridge or Horton but were Milton's heritage from literary convention. So, too, with only one exception, were Shakespeare's. Rivers, whether placid or in flood, the sea, woods, fields, gardens afforded him image after image. References to mountains and even to hills are infrequent. Edgar's description of the cliff in *Lear* is realistic as is no other passage in which Shakespeare mentions or describes the wild and irregular in nature. "He that can read it without being dizzy," Addison remarked, "has a very good head, or a very bad one." But apart from this, there is no evidence that Shakespeare had any feeling for high hills, which he had probably never seen. He might write charming lines in which mountains were mentioned, yet the verses usually came not from observation but from literary tradition, as when Romeo and Juliet watched the dawn:

> Look, love, what envious streaks
> Do lace the severing clouds in yonder east.
> Night's candles are burned out, and jocund day
> Stands tiptoe on the misty mountain tops.

In the most familiar passages, Shakespeare's language showed his literary heritage. The phrases Othello used to describe strange places echoed classical poets:

> Of antres vast, and deserts idle,
> Rough quarries, rocks and hills whose heads touch heaven
> It was my hint to speak.

When Shakespeare described Hamlet's father with

> Hyperion's curls, the front of Jove himself,
> An eye like Mars, to threaten or command,
> A station like the herald Mercury
> New-lighted on a heaven-kissing hill,

his memory went back to Virgil's description of Mercury on Mount Atlas. When Hamlet and Laertes vied in their mountain imagery over Ophelia's grave, they were echoing the *Georgics*.

The classical heritage was so powerful in the early seventeenth century that we find few literary mountain passages that were not borrowed from either the Greeks or the Romans. Only in one direction did the English writers strike out paths for themselves. "Make Ossa like a wart," said Hamlet. Poole has told us that in 1657 "Dugs, Risings, Tumors, Blisters, Warts" were proper epithets for mountains. Both the Greeks and the Romans —the Romans more than the Greeks—had described mountains in anatomical terms, implying analogies with animals and human beings. Mountains had "brows, foreheads, shoulders, backs, breasts, ribs." When Milton in his early paraphrase of Psalm 114 spoke of "huge-bellied mountains," he had good classical authority. Renaissance writers became still more interested in figures of speech implying the abnormal, the degenerative, the pathological. Here, too, were memories of Latin authors who had spoken of the wrinkles, the furrows, and the baldness of hills. Occasionally classical writers had used such figures as "excrescences," abnormal swellings indicating disease whether in hills or in plants; we find *verruca* and even *ulcera*. The tendency toward personification in mountain description had gone further among Italians who added figures descriptive of articles of clothing: "cappello," applied to the cloud encircling a mountain; "scarpa" (*shoe*), used in such phrases as "la scarpa del monte," "monte scarpato"; "vestito" (*garment* or *clothed*), as in "Colle Vestito" and "Passo del Vestito."

Yet even among Italians there was little to explain the most characteristic vocabulary of seventeenth-century English poets: "Wens, Warts, Pimples, Blisters, and Imposthumes." Indeed this tendency was largely responsible for almost the only originality we find among most of the lesser and some of the greater English poets—transformation of old classical figures into something more modern, reflecting not only metaphysical style but growing interest in medicine, particularly in pathology.

The second important literary heritage of the seventeenth century served in some ways to offset, in others to augment the Greek and Roman. In the Bible, as in the classics, seventeenth-century poets found an implicit dualism, for the Old and New Testaments differed as did the Greeks and Romans in their attitude toward grand nature. Familiar passages from the Old Testament recalled ancestors who had felt the peace of the everlasting hills, had lifted up their eyes to the mountains. No associations of evil or terror surrounded hills that skipped like young rams. Sinai and Ararat had long been sacred in literature and art. Others than Milton visualized "the shepherd who first taught the chosen seed" as walking familiarly with God upon a mountain. Mountains were to bring peace to the people, and the little hills, righteousness. In Hebraic literature as in Greek was a sense of the Sublime, alien to the Christian Scriptures.[9]

The New Testament drew less from this strain of exaltation of Nature than from another attitude in the prophetic books. The Apostles knew the words of Isaiah: "How beautiful upon the mountains are the feet of him that bringeth good tidings, that publisheth peace," yet the Messiah of the Christians showed little feeling for mountains loved by the patriarchs. He remembered rather, as did Luke, another verse of Isaiah: "Every valley shall be exalted, and every mountain and hill shall be made low." Whether in external Nature or in the social scene, what was "high" was suspect; what was "low," more worthy. Mountains were "high," "rough," "crooked," symbolic of a perverse generation. Into them was read a social philosphy implied in verses in Luke: "He hath put down princes from their thrones; and hath exalted them of low degree. The hungry he hath filled with good things, and the rich he hath set empty away." Many English Puritans, living in a time of political and social change and chaos, read into mountains and valleys their own equalitarian philosophy. Laurence Clarkson put the matter

---

[9] This is a point that merits fuller consideration than I can give it here. It is interesting that the only nonclassical illustration of the "sublime" style used by Longinus was the first verse of Genesis. Montesquieu stressed the difference between the two religions, so far as the Sublime was concerned, in his "Essai sur le Gout" in *Pensées et Fragments inédits* (Bordeaux, 1899–1901), I, 221–222: "There is, in the system of the Jews, a great deal of proneness toward the Sublime, for they were in the habit of attributing all their thoughts and actions to special inspirations of the Deity; and this gave them a very great incentive. . . . The Christian system (I use the term, inapt though it may be) seems to give us a greater incentive by giving us more healthy notions about the Deity. But as this incentive neither engenders nor is involved in any passions, it follows naturally that the Sublime is destroyed by it. Indeed the mysteries are sublime to reason rather than to the senses."

succinctly when he said: "If you would understand the Scriptures, you shall read it calleth rich men wicked Mountains, and
poor believing men Valleys." [10]

Bunyan's attitude toward mountains suggests the symbolism
read into them by lower-class preachers. In spite of his phrase
"Delectable Mountains," the untraveled Bunyan nowhere showed
any knowledge of actual mountains. In *Pilgrim's Progress*, his
hills were only symbols of the ups and downs of life. Even the
Delectable Mountains were entirely allegorical. Mountains were
"Immanuel's Land," but their beauty lay less in themselves than
in the fact that from them Pilgrim could see the heavenly city.
In his sermons Bunyan went further, interpreting mountains
and valleys in terms of his social philosophy: "Water naturally
descends to and abides in low places, in valleys and places which
are undermost; and the grace of God and the Spirit of grace is
of that nature also." [11] The valleys are watered by rivers and
streams; the mountains are barren and dry. The mountains are
the "proud"; the valleys, the "humble."

The Scriptural dualism in regard to mountains is reflected in
a forgotten work of William Prynne, written about 1640, while
its author was temporarily imprisoned in a Channel Island castle.[12] Looking out upon massy piles of rocks and long wastes
of the sea, Prynne occupied himself with versifying Biblical
passages concerning these phenomena. In "Rockes Improved . . .
a barren and harsh Soyle, yet a Fruitful and Delightfull subject of Meditation," we find both the Old Testament and the

[10] "The Right Devil Discovered," quoted in William York Tindall,
John Bunyan, Mechanick Preacher (New York, 1934), p. 115. Mr. Tindall
writes: "Like the Quakers Bunyan esteemed for its social implications
the biblical imagery of mountains, valleys, and waters."

[11] "The Water of Life," in Bunyan, *Works* (Glasgow, 1853), III, 541.

[12] *Mount-Orgueil; or, Divine and Profitable Meditations, Raised from
the Contemplation of These Three Leaves of Natures Volume, I. Rockes;
2. Seas; 3. Gardens, Digested into Three Distinct Poems* (London, 1641).
The quotations may be found on pp. 20, 18, 12.

New, conventional justification of mountains and equally conventional condemnation. On the one hand, rocks are like ungodly men, shameless, impudent, obdurate, proud, hard, barren, deaf, cold, dumb, lifeless. Yet rocks and mountains are not wholly evil. God was revealed to Moses upon a mountain; often in Holy Writ, Christ "a Rocke is stil'd"; upon a rock Christ founded His Church; His death "Rockes did lament"; entombed within a rock, Christ rose in glory. Though mountains may symbolize the "heavy, bruising, cold, fixed, hard" aspects of sin, they are also models of patience, watchfulness, humility; enduring through tempest, bare, ragged, they are like God's elect. So Prynne weighed and balanced the virtues and defects of rocks and hills; so he praised and condemned, turning now to the Old Testament, now to the New for his authority. Yet rocks and mountains were only allegory and symbol to him as to Bunyan.

Like the underground rivers which captivated the imaginations of our ancestors, these two streams of tradition flowed down for centuries. For a time we shall be conscious of one rather than of the other, a mountain attitude reflecting either the distaste of the Romans or the distrust of primitive Christians for "that which is high." But ultimately the other spirit will triumph—the heritage from Greeks who worshiped their gods on Olympus and Hebrews who, lifting up their eyes to the hills, remembered men who had walked familiarly with Deity upon "the Lord's holy hill":

> Moses, Aaron, Nadab and Abihu
> Climbed and saw the very God, the Highest,
> Stand upon the paved work of a sapphire.
> Like the bodied heaven in his clearness
> Shone the stone, the sapphire of that paved work,
> When they ate and drank and saw God also! [13]

[13] Robert Browning, "One Word More."

III

No modern literary student can believe—as scholars and students did for many years—that during the Dark and Middle Ages interest in external Nature ceased, to stir again only with the supposed Renaissance spirit. Historians of painting, architecture, science, literature have put an end to that old fallacy. Although the most acute observation of Nature appears in the depiction of her smaller rather than grander phases, religious painters carried on the Hebraic exaltation of mountains, particularly Sinai and Ararat. In literature allegorization, personification, and abstraction were so persistent that they have tended to overshadow more realistic treatments of Nature. There was nothing abstract or allegorical about the scenery around the haunted mere, the home of Grendel and his dam in Beowulf:

> A hidden land they inhabit,
> Wolf-haunted valleys, perilous fen paths
> And windswept headlands, where the mountain stream
> Descends beneath the shadow of the cliffs,
> A torrent down the crags. Measured by miles
> It is not far from here that the mere lieth;
> Rime-frosted groves hang over it, a wood
> Fast rooted overshadoweth the wave. . . .
>   'Tis not a pleasant spot;
> Dark toward the clouds the turmoil of the waves
> Leaps upward from it, when the tempest stirs
> Disastrous storms, until the heaven grows dark
> And the skies weep.[14]

Wild and rugged and dangerous—and perhaps, as we shall see, haunted by more than monsters—the scene is extraordinarily

[14] *Beowulf in Modern English*, trans. by Mary E. Waterhouse (Cambridge, Eng., 1949), pp. 48–49, ll. 1357 ff. There are more parallels for this kind of scenery in German than in English literature. See Gertrud Stockmayer, *Ueber Natur gefuhl in Deutschland im 10. und 11. Jahrhundert* (Leipzig, 1910); B. Q. Morgan, *Nature in Middle High German Lyrics* (Göttingen, 1912).

realistic. The "Gawain poet," too, wrote of wild Nature as if he knew the northern country intimately, as perhaps he did.

Nevertheless the dominant tendency of medieval literature was toward abstraction and moralization, so far as most nature imagery was concerned. Indeed, so powerful was the negativistic influence of the Latin classics and Christian allegorization that even theologians and poets who lived among them seemed to see mountains not as they were but as tradition and convention had made them seem. Augustine and Dante may serve as illustrations. "No one who has read extensively in the writings of St. Augustine," writes a modern critic, "can fail to be impressed by the wealth of allusions in them to the world of nature." [15] Augustine knew mountains well and, responsive as he was to light and color, often paused to describe the surface of the hills at Casciago. In the passage of the *Confessions* that Petrarch remembered on Mont Ventoux, he said:

And men go forth to admire the peaks of mountains, the vast billows of the sea, the wide courses of rivers, the winding expanse of Ocean, the revolutions of the stars, and they leave themselves behind; nor do they marvel that when I was speaking of all these things, I was not viewing them with my eyes, not yet could I speak of them unless I were beholding in my memory these mountains, billows, and stars, which I have seen, and the Ocean which I have come to know by hearsay, in as vast a compass as if I were beholding them externally.

Yet for the most part Augustine used mountain imagery only to point a moral. The symbolism of the Gospels is reiterated: "Hills and mountains are elevations of the earth; but valleys are depressions of the earth. Do not despise the depressions, for from them springs flow. . . . The heavens are indeed the higher bodies of the world. . . . But it is not written that God is near to tall men, or to those who dwell on the mountains, but it is written, 'The Lord is nigh unto them that are of a broken heart,'

[15] Sister Mary Jane Holman, *Nature-Imagery in the Works of St. Augustine* (Washington, 1932), pp. ix, 114, 54, 64, 99.

which refers to humility." Augustine carried his nature imagery to no such extremes as did some Fathers, but allegory and moralization were always there.

There is no question of the personal reminiscence of a mountain in Dante's realistic account of the ascent of Bismantova:

> Up through the riven rock we made our way;
> Cliffs hemmed us in on either side; the ground
> Beneath called feet and hands both into play. . . .
> Surpassing sight, the summits pierce the sky. . . .
> Forcing myself, I crawled up after him
> Until the ledge was underfoot at last.[16]

Nowhere, however, did Dante suggest the slightest aesthetic gratification in this or any other mountain ascent. Whether because of his own experience or because of his literary and theological heritage, Dante did not *like* mountains. Ruskin's comments are not unjust:

To Dante mountains are inconceivable except as great broken stones or crags; all their broad contours and undulations seem to have escaped his eye. It is, indeed, with his usual overtone of symbolic meaning that he describes the great broken stones, and the fall of the shattered mountain. . . . In no part of the poem do we find allusions to mountains in other than a stern light; nor the slightest evidence that Dante cared to look at them. . . . And whenever hills are spoken of as having any influence on character, the repugnance of them is still manifest; they are always causes of rudeness or cruelty.

The Mount of Purgatorio remains not a mountain but a symbol and an allegory—the greatest of all variants upon Hill Difficulty.

Even in such accounts of their experiences as those of John of Salisbury and Petrarch—long isolated from their backgrounds

[16] "Purgatorio," IV, 31 ff., in *Divine Comedy*, trans. by J. B. Fletcher (New York, 1931). Ruskin's comment may be found in *Modern Painters*, vol. III, pt. IV, ch. xvi.

and considered unique in their periods [17]—we find the characteristic response to classical or religious traditions. John of Salisbury,
writing from the Grand St. Bernard, left a vivid account of
the perils he encountered, the danger of ascent, ice and snow
and cold so intense that his ink was frozen. Toward the end of
his letter he said: "I have been on the mount of Jove; on the
one hand looking up to the heaven of the mountain; on the
other shuddering at the hell of the valleys; feeling myself so
much nearer to heaven that I was more sure that my prayer
would be heard." Yet almost immediately he concluded: "Lord,
I said, restore me to my brethren, that they come not into this
place of torment." [18]

Petrarch's reaction was strikingly different. His ascent of

[17] Cf. Lynn Thorndike, "Renaissance or Prenaissance?" *J.H.I.*, IV
(1943), 71–72: "Not only has it been demonstrated that the thirteenth
and fourteenth centuries were more active and penetrating in natural
science than was the quattrocento, but the notion that 'appreciation of
natural beauty' was 'introduced into modern Europe by the Italian
Renaissance' must also be abandoned. Burckhardt admitted that medieval
literature displayed sympathy with nature, but nevertheless regarded
Petrarch's ascent of Mont Ventoux (which is only 6260 feet high) in
1336 as epoch-making. Petrarch represented an old herdsman who had
tried in vain to climb it fifty years before as beseeching him to turn
back on the ground that he had received only torn clothes and broken
bones for his pains and that no one had attempted the ascent since. As
a matter of fact, Jean Buridan, the Parisian schoolman, had visited it
between 1316 and 1334, had given details as to its altitude, and had waxed
enthusiastic as to the Cevennes. So that all Petrarch's account proves
is his capacity for storytelling and his ability to make a mountain out
of a molehill. Miss Stockmayer, in a book on feeling for nature in Germany in the tenth and eleventh centuries, has noted various ascents and
descriptions of mountains from that period. In the closing years of his
life archbishop Anno of Cologne climbed his beloved mountains more
often than usual."

[18] John of Salisbury's letter is quoted by Edward Tompkins Mc-
Laughlin, *The Mediaeval Feeling for Nature* (New York, 1894), p. 6.
Petrarch's account has been quoted so often that it seems unnecessary to
give it in any detail. It may also be found in McLaughlin, pp. 2 ff.

Mount Ventoux in April, 1335, was of his own volition, not forced upon him by necessity. Delight and aesthetic gratification ring through his tribute to grandeur and majesty, an attitude so modern that his comment has been frequently quoted in anthologies for mountain climbers. Yet at the moment of his deepest emotion, tradition conquered feeling. Taking out a copy of the *Confessions*, Petrarch "closed the book, angry with myself for not ceasing to admire things of the earth, instead of remembering that the human soul is beyond comparison the subject for admiration. Once again, as I descended, I gazed back, and the lofty summit of the mountain seemed to me scarcely a cubit high, compared with the sublime dignity of man." For a moment upon Mount Ventoux, Petrarch had seen the "Mountain Glory." The moment passed, and his eyes were darkened by the "Mountain Gloom," inherited from Roman poets and the Christian preachers.

IV

Throughout the Middle Ages, indeed throughout the Renaissance, allegorization, abstraction, and personification so overshadow realism that the characteristic mountain imagery of the earlier seventeenth century is little more than a series of conventional stereotypes. Two in particular became clichés in the hands of the lesser and some of the greater poets. Donne wrote in his third satire:

> On a huge hill
> Cragged and steep, Truth stands, and hee that will
> Reach her, about must, and about must goe;
> And what the hills suddenness resists, winne so;
> Yet strive so, that before age, deaths twilight,
> Thy Soule rest, for none can worke in that night.

The basic figure is at least as old as Prodicus' apologue to the *Choice of Heracles*, made familiar by Xenophon. Allegorized in various forms during the Middle Ages, it merged with other figures, some undoubtedly drawn from the many treatments of the Goddess Fortuna, who throughout her long history was usually associated with a mountain.[19] By the time of Claudian she had been transported from the Earthly Paradise to a mountain top. Her dwelling place, variable as the goddess herself, might be either beautiful or dangerous. In the *Anticlaudianus* of Alanus de Insulis the two strains were merged. Seen from one aspect, Fortune's house was ugly and dangerous, from another it "gleamed with silver and sparkled with gems." As the legend grew, so did the dualism, so that the summit was both desirable and terrible, always distant and remote. At some time the apologue merged with the equally venerable *Tabula* of Cebes,[20] never more brilliantly than in Holbein's *Table of Cebus,* where young people frolic at the foot of the mountain while wiser and more mature men and women struggle up the steep and narrow path. So Milton interpreted the old allegory when he wrote "To a Virtuous Young Lady":

> Lady that in the prime of earliest youth
> Wisely hath shunn'd the broad way and the green,
> And with those few art eminently seen
> That labor up the Hill of Heav'nly Truth.

Whether the Hill of Virtue, the Hill of Truth, or the Hill of Learning, it was always, as to Bunyan, Hill Difficulty.

The other persistent convention, even more frequently re-iterated, traced its ancestry to the Christian interpretation of Isaiah's prophecy of the exaltation of the valleys and the abasement of the hills, interpreted by Augustine and other Fathers

[19] See Howard Patch, *The Goddess Fortuna in Mediaeval Literature* (Cambridge, Mass., 1927), particularly ch. iv.

[20] Dr. Edwin C. Heinle has made a study of the Prodicus and Cebes allegories as they developed during the Middle Ages and passed down to the eighteenth century in his "Eighteenth Century Allegorical Essay" (1957; available on microfilm in the Columbia University Libraries).

until it had become a stock in trade of preachers everywhere. In the "July Eclogue" of the *Shepheards Calender*, "made in the honour and commendation of good shepheards, and to the shame and disprayse of proud and ambitious pastours," Spenser borrowed the theme of his "sacred hills" from Mantuan, but drew a different lesson. In the earlier version the "shepherd of the mountains" won the victory, while in Spenser's eclogue the humble valley conquered in the rhetorical struggle. "How can a lofty hill," wrote Phineas Fletcher in one of his pastorals, "To lowly shepherd's thought be rightly fitting?" The same symbolism appears in William Habington's "Et Exultavit Humiles," the title of which sufficiently suggests its argument. Hill follows hill in such tedious succession as a symbol of overweening ambition, excessive aspiration, and ugly pride that to quote, even to list them, would result in a mere dull catalogue of common things. "Prouder than haughty hills, harder than rocks" —so Giles Fletcher succinctly stated the most conventional attitude toward mountains, persistent for generations under the influence of Latin poetry and Christian moralization.

In a time of turmoil and strife, when England beheaded a king, and Cavalier and Puritan divided sharply on their interpretation of true "greatness," traditional mountain imagery served on both sides. Henry King might have been writing for the Puritans when he said:

> Put off your giant titles, then I can
> Stand in your judgment's blank an equal man.
> Though hills advanced are above the plain,
> They are but higher earth, nor must disdain
> Alliance with the vale; we see a spade
> Can level them, and make a mount a glade.[21]

Since "Cooper's Hill" was written in honor of the exiled monarch and his father and was filled with praise of monarchs and mon-

[21] Henry King, "A Letter," in *Minor Poets of the Caroline Period* (Oxford, 1906), III, 200.

archy, Denham could not follow the conventional opposition of "high" and "low." His mountain was proud, but pride was not arrogance or disdain; it was the fitting mien of majesty. Grand and majestic, the monarch-mountain does not despise the valley, but shelters it from storms he himself bears. Yet although Denham was describing real hills familiar to all Londoners and although he established a pattern of topographical poetry that was to last for a century, "Cooper's Hill" still echoes old abstraction and allegorization:

> But his proud head the aery Mountain hides
> Among the Clouds; his shoulders, and his sides
> A shady mantle cloaths; his curled brows
> Frown on the gentle stream, which calmly flows,
> While winds and storms his lofty forehead beat:
> The common fate of all that's high and great.
> Low at his foot a spacious plain is plac't,
> Between the mountain and the stream embrac't:
> Which shade and shelter from the Hill derives.

Drayton's *Poly-Olbion* [22] is a remarkable example of the persistence of old literary conventions in the earlier seventeenth century. Even more than Denham, Drayton was writing an *English* poem, "a chorographicall Description of all the Tracts, Rivers, Mountaines, Forests, and other Parts . . . of Great Britain." In some forty "Songs," which are less songs than leisurely topographical descriptions and antiquarian digressions, he celebrated all the shires of Britain, calling upon his not inconsiderable learning to do so. The project he had set himself required the sort of ingenuity in debate that Drayton and his contemporaries had learned from seventeenth-century schoolmasters: ability to uphold either side of a moot question. When

---

[22] Michael Drayton, *Poly-Olbion: A Chorographicall Description of All the Tracts, Rivers, Mountaines, Forests, and other Parts of This Renowned Isle of Great Britain* (printed, from the 1622 ed., by the Spenser Society, London, 1889). My references are to I, 65, 229–233; II, 164.

the "low counties" speak in *Poly-Olbion,* Drayton turned back
to the Latin poets and the Scriptures for epithets and adjectives
condemning the "warts and wens" of Nature. Mountains were
inhospitable, desolate, hostile, obdurate, barren, hard, and proud.
But in the songs that deal with northern and western counties
—as in the Fourth Song treating Monmouthshire—the mountains become mighty warriors, bold and magnificent in their
strife, contending for the glory of England or of Wales. The
cumulative impression of *Poly-Olbion* is that Drayton himself
was *for* mountains rather than against them. He could abase
the hills in order to exalt the valleys when expediency demanded,
but when the Muse makes "mighty Malverne speake his mind
In honour of the Mountaine kind," Drayton comes stoutly to
the defense of mountains in general:

> And more, in our defence, to answere those, with spight
> That tearme us barren, rude, and voide of all delight;
> Wee Mountaines, to the Land, like Warts or Wens do bee,
> By which, fair'st living things disfigur'd oft they see; . . .
> Yet, falling to my lot, This stoutlie I maintaine
> 'Gainst Forrests, Valleys, Fields, Groves, Rivers, Pasture,
> Plaine. . . .
> The Mountaine is the King. . . .
> For Mountaines be like Men of brave heroique mind,
> With eyes erect to heaven, of whence themselves they find;
> Whereas the lowlie Vale, as earthlie, like it selfe,
> Doth never further looke then how to purchase pelfe.

The Cambrian Hills led him to his finest passage in praise of
mountain scenery, in which, although the vocabulary is still
derivative, there seems a personal feeling for grand nature. He
lavished his rhetoric, with overtones drawn from Greek rather
than Roman literature, upon "proud Skiddo that doth show the
high'st . . . most like Parnassus selfe . . . Having a double
head, as hath that sacred Mount." Head uplifted, "Skiddo"
surveyed the grand scenery of which he was himself part and

center. From his "glorious heights" he overlooked the "rough Hibernian Sea" and the long extended "Hills farre under me." When he was crowned with the "Helme of Clouds," the valleys trembled, but "Skiddo" their protector and their king stood firm, unshaken, grand, gazing proudly over that "row of Mountaines tall . . . which we our English Alpes may very aptly call." *Poly-Olbion* was probably written by a poet turning over books and maps in his study. Perhaps Drayton had traveled no farther than his native Warwickshire, though in the northern and western songs a modern reader feels an emotional response to the grand, the wild, the irregular in nature. Yet on the whole Drayton's mountain passages—there are more in *Poly-Olbion* than in any other poem of the century—prove the persistence of the literary conventions stemming from classics and Scripture.

But what of poets who had been to Wales or Scotland? We might use as a touchstone of taste the precursor of the "Peasant Poets" of the next century, John Taylor, "the Water Poet," since certainly he was not weighed down by classical learning. Summarily ejected from the only school he attended when he became "mired" in Latin grammar, and apprenticed to a barge-man, he nevertheless became a far traveler and one of the most voluminous versifiers of his day. His "Pennyles Pilgrimage" and "Moneylesse Perambulations" took him not only to Wales and Scotland but even to the continent. Disciple and rival of Thomas Coryat, he journeyed on foot from London to Scotland, where he was entertained with a day's hunting by one of the generous hosts who made his a penniless pilgrimage. His gratitude overflowed in doggerel [23] in which there are still reminiscences of his slight classical learning:

> If Sport like this can on the Mountaines be,
> Where Phoebus flames can never melt the Snow:
> Then let who list delight in Vales below,

[23] John Taylor, *Works* (published by the Spenser Society, London, 1870), pp. 12–13, 136.

> Skie-kissing Mountaines pleasure are for me. . . .
> Lowland, your Sports are low as is your Seate,
> The High-land Games & Minds, are high and great.

But it was the hunting rather than the mountains that Taylor really enjoyed. Later he went to Wales, a journey, he says, "Performed by the Riding, Going, Crawling, Running, and Writing of John Taylor." One ascent on horseback—"I mounted Dun, Dun mounted Penmen Mawre"—was enough:

> there are other Hills accounted higher,
> Whose lofty tops I had no mind t'aspire:
> As Snowdon, and the tall Plinnilimon,
> Which I no stomach had to tread upon.

More lettered—and often less traveled—poets on the whole agreed with Thomas Carew who, after a visit to Scotland, wrote to a friend:

> I breathe, sweet Ghib, the temperate air of Wrest,
> Where I no more with raging storms oppress'd
> Wear the cold nights out by the backs of Tweed,
> On the bleak mountains, where fierce tempests breed,
> And everlasting Winter dwells; where mild
> Favonious, and the vernal winds exil'd,
> Did never spread their wings; but the wild North
> Brings sterile fern, thistles, and brambles forth.[24]

William Drummond was born and bred in Scotland and lived amid wild and irregular scenery at Hawthornden by choice. There are momentary glimpses of real northern scenery in his poetry, particularly in "Tears on the Death of Moeliades," where the Clyde flows down "steepy rocks and Tweed through her green mountains clad with flocks." As a Scot he felt mountains symbols of liberty, "bulwark of our freedom, giant walls, which never friends did slight, nor sword made thralls." In stern

[24] Thomas Carew, "To My Friend G. N.," in *Minor Poets of the Seventeenth Century* (New York, 1931), p. 134.

Caledonia, men are "hard primitivists," who "run over panting mountains crown'd with ice." Yet even when he describes the country that he loved, Drummond's vocabulary and idiom are as much a pastiche of the classics as those of poets who had never left London. Old literary traditions persist in "the mountain's pride," in hills that "menace the spheres," in "the horrid mountains' helms of snow":

> Here grow green woods, here silver brooks do glide.
> Here mountains stretch them out with painted pride;
> Embroid'ring all the banks, here hills aspire
> To crown their heads with the ethereal fire.[25]

Drummond had traveled on the continent—though there is no evidence that he had crossed the Alps. His one Alpine reference is, like Pope's more famous lines, a reminiscence not of mountains but of Lucretius and Silius Italicus:

> Ah! as a pilgrim who the Alps doth pass,
> Or Atlas' temples crown'd with winter glass,
> The airy Caucasus, the Apennine,
> Pyrenees' clifts, where Sun doth never shine,
> When he some craggy hills hath overwent,
> Begins to think of rest, his journey spent,
> Til mounting some tall mountain, he do find
> More heights before him than he left behind.

Henry Vaughan loved the mountains among which he spent most of his life. "Swan of Usk" though he was, his feeling for the Welsh mountains was second only to his love for the river. Yet there are no extended descriptions of mountains in his poetry, and his allusions are couched in literary language. Drummond turned more naturally to the classics, Vaughan to the Scriptures. He heard "the hills and valleys into singing break"; with the Psalmist he looked "up to those bright, and gladsome

---

[25] William Drummond, "Flowers of Sion" and "The River of Forth Feasting," in Chalmers, *English Poets*, V, 670–682.

hills." Yet in spite of Biblical language, there are memories of real scenery in his poetry. Writing upon such a conventional subject as the Mount of Olives, Vaughan makes us remember that this was a hill, as real as English hills:

> *Cotswold* and *Cooper's* both have met
> With learned swaines, and Eccho yet
>   Their pipes, and wit;
> But thou sleep'st in a deepe neglect
> Untouch'd by any.

Loving mountains as he did, Vaughan believed that Jesus must have sought the comfort and peace of the everlasting hills. He liked to think that, during the periods of His life not treated in the Gospels, Jesus had found solace in Nature. "What happy, secret fountain, Fair shade, or mountain . . . Was then thy dwelling?" He recalled with joy and sadness two supreme moments in the life of the Savior, both associated with hills:

> Their Lord with thee had most to doe;
> He wept once, walkt whole nights on thee,
> And from thee (his suff'rings ended,)
>   Unto glorie
>   Was attended.

In Vaughan's most familiar lines, the mountain imagery is almost divorced from the Biblical idiom common in most of his poetry. "Looking Back" makes us feel that Vaughan had known hills and mountains and loved them for themselves as later for their evocation of great passages in the Bible:

> Fair shining Mountains of my pilgrimage,
>   And flow'ry Vales, whose flow'rs were stars;
> The days and nights of my first happy age;
>   An age without distaste and warres;
> When I by thought ascend your sunny heads,
>   And mind those sacred, midnight Lights;

> By which I walk'd, when curtain'd Rooms and Beds
>   Confin'd or seal'd up to other sights,
>   O then how bright
>   And quick a light
> Doth brush my heart and scatter light.[26]

But the theme, the language, and the mood are all derivative from poetic habits established for generations. Even Henry Vaughan, who spent most of his life among them, wrote of mountains as convention and tradition had taught him to write.

But surely—the modern reader may well feel—although academic training and lessons learned in church dimmed the eyes and dictated the vocabularies of men sitting in their London studies, and even of a Scot and a Welshman, men who crossed the Alps must have been overwhelmed by an experience that has moved modern poets to their most lyrical language. Let us try three of the best-known travelers of the seventeenth century, Thomas Coryat, James Howell, and John Evelyn, two of them writing in the earlier years, one at mid-century.

A curious "Oration Made by Hermanus Kircherus," supposedly "Professor of the University of Marpurg," prefixed to *Coryat's Crudities*, may give us momentary pause, for in this lyrical rhapsody we find more excessive praise of mountains than we have yet encountered. The unknown professor wrote:

What I pray you is more pleasant, more delectable, and more acceptable unto a man than to behold the heighth of hilles, as it were the very Atlantes themselves of heaven? to admire Hercules his pillars? to see the mountaines Taurus and Caucasus, to view the hill Olympus, the seat of Jupiter? to passe over the Alpes that were broken by Annibals Viniger? to climbe up the Apennine promontory of Italy? from the hill Ida to behold the rising of the Sunne before

[26] Henry Vaughan, *Works*, ed. by L. C. Martin (Oxford, 1914), II, 411, 414–415, 440, 516.

the Sunne appeares? to visite Parnassus and Helicon, the most celebrated seats of the Muses? Neither indeed is there any hill or hillocke,
which doth not containe it in the most sweete memory of worthy
matters.[27]

"Professor Kircher's" emotions, however, were aroused by classical mountains he had visited only between the covers of classical
authors, though, unlike most of the poets we have read, he
turned to Greek rather than Latin. Let us see how Coryat himself felt on the solitary journey on which he wore out the shoes
he immortalized in his illustrations. During his wanderings in
1611, Coryat entered Savoy by way of Aiguebelle, as will many
of our later travelers. His first ascent was made on foot, since,
as he candidly acknowledged, he was afraid to go on horseback.
Later his bravado failed, and he hired natives to carry him in a
crude chair, rigged for the occasion. Terrified every moment,
he experienced all the fear of later travelers, yet never for a
moment their "rapture" or "ecstasy." The classical reminiscences
that came to his mind were very different from those of
Kircherus: "When I had *tandem aliquando* gotten up to the
toppe, I said to my selfe with Aeneas in Virgil: *Forsan & haec
olim meminisse juvabit.*"

Safe in his study among his books, Professor Hermanus
Kircherus responded to the majesty of Taurus and Caucasus
that he had never seen, to sunrise over mountains that were his
heritage from classical literature. But Thomas Coryat, limping
on his journey and finding the Alps an almost impassable barrier
between himself and England, crossed them grimly, fearfully,
exasperated that they should be there at all, retarding him on
the most curious "record-breaking" Grand Tour of which
written record remains.

In his *Familiar Letters* [28] James Howell showed little interest

---

[27] *Coryat's Crudities* (Glasgow, 1905), I, 143–144, 217.
[28] *Epistolae Ho-Elianae: The Familiar Letters* (London, 1890), pp. 41,
95.

in scenery. He wrote to his father on September 7, 1619, comparing the topography of France with that of England:

There is not upon the Earth a richer Country, nor poorer People. 'Tis true, England hath a good repute abroad for her Fertility: yet . . . there be many more Heaths, Commons, bleak barren Hills and waste Grounds in England by many degrees, than I find here, and I am sorry our Country of Wales should give more Instances hereof than any other Part.

Another of Howell's entries might have served as a source for Joshua Poole's list of descriptive adjectives and epithets. He wrote from Lyons in 1621:

I am now got over the Alps and return'd to France; I had crossed and clambered up the Pyreneans to Spain before; they are not so high and hideous as the Alps; but for our mountains in Wales, as Eppint and Penwinmaur . . . they are but Molehills in comparison of these; they are but Pigmies compar'd to Giants, but Blisters to Imposthumes, or Pimples to Warts.

John Evelyn's emotions were more mixed, though any reader of the *Diary* is aware that Evelyn consistently preferred the works of Art to those of Nature. Nevertheless his first extended comment upon the Alps suggests that he was at least susceptible of emotions felt by later travelers.[29] On November 2, 1644, he made a partial ascent of Monte Pientio. Entering the clouds, "we seemed to be rather in the Sea than the Clowdes, till we having pierc'd quite through, came into a most serene heaven." This was, he said, "one of the most pleasant, new and altogether surprizing objects that in my life I ever beheld." Other comments, however, are conventional. Immediately after that experience, he commented on "heapes of Rocks so strangely congested and broaken . . . as would affright one with their horror and

[29] *Diary of John Evelyn*, ed. by E. S. de Beer (Oxford, 1955), II, 208–209, 507–511.

menacing postures." In 1646 Evelyn crossed the Simplon Pass, of which his chief memories were the dangers and discomforts of the journey even in May, "the Way having (tis sai'd) ben cover'd with Snow since the Creation." On muleback the travelers made their way "through very steepe, craggy, & dangerous passages . . . through strange, horrid & firefull Craggs & tracts abounding in Pine trees, & onely inhabited with Beares, Wolves, & Wild Goates . . . the horizon being terminated with rocks, & mountines, whose tops . . . seem'd to touch the Skies." From the mountains descended "greate Cataracts of Mealted Snow, and other Waters, which made a terrible roaring." Waste places of the world Lucretius had called mountain ranges. The seventeenth-century translator of Lucretius went even further. Arrived one night at Mergozzo, he saw the Alps, "which now rise as it were suddainly, after some hundred of miles of the most even Country in the World, and where there is hardly a stone to be found, as if nature had here swept up the rubbish of the Earth in the Alps, to forme and cleare the Plaines of Lombardy."

Clearly, no one of these travelers experienced the "ecstasy" or "rapture" common in the next century. Mountains were warts, blisters, imposthumes, when they were not the rubbish of the earth, swept away by the careful housewife Nature— waste places of the world, with little meaning and less charm for men who crossed the Alps only to reach the plains.

V

In *Pride and Prejudice* the "Peak" district of the Derbyshire Highland was "Mr. Darcy's county" to which Elizabeth Bennett traveled with her aunt and uncle "because of its known beauties." This was the place in which Anna Seward, "the Swan of Litchfield," spent her youth, of which she wrote: "The first scenic objects that met my infant glance, and impressed me with their lovely and romantic grandeur, were the mountains, the rocks, and the vales of Derbyshire." [30] In the period of High Romanticism, travelers sought the "Peak" for its strangeness and mystery and found there both the "romantic" and the "sublime."

What did the seventeenth century make of the "Peak"? Some journeyed there because they must; others because they were guests of various Earls of Devonshire, whose magnificent home, Chatsworth, was in the Devonshire Highlands, close to the border of Staffordshire. Even in the seventeenth century some travelers went from curiosity, for the "Wonders of the Peak" were already famous:

> Of the high Peak, are Seven wonders writ,
> Two Fonts, two Caves, one Palace, Mount, and Pitt.

Chatsworth was the work of Art; the others were the caprice of Nature who showed herself here in grotesque mood, in peaks that seemed to rise to prodigious height, in spouting geysers and caves. Geologically the district was different from anything the Londoner had seen.

In *Poly-Olbion* Drayton chose only unpleasant figures for this district:

> to th' unwearied Muse the Peake appeares the while,
> A withered Beldam long, with bleared watrish eyes . . .
> Her meager wrinkled face, being sulyed still with lead.[31]

Rehearsing her "Wonders," the "withered Beldam" called upon her children:

[30] Anna Seward, *Letters Written between the Years 1784-1807* (Edinburgh, 1811), III, 131; see also *Poetical Works, with Extracts from Her Literary Correspondence*, ed. by Walter Scott (Edinburgh, 1810), I, cliii–clxvi.

[31] Twenty-sixth Song in *Poly-Olbion*, II, 123-124. John Taylor visited the district in 1639 by chance rather than design. He was particularly impressed—not pleasantly so—by the caves and the "Devills Arse," where

My dreadfull daughters borne, your mothers deare delight,
Great Natures chiefest worke, wherein shee shewed her might;
Yee darke and hollow Caves, the pourtraitures of Hell,
Where Fogs and misty Damps continually doe dwell . . .

The epithets grow in ugliness until they reach a climax in the description of the "Devils-arse," that curious peak even more grotesque in the metaphysical sketch of Drayton's illustrator than in the poem itself. The "devils-arse" is black and swarthy —but not comely!

In the second part of Walton's *Compleat Angler*,[32] Charles Cotton described his meeting with a stranger from London, whom he invited to stop and fish with him in the "Peak" district. As they made the first ascent, "Viator" looked about him in consternation: "Bless me, what Mountains are here!" Like Coryat he was too frightened to continue on horseback, and more terrified still when he found the descent as "steep as a Penthouse." Arrived in Staffordshire, he drew a long breath and declared that if he ever lived to get back to London he would "sit down and write my Travels, and like Tom Coriate, print them at my own charge." Never again would he ascend the horrid hills; "so farewell Hanson Toot; I'll no more on thee; I'll go twenty Miles about first. Puh. I sweat, that my shirt sticks to my back."

The distaste of Cotton's traveler from the lowlands may be explained by his lack of experience or even by his reading of *Coryat's Crudities*. But worse is yet to come. In 1636 the still unknown tutor of the youthful William Cavendish, later second

---

he paused to write three addresses to His Satanic Majesty, "three jerks with my pen," concluding

> I know that many fooles will jeere and frumpe,
> That I dare come so neare the Divells Rumpe.

Taylor's account may be found in his "Pennyles Pilgrimage" mentioned above.

[32] Cotton's account is in part II, chapter ii. My quotations are from *The Complete Angler* (New York and London, 1847), pp. 40–48.

Earl of Devonshire, set himself the task of celebrating the district in which his patron lived, and Thomas Hobbes—who considered himself at this time a man of letters rather than a philospher—produced a poem, *De Mirabilibus Pecci Carmen*.[33] Hobbes was quite at home at Chatsworth. He had also traveled abroad with his pupil. He had experienced dangers of travel compared with which the Derbyshire Highlands were only child's play. Certainly he could not really have felt the fear and distaste he expressed in his poem, but was obviously describing the scenery about Chatsworth as Latin tradition dictated.

Although the *De Mirabilibus Pecci Carmen* may offer some material to a reader interested in manifestations of semiscientific curiosity, the student of literature is likely to remember it rather because Hobbes, when he attempted to be a poet, left behind him one of the worst examples of "metaphysical" grotesquerie:

> Behind a ruin'd mountain does appear
> Swelling into two parts, which turgent are
> As when we bend our bodies to the ground,
> The buttocks amply sticking out are found.

Such was the mountain poetry of the philosopher who was to give new direction to aesthetics and literary criticism.

If Hobbes's attitude seems strange, Charles Cotton's is quite inexplicable unless dictated by literary tradition. Hobbes had written his poem early in the century; it was translated into

[33] *De Mirabilibus Pecci Carmen: Being the Wonders of the Peak in Darbyshire . . . in Englishe and Latine; the Latine Written by Thomas Hobbes of Malmesbury, the Englishe by a Person of Quality* (London, 1678). My quotations may be found in this edition, pp. 16, 38, 30, 81. I have sometimes wondered whether the "Person of Quality" who translated Hobbes's poem was Charles Cotton, for in his *Wonders of the Peak* he frequently uses very similar phrases. During the latter part of the century English travelers sought the "Peak" district to see the "Wonders" which Defoe at least thought much overrated. See his *Journey through Scotland and Wales* (Everyman's Library), II, 157–179.

English only in 1678, about the time of his death. In 1679, Charles Cotton wrote his *Wonders of the Peak* to flatter a later Earl of Devonshire. The mantle of Elijah fell upon Elisha—with a vengeance. Although Hobbes had spent many years in the "Peak" district, he was, after all, an outlander. Charles Cotton had been born there and knew the "Peak" in all its moods. Except in this one poem, he shows such strong feeling for his native county that he has frequently been called an early Romanticist. He loved Nature most in her extremes, as in "Winter" and "Storm." In the "Stanzas Irreguliers," written to Izaak Walton, his fellow fisherman, he wrote lyrically of the "beloved rocks," from which he looked down "giddy with pleasure," of the strange caves that charmed him as much as the heights.[34]

And yet in the long formal poem on Chatsworth,[35] Cotton's adjectives and epithets might have been taken verbatim from Poole's *English Parnassus*. Why, he expostulates, has Heaven damned him to a place

> Where Nature only suffers in Disgrace,
> A Country so deformed, the Traveller
> Would swear that those parts Nature's Pudents were:
> Like Warts and Wens, Hills on the one side dwell
> To all but Natives Inaccessible;
> Th' other a blue scrofulus Scum defiles
> Flowing from th' Earth's imposthumated Boyles;
> That seems the steaps (Mountains on Mountains thrown)
> By which the Giants storm'd the Thunderers Throne.
> This from the prospect seems the sulph'rous Flood,
> Where sinful Sodom and Gomorrah stood.

Only the river Dove is exempt from the insults Cotton hurls at the whole region. If we are to believe what he says here,

[34] Charles Cotton, *Poems*, ed. by John Beresford (New York, n.d.), pp. 45–47.

[35] Charles Cotton, *The Wonders of the Peak*. The first edition appeared in 1681; my references are to the fourth edition of 1699, pp. 1, 46, 73.

rather than elsewhere, the river alone afforded him compensation for all the evils of the district, for the "Storm" and "Winter" he had once loved, the ugliness he had once found beautiful, the solitude in which he had taken such pleasure in the "Stanzas Irreguliers."

Cotton describes in even more detail than Hobbes the "Wonders" of the district. The "Peak" leads him to the most conventional rhetoric of disparagement:

> On your right hand close by, your Eye is strook
> With a stupendious Rock, raising so high
> His craggy Temples tow'rds the Azure sky,
> That if you should this with the rest compare,
> They Hillocks, Mole-Hills, Warts, and Pibbles are.

The ugliness of Nature enhances the beauty of Art: man has triumphed where Nature failed. A final compliment to Chatsworth led Cotton to the most drastic condemnation ever uttered of his native county:

> Environ'd round with Nature's Shames and Ills,
> Black Heaths, wild Rocks, black Crags, and naked Hills,
> And the whole prospect so inform, and rude,
> Who is it but must presently conclude?
> That this is Paradise, which seated stands
> In midst of Desarts and of barren Sands?
> So bright a Diamond would look if set
> In a vile socket of ignoble Jet,
> And such a face the new-born Nature took
> When out of Chaos by the Fiat strook.

Seventeenth-century travelers, diarists, essayists, poets, whether of the first rank or the third—all were conditioned in their attitudes toward the grander aspects of nature by their literary and religious heritage to such an extent that they described mountains only as books had taught them to speak.

VI

"High objects, it is true, attract the sight," Dryden wrote in the Dedication to his *Indian Emperor*, "but it looks up with pain on Craggy Rocks and Barren Mountains, and continues not long intent on any object, which is wanting in shades of green to entertain it." Here, merely in passing, is a suggestion of a psychological approach to scenery which will become common in the eighteenth century, when men of letters will be as much interested in the reasons for their reactions to nature as in nature itself. We have found nothing of this among earlier seventeenth-century poets whose aesthetics—if we may use a word they did not—remained as conventional and derivative as their landscape descriptions.

Marvell, with whom we began, is a good example of a poet into whom modern criticism is reading a self-conscious theory of art, yet whose aesthetics was primarily ethics. His condemnation of mountains was based upon Christian ideas of pride and humility and classical belief in limitation and proportion. The low hill at Bill-borow, with which the "unjust" mountain was contrasted, was beautiful in its restraint, suggesting as it did the Circle of Perfection the seventeenth-century poets found in a Divine Geometry that taught men lessons of moderation:

> The Beasts are by their Dens exprest,
> And Birds contrive an equal Nest;
> The low-roof'd Tortoises do dwell
> In cases fit of Tortoise-shell.

"Of all things, only Man unrul'd" built "unproportion'd" dwellings—this was the way Marvell felt as he contrasted the noble restraint of Appleton House with the disproportion of most contemporary architecture. In Appleton House he found an ethical order and harmony essential to beauty:

> Humility alone designs
> Those short but admirable Lines,

> By which ungirt and unconstrain'd,
> Things greater are in less contain'd.

"Lowness" is more worthy than "Greatness." Like poets before and after him, Marvell turned for his basic lesson to what he called "Nature"—that watchword of both classicist and Romanticist—and found it rather in a parable of Jesus:

> But all things are composed here
> Like Nature, orderly and near:
> In which we the dimensions find
> Of that more sober Age and Mind,
> When larger sized Men did stoop
> To enter at a narrow loop;
> As practising, in door so strait,
> To strain themselves through Heavens Gate.[36]

To Marvell, as to other classical and Christian poets, beauty was, as Aristotle and the Fathers had taught, a mean between extremes, appealing to Reason that recognized proportion, limitation, and restraint as qualities imposed by God upon Nature when he brought order out of chaos.

Although the seventeenth-century poets recognized the beauty of Nature—in the small, if not yet in the large—they seldom paused to consider the nature of Beauty and, when they defined Beauty, did so in terms of conventions they had inherited. "The worlds beauty is decai'd and gone," Donne wrote in "The First Anniversary"—"Beauty, that's colour and proportion." He was saying only what Augustine had said, paraphrasing words of Cicero that were probably already a commonplace when Cicero used them: "Beauty is a proportion of the parts, together with a certain agreeableness of color." Bacon wrote essays "Of Deformity" and "Of Beauty" in which there was nothing original. He and others who wrote on these topics associated *beauty*

---

[36] "Upon Appleton House," Stanzas ii, vi, iv, in Marvell, *Poems and Letters*, I, 59–60.

with human beings, not with external nature. "There are no Grotesques in Nature," [37] said Sir Thomas Browne, who had learned from both the Book of God's Words and the Book of God's Works that "there is a general beauty in the works of God":

I cannot tell by what Logick we call a Toad, a Bear, or an Elephant ugly; they being created in those outward shapes and figures which best express the action of their inward forms, and having past the Visitation of God, who saw that all he made was good.

Browne was remembering Genesis but also the long school of classical thought, going back at least to Plato, which taught that "that is beautiful which can do its particular work well."

Beauty was associated with living things—women, flowers, birds—rather than scenery and with the small rather than the large. Temperamentally most poets of the earlier seventeenth century, like Sir Thomas Browne, went "to School to the wisdom of Bees, Ants, and Spiders" and preferred "Regio-Montanus his Fly before his Eagle." "Ruder heads stand amazed," Browne wrote, "at those prodigious pieces of Nature, Whales, Dromidaries, and Camels . . . the Colossus and majestick pierces" of Nature's hand. But in "Nature's narrow Engines" he found a more "curious Mathematicks" and a truer reflection of "the Wisdom of their Maker." Those who were ready to feel another attitude in the presence of "the Colossus and Majestick pieces" of Nature were in a small minority. "I confess," wrote Abraham Cowley,[38] "I love littleness almost in all things. A little convenient Estate, a little cheerful House, a little Company, and a very little Feast. If I were ever to fall in love again (which is a Great Passion, and therefore I hope, I have done with it) it would be, I think, with Prettiness rather than Majestical Beauty." Cowley

[37] *Religio Medici*, in Sir Thomas Browne, *Works*, ed. by Geoffrey Keynes (London, 1928), I, 21–22.

[38] "Of Greatness," in *Essays, Plays, Sundry Verses*, ed. by A. R. Waller (Cambridge, Eng., 1906), p. 429.

was writing lightly, but the mood was the dominant one of his century.

Denis the Carthusian once wrote a treatise *De Venustate Mundi et Pulchritudine Dei* in which he implied that what man calls *beautiful* in the world is at most *pretty*, since Beauty belongs to God alone. So the poets of the earlier century felt that "greatness" and "vastness" were attributes of Deity rather than of landscape. Man's concern, as Donne suggested in his "Elegie for Prince Henry," was with "quotidian things . . . shut in for Man in one Circumference." God's were "th' enormous Greatnesses." "O rack me not to such a vast extent," said Herbert. "Those distances belong to Thee." Herbert and Marvell, Drayton and Denham, Coryat and Evelyn were not yet ready to experience the "Sublime" in external Nature. Conditioned by their classical and Biblical heritage, following classical and Christian teachers in an aesthetics subordinated to ethics, they were still living in a limited, circumscribed universe.

But the Circle of Perfection was to be shattered. Before we can understand the revolution in taste that occurred in this century which seems so conservative, we must turn back to the authors we have been reading to see that some of them at least —sometimes in the very works that have been quoted—were aware of other ideas that throw a different light upon the feeling of distaste and disparagement of grand works of Nature. In his passage on monstrosities and grotesques, Sir Thomas Browne did not mention mountains, though they might have served him to even better purpose than the toad, the bear, and the elephant. If God created mountains, must they not also be beautiful? But did God create mountains? Were they original with the world, or did they rise at some later period, as a result of human sin, and so remain to man a warning and rebuke, a visible reminder of the sin of man and the wrath of God?

Chapter Two

The Theological Dilemma

"The Lord's Controversy"

"HEAR, O ye mountains, the Lord's controversy!" Micah's phrase in peculiarly apt for our purposes, for a "Lord's controversy" in respect to external nature in general and mountains in particular seems to have gathered momentum during the Middle Ages, continued throughout the Renaissance and Reformation, and passed down to the seventeenth century, when the oppositions were faced and the controversy began to be resolved. Like Alph the sacred river, this was a stream that ran through caverns, sometimes flowing on the surface, sometimes seeming to disappear as it took its way through subterranean passages, emerging again to toss its waters into the air, like Alpheus in the fountain Arethusa.

We have found that our British ancestors—most of them lowlanders—had inherited from the classics and the Bible long-established traditions that were reflected in their descriptive poetry. Yet literary convention alone will not explain all the attitudes shown by Coryat, Howell, Evelyn on their travels or by Marvell and Drayton, Hobbes and Cotton in their poetry. Theology was equally important. During centuries of pondering upon crucial passages in the Bible, Christian and Hebrew Fathers had read into the first chapter of Genesis much that does not appear on the surface. The original earth, which God called good, should have been the ultimate model of beauty. When Deity created a world from chaos, what kind of world did He create? In the answers to this question we shall discover a dichotomy less familiar and more complex than the simple dualism of the seventeenth-century literary heritage.

I

The conventional idea most of us accept insofar as we ever consider the matter is that Adam and Eve found themselves in a world topographically much like our own:

"His hands prepared the dry land." Up to that moment the earth had been *void*, for it had been *without form*. The command that the waters should be gathered was the command that the earth should be sculptured. The sea was not driven to his place in suddenly restrained rebellion, but withdrawn to his place in perfect and patient obedience. The dry land appeared, not in level sands, forsaken by the surges, which those surges might again claim for their own; but in range beyond range of swelling hill and iron rock, for ever to claim kindred with the firmament, and to be companioned by the clouds of heaven.[1]

This happens to be Ruskin, but the idea had been widely accepted throughout Jewish and Christian history. Du Bartas and Milton are examples of Renaissance poets who followed the conventional interpretation when they described the emergence of the earth from chaos. Du Bartas began his description of the miracle of the third day with a passage indicating that mountains were original with the creation:

> All these steep mountains, those high horned tops
> The misty cloak of wandring clouds enwraps,

[1] John Ruskin, *Modern Painters* (New York, 1857), V, 86–87.

Under first waters their crump shoulders hid
And all the earth as a dull pond abid,
Until the all Monarchs bounteous Majesty . . .
Commanded Neptune straight to marshal forth
His floods apart, and to unfold the earth. . . .
Even so the sea to 'tself itself betook,
Mount after mount, field after field, besook.[2]

Milton, too, took for granted that after the third day the external earth was in general as it was in his own time:

God said,
"Be gathered now, ye waters under Heaven,
Into one place, and let dry land appear!"
Immediately the mountains huge appear
Emergent, and their broad bare backs upheave
Into the clouds; their tops ascend the sky.[3]

There is much more of this among seventeenth-century writers, but the idea is so familiar that we may turn to a less obvious conception, using as transition two homely illustrations that touch lightly upon opposed ideas of the original shape of the world.[4] Dekker in *The Gull's Hornbook* spoke of the world "as it was at first, with all the ancient circles, lines, parallels, and figures; representing indeed all the wrinkles, cracks, crevices, and flaws (like the mole on Helen's cheek, being *cos amoris*) stuck upon it at the first creation, and made it look more lovely." But in a song in "Britannia's Pastorals," William Browne suggested lightly that "the Cockle picked by Plow-men" was a tiny microcosm, and he implied two stages in its appearance, an early one when it was round, full, and unblemished and a later when it was marked by irregularities:

[2] Joshua Sylvester, trans., *Bartas: His Divine Weekes and Workes* (London, n.d. [1st ed., 1598]), III, 1–5, 7–8, 17–18.

[3] *Paradise Lost*, VII, 282–287.

[4] Thomas Dekker, *The Gull's Hornbook*, ed. by R. B. McKerrow (London, 1904), p. 17; William Browne, "Britannia's Pastorals," bk. II, Song iii, ll. 328–331, in William Browne, *Whole Works*, ed. by W. C. Hazlitt (London, 1869), II, 35.

> For being round and full at his halfe-birthe
> It signified the perfect Orbe of Earth;
> And by his inequalities when blowne
> The Earths low Vales and higher Hills were showne.

Marvell's "hook-shouldered" mountains deformed the earth. Let us look at the contrasting hill in the first stanza of the same poem:

> See how the arched Earth does here
> Rise in a perfect Hemisphere!
> The stiffest Compass could not strike
> A Line more circular and like;
> Nor softest Pensel draw a Brow
> So equal as this Hill does bow.
> It seems as for a Model laid,
> And that the World by it was made.

"The World by it was made." What kind of world? Certainly not the present deformed and disproportioned earth in which monstrous excrescences threaten the balance of the whole. A similar metaphor about the primitive earth was in Marvell's mind when he wrote "Upon Appleton House":

> This Scene again withdrawing brings
> A new and empty Face of things;
> A levell'd space, as smooth and plain,
> As Clothes for Lilly stretched to stain.
> The World when first created sure
> Was such a Table rase and pure.[5]

Later in the poem he made the contrast more explicit:

> 'Tis not what once it was, the World;
> But a rude Heap, together hurl'd;
> All negligently overthrown,
> Gulfes, Deserts, Precipices, Stone.

---

[5] "Upon Appleton House," stanzas lcvi, lxxxvi, in Andrew Marvell, *Poems and Letters*, ed. by H. M. Margoliouth (Oxford, 1927), I, 72, 82.

We have already considered briefly some of Donne's lines about "a Tenerif, or higher Hill," but we may well reread the whole passage in its context:

> But keepes the earth her round proportion still?
> Doth not a Tenarif, or higher Hill
> Rise so high like a Rocke, that one might thinke
> The floating Moone would shipwrack there, and sinke?
> Seas are so deepe, that Whales being strooke to day,
> Perchance to morrow, scarce at middle way
> Of their wished journies end, the bottome, die.
> And men, to sound depths, so much line untie,
> As one might thinke, that there would rise
> At end thereof, one of th' Antipodies.
> Are these but warts and pock-holes in the face
> Of th' earth? Thinke so; but yet confesse, in this
> The worlds proportion disfigured is.[6]

In "The First Anniversary" Donne was brooding over the chaos he felt everywhere around him: in the sudden death of youth, in his own personal problems, in the social and political milieu after the death of Elizabeth. The "decay of nature," his main theme, showed itself most immediately in the decay and death of man, the microcosm. But shortly before Donne wrote the poem, Galileo's telescopic discoveries made it appear that decay extended to the macrocosm, the universe. Donne's pervasive pessimism led him to find degeneration and decay equally in the geocosm, "the worlds whole frame." "Keepes the earth her round proportion still?" Donne asked, and answered his question in the negative. Once completely spherical and solid, the earth is no longer solid or round, but marked by "pock-holes," the unfathomable depths of the sea, and by "warts," the hills and mountains, all marring the once-smooth sphere of perfection.

[6] "The First Anniversary," ll. 284–301, in Donne, *Complete Poetry and Selected Prose*, ed. by John Hayward (Bloomsbury, 1929), pp. 204–205.

In Marvell and Donne we find a tradition different from that followed by Milton and Du Bartas. The original earth was not the world we see. The Great Sculptor had not carved out hills and mountains, valleys and depths of ocean. He was rather a classical aesthetician to whom symmetry, proportion, and the restraint of the circle were of first importance. Something had happened to cause the "warts and pock-marks." It is difficult today, in an age when social, economic, and international problems are paramount, to think ourselves back to a time when these were of far less importance than theological issues. We are so much more intent upon what man has made of man than upon what God originally made of him, so much more concerned with what man may make of Nature than with the Nature originally created by God, that once-burning issues seem trivial. But it is impossible to go far in our present problem of changing attitudes toward external nature unless we attempt to disentangle various strands of theological interpretation which generations of commentators had read into basic passages of Genesis.[7] Important though literary convention was, more basic were opposed points of view that had gradually developed among Jewish and Christian thinkers and came to a climax in the

[7] In spite of the vast amount of commentary upon Genesis, there seems no systematic treatment of the ideas most important in this study. I found some assistance in F. E. Robbins, *The Hexaemeral Literature: A Study of the Greek and Latin Commentaries on Genesis* (Chicago, 1912). With the original help of Aileen Ward, I attempted to follow the development of these problems by reading the commentaries on Genesis by many of the authorities in the *Patrologia Latina*, testing them particularly on these themes: the first and third days of Creation; the location and description of Paradise; the judgment on Adam and Eve; the Deluge. It is impossible to refer to all authorities consulted and fortunately unnecessary since so many of them simply repeat each other. In my original version I dealt at greater length with commentaries on the Deluge, but Don Cameron Allen has covered so much material in his *Legend of Noah: Renaissance Rationalism in Art, Science, and Letters* (Urbana, 1949) that I have shortened my discussion of the Flood, both here and in Chapters Five and Six.

periods of the Renaissance and Reformation. When did mountains appear on the earth, and why?

II

The "Notion of the Mundane Egg, or that the World was Oviform," wrote Thomas Burnet in *The Sacred Theory of the Earth*,[8] "hath been the Sense and Language of all Antiquity, Latins, Greeks, Persians, Aegyptians, and others." In their theological, as in their literary heritage, our ancestors found dualism in classical and Scriptural traditions. We need not go back, as did Burnet, to Persian, Egyptian, or other Oriental legends of the "cosmic egg." In either classical or Christian writers, poets like Donne and Marvell could have found the idea that the original earth was smooth and round. Ovid was repeating what had long been said when he began the *Metamorphoses* with an account of the emergence of the world from chaos.[9] When a god created the earth

his first care was to shape the earth into a great ball, so that it might be the same in all directions. After that, he commanded the sea to spread out this way and that, to swell into waves under the influence of the rushing winds, and to pour themselves around earth's shores.

Only later—there is no indication of the time involved—did the god ordain that the valleys should sink down and mountains rise up. Interested as Ovid was in *change*, which is his basic theme ("I should believe that nothing lasts long under the same form"), Ovid implied various metamorphoses in earth's surface, stressing the vicissitudes of sea and land that had been

[8] This work, published in 1681 as *Telluris Theoria Sacra* and translated into English in 1684, will be discussed in detail in Chapter Five. I quote throughout from the edition published at London in 1726. The quotation here is from vol. I, p. 86.

[9] Ovid, *Metamorphoses*, trans. by Mary McInnes (Penguin Books, 1955), bk. I, p. 32, bk. XV, p. 371.

posited by various classical philosophers. "I have seen what once was solid earth now changed into sea, and lands created out of what once was ocean. . . . Mountains have been washed away by floods, and levelled into plains." But classical writers who pictured the emergent earth as a great ball were not responsible for other conceptions that lie behind the seventeenth-century writers. These were inherited from commentators who had interpreted the most mysterious and provocative passages in the Bible, the first chapters of Genesis.

This is no place to enter into a discussion of the long controversy over "Bara: the Creation" (the first verse of Genesis) on which every important Jewish and Christian Father expressed himself.[10] Our present concern is only with those verses that were interpreted in connection with the structure and shape of the original earth. We may again take our departure from a familiar passage in Milton, even though he did not accept the theory of a primitive smooth earth. But on two occasions he implied the conception of the "Mundane Egg," which Burnet said had been "the Sense and Language of all Antiquity." In the first of the prologues in *Paradise Lost*, which begin as invocations to a classical Muse and end as prayers to the Holy Spirit, Milton wrote:

> Instruct me, for Thou know'st; Thou from the first
> Wast present, and with mighty wings outspread
> Dove-like satst brooding on the vast Abyss
> And mad'st it pregnant.[11]

Later when Raphael described the Creation to Adam and Eve, Milton said:

[10] The literary student, interested to see the importance of this to even a layman like Milton, will find a discussion in chapter v of George Newton Conklin, *Biblical Criticism and Heresy in Milton* (New York, 1949).

[11] *Paradise Lost*, I, 19–22; VII, 233–237. Milton was here following Jerome's interpretation which had been developed by Ambrose, Augustine, Strabo, and others.

> Darkness profound
> Cover'd th' Abyss; but on the watrie calme
> His brooding wings the Spirit of God outspred
> And vital vertue infus'd, and vital warmth
> Throughout the fluid mass.

Milton's figure shows that he is not translating the second verse of Genesis as did the King James scholars, "the Spirit of God *moved* upon the face of the waters." Following a host of patristic commentators he went back to the Hebrew word which might imply various "movements," among them "hovering" or "fluttering." [12] Whatever the meaning of the original, it served as authority to Christian expositors, who, desirous of reading the Christian conception of the Trinity into the Hebrew text, seized upon a possible bird image to equate the "Holy Spirit" (*rauch —pneuma—spiritus*) with the Holy Ghost in the form of a Heavenly Dove. By the fourth century A.D. Basil in the *Hexaemeron* had established the interpretation that the original text of Genesis 1:2 implied the conception of a bird sitting upon its eggs. Basil was followed in this interpretation by various others who further developed the figure, though among the earlier Fathers the "Mundane Egg" was largely allegorical. As time went on, however, there was growing interest in the physical nature of the egg. Abelard established its elemental structure by

[12] A passage from Sir Walter Ralegh's *History of the World* (London, 1687; pt. 1, bk. i, ch. vi, p. 4) may assist the reader:

"After the Creation of Heaven and Earth, then void and without form, the Spirit of God moved upon the waters. The Seventy Interpreters use the word *superferebatur*, moved upon or over; *incubabat* or *fovebat* (saith Hierome) out of Basil; and Basil out of a Syrian Doctor; . . . which words *incubare* or *fovere*, importing warmth, hatching, or quickening, have a special likeness. . . . *The Word is taken of birds hatching their young, not corporally, but in a spiritual and unexpressible manner.* [Marginal Gloss: Junius.]

"Some of the Hebrews convert it to this effect, *Spiritus Dei volitabat; The Spirit of God did flutter.* . . . And therefore, whether that motion, vitality, and operation, were by incubation or how else, the manner is onely known to God."

the long-honored doctrine of "correspondence," the yolk corresponding to earth, the white to water, the membrane to air, the shell to fire. Within the curious shell of a little world made cunningly of elements, expositors discovered a possible explanation for one of the problems that had taxed their ingenuity—the source of the waters that inundated the world. But before we are ready to consider the relationship of the Deluge to mountains, we must return to other passages in Genesis.

There seems to have been an inherent dualism in Jewish thought about the appearance of the external earth at the time of Creation. Certainly a layman, reading the Bible, would take for granted that mountains were original, since Genesis says that, at the time of the Deluge, "all the high mountains that were under the whole heaven were covered." A particular mountain was named when the ark was said to have rested upon Ararat. But while mountains were mentioned in connection with the Flood, they were not mentioned earlier, and Biblical exegetes always seized as eagerly upon negative as positive evidence. Moses had described the four rivers of Paradise; if there were hills and mountains, why did he not speak of them? Both Jewish legend and the works of the Fathers indicate that each of the traditions we have found in the seventeenth century was familiar, although, as in the Christian interpretation, one was more customary than the other.

"Up to this time," declared various rabbinical exegetes, commenting upon the work of the third day of Creation,[13] "the earth was a plain, and wholly covered with water. Scarcely had the words of God, 'Let the waters be gathered together,' made themselves heard, when mountains appeared all over and hills."

[13] Louis Ginzberg, *The Legends of the Jews* (Philadelphia, 1913), I, 18. This is Professor Ginzberg's paraphrase of a number of commentators, to whom he refers in his notes, who held the conventional opinion. In this particular edition, the notes are not in the original volume, but in vol. V (Philadelphia, 1925). On this sentence and the one that follows, see V, 26, note 71. The passage about mountains flying like birds Ginzberg attributes to Tehellim (ed. by Buber [Wilna, 1891]), 90: 391.

Sometimes the imagery is more specific: "The mountains flew over the water as birds, whereupon God distributed them in accordance with the nature of the earth. . . . And God took earth and threw it upon the waters and they became land; then the small stones that were within the earth turned into mountains and hills." The other theory we have discovered, however, seems to have been even more common among Jewish than among Christian interpreters. Louis Ginzberg noted in *The Legends of the Jews:* "The conception that the mountains did not originally belong to the earth's form is prevalent in legend." [14] Jewish and Christian expositors who held the theory that mountains emerged at some time after the Creation were in agreement in attributing the blemishes on Nature to human depravity. A majority of the Christian thinkers blamed mountains upon the sins of the generation of Enosh, but Jewish legend often chose an earlier date. The belief that mountains arose as a result of the sin of Cain seems to have been frequently expressed. The account in Genesis reads: "And now cursed art thou from the ground which hath opened her mouth to receive thy brother's blood from thy hand." More than one rabbinical commentator interpreted: "The earth, which originally consisted of a level surface, became mountainous as a punishment for receiving Abel's blood . . . and the earth will not become level again until Messianic times." [15] So pervasive was this legend that, as Professor Ginzberg has shown, it is to be found not only in commentaries upon the Cain story in Genesis, but in interpretations of the Revelation upon Mount Sinai and of the destruction of the Egyptians in the Red Sea, when both sea and land refused to accept the bodies of the dead, earth because she "remembered with terror the curse that had been pronounced for having sucked up Abel's blood." [16]

[14] *Legends of the Jews*, V, 142.   [15] *Ibid.*, note 31.

[16] *Legends of the Jews* (Philadelphia, 1911), III, 31 and 91. At the time of the Revelation on Mount Sinai, earth "thought the resurrection of the dead was about to take place, and she would have to account for the blood of the slain she had absorbed."

Even more frequent, it would seem, was the belief that mountains, like other distortions of the earth, were an immediate result of the sin of Adam and Eve. Tenfold punishments were inflicted at that time on Adam, on Eve, and on the serpent, and—according to some interpretations—on earth also. Among these judgments were two of importance in our particular study: "Thenceforth she was to be divided into valleys and mountains . . . and finally she shall, one day, 'wax old like a garment.' " [17] The idea that the world was growing old and wearing out, based on the analogy of human senescence, was of course familiar in classical thinking, and the theme of the "decay of Nature" in Christian thought has often been traced. But the conception of progressive "decays of Nature" in both man and the external world seems to have been even more marked in Hebraic than in Christian thinking. The macrocosm reflected the microcosm, and degenerations in man were paralleled by corresponding deteriorations in the external world, among which the emergence of mountains was one of the most spectacular. Whether at the time of Adam or Cain or the generation of Enosh, man, as Henry Vaughan said in "Corruption," drew "the Curse upon the world, and Crackt the whole frame with his fall." According to one tradition, then, mountains are symbols of human sin, monstrous excrescences on the original smooth face of Nature. Here is a central issue in "the Lord's Controversy": was the punishment of human sin limited to man, or was it also extended to Nature? This leads us to the account of the judgment in Genesis 3: 14–20.

"It was taught in R. Nathan's name," reads the *Midrash Rabbah*, "*three* entered for judgment, yet *four* came out guilty. Adam and Eve and the serpent entered for judgment, whereas the *earth* was punished with them." [18] The earth was punished with man, but how are we to understand the word *earth*, ambig-

[17] *Legends of the Jews*, I, 77–81.
[18] *Midrash Rabbah*, ed. by H. Freedman and Maurice Simon (London, 1939), I, 39.

uous in other languages as in English? I must leave to others the dichotomy inherent in Jewish thinking and confine myself to Christian Fathers. "The Lord's Controversy" seems to go back ulitimately to one verse in Genesis, which led at first to dispute over words rather than ideas. In the Vulgate, Jerome incorrectly translated phrases in Genesis 3:17 as "maledicta terra in opere tuo," rather than "maledicta humus propter te." Aquila, in his early translation from Hebrew to Greek, had read the phrase correctly. Yet Jerome had authority for his reading in the Septuagint and in Origen, although the latter gave also Aquila's reading and others in the *Hexapla*.[19] Jerome's translation, however, persisted until finally, in the decision of the Council of Trent that "ipsa vetus et vulgata editio" should be the official Bible, it became and remained the standard reading of Roman Catholics. If, for convenience, we follow the English translation in the Roman Catholic Douay version on the one hand and the Protestant King James version on the other, we may see the distinction that developed. The Douay reading is, "Cursed is the earth in thy work." The King James scholars translated, "Cursed is the ground for thy sake."

"Men believe that their reason governs words," wrote Bacon, "but it is also true that words impose upon the understanding." So it proved in "the Lord's Controversy." In the two translations lurks a chiasmus. Had Jerome written, "Cursed is the *earth for thy sake*," and the opposition declared, "Cursed is the *ground in thy work*," the issue would at least have been clear-cut, and although dualism would still be present, the waters of controversy might well have divided into two main streams, rather than flowing on together with periodic eruptions. The chief problem was whether the "earth" was cursed *for man's sake* or only *in man's work*. If the curse was limited to the *humus* or soil,

[19] Cf. *Origenis Hexaplorum*, ed. by Fredericus Field (Oxonii, 1895), I, 16. Origen notes: "Et Aquila non discordit, dicens: Maledicta humus propter te."

external nature was not necessarily changed in appearance, and the topography of primitive earth may well have been as it now is. Adam's punishment—if *earth* means only *humus*—consisted chiefly in the fact that the once-fertile soil now brought forth thorns and thistles and stubbornly denied that ease of life which Milton's Adam and Eve remembered in Eden when

> after no more toil
> Of their sweet gardening labor than sufficed
> To recommend cool Zephyr, and made ease
> More easy, wholesome thirst and appetite
> More grateful, to their supper fruits they fell.[20]

But if the curse of God had passed from man to *terra*, then Nature too was cursed, and the earth may have changed as much in physical appearance as has man.

The earlier Fathers recognized the possible implications in Jerome's passage but did not labor them. Dispute over the passage was for many years confined to words rather than ideas. Augustine's authority was undoubtedly influential in stemming the implicit controversy, for although he followed Jerome in accepting the word *terra*, his comments on the passage indicate that the curse was laid on the *soil* rather than on the whole *earth*.[21] In the eighth and ninth centuries the problem involved in Jerome's translation became more important. Various Fathers who followed Jerome in using the word *terra* paused to consider the connotations. Alcuin did not specifically gloss the passage on the curse, though he indicated in passing that *humus* rather than *terra* was implied. Rabanus Maurus, still following the Jerome

---

[20] *Paradise Lost*, IV, 327–331.

[21] In *De Genesi contra Manichaeos*, caput xx (*Patrologia Latina*, XXXIV, 211–212), Augustine wrote: "Maledicta terra erit in omnibus operibus tuis"; here he mentioned the thorns and thistles and discussed man's difficulty in wresting his living from the soil. He concluded: "Ipsi sunt labores et tristitiae quas habet homo ex terra." In *De Genesi ad Litteram*, caput xxxviii (*P.L.*, XXXIV, 450), he again confined his discussion to the soil tilled by man.

translation, discussed the passage at some length. Strabo quoted several interpretations, indicating that by his time the verse was becoming an important *locus*. He seemed particularly interested in an idea implied rather than developed by Augustine, that the curse was upon *earth* in contradistinction to *water*, which remained blameless. More and more, the ambiguous *earth* cursed by God was coming to mean the world, the curse extending from man to Nature.[22]

Important though the theme of the "decay of nature" had been among the Greeks and Romans, at least from the time of Hesiod, the basic emphasis in the legend of the Four Ages was upon the degeneration of man rather than the deterioration of external nature. There was little in the classics to correspond to the Jewish and Christian parallelism between decay in one and the other, nothing like the brooding upon possible causal relationship between the sins of man and changes in the appearance of the world. Even those Christians who limited the curse of God to the *ground* agreed that the sin of Adam had some effect upon external nature. Milton, who followed the Protestant wording, quoted the Son of God as saying to Adam, "Cursed is the *ground for thy sake*." He was following a long train of early commentators when, in his description of the temptation, he indicated that the sins of both Eve and Adam were immediately reflected in the physical world.[23] When Eve ate the apple,

> Earth felt the wound, and Nature from her seat,
> Sighing through all her works, gave signs of woe.

When Adam "scrupled not to eat, Against his better knowledge, not deceived," there was again an immediate response of external nature:

[22] Alcuin, *Interrogationes et Responsiones in Genesin* (P.L., C, 53); Rabanus Maurus, *Commentaria in Genesin* (P.L., CVII, 519). Cf. Petrus Comestor, *Historia Scholastica* (P.L., CXCVII, 1084–1085).

[23] The passages are from *Paradise Lost*, bk. IX, beginning with ll. 782 and 997.

> Earth trembled from her entrails, as again
> In pangs, and Nature gave a second groan;
> Sky loured, and, muttering thunder, some sad drops
> Wept at completing of the mortal Sin
> Original.

He was following old authority, too, in the long passage in which he recounted in detail charges given by God to Nature: the sun bidden "so to move, so shine, As might affect the Earth with cold and heat Scarce tolerable"; the planets to perform motions "Of noxious efficacy . . . to join In synod unbenign"; the winds "with bluster to confound Sea, air, and shore." Conflicting opinions from the Fathers were in Milton's mind when he continued:

> *Some say* he bid his Angels turn askance
> The poles of earth twice ten degrees and more
> From the Sun's axle; they with labour pushed
> Oblique the centric Globe; *some say* the Sun
> Was bid turn reins from the equinoctial road.

Yet no matter how many earlier commentators Milton followed, he consistently developed the interpretation, "Cursed be the *ground for thy sake*," since all the changes in Nature that he listed caused only "heat and cold Scarce tolerable," affecting the *ground* from which Adam was to earn his bread in the sweat of his brow.

Whatever the division of opinion on this point, there was common consent among Biblical expositors that the Deluge, that judgment of God upon two millennia of human sin, must have affected external nature. With the exception of the first chapter of Genesis, there was no section of the Bible so interesting to the commentators as the account of the Flood. Was the Deluge localized or universal? Was Deucalion's Flood the same as Noah's? What effect did the Flood have upon Paradise? How did Noah find room in the ark, the dimensions of which were specifically ordained by God, for "two of every sort" of living things? What was the origin of the waters that inundated the globe? We cannot enter into these questions now,[24] though we shall return to them when old and new theories break forth afresh during the Burnet controversy. At present we are concerned with interpretations of the Flood only insofar as they touch upon our problem of the origin of mountains. Sir Walter Ralegh, who devoted a lengthy section of his *History of the World* to events reported in Genesis, suggested the two most frequent opinions when he was discussing the tradition that the seat of Paradise was effaced by the Flood:

Whereas it is supposed by Aug. Chrysamensis, that the Flood hath altered, deformed, or rather annihilated this place, in such sort, as no man can find any mark or memory thereof (of which opinion there were others also), ascribing to the Flood the cause of those high Mountains, which are found on all the Earth over, with many other strange effects.[25]

Having stated the most extreme position, Ralegh went on to the other:

For mine own opinion, I think neither the one, nor the other to be true. For although I cannot deny, but that the face of Paradise

[24] All these problems are discussed by Don Cameron Allen in *The Legend of Noah*, referred to above. Mr. Allen says (pp. 84–85): "The patristic writers had faced the question of whether the Flood had been universal when the pagans shouted that it was simply a local affair; but throughout the Middle Ages, save for an occasional announcement that the whole world was drowned, the matter had been forgotten. The scientific activities of the Renaissance brought this difficulty to the forefront again, for the men of that age wanted to know where the water came from and where it went after the Flood was over. The Catholic theologians met this difficulty by saying that the impossibility of explaining the mechanics of the Flood showed that it was a miracle, but the Protestants who were anxious to prove that all of the Bible accorded with reason sat down to work out coldly scientific solutions. They failed, of course, to produce such a solution, and with this failure, the inspired history of Noah became simply a Jewish myth."

[25] *History of the World*, pt. i, ch. ii, bk. v, p. 22.

was after the Flood withered, and grown old, in respect of the first beauty (for both the ages of men, and the nature of all things Time hath changed) yet if there had been no sign of any such place, or if the soil and seat had not remained, then would not Moses, who wrote of Paradise about 850 years after the Flood, have described it so particularly.

Ralegh named only one authority, though he added, "There were others also." Thomas Burnet was more specific. Discussing certain traditions about the primitive earth which he said were "common to both Jews and Christians," he mentioned among the more important: "That there was no Rain from the beginning of the World until the Deluge, and that there were no Mountains till the Flood." [26] His list of authorities included, "the ancient ordinary Glosse [upon Genesis] which some make eight hundred years old . . . Historia Scholastica, Alcuinis, Rabanus Maurus, Lyranus, and such Collectors of Antiquity. Bede relates that of the Plainness or Smoothness of the Antediluvian Earth." Certainly the reader of commentaries upon Genesis in the *Patrologia Latina* finds plenty of evidence for a theory that the original earth had been smooth and round and that mountains emerged for the first time after the Flood. But though the authorities cited by Burnet repeat the legend, no one of them held it as an article of faith. They were all content with a position established by Augustine. In the *De Genesi contra Manichaeos*, although he had something to say about the Deluge, Augustine did not mention mountains. In the *Enerratio in Psalmum LXXXIX* he implied that mountains emerged before the Flood, presumably on the third day of Creation. In the *De Genesi ad Litteram*, however, he made the suggestion which most of his followers accepted, but which, in the period of the mountain controversy,

[26] *The Sacred Theory of the Earth*, I, 394. Burnet referred to the *Glossa Ordinaria* of Walafrid Strabo; Rabanus Maurus, *Commentaria in Genesin*; Petrus Comestor, *Historia Scholastica*; Alcuin, *Interrogationes et Responsiones in Genesin*.

afforded ammunition on both sides. On the one hand, he said that, in reaching over Olympus, the waters of the Deluge rose so high as to dissolve the first heavens, thereby indicating that mountains were already in existence. On the other hand, he entered into a discussion of the difficulty of watering the primitive earth from one source of waters in Paradise, which led him to postulate a large fountain from which and to which the waters flowed and reflowed at the same time, as in the Nile Valley, aided by a system of underground channels and caves. This was made easier, he said, because "it is highly probable that in the early days of the earth most, but not all, areas were flat, so that there could be wider dispersion and expansion of the waters as they broke forth." [27] Later commentators interpreted this as meaning that, although some mountains might have existed since the Creation, they were few and less rugged than those we know today. Some force—presumably the Deluge—had raised them higher and as a consequence the valleys and the depths of ocean were more profound.

This was in general the position held by the commentators to whom Burnet alluded, even by Bede whom he particularly emphasized as an adherent of the smooth, plain antediluvian earth. Burnet was not alone in this interpretation, since among later commentators the idea of an original smooth earth was attributed to Bede more often than to any other Christian thinker. Bede's most extreme position was expressed in his *Expositio super Epistolas Catholicas*, in which he implied that the original earth was annihilated by the Flood and the one that emerged was rugged and irregular. But in the *De Sex Dierum Creatione Liber* (attributed to Bede by some but not all scholars) he repeated the Augustinian position that the original earth had been less rugged

---

[27] Augustine's words were: "Tunc in novitate terrarum, etsi non omnia, plura tamen plana fuisse credibile est, quo latius possent erumpentia fluenta dispergi atque distendi."

than it afterward became.[28] His commentary on II Peter 2:5,[29] "And God spared not the ancient world," is as ambiguous as the original is mysterious:

And he did not spare the original world: The world which the human race now inhabits is the same as the one occupied by people before the flood. Nevertheless, it is truly original, using the term as if it meant "different," as appears from later statements in this epistle. The world of that time perished, overwhelmed in a deluge of water. The former skies, in other words the tracts of turbulent air, were removed by the height of the accumulated waters and the earth took on a different appearance as the waters receded. It is believed that some mountains and valleys were originally created but not to the extent that they are now found on the earth's surface. It might be possible to deny this if it were not for the fact that we are able to observe changes every year brought about on the earth by the action of water. Thus it is all the more credible that such changes took place at that time, when the action of the waters attacking the earth was more powerful and of longer duration.

[28] The passage in the *Expositio* may be found in *P.L.*, XCIII, 75. In the *De Sex Dierum Creatione* (*P.L.*, XCIII, 75), the older text reads "plana," the later "plena." "Plana" is clearly correct in this context.

[29] Bede wrote (*P.L.*, XCIII, 85): "*Et originali mundo non pepercit:* Idem ipse mundus est, in quo nunc humanum genus habitat, quem inhabitaverunt hi qui ante diluvium fuerunt. Sed tamen recte originalis mundus ille, quasi alius dicitur, quia sicut in consequentibus huius epistolae scriptum continentur, ille tunc mundus aqua inundatus periit, et coelis videlicet qui erant prius, id est, cunctis aeris huius turbulenti spatiis aquarum accrescentium altitudine consumptis, terra quoque in alteram faciem excedentibus aquis immutata. Nam etsi montes aliqui atque convalles ab initio facti creduntur, non tamen tanti quanti in orbe cernuntur universo. Quod negari forte potuisset, si non etiam nunc omnibus annis terrarum faciem cerneremus aquarum subversione mutatam. Quod tanto magis tunc fuisse factum creditur, quanto maior ac diuturnior aquarum impetus terram obsidens alluebat." I am indebted to my colleague, Professor W. T. H. Jackson, for the translation.

Throughout all these passages from Augustine and Bede—and the writings of many other Fathers on the subject of the topography of the primitive earth—the word *plana* (level) echoes like a motif. Is it possible that this constant repetition of the idea of a more level or "flatter" earth was responsible for the growth of the legend that in the Dark Ages men believed the earth was flat—an old wives' tale still unfortunately taught to school children? Classical and patristic philosophers, with only a few exceptions, accepted the idea that the earth was round. But if even an excellent scholar like Burnet read from the Fathers what he wished to find—his beloved Mundane Egg—less expert clergy, finding the persistent repetition of "plana," might well have come to think that for centuries learned men believed the earth was flat.[30]

The poets, with whom we began and to whom we return, were not as concerned as the theologians with orthodoxy or heterodoxy in their descriptions of the smooth original earth. Neither Marvell nor Donne mentioned the Flood as the cause of the destruction of their circular smooth worlds. Except for the last two lines quoted, Marvell's imagination might well have gone back only to classical writers, without the intermediary step of Genesis, and though Donne's passage has definite theological overtones, he did not localize in time or place the destruction of his perfect globe. Michael Drayton, who as we know was able to adapt many traditions, made use of the most extreme position in his Ninth Song, in which the water nymphs replied to the mountain nymphs:

[30] F. E. Robbins in his *Hexaemeral Literature* and Arnold Williams in his *Common Expositor* both mention in passing a few Fathers who held the idea of a flat earth. The most interesting study I have found is Charles M. Jones, "The Flat Earth," *Thought,* IX (1934), 296–307. Aristotle, Ptolemy, and many others had taught that the earth was round; only a few of the Church Fathers—with the exception of Lactantius, none familiar to the general reader—held the other opinion.

Tell us, ye haughtie Hils, why vainly thus you threat,
Esteeming us so mean, compar'd to you so great.
To make you know your selves, you this must understand
That our great Maker layd the surface of the Land
As levell as the Lake untill the generall Flood,
When over all so long the troubled waters stood:
Which, hurried with the blasts from angry heaven that
    blew,
Upon huge massy heapes the loosened gravell threw!
Which, since, in tract of time, your selves did Mountaines
    name.
So that the Earth, by you (to check her mirthfull cheere)
May alwaies see (from heaven) those plagues that poured
    were
Upon the former world; as t'were by scars to showe
That still she must remain disfigur'd with the blow:
And by th' infectious slime that doomfull Deluge left,
Nature herself hath since of puritie been reft;
And by the seeds corrupt, the life of mortall man
Was shortned. With these plagues yee Mountains first
    began.[31]

In his stanzas "Of Divine Deity," Edmund Waller celebrated
Moses who had hymned the Creation and in as sublime strain
described the destruction of the world by Flood:

How the Flood drowned the first offending race,
Who might the figure of our world deface.
For new-made earth, so even and so fair,
Less equal now, uncertain makes the air;
Surprised with heat, and unexpected cold,
Early distempers make our youth look old;
Our days so evil, and so few, may tell
That on the ruins of that earth we dwell.[32]

[31] *Poly-Olbion*, bk. IX, ll. 105–122.
[32] Edmund Waller, *Poetical Works*, ed. by George Gilfillan (Edinburgh, 1857), p. 195.

The sixteenth-century Scottish poet David Lyndsay drew a graphic picture of Noah emerging from the ark to see a strange postdiluvian world.[33] "We may believe his heart was sore," said Lyndsay, as Noah remembered the earth he had known, "so plesand and perfyte, Quhilk to behold was gret delyte." Of the many physical changes that had occurred, Noah was most appalled by the deformed monstrosities, the mountains:

> The Erth, quhilk was so fair formit,
> Wes, be that curious Flude, deformit;
> Quhare unquhyle wer the plesand planis,
> Wer holkit glennis, and hie montanis;
> From clattrying cragis, gret and gray,
> The erth was weschin quyte away.

Among the Fathers and the poets we have found a series of disparate ideas, which have been isolated and analyzed, since they are basic to the Burnet controversy that was to bring them all sharply into focus. In none of the Fathers and in none of the poets have we found exactly the combination of ideas we shall discover at the end of the seventeenth century, when old "fundamental assumptions" and "unconscious presuppositions," long flowing underground, will mingle their waters of discord with the waters of new fountains. Yet all the elements are really before us, as they were in Abelard's smooth Mundane Egg. Each of these elements goes back to mysterious verses in Genesis or to commentaries upon those verses. If we are finally to understand the change that has taken place in modern thinking about mountains, we must remember the negative evidence of Genesis about mountains before the Flood; the long history of the mundane or cosmic egg, which, in the treatments of medieval commentators,

---

[33] "Dialogue betuixt Experience and Ane Courteour of the Miserabyll Estait of the World," in David Lyndsay, *Poetical Works*, ed. by David Laing (Edinburgh, 1879), II, 269–284. Lyndsay did not say that there were no mountains before the Flood; indeed, when the rains came, "sum to heychast montanis fleid." His emphasis is upon the havoc wrought in the physical earth by the effects of the Flood.

on the one hand was reverently read into the Holy Dove, on the other developed gradually the conception of a world made of elements, containing within itself one cause of its own destruction; the long dispute about the effects of the Deluge; and the curse laid by God upon the *earth*, which may have been either upon the *soil* or the *world*. Of them all, the last was undoubtedly the most pervasive "unconscious presupposition"—and to literary students the most important.

"Cursèd is the earth"—perhaps in this old idea, so old that we had forgotten it, lies one explanation of the superstitious awe with which Nature was surrounded, from the Dark Ages to Rip Van Winkle, in the minds of men to whom the "haunted air and gnoméd mine" were filled with malign and awful presences and powers. Is it possible that this idea helped to make the vague, mysterious landscape of the haunted mere in *Beowulf* so fearful? It is not all a matter of reptiles and dragons and water creatures with fierce tusks, or the elemental danger of "wolf-haunted valleys, perilous fen paths," awesome caves and caverns, mountains with rushing cascades and rivulets, or even the dread of primitive man for a Nature he does not understand. The author of *Beowulf* was reflecting more than primitive superstition. Conscious and perhaps unconscious presuppositions of theology hover over the poem. Grendel's dam and Grendel himself, "haunter of the borderlands," inhabited "the land of monsters" because their ancestry went back to Cain:

> The everlasting Lord avenged
> The death by which he slew his brother Abel;
> Nor gained he by that deed, since for the crime
> Far from mankind the Ruler banished him.
> Of him all monstrous things were brought to life,
> Ogres and goblins and accursed creatures,
> And giants, also, who long strove with God.[34]

[34] *Beowulf in Modern English*, trans. by Mary E. Waterhouse (Cambridge, Eng., 1949), p. 6; Introduction ll. 107-113.

As the curse of Cain consciously hovers over the poem, so perhaps unconsciously did the curse of God upon the earth—which contemporary theologians were arguing at the time *Beowulf* was written.

Perhaps the same unconscious presupposition may have lingered in Chaucer's mind when in the "Franklin's Tale" he added to the soliloquy of Dorigen [35] theological details which sound strange upon the lips of the "wyf That loveth hire housbonde as hire hertes lyf." Mourning his absence across the sea, she sat on the cliffs looking over the "grisly rokkes blake" of the stern coast, wondering at the strange providence of God, who presumably made nothing in vain ("In ydel, as men seyn, ye no thyng make"). Her dread of rocks upon which so many mariners have perished is understandable enough, but her pondering is couched in theological vein:

> But, Lord, thise grisly feendly rokkes blake,
> That semen rather a foul confusion
> Of werk than any fair creacion
> Of swich a parfit wys God and a stable,
> Why han ye wroght this werk unresonable?
> For by this werk, south, north, ne west, ne eest,
> Ther nys yfostered man, ne bryd, ne beest.

Dorigen's cry echoes and anticipates that of men more learned than she who, looking at broken rocks and stones on seacoast or among mountains and finding no order, but only wild asymmetry and multifarious confusion, could not persuade themselves that this was the world that the Lord had made and felt themselves rather standing upon the ruins of a broken world.

III

Insofar as critics have considered the feeling against external nature in the period of the Reformation, they seem to have taken

---

[35] "Franklin's Tale," ll. 865–893. I follow the text of the Robinson edition (Cambridge, Mass., 1933), p. 165.

for granted that the negativistic attitude was Calvin's.[36] For that reason I shall violate chronology and consider Calvin's attitude toward external nature in general and mountains in particular before turning to Luther. On this issue, as on many others, the two great Protestant reformers stood opposed. Perhaps this particular difference was not entirely the result of dogma and theology. Calvin spent much of his life among mountains, whereas Luther was a lowlander who, on his journey over the Alps, shared the fright and distaste of travelers like Coryat.

A natural lover of nature, Calvin could not believe that Nature, created by God, was other than good, nor could he read into it any reflection of the sin of man. His position may be seen in an important chapter in the *Institutes*, in which he developed the theme, "Man, unable to appreciate nature, because of his lapsed condition." He said:

God . . . hath manifested himself in the formation of every part of the world. . . . On all his works he hath inscribed his glory in characters so clear, unequivocal, and striking, that the most illiterate and stupid cannot exculpate themselves by the plea of ignorance. . . . But herein appears the vile ingratitude of men; that, while they ought to be proclaiming bounties bestowed upon them, they are only inflated with greater pride. . . . Notwithstanding the clear representations given by God in the mirror of his works, both of himself and of his everlasting dominion, such is our stupidity that, always inattentive to these obvious testimonies, we derive no advantages from them.[37]

External nature, far from being evil, was a supreme evidence of the goodness of God; evil existed not in external nature but in *man*. This is not to say that Calvin held that the external earth

[36] Cecil Moore in his pioneer essay, "The Return to Nature in English Poetry," to which I have referred above, accepted without question the idea that Calvinism led to a feeling of withdrawal from external nature. The idea was common among the older writers on the subject of attitudes toward nature.

[37] *The Institutes of the Christian Religion*, I, 58, 61, 69 (New Haven, 1816), bk. I, ch. v. The *Institutes* was written before Calvin went to Switzerland.

today was as beautiful as it had been in the days of Eden. His position was in general Augustine's. In a long passage in his commentary on Genesis,[38] discussing the opinion of those who insist that the whole face of nature was changed by the Flood, he admitted that some of the original beauty of earth had been damaged by the Flood; yet he concluded, "Notwithstanding I say that it is the same earth which was created in the beginning."

Calvin is one of the few commentators upon Genesis who at this late date did not enter into the mountain controversy, which had become at least a minor skirmish by this time. Neither in his comment on the work of the third day nor in his interpretation of the Deluge did he discuss mountains. Yet it is possible to reconstruct his attitude on various issues involved.

To Calvin, as later to Milton, the original Paradise was the Garden of Eden, a limited and circumscribed portion of the earth.[39] "I state this expressly," he says, "because there have been authors who would extend this garden over all regions of the

[38] *Commentaries upon the First Book of Moses Called Genesis*, ed. by John King (Edinburgh 1847), I, 113–114, 174–175.

[39] The problem of the location and size of the original Paradise had a long history among the Fathers. The expositors divided into two main groups, one holding that the original Paradise was comparatively small and limited to the actual Garden of Eden, the other asserting that Paradise constituted a major part of the earth. There was general agreement that Paradise disappeared, but authorities disagreed on when the disappearance occurred, some holding that it came about immediately after the expulsion of Adam and Eve, others (like Ralegh in the quoted passage) insisting that since the place of Paradise was known by Moses it continued to exist until the time of the Flood. In the passage quoted in the text, Calvin is following Augustine and opposing the other party. Milton's account of the destruction of Paradise follows one of the most interesting theories (*Paradise Lost*, XI, 825 ff.):

> then shall this Mount
> Of Paradise by might of waves be moved
> Out of his place, pushed by the horned flood,
> With all his verdure spoiled, and trees adrift
> Down the great river to the opening gulf,
> And there take root, an island salt and bare,
> The haunt of seals and orcs, and sea-mews clang.

world." On the problem of the curse God laid upon the earth, Calvin was equally specific. The original "blessing of earth" consisted in "that fertility which God infuses by his secret power"; the curse is "nothing else than the opposite privation, when God withdraws his favor." The earth itself is innocent. "This whole punishment is exacted, not from the earth itself, but from man alone." Nature is changed to man, but Nature herself is not fundamentally changed, because Nature is the work of God. Many had said that external nature like man decays, degenerates, passes through various stages. This Calvin denied: "It has been falsely maintained by some, that the earth is exhausted by the long succession of time, as if constant bringing forth had wearied it. They think more correctly that, by the increasing wickedness of man, the remaining blessing of God is gradually diminished and impaired."

If Calvin did not discuss mountains, he left a map of the original Paradise, with the words: "I will now submit a plan to view, that the reader may understand." [40] The map shows mountains as well as rivers in Eden. To be sure, these are neat and decorous hills, again reminding us of the theory of Augustine that, though mountains were original with the earth, they were greatly increased by the Flood. One of Calvin's important British interpreters, John Mercer, whose commentary on Genesis was widely read in the British Isles, suggested more specifically the point of view of Calvinism. In his commentary, Mercer followed Calvin point by point, though he sometimes expanded ideas Calvin touched only slightly. On this problem Mercer insisted that those who believed that mountains did not exist before the Flood and that they were cast up by the force of the Deluge were wrong; Genesis clearly showed that mountains and valleys were original with the Creation.[41] If man, lifting up his eyes to the hills,

[40] The map was published in the Geneva Bible; it is also to be found in many early editions of Calvin's *Commentaries*.

[41] *Ioannes Merceri Regii: In Genesin Primum Mosis Librum* (Geneva, 1597), pp. 172–173. It is interesting to see that both Protestant

failed to appreciate these or any other evidence of God's handiwork, the fault to Calvin was not in nature but in man's "lapsed
condition." Luther had held a different opinion.

In two commentaries upon Genesis,[42] Luther combined into
a pessimistic whole various elements of the Fathers which we
have considered. Of all his great body of works, these commentaries are the most important for our purpose, in part because
of the lucidity with which Luther brought order out of preceding chaos, in part because they were written in the last years
of Luther's life and embodied his final thinking on many important points. Luther did not doubt that the Flood destroyed

---

and Catholic expositors pay a good deal of attention to the mountain
controversy. One of the most widely read Catholic commentaries of this
period was the *Commentariorum et Disputationum in Genesin* by Bene-
dict Pererius, a Jesuit. In the 1601 edition, published at Cologne, p. 47,
Pererius discusses at some length the question: "Whether the difference
between mountains and valleys existed before the Flood?" He brands as
false the opinion of those who assert that the primeval earth was smooth,
without inequalities. He quotes extensively from other books of the
Bible to prove that the irregularities were there from the beginning and
then defends mountains because they add materially "ad decorum, ornatum
& commoditatem terrae." He also brings in the familiar pragmatic defense of the usefulness of hills and mountains. He returns to the subject
again, pp. 482 ff., in connection with his discussion of the Deluge. Another Catholic commentary that treats the subject extensively is Cornelius
Cornelii a Lapide, *Commentaria in Pentateuchem Mosis* (Antwerp, 1618),
pp. 43 ff. Most of the commentaries of this period that I have examined
go into the matter at least briefly, but these two are particularly detailed.

[42] References in this section are chiefly to two volumes: *Critical and
Devotional Commentaries on Genesis* (vol. I, *Luther on the Creation*;
vol. II, *Luther on Sin and the Flood*) in Martin Luther, *Precious and
Sacred Writings*, ed. by J. M. Lenker (Minneapolis, 1904). The only
one of the ideas I have mentioned which Luther does not discuss is the
breaking of the "Mundane Egg." He was much interested in the "Mundane
Egg," however, and discussed some of the interpretations. In his own
interpretation of Genesis 1:2, he wrote: "And as a hen sits upon her
eggs that she may hatch her young, thus warming her eggs and as it
were infusing into them animation, so the Scriptures say the Holy Ghost
brooded."

the place of Paradise; there was no question in his mind that Paradise was no small Garden of Eden. It was not "a confined garden of a few miles extent. It was doubtless the greater and better part of the earth. And my judgment is, this garden continued till the Deluge." The original earth had been a model of beauty. But beauty began to fade from external nature at the time of the Fall of Adam and continued to disappear in progressive stages of degeneration. One of the tragedies man must face is that "even the earth, which is innocent in itself and committed no sin, is nevertheless compelled to bear sin's curse." "All these things were deformed by sin and remain deformed still. . . . All creatures, yea, even the sun and the moon, have as it were put on sackcloth. They were all originally 'good,' but by sin and the curse they have become defiled and noxious. At length came the greater curse of the Flood, which destroyed Paradise, and the whole human race." [43] To Luther the evil effect seems always to have been from man to Nature, rather than from Nature to man.

Changes in external Nature did not occur at once. One of Luther's persistent emphases is that the deterioration of both man and Nature has been a long and steady descent. His translation of the disputed passage on the curse is significant. In his commentary he specifically took issue with Jerome's *terra*. His own translation was: "verflucht sei der Acker um deinetwillen." [44] The original curse was merely upon "Acker," the fields, the ground, not upon "Erde." But as time went on (Luther wrote) and "as the sins of men increased, the punishments of those sins increased also; and . . . all such punishments and evils were added to the original curse of the earth." The punishments imposed upon Adam were "lighter and more tolerable" than those of his progeny. The sin of Cain produced still other malign effects in Nature, though Luther did not state in detail the exact punishments man and Nature then suffered. As the

[43] *Luther on the Creation*, pp. 152–153.   [44] *Ibid.*, pp. 314–316.

sins of the generation of Enosh increased, the punishment inflicted on man and external Nature grew, until the climax came
in the Deluge.

Among changes in the appearance of Nature after the Deluge,
Luther specifically mentioned the emergence of mountains:

As therefore since the Flood mountains exist where fields and fruitful plains before flourished, so there can be no doubt that fountains
and sources of rivers are now found where none existed before,
and where the state of nature had been quite the contrary. For
the whole face of Nature was changed by that mighty convulsion.[45]

From this observation, Luther proceeded as always to a moral
lesson:

How much excellency has perished from our bodies through sin.
Wherefore the sum of the matter under discussion is that we must
speak of the whole nature since its corruption, as an entirely altered face of things: a face which nature has assumed, first by
means of sin, and secondly by the awful effects of the universal
Deluge. Nor has God ceased to act in the same way. When he
punishes sin he still curses at the same time the earth also.

To Luther the Deluge was a climax of man's early sins, but it
was only one such climax. "The whole world degenerates and
grows worse every day." This is his persistent refrain echoed by
many in the late Reformation period. As Luther read history,
he found the "decay of Nature" in every part of the microcosm
and macrocosm. The present tense he used so frequently was not
only a rhetorical but a historical present. He was trying to bring
home to his generation their parlous state, a condition even
worse than that of the generation of Cain or the generation of
Enosh because it occurred later. Behind Luther's exposition of
Genesis lay his philosophy of history which may be found in
many places in his works but most succinctly in the *Supputatio*

[45] *Ibid.*, pp. 164–165.

Annorum Mundi, written in 1541, and both in the original and in translation of great influence in Protestant countries.[46]

Augustine, following Hebraic and Christian traditions, had developed the classical conception of the "four ages"—gold, silver, brass, and iron—into "seven ages" of the world and of man, corresponding to the seven days of Creation.[47] "Sex milibus annorum stabit Mundus," stated *Elia Propheta,* "Septimus Dies Sabbatum aeternum est." The world created in 4000 B.C. (Luther conveniently used round numbers) would continue for six thousand years; after that would come the Millennium, the Sabbath corresponding to the seventh day upon which God rested. Five ages had already passed. Luther's sixth age was the Age of the Pope, but the Pope, he wrote, "will not complete his millennium." The world had become so evil that God would not permit it to continue until 2000 A.D. In his *Table Talk* Luther dated its end as early as 1560. "The last day is already breaking. . . . The world will perish shortly. . . . The last day is at the door, and I believe the world will not endure a hundred years."[48] It is an intensely pessimistic picture of the history of mankind: always

[46] Preserved Smith, *History of Modern Culture* (New York, 1930), I, 289, mentions an English translation of the *Supputatio,* 1576. I have not been able to find a copy of this translation, nor is it mentioned in either the *Short Title Catalogue* or the *British Museum Catalogue.* The Latin version is available in the Weimar edition of *Luthers Werke,* LIII, 1 ff. Consisting as it does largely of tables showing the world's history, the work is not so interesting and dramatic as Luther's treatment of the world's chronology in his commentary on Genesis, *Conversations,* and *Table Talk.* I have discussed these ideas of Luther's in my *Breaking of the Circle* (Evanston, Ill., 1950). There is some repetition in this section.

[47] The idea of the seven ages of man was a commonplace among early Jewish hexaemeral writers. See Robbins, *Hexaemeral Literature,* p. 27. Augustine developed the idea of the ages of the world in *De Genesi contra Manichaeos,* I, 23 (*P.L.,* CLXXII). It was further developed by Abelard in *Genesis* (*P.L.,* CLXXVIII, 771) and by Honorius in *De Imagine Mundi,* II, 75 (*P.L.,* CLXXII).

[48] *Conversations with Luther,* ed. by Preserved Smith and H. P. Gallinger (New York, 1913), pp. 245, 150.

man sins, and always his sins affect not only man but nature. "All creatures, yea, even the sun and moon, have put on sackcloth." The innocent earth has been forced to bear man's curse. Nature has decayed with man, and the world degenerates and grows worse every day. "Change and decay in all around" Luther saw. Two things alone remained constant—the sin of man and the wrath of God. "The end is at hand, at the very threshold. . . . The joys of the world are played out."

IV

Upon a generation conditioned more than they realized by such pessimism [49] dawned the "new star" of 1572—clear indication to many that this was God's omen proclaiming the end of the world. No matter what astronomers might say, Christians everywhere must have feared that this aberration of cosmic nature presaged the day of doom. Orthodoxy had long accepted the idea of the decay of human nature. But even among the most pessimistic, decay had been limited to sublunary nature in this world. Now corruption and decay had been extended by the wrath of God—and the sin of man—to the whole cosmos. The star of 1572 presaged it; the star of 1604 proved it; Galileo's telescopic discovery of spots in the moon and sun, implying that those celestial bodies too suffered degeneration, sealed the doom. "When we look for incorruption in the heavens," Sir Thomas Browne wrote, "we finde they are but like the Earth; Durable in their main bodies, alterable in their parts; whereof beside Comets and new Stars, perspectives begin to tell tales. And the spots that wander about the Sun, with Phaetons favour, would make clear conviction." Not only the world but the universe was approaching its end.

[49] If in this chapter I have stressed the medieval and Reformation background of the "decay of nature," it is merely because the Renaissance backgrounds have been made so familiar by scholars such as Richard F. Jones, George Williamson, Don Cameron Allen, Charles Monroe Coffin, and Victor Harris.

I see the World grows old, when as the heat
Of thy great love once spread, as in an urn,
Does closet up itself and still retreat.

So Herbert and so a dozen other poets. Sir Thomas Browne
wrote: " 'Tis too late to be ambitious. The great mutations of
the world are acted, or time may be too short for our designes.
. . . We whose generations are ordained in this setting part of
time, are providentially taken off from such imaginations." But
in another mood, Sir Thomas Browne the scientist could say:
"I believe the World grows near its end, yet is neither old nor
decayed, nor shall ever perish upon the ruines of its own Principles." [50]

It was natural that in such a period men's minds should turn
to the implications of a basic Aristotelian conception, long
opposed by the Fathers—the eternity of the world. The controversy over this idea in the sixteenth and seventeenth centuries
was no mere academic disputation. It was involved with a subconscious struggle for human survival and the survival of a
familiar world and universe. Among those who longed to uphold
the ancient "heresy" were men who, in revolt against the more
somber teachings of Christianity, strove to save their world
from extinction, if only by logic. Arrayed against them were
others, equally sincere, who felt it their duty to uphold orthodoxy even at the cost of humanity, the cost of the world. Dual
streams of optimism and pessimism which we have found in the
Fathers and the reformers broke into the open, flinging the waters
of discord high into the air. In the Goodman-Hakewill controversy, we find a result of the various trends of thought we
have been following.

Godfrey Goodman, "her Maiesties Chaplaine," later Bishop of
Gloucester, published *The Fall of Man* in 1616, with a second

[50] "Hydriotaphia," in Sir Thomas Browne, *Religio Medici and Other
Writings* (London, 1934), pp. 137, 133–134.

edition in 1618.[51] It was not directly challenged until 1627 when George Hakewill published his *Apologie of the Power and Providence of God,* which appeared again in 1630 and in an enlarged third edition in 1635, including a new section of 226 pages that comprised a point-by-point debate between the author and "G. G. a Reverent Prelate." [52] Goodman, now Bishop of Gloucester, had returned to the fight with some reluctance, it would seem, since by 1635 the temper of the age had changed from the pervasive melancholy of 1616. Basic issues on which Goodman and Hakewill disagreed may be seen more briefly in Milton's youthful Latin poem "Naturam non Pati Senium," a Cambridge exercise of 1628 presumably patterned upon the 1627 edition of Hakewill's *Apologie.* Milton was echoing Hakewill's belief that "decay" had not passed from microcosm to macrocosm. Decay is not in Nature, wrote the young poet; it is man who reads his own shortcomings and sin into the external world. "Driven and wearied by perpetual error," he wrote, man "dares to measure the deeds of the gods by his own, to his own laws he likens those graven on eternal adamant." If the "law" of man has

[51] *The Fall of Man; or, The Corruption of Nature proved by the Light of Our Naturall Reason* (London, 1616). For complete bibliography see R. F. Jones, *Ancients and Moderns* (St. Louis, 1936), pp. 292–294. Goodman's book is excessively rare. When I used it in England before the last war, I was not interested in the mountain controversy and made no notes upon it. Mr. Victor Harris was good enough to copy some pertinent passages from the microfilm of *The Fall of Man* in the University of Chicago Library. Most of the important points were made by Goodman again in the debate which was added by Hakewill to the 1635 edition of his own work.

[52] George Hakewill, *An Apologie or Declaration of the Power and Providence of God in the Government of the World,* divided into six books (Oxford, 1635). The Goodman-Hakewill debate is added as "Liber V," repaginated as pp. 1–226. The Goodman-Hakewill controversy has become increasingly familiar to scholars since R. F. Jones first pointed it out in his early *Background of the Battle of the Books* (St. Louis, 1920). Mr. Jones carried his study further in *Ancients and Moderns.* Victor Harris deals with the controversy in *All Coherence Gone* (Chicago, 1949).

been decay since the sin of Adam, there is no such law in Nature. "Shall the universal mother grow sterile with age?" he asks. "Shall she go stricken with eld, her steps uncertain, her starry head palsied?" He considered the implications of the new astronomy: "Shall the hideousness of age, and filth, and wasting, and the eternal famine of the years, vex the stars?" Has decay passed from man to the cosmos? Milton denied it and briefly reflected the mountain controversy, implying here, as later in *Paradise Lost*, that mountains were not evidences of the decay of the world, not "wrinkles and furrows" upon the face of a Nature now grown old.

In the third edition of the *Apologie*, with its debate between the pessimist and the optimist, the relation of the mountain controversy to the whole problem of the decay of Nature became explicit. Goodman believed that there was a "natural corruptibility" in the earth as in man. Hakewill insisted that the Divine Creator would not have made a corruptible earth. The apparent changes were the result not of *decay* but of *mutability*. Natural law is everywhere in operation: fertility follows barrenness, as barrenness fertility. In the seeds and springs of things are generation and regeneration.

Goodman was correct in his insistence that Hakewill's arguments, if carried to their logical conclusion, would lead his opponent to accept the Aristotelian heresy. Indeed Goodman pressed his lance into the weakest spot in Hakewill's logical armor, for in his heart Hakewill *was* arguing for the eternity of the world, yet attempting to keep from heresy. In his later preface "To the Christian Reader" Hakewill insisted that he did not actually argue the world's eternity in his earlier work, "but onely a possibilitie thereof in the course of nature, had not the God of nature by his supernatural power decreed to set an end to it." Hakewill's position seems to have been this: Nature, following her own course, would never decay. God, however, can and will put an end even to Nature. The world must end, but the end would come not by any defect in Nature herself but by the fiat of Deity.

In order to uphold their basic positions, both Goodman and Hakewill inevitably turned back to the various interpretations of Genesis we have considered and raised again the problems of the appearance of the original earth, the curse laid upon man and perhaps Nature, the effect of the Deluge upon the topography of the globe. Goodman followed the more pessimistic strain in the Fathers and the reformers, insisting upon steady progressive stages in the degeneration of both man and Nature.[53] The curse of God was not limited to man. "As man was corrupted . . . so it stood with the uniformitie of Gods judgments, that nothing should remain untouched, no not the elements themselves." Man was "totally defaced"; the world likewise, for even though it was His own work, "God at length in his wisdome for our sins, thought fit to deface it." The original earth had been very different from the one Goodman saw about him. "Before the deluge the earth was more levell, and framed according to a better rule of a Globe or a Center." That great catastrophe, the "generall confusion of nature," completely changed the face of the globe:

I suppose likewise, that the un-eveness of the earth (the hils and the vales) were much caused by this generall deluge; for ye shall observe, that the highest mountaines upon earth, carrie some proportion to the lowest bottom at Sea: . . . that God might observe some kinde of proportion in the inequalite.

Unlike many of the Fathers who had preceded him, Goodman did not confine himself only to theology and to logic. Personal observation played a part in his discussion of mountains. He was clearly interested in fossils, which he held, in orthodox fashion, to be results of the Deluge. He had noticed around him various phenomena which he felt could be explained only in terms of a great catastrophe:

[53] Goodman, *The Fall of Man*, pp. 280–281, 285.

I have observed rockes and stones seeming to hang in the ayre, without any circumiacent earth . . . and standing thus they did daily decay and decline, and therefore certainly were not thus from the first creation, but the conflux of waters hath uncovered them of earth, and left them naked and bare, to be the immoveable markes of the great deluge.[54]

Hakewill, too, had observed the supposed decay of rocks and mountains, but he refused to draw Goodman's conclusions. "If you please to reexamine them," he wrote, "you shall finde them either to be no necessary effects of a deluge, or at leastwise not of any universall floud; nor that the violence of Noah's floud did so much alter and deface the earth, or was the chief cause of mountaines and vallies as you pretend." He had noticed that the natural forces that seem to destroy serve also to rebuild. He replied not only to Goodman but to Isaiah:

But beside this, if any mountaines bee humbled into valleys, meanes are not wanting for the proportionable raising of valleys into mountaines, sometimes by inundations, it being the opinion if not of all yet I daresay both of the greatest and soundest part of Divines, that the mountaines, though made perchance they were not, yet were they much increased by the general floud.[55]

This led Hakewill into a spirited defense of the place of mountains in the scheme of the world. Like Goodman he went back to the classics and to the Fathers, but deliberately chose among his sources arguments that led to optimism rather than to pessimism. If mountains are less fruitful than valleys, they are not therefore less valuable and useful. Hakewill's pragmatic defense of mountains looked back to Pliny, but it also looked forward to John Ray whose listing of twenty instances of the usefulness of mountains in his *Wisdom of God* became a model for eighteenth-century poets. "To imagine the mountaines were not made by God as we now see them," Hakewill concluded his

[54] *Ibid.*, pp. 286–287.
[55] Hakewill, *Apologie* (1635), pp. 62, 69, 71 ff.

defense, "is in my judgment not to consider sufficiently of his worke."

But Hakewill's was more than a pragmatic defense. His mountain vocabulary is singularly free from the conventional epithets of disparagement. Clearly he liked the "pleasing variety of mountaines and vallies" and preferred a varied Nature to one too smooth and plain. Everywhere in the universe Hakewill found variety. A world less diversified would be a world less good, a world less beautiful. One of the longest and most rhetorical passages in the *Apologie* is that in which Hakewill, looking through Nature up to Nature's God, emphasized *variety* as a principle of the universe.[56] He who created the angels did not make them all seraphim; He who created the stars did not make all suns. There is variety and diversity among men, among animals, among vegetables, everywhere in the Great Chain of Being. Variety is found even in inorganic matter, for "he who created the stones, made them not all diamonds." Why, then, should we desire all parts of the earth alike? Hakewill concluded:

Truly, my Lord, I ever conceived that varietie, and disparitie, serving for ornament, use, and delight, might likewise thereby serve to set forth the wisedome, power and goodness of the Creator, no less than his greatest and most glorious workes. . . . I thinke that all things considered, wee have no less reason to blesse God for the less fruitfull mountaines, than for the fat and fruitfull vallies.

V

Neither Goodman nor Hakewill has said anything really original about the mountain controversy. They have merely brought in to sharper perspective latent issues involved. Goodman responded to the strain of pessimism we have found in one group of the Fathers and in Luther; his philosophy of history emphasized progressive degeneration in every age in man and in

[56] *Ibid.*, pp. 142-143.

Nature. Hakewill followed the more optimistic teachings of both the Middle Ages and the Renaissance. His theory of history was cyclical, but in his discussion of mutabilities of man and of Nature, he emphasized the rise rather than the fall. Hakewill was a man of modern if not yet of scientific cast of mind. Had it not been for the necessity of acknowledging the destruction of the world by God's fiat, he might have gone further in laying a basis for later scientific thinking. The "Bacon-faced generation" forgot his theology but remembered his optimism; well down into the latter part of the century, Hakewill remained in their minds a greater apostle of progress than he actually was.

The Goodman-Hakewill controversy, rich in innuendoes, was not unique in the earlier seventeenth century, but it serves better than any other series of writings to remind us of the point we have reached in our search for the origins of modern attitudes toward external Nature. We have come a long way from that early reading of Jerome which perhaps helped to bring "death into the world, and all our woe." We have followed the winding paths of a few Fathers who realized only vaguely the ultimate significance of problems they raised about the earth. We have heard men pondering the curse laid upon the earth—what *earth* involved, whether it was cursed "for man's sake" or only "in man's work." Confusion has never ceased to surround the cryptic passage. The problem implicit in the Fathers, more explicit in the period of the Reformation, came to one of its climaxes in the early seventeenth century when its proponents showed themselves opposed on many points but on none more basic than the question whether Nature has degenerated as has man.

Three strands of pessimism in regard to Nature have come together. Orthodoxy had long accepted the Christian conception of the "decay of human nature." Vaguely during the Middle Ages, more clearly during the Reformation, decay had passed from man to external Nature—to *terra*, as distinguished from *humus*—showing itself most markedly in the heights of mountains and depths of ocean. In 1572 and in 1604, decay was still further extended, and man faced the possibility of degeneration in the heavenly bodies—the decay, not only of man and of the earth, but of the cosmos. Yet each of these "decays" aroused opposition. Against the orthodox conception of the decay of Nature in man was the humanistic defense of the essential goodness of man. In opposition to the idea of the decay of Nature in the earth, we find one group of theologians stanchly insisting that the *earth* was not cursed, that this still is the world that the Lord hath made, and other men, like Hakewill, declaring that, even though God may and will destroy it, Nature in itself has no seeds of decay, but operates upon orderly laws. If momentarily the "new philosophy," which seemed to prophesy the decay of the cosmos, called all in doubt, the implications of the Galilean discoveries were to lead in the opposite direction, to exultation rather than despair. But the issues will not be finally resolved until old theology has come face to face with new science.

In the meantime we must leave "the Lord's Controversy" to consider still other oppositions which may seem of more moment today than these almost forgotten theological problems. We are wandering between two worlds. "It is as natural to die as to be born," said Bacon, "and to a little infant, perhaps, the one is as painful as the other." The seventeenth century suffered the throes of birth and death. As "the Lord's Controversy" died, other controversies arose to take its place.

Chapter Three

New Philosophy

"New Distant Scenes of Endless Science Rise"

IMPORTANT though "the Lord's Controversy" was, it would be unjust to the complex seventeenth century to imply that theological issues were the sole or even the most important cause of the volcanic eruption that occurred during the last years of the period. This was a "century of revolutions," affecting every field of thought. The quarrel over mountains merged in the late Restoration period with the Battle of the Books. Both were skirmishes in a long engagement, the war of Ancient versus Modern. Each had its part in the still more protracted warfare between science and religion. But this was also a "century of genius," the effect of which was shown in the advancement of "Scientia," which in the seventeenth century included both science and philosophy; it was natural history, rather than "science" in our restricted use of the term. It will be no surprise to find the "new distant scenes of endless science" leading to geology, but that search for the origin of modern mountain attitudes should involve astronomy may at first seem perplexing. Yet at some time we must set off on one of those "cosmic voyages" popular in the seventeenth and eighteenth centuries, follow Burton's long-winged hawk on a celestial journey, perhaps even lose ourselves in an "O Altitudo." From a journey into space, we may return to earth with new eyes. Experiencing "vastness" in the cosmic reaches, we may come back with new imaginations to the relative vastness of this punctual spot, our earth.

I

One intellectual world, as we have seen, was dying, another striving for being. It would be possible to follow the fading beliefs and the emergent attitudes through the works of many philosophers, scientists, and poets. But various issues faced by the seventeenth century, with the implicit contradictions and vacillations of opinion, will be more clearly understood, I believe, if I use as weather vane one philosopher of the mid-century who responded now to one, again to another, of the winds of doctrine affecting the climate of opinion.

I shall take my departure from Henry More, the Cambridge Platonist, philosopher, and poet. Only the scholar now reads More's tortuous *Philosophical Poems*, his cabbalistical interpretations of Daniel and the Apocalypse, his verbose theological works. Unfortunately More lacked the gift of true poetry, yet in spite of the ineptitude of his meter and rhyme, the harshness of his style, the abstruseness of his allegory, his "Platonic Poems" were contagious. The verbosity and superabundance of his prose did not disturb his contemporaries. His philosophical and theological works were widely read. Even more important was the fact that More was one of the most persuasive and compelling teachers of his generation. The charm of his personality, his native enthusiasm, his gentle mysticism laid its spell upon students who went out from Cambridge to teach his philosophy to another generation of pupils.

More's influence lived on in his pupil's pupil, Isaac Newton, in Leibniz, who found him one of the most congenial of English philosophers, in Barrow and Berkeley, in Shaftesbury, who acknowledged his debt, yet still owed him more than he knew. It was revived again in Coleridge, whose philosophy was even more influenced by the Christian Platonists than by the German idealists, and it powerfully affected the "Vermont Transcendentalists," who gave new direction to American idealism in the nineteenth century. Today we have been discovering More again and beginning to realize the extent to which he anticipated modern movements of thought. However, it is not primarily because of More's influence that I select him as a guide to the seemingly confused issues of the mid-century in which he lived but because he affords a better index to tendencies of his generation than would a more systematic thinker, such as Hobbes or Descartes. Henry More was immensely susceptible to ideas and often uncritical of those he accepted. His response was frequently emotional rather than logical. He was touched by the "enthusiasm" against which he warned his generation. I shall use him as a seventeenth-century weather vane to point various directions of winds of doctrine.

In 1652 More published his first important philosophical work, *An Antidote against Atheism,* one of the most important encyclopedias of the age and a model for such later "physico-theologies" as the Boyle Lectures. Encyclopedias were as popular in the seventeenth century as they are today, but their aim and scope were different. In our modern reference books knowledge is broken up into small segments. The desire of the seventeenth-century encyclopedists was to bring knowledge together, interpreting the facts of the external world in the light of one central premise. In the *Antidote against Atheism* More's contemporaries found information about flora and fauna, about the anatomy of animals and the physiology of man; they found the information offered, however, not for its factual value, but as proof of More's central thesis that all parts of the created universe argued "the power and Providence of God," that understanding of the central design in the creation of the world and of man would prove, as the title implied, "an antidote against atheism."

Wherever he looked in external Nature, More saw design and plan. "The Fabrick of Bodies of Animals argues a Deity; so too the bodies of men, and the seminal principle inherent in plants. . . . All things in nature, animate and inanimate, bespeak the providence and plan of Deity; Nothing made by Him can be other than good." Such is More's central thesis. Where did it lead him when he came to consider the warts and blisters of Nature?

Unlike Sir Thomas Browne, More entered into a consideration of the place of mountains in the created world,[1] proposing that we "swiftly course over the Valleys and Mountains," which to the atheist are "silent, and say nothing of a God."

To begin at the Top first, even those rudely-scattered Mountains, that seem but so many Wens and unnatural Protuberances upon the Face of the Earth, if you consider but of what consequence they are, thus reconciled you will deem them Ornaments as well as useful. For these are Nature's Stillatories, in whose hollow Caverns the ascending Vapours are congealed to the universal *Aqua vitae*, that good fresh-water, the Liquor of Life, that sustains all the living Creatures in the World.

Starting with the accepted theory that mountains were valuable because of their condensation of salt water into fresh, More listed many other uses, as Hakewill and others had done. All that he said about the usefulness of mountains had been said before, most of it for centuries, particularly by Pliny, whose pragmatic arguments had been reiterated by John Wilkins, an important popularizer of science, not long before More wrote his *Antidote*: Nature (saith Pliny) purposely framed them for many excellent uses; partly to tame the violence of greater rivers, to strengthen certain joints within the veins and bowels of the earth, to break

---

[1] *An Antidote against Atheism*, in *A Collection of Several Philosophical Writings of Dr. Henry More* (London, 1712), bk. I, ch. iii, pp. 47 ff., "The Great Usefulness of Hills and Mountains."

the force of the sea's inundation, and for the safety of the earth's inhabitants, whether beasts or men.[2]

More added little to Pliny's arguments, though ironically enough —so it seems to a reader who has lived through modern wars—he emphasized the part played by mountains in raising war from savagery to dignity:

Had it not been for the forenamed provision of Iron, Steel, and Brass, and such like necessary Materials, instead of all this glory and solemnity there had been nothing but howlings and shoutings of poor naked men, belabouring one another with shag'd sticks, or duly falling together by the ears at Fist-cuffs.

The *Antidote against Atheism* had a specific purpose. In 1640 Thomas Hobbes had circulated in manuscript a pamphlet that contained the germ of his philosophy. This he expanded into the *De Cive* and in 1651, the year before More's *Antidote*, into the *Leviathan*. Of all the atheisms of the century, none seemed so dangerous to Henry More as that of the "Arch Heretic," whose conceptions of the nature of God, of man, and of the universe were diametrically opposed to the fundamental religious, ethical, and metaphysical beliefs of the Cambridge Platonists. There is no need to rehearse here the series of controversies to which Hobbes gave rise. It is enough to say that More's *Antidote* was recognized as one of the early important replies to Hobbes and that the Cambridge Platonists were as much united by their opposition to Hobbes as by their Platonism.

What had Hobbes to do with the mountain controversy? To be sure, he has crossed our pages with his curious poem on the "Peak" district. Yet in his philosophical works Hobbes did not discuss mountains. Even in his rhetorical imagery, he showed no response, favorable or unfavorable, to hills and mountains.[3] Nev-

[2] John Wilkins, *That the Moon May Be a World, in Mathematical and Philosophical Works* (London, 1802), I, 63.

[3] A Master's candidate at Columbia University, Miss Elizabeth Falck, made a study of Hobbes's imagery in a Master's essay, which is on file in the Carpenter Library. Hobbes seldom referred to either mountains

ertheless in his passage on mountains More was denying implications in Hobbes whom he considered primarily responsible for bringing back into modern thought the "Epicurean heresy." In his *Antidote* More entered into the "Holy War," basic to many of the works of the Cambridge Platonists, notably Cudworth, whose *True Intellectual System of the Universe* and *Eternal and Immutable System of Morality* were the most complete antidotes to Hobbes offered by the Cambridge philosophers.

With our historical perspective, it is possible to discriminate between "atomism" as a scientific hypothesis and Lucretianism —or rather, pseudo-Epicureanism—with its supposed easy hedonistic morality. The distinction was not so easy in the seventeenth century. Robert Boyle, the most important atomist in English, felt it expedient to state frequently that he was following a scientific method, not theological dogma. He considered himself a "Christian Virtuoso." In his will he established the Boyle Lectures for the express purpose of stemming heresies in England. As the century proceeded, the power of the "Lucretian atheists" in science and philosophy grew. The more fully atomism proved its value as a scientific hypothesis, the more violently its supposed ethical and religious implications were attacked. "Of all the sects and factions which divide the world," Isaac Barrow wrote about 1665, "that of Epicurean scorners is become the most formidable." Somewhat later William Nichols, another leader in the crusade, declared: "Atheism and Theism are now got from the Court to the Exchange; they begin to talk of them in Shops and Stalls, and the Cavils of Spinoza and Hobbes are grown common even to the very Rabble." [4]

In his mountain passage in the *Antidote* More was really replying less to Hobbes than to Lucretius who was supposedly

---

or hills, and his imagery indicates no interest in either. This bears out my belief that his poem on the "Peak" was a mere rhetorical exercise.

[4] Isaac Barrow, *Theological Works* (Oxford, 1830), IV, 232; William Nichols, *A Conference with a Theist* (London, 1723), I, v.

responsible for the belief, persistent in many generations, that
mountains and other waste places of the world were evidence
of the fortuitous emergence of earth. Lucretius had written:

> Nature
> Has by no means been fashioned for our benefit
> By divine power; so great are the defects
> Which are her bane. First, of the whole space,
> Covered by the enormous reach of heaven,
> A greedy portion mountains occupy
> And forests of wild beasts; rocks and waste swamps
> Possess it, or the wide land-sundering sea. . . .
> For in truth, not by design
> Did the primordial particles of things
> Arrange themselves each in its own right place
> Intelligently.[5]

So far as mountains were concerned, More was thinking of these
words written centuries earlier and also of such contemporary
atomists as Pierre Gassendi, associate of Hobbes, who in a work
ostensibly devoted to the same purpose as that of Henry More
had insisted that mountains were evidence that man lives upon
ruins.[6] Gassendi's God seemed to More an arbitrary Deity, gloat-
ing over His power, a God who permitted ugliness in Nature.
"It were better to have no opinion of God at all," Bacon had
said and More believed, "than such an opinion as is unworthy
of him."

Later in his *Divine Dialogues* More replied in more detail to
the arguments of the *De Rerum Natura* in regard to mountains:

[5] *De Rerum Natura*, trans. by R. C. Trevelyan (Cambridge, Eng.,
1937), bk. V, ll. 198–225. On early seventeenth-century attitudes toward
atomism see Charles Harrison, "Ancient Atomists and English Literature
of the Seventeenth Century," *Harvard Studies in Classical Philology*,
XIV (1934), 1–80, and "Bacon, Hobbes, Boyle, and the Ancient Atomists,"
Harvard Studies and Notes in Philology and Literature, XV (1933),
191–218.

[6] Gassendi, *Abrégé de la Philosophie* (Lyon, 1684), II, 71–72.

Now for these Allegations, That Rocks and Mountains and Woods and the Sea take up so great a part; whatever elegancy there may be in Lucretius his Poetry, the Philosophy of such Objections, I am sure, lies very shallow. For it is as unskilfully alledged against Nature that all the Earth is not soft molds, as it would be that any Animal is not all Flesh, but that there is Blood also and Bones. The Rocks, therefore, beside other uses for conveying the subterraneous Waters, may serve also for consolidating the Earth. And it is manifest that the Hills are usually the Promptuaries of Rivers and Springs. . . . But the Poet seems to speak so unskilfully, as if he expected all the face of the Earth should be nothing else but rank green Meadow.[7]

When Henry More wrote his *Antidote* in the mid-century, Epicurus and Lucretius were still only potentially dangerous. "Little of the Epicurean philosophy was then known amongst us," John Evelyn noted in his diary on May 12, 1656, the year in which both he and Walter Charleton published their partial translations of Lucretius. For nearly a century Epicureanism had been more powerful in France than in England, where no complete translation of the *De Rerum Natura* appeared before 1675. Earlier English treatments had been concerned chiefly with the supposed morals of Epicurus, and the translators usually spent more time in apologies for their temerity in treating the author at all than in attempts to justify the position of either Epicurus or Lucretius.

Interest in literary, philosophical, and scientific Epicureanism grew steadily in England. During the Commonwealth years, when many Englishmen followed the King to France, men of letters as well as scientists and philosophers came into contact with French atomists, particularly Gassendi. Before and during the Restoration they returned to England with new interest in Epicureanism among their Gallic enthusiasms. Henry More had laid aside his philosophical pen before the publication of Creech's

[7] *Divine Dialogues* (2d ed.; London, 1713), p. 103.

English translation that remained standard for a century. Close to the end of his life, he paid no attention to the *annus mirabilis* of English Lucretianism, 1685, during which Dryden and Sir William Temple in England and Saint-Evremond in France published translations, letters, and essays that caused a literary vogue. The "Holy War" continued, and as we shall see, the Lucretian position in regard to mountains took on new importance after the publication of Burnet's *Sacred Theory of the Earth*. But we must go back to our mid-century barometer to detect still other changes in the climate of opinion, for although opposition to Epicurus, Lucretius, and Hobbes played some part in the mountain controversy, it was not of the first importance in the change in taste. Philosophers might have continued indefinitely to justify mountains for their usefulness, to present logical arguments proving their purpose in the scheme of things, and yet have felt no more stirring of the emotions than did Coryat, Howell, and Evelyn.

II

More's mountain arguments were not original. Even when he went beyond the usual pragmatic defense to say, "You may deem them *ornaments* as well as *useful*," he was merely repeating inherited commonplace. When he added that it was "better" not only for the *convenience* but for the *delight* of human life, that there should be distinction between mountain and valley, land and water, he was approaching a principle that was later to be of importance to him, but he did not go further in this early work than the poets and essayists we have read. *Variety* and *diversity* were still ethical rather than aesthetic principles. Yet Henry More was not uninterested in aesthetics. Indeed, in a later chapter in the *Antidote* [8] he developed at some length the thesis that "there is such a thing as Beauty, and that it is the Object of our intellectual Faculties." But beauty was still associated in More's

[8] *Antidote against Atheism*, pp. 52–53.

mind, as in Browne's, with the small and exquisite rather than with the large and grand. "I think it undeniable," he wrote, "but there is comely Symmetry and Beautifulness in sundry living Creatures, a tolerable useful Proportion of parts in all." More's vocabulary in the section that follows is interesting. Birds, he said, are "goodly things and beautiful," but at once corrected himself to write, "or at least elegant and *pretty*." But even in the animal kingdom More found creatures that aroused a different kind of admiration. "For *Stateliness* and *Majesty*," he asked, "what is comparable to a Horse?" Or what could vie with "that grave *Awfulness*, as in your best breed of Mastiff?"

Like the poets, More was conditioned by his literary heritage. His vocabulary in his mountain passages is the old one, "Wens and unnatural Protuberances upon the Face of Nature." Intellectually he was persuaded of the value of mountains, but emotionally he was unmoved by them. As with so many of his contemporaries, More's mountains came to him only from books. Born in the low counthy of Lincolnshire, he spent most of his life among the Cambridge fens. At this time he had been no farther afield than the rolling county of Warwickshire. And yet limited experience alone is not sufficient to explain his attitude: Henry More never saw a mountain. Neither did Immanuel Kant. There is, however, a great difference in their aesthetic attitudes toward the grand in Nature.

When he wrote the *Antidote* Henry More had fallen under the influence of Descartes. Indeed, he was one of the earliest English Cartesians and for some years one of the most influential, writing in praise of Descartes, teaching Cartesianism to his students at Christ's College. In 1652 his aesthetic was a fusion of sources: Plato and Pythagoras, as interpeted by Alexandrian and Renaissance Neoplatonic commentators; medieval Fathers, particularly Augustine; Descartes, as interpreted by More who did not yet fully grasp the implications of Cartesianism. He was quite prepared to agree with the aesthetic attitude implied in a passage in the *Discourse on the Method* [9] in which Descartes said that "those ancient cities which, originally mere villages, have become in the process of time great towns, are usually badly constructed in comparison with those which are regularly laid out on a plain by a surveyor" and with Descartes's belief that there is less perfection in a building "composed of several portions and carried out by the hands of several members, than in those on which one individual alone has worked." Like Descartes, More had no admiration for Gothic architecture.

As a Platonist, More remembered the "regular solids" of the *Timaeus*, repeated throughout the universe, the graphic pictures of the creation of the world from "geometrical seeds" of isosceles and scalene right-angled triangles, and the Platonic emphasis upon the harmony of the universe found in proportions existing everywhere in the cosmos. As a Christian he was equally familiar with Augustine's adaptation of earlier ideas to his own mathematical conception of the nature of the universe, his stress upon harmony in music and proportion in architecture and in the human body. Indeed, he was even more influenced by Augustine than by Plato, for it was Augustine who had equated these mathematical forms with the *beauty* he found on earth. Discussing the "steps of ascent" in the *De Ordine*,[10] Augustine had said: "From this stage, reason advanced to the province of the eyes. And scanning the earth and the heavens, it realized that nothing pleased it but beauty; and in beauty, design; and in design, dimensions; and in dimensions, number." To Augustine, God was the Divine Architect creating according to measure, number, and geometrical form. Human architects too should build in measure and proportion. There is a symmetry that pleases the Reason. "It pleases because it is beautiful, and it is beautiful because the parts are like and are brought by a certain bond to a single harmony."

Another passage from the *Antidote against Atheism* will show that in 1652 Henry More was far from feeling any enthusiasm for the irregular:

I appeal to any Man that is not sunk into so forlorn a pitch of Degeneracy, that he is as stupid as the basest of Beasts, whether, for example, a rightly-cut Tetrædrum, Cube, or Icosædrum, have no more pulchritude in them, than any rude broken Stone lying in the Field or High ways; or to name other solid Figures, which though they be not Regular, properly so called, yet have a settled Idea and Nature, as a Cone, Sphear, or Cylinder, whether the sight of these do not gratify the Minds of Men more, and pretend to more Elegancy of Shape, than those rude cuttings or chippings of free-stone that fall from the Mason's hands. . . .

It is observable, that if Nature shape any thing near this Geometrical accuracy, that we take notice of it with much content and pleasure; as if it be but exactly round . . . or ordinately Quin-quangular, or have the sides but Parallel, though the Angles be unequal. . . . These Stones, I say, gratifie our Sight, as having a nearer cognation with the Soul of Men, that is Rational and Intellectual, and therefore is well pleased when it meets with any outward Object that fits and agrees with those cogenite Ideas her own Nature is furnished with. For *Symmetry*, *Equality*, and *Correspondency of Parts*, is the discernment of *Reason*, not the Object of *Sense*.[11]

Beginning with the "regular solids" and "geometrical seeds," More has added other elements from Plotinus, Augustine, Ficino. He would have agreed with Sir Christopher Wren: "Beauty is a Harmony of Objects, begetting Pleasure by the Eye. There are two Causes of Beauty—natural and customary. Natural is from Geometry, consisting in uniformity (that is Equality). . . . Always the true test is natural or geometrical Beauty. Geometrical Figures are naturally more beautiful than any other irreg-

[11] *Antidote against Atheism*, p. 54.

ular; in this all consent, as to a Law of Nature." [12] The appeal of geometrical accuracy was to Reason. Nothing could be beautiful that was not rational. Certainly there was little in this early aesthetic of Henry More to justify *irregularity* as an aesthetic norm, nothing to make him feel the charm of ruins and grottoes and Gothic cathedrals, of clouds and mountains with their violation of geometrical pattern, little indeed to anticipate More's own later aesthetic in the *Divine Dialogues*.

III

The Cartesian aesthetic was only incidental, so far as More was concerned, since there was nothing in the passages in the *Discourse* that had not been implied by earlier writers. But other Cartesian ways of thinking remained with More even after he departed from his discipleship. Although he could not agree with Descartes's atomism, he was persuaded of the truth of the Cartesian insistence on the operation of regular laws of nature, mathematical and predictable, persuaded too of the truth of the idea of progress, in the development of which Descartes played an important part. But the proof More found for belief in progress differed radically from the Cartesian, for More was what Descartes had no desire to be—a religious philosopher. Only recently have we become aware of the important position held by More and certain other Cambridge philosophers and theologians in developing some of the most far-reaching implications in the modern idea of progress. Ernest Lee Tuveson in *Millennium and Utopia* has uncovered a neglected chapter in the development of the idea in the apocalyptical interpretations of seventeenth-century divines. [13]

[12] Sir Christopher Wren, *Parentalia*, in Sir Lawrence Weaver, *Sir Christopher Wren* (London, 1923), p. 150.

[13] Ernest Lee Tuveson, *Millennium and Utopia: A Study in the Background of the Idea of Progress* (Berkeley and Los Angeles, 1949). Mr. Tuveson, who studied with me at Columbia University, gives me much more credit than I deserve in his Preface. It is true that I suggested to

Today we have departed so far from our ancestors that we dismiss impatiently the seeming obsession of seventeenth-century theologians with the interpretation of prophetic books. Historians of science apologize for the fact that Isaac Newton considered his interpretation of Daniel more important than the *Principia*. Yet from the point of view of men like Henry More, interpretation of the apocalyptic prophecies *was* of much more moment to humanity than discovery of the law of gravitation. More and Newton believed that the prophetic books, properly interpreted, disproved completely the "sorrows of Cyprian," the despair of men who believed themselves living in the "setting part of time." Following Joseph Mede, the greatest apocalyptical expositor of the century, More had developed a conception of the Millennium very different from that of the Fathers and of Luther. Joseph Mede, writes Mr. Tuveson, began "the process of changing a purely secular and fortuitous theory of progress into one of predestined advancement toward a shortly to be expected apocalyptic event, and began to fasten on the 'modern' world the notion that it has a special role to play and a unique degree of enlightenment. . . . We stand, Mede told his contemporaries, close to the apex rather than the nadir of time." [14] Not only was there no need for despair; there was reason for the

him a study of Thomas Burnet and the Cambridge Platonists, yet I did so with no idea that he would reach the important conclusions he has found. His book was written independently at the Huntington Library. The first draft he sent me so closely paralleled this study, upon which I had been engaged for a number of years that, although I was glad to find that his conclusions agreed in the main with my own, I felt that his briefer study added little to my longer one. From that first draft he developed some papers, to some of which I refer below. I did not see his second study until I met him at the Huntington Library, when I was both surprised and delighted to discover his new approach. I may add that I was also chagrined, since I myself had too easily dismissed the apocalyptical studies of the Cambridge Platonists during the years I spent working on Henry More for my own doctoral dissertation and its development into the *Conway Letters*.

[14] Tuveson, *Millennium and Utopia*, pp. 84–85.

greatest possible optimism, evidence for which lay in the most sacred of all sources—the Book of God's Words.

Mr. Tuveson has shown in detail the new basis for optimism, laid down by these apocalyptical students. I shall not repeat his proof, but merely avail myself of some of his conclusions. Mede and More went further than the humanists in their insistence upon the *perfectibility of man*, further than Bodin, Le Roy, Bacon, and other earlier progressivists in their vision of the future. They did not look back to the past. The Millennium was not to be the end of all things but the beginning—the greatest age when man would live in a "Paradise happier far" than that lost by Adam and Eve. From the ruins of an old world would emerge a new and better one in which man, stripped of grossness, would rise with glorified body and glorified mind, a greater Phoenix soaring from the ashes.

Christian philosophers like Henry More did not fear death. What they had feared had been extinction—in this generation perhaps extinction of *mind*, even more than of body. If the world must be destroyed, the sooner the better, since that temporary destruction meant the coming of an era in which both mind and spirit would be possessed of powers far greater than at present. The Christian Platonists did not desire the everlasting rest. They anticipated rather a Millennium during which they would continue the intellectual activities that had engaged their minds on earth. More's "Middle Period" was neither on earth nor in Heaven. In the "middle regions" of the air he laid his Utopia, a new Jerusalem where men, furnished with "subtil aethereall bodies" that had sloughed off grossness, would "entertain themselves with Intellectual Contemplations, whether Naturall, Mathematical, or Metaphysicall . . . and administer much content to one another in mutual conferences concerning the nature of things." Milton's fallen angels engaged in "discourse more sweet," but their conversation was of foreknowledge, will, and fate, from which they "found no end in wandring mazes lost." More's ethereal spirits were likely to be discovered continuing such arguments as "whether Pythagoras' or Ptolemies Hypothesis be true concerning the Motion of the Earth; and whether the Stars be so bigge as some define them."

Robert Boyle spoke comfortable words of assurance "to those Christian virtuosi that are afraid to quit this world, chiefly, because they fear to lose the delightful philosophical knowledge they have of it." [15] Let them cease to fear. "It is as likely that all our faculties will, in the future blessed state, be enlarged and heightened; so will our knowledge also be, of all things that will continue worth it, and can contribute to our happiness in that new state." In this world or in that "middle region" to which ethereal spirits ascend, wrote John Ray, in his vision of the future, man would find

matter enough to exercise and employ our Minds, I do not say to all Eternity, but to many Ages. . . . Let us endeavour to promote and increase this knowledge, and make new Discoveries, not so much distrusting our own Parts, or despairing of our own Abilities, as to think that our Industry can add nothing to the Invention of our Ancestors, or correct any of their Mistakes. Let us not think that the Bounds of Science are fixed, like Hercules Pillars, and inscrib'd with a *Ne plus ultra;* . . . the Treasures of Nature are inexhaustible; here is Employment enough for the vastest Parts, the most indefatigable Industries, the happiest Opportunities, the most prolix and undisturb'd Vacancies.[16]

Whether before or after the Conflagration, the Millennium was at hand, and men began to look forward not with dread but with anticipation. The "Mechanist New Jerusalem," as Mr. Tuveson calls it, differed in many ways from older conceptions of Heaven. The new Paradise presupposed no "torpid and unactive State" consisting only "in an uninterrupted and endless

[15] Robert Boyle, *The Christian Virtuoso,* in *Works* (London, 1672), VI, 789.

[16] John Ray, *Wisdom of God Manifested in the Works of Creation* (10th ed.; London, 1735), pp. 199–200.

Act of Love." "Contentment is a sleepy Thing," said Thomas Traherne, and so Henry More felt. Man was perfectible, capable of greater things in the future than in the past. Progress was not only possible but inevitable, the main "plot" of God's great drama. In the cryptic riddles of the prophetic books, seventeenth-century optimists found God's promise of a new heavenly city of philosophers and scientists.

Read against this background, one of Henry More's few personal references to Isaac Newton [17] takes on added significance. Newton had come up to Cambridge from the Grantham Grammar School—which More also had attended—where his teacher had been Dr. Joseph Clark, one of More's former pupils, who had instilled into the young Newton many of the principles of Cambridge Platonism, as Newton's commonplace books show. Newton's Cambridge association with More continued until the latter's death. Writing to Dr. John Sharp on August 16, 1680, More said:

I remember you . . . asked me about Mr. Newton and my agreement in Apocalyptical Notions. And I remember I told you how well we agreed. For after his reading of the Exposition of the Apocalypse which I gave him, he came to my chamber, where he seem'd to me not onely to approve my Exposition as coherent and perspicuous throughout, but (by the manner of his countenance which is ordinarily melancholy and thoughtfull, but then mighty lightsome and cheerfull, and by the free profession of what satisfaction he took therein) to be in a manner transported.

In that chamber at Christ's College, Newton seems a symbol of his age. Discovering the "truth" embedded in the prophetic books

[17] *Conway Letters*, ed. by Marjorie Hope Nicolson (New Haven, 1930), pp. 478–479. In the following passage More takes exception to a "conceit" of Newton's in his interpretation of "the seven Vials" and adds a reproving comment about his pupil's pupil: "Mr. Newton has a singular Genius to Mathematicks, and I take him to be a good serious man. But he pronounces of the Seven Churches, not having yett read my Exposition of them."

of the Bible, he saw a new future for the world, for man, and for the advancement of learning and showed the effect of that discovery in a complete change of expression. The previous age had been "melancholy and thought full." The age of More and of Newton became "mighty lightsome and chearfull . . . in a manner transported." The vision of a New Jerusalem had put an end to former dread of intellectual extinction.

IV

For a time Henry More was a Cartesian; during a longer period he was an opponent of Hobbes. Before, during, and after those periods he was a "Platonist," with all the confused connotations of that term in his century.[18] How well he knew the Platonic dialogues at first hand is not important, since his Platonism was largely drawn from Alexandrian and Renaissance commentators and interpreters. Such Platonists were peculiarly receptive to the astronomy of Copernicus, since the heliocentric theory did not seem new to them, but rather a return to doctrines propounded by early Greek philosophers. "Then in the middle of them all stands the sun," wrote Copernicus. "For who, in our most beautiful temple, could set this light in another or better place, than that from which it can at once illuminate the whole? . . . Trimigistus calls it the visible God; Sophocles' Electra, the All-Seer. And in fact does the sun, seated on his royal throne, guide his family of planets as they circle round him." [19]

As a Platonist, More stoutly opposed the "stiff-standers for ag'd Ptolemee" and devoted a long canto of his *Immortality of*

[18] Inevitably there is a certain amount of repetition in this section of what I have said in *The Breaking of the Circle* (Evanston, Ill., 1950), where I dealt with More's attitude toward the idea of infinity. In the other study I developed in much more detail the mood of "aspiration" as it shows itself in Traherne and other writers.

[19] Copernicus, *De Revolutionibus*, quoted by Edwin A. Burtt, *Metaphysical Foundations of Physics* (New York, 1932), p. 45.

the Soul [20] to prove that "Pythagore's position's right, Coper-
nicks, or whosever dogma's hight," and to praise those

> Blest souls first Authors of Astronomie!
> Who clomb the heavens with your high reaching mind,
> Scal'd the high battlements of the lofty skie,
> To whom compar'd this earth a point you find.

All the discoveries reported by Galileo appear in More's poems:
the "stars innumerable," the Milky Way, the phases of Venus,
"the Medicean four [that] reel about Jove." Like most laymen
of his period More was particularly interested in Galileo's description of the moon, a little world dark in itself, shining by
reflected light:

> the Planets dark opacitie,
> Which long time hath been found in the low Moon:
> Hills, Valleys, and such like asperitie
> Through optick glasses thence have plainly shone.[21]

Galileo's discovery of the mountains of the moon seemed proof
that the moon and probably the planets were worlds like our
own, a theme to which More frequently returned in prose and
poetry.

Telescopic proof of the existence of mountains in the moon
afforded new arguments about mountains on earth. John Wilkins
wrote in *That the Moon May Be a World:*

Though there are some who think mountains to be a deformity to
the earth, as if they were either beat up by the flood, or else cast up
like so many heaps of rubbish left at the creation; yet if well considered, they will be found as much to conduce to the beauty and
conveniency of the universe, as any other parts.[22]

[20] *Psychathanasia; or, The Second Part of the Song of the Soul Treating
of the Immortality of Souls, Especially Mans Soul*, in *Complete Poems
of Dr. Henry More*, ed. by Alexander Grosart (Edinburgh, 1878), bk.
III, canto iii, stanza 1.

[21] *Ibid.*, III, iii, 62.   [22] *That the Moon May Be a World*, I, 63, 74.

"A good author," he added, "doth rightly call them nature's bulwarks, cast up at God Almighty's own charges, the scorns and curbs of victorious armies." Surely "such useful parts" were not the result of human sin, "but rather at the first created by the goodness and providence of the Almighty. . . . Since providence hath some special end in all its works, certainly then these mountains were not produced in vain; and what more probable meaning can we conceive there should be, than to make that Place convenient for Habitation." As on earth, so in the moon; as in the moon, so on earth.

Although Wilkins suggested that there was "beauty" in hills, the seventeenth century had inherited a quite different picture of lunar mountains from Kepler's *Somnium*.[23] The single piece of fiction written by the great scientist offered the most exact description of telescopic lunar hills and valleys, a vivid if forbidding spectacle of vast towering mountains, profound chasms and abysses into which crept for protection the strange denizens of the moon world, creatures of "a serpentine nature," fearful prehistoric monsters. From the *Somnium* passed into literature (even down to the nineteenth century) a grim, austere, yet majestic picture of lunar mountains, in which were combined the grandeur and terror of the later "Sublime."

There were, however, more profound implications in the new astronomy which, though they may seem at first to have little relationship to the mountain problem, were basic, I believe, to our modern feeling for the sublimity of external nature. For centuries man had turned to the supposedly eternal and immutable heavens for proof of his ethics and aesthetics. Change and decay might be everywhere in our terrestrial world, but until the seventeenth century they had been limited to sublunary regions. Beyond the orb of the moon, the heavens remained as the

[23] I have discussed Kepler's graphic description of lunar hills in "Kepler, the Somium, and John Donne," *J.H.I.*, I (1940), 259 ff.; see also my *Voyages to the Moon* (New York, 1948), pp. 46–47.

finger of God had made them, presumably even then arranged in the familiar constellations that for centuries had imposed an artificial pattern on the skies. But the cosmos was changing. Novae had appeared more than once in the supposedly immutable heavens. Galileo had discovered stars—and, he thought, planets —never seen before and had found spots on the sun and moon, arguing decay in those heavenly bodies. Man looked up at night to skies both familiar and strange. The pattern was breaking, and old ideals of order, proportion, restraint everywhere were threatened.

Elsewhere I have tried to show varying responses of the poets to the new astronomy: the early pessimism of Donne; Herbert's "content" with the old and refusal to be disturbed by the new implications; the "delight in disorder" of more daring spirits. As Henry More wrote:

> The meaner mind works with more nicetie
> As Spiders wont to weave their idle web.
> But braver spirits do all things gallantly
> Of lesser failings not at all affred:
>   So Natures carelesse pencill dipt in light
>   With sprinkled starres hath spattered the Night.[24]

Pascal's terror before infinite space was not characteristic of the Mores and Trahernes in England. Conditioned though they still were by ideals of order, these "soaring souls" sought and found another Order in the cosmos, transcending in magnificence the familiar but limited design. If man could see the heavens as they must appear from the true center, the sun, he would find a pattern more beautiful than that of the artificial constellations:

> But though these lights do seem so rudely throwen
> And scattered throughout the spacious sky,
> Yet each most seemly sits in his own Throne
> In distance due and comely Majesty. . . .

[24] "Cupid's Conflict," in *Complete Poems*, p. 172.

> Keeping a well-proportionated space
> One from another.[25]

Yet even from the sun he would observe the pattern of only one universe. Of all implications of the new astronomy, none so captivated the imagination of free spirits like More as the idea of a plurality of worlds, the theory that the fixed stars were suns, each the center of its universe:

> The Centre of each severall world's a Sunne . . .
> About whose radiant crown the Planets runne,
> Like reeling moths around a candle light;
> These all together, one world I conceit,
> And that even infinite such worlds there be,
> That inexhausted Good that God is hight,
> A full sufficient reason is to me,
> Who simple Goodness make the highest Deity.[26]

"INFINITIE OF WORLDS!" More had written when he first faced the ultimate implications of the new astronomy, "A thing monstrous if assented to, and to be startled at." [27] But his recoil was momentary, for, granted the God of Plenitude in whom More believed, the idea of an infinity of worlds was not monstrous but inevitable, not appalling but enthralling.

Henry More was the first English poet to express and the first English philosopher to teach the idea of infinite space and an infinity of worlds. "Roused up," as he said, "by a new Philosophick furie," he denied "the Hypothesis of either the world or time being infinite; defending the infinitude of both." He forgot the Reason he had so carefully cultivated and gave free rein to his own native enthusiasm. He broke the bonds of finite time and space and shattered the Circle of Perfection from which he had formerly deduced an ethics and aesthetics of limitation, restraint, and proportion.

As a philosopher Henry More's greatest contribution to the

[25] Henry More, *Democritus Platonissans; or, An Essay upon the Infinity of Worlds*, in *Complete Poems*, stanza 55, p. 96.
[26] *Ibid.*, stanza 51, p. 95.   [27] *Ibid.*, Preface.

history of thought lies in his development of the concept of absolute space and, to a lesser degree, absolute time. More's ideas on the subject first appeared in his poem, *Democritus Platonissans; or, An Essay upon the Infinity of Worlds Out of Platonick Principles*, published in 1646. They were further developed through his correspondence with Descartes and most fully discussed in the *Enchiridion Metaphysicum* and *Divine Dialogues*, though many of his later works treat the ideas of space that lay behind Barrow, Newton, Locke, and Berkeley. Space was the vehicle of Deity, by means of which finite man might come closer to comprehension of the true Infinite, God. We do not know it with our intellects, as we do not know God, yet we feel and sense it. And think as we will, we cannot think away space, as we cannot think away God. In his *Enchiridion Metaphysicum* More transferred to space some twenty attributes formerly associated with God:

This infinite and immobile space which is so certainly discerned in the nature of things will seem . . . to be something not merely real but divine. . . . The divine names and titles which precisely harmonize with it . . . are these which severally belong to Metaphysical Primal Being. As *Unum, Simplex, Immobile, Aeternum, Completum, Independens, A se existens, Per se subsistens, Incorruptible, Necessarium, Immensum, Increatum, Incircumscriptum, Incomprehensible, Omnipraesens, Incorporeum, Omnia permeans et complectens, Ens per Essentiam, Ens actu, Purus Actus*. There are no fewer than twenty epithets by which the divine Deity is wont to be described which harmonize most exactly with this infinite internal place which we have demonstrated to exist in the nature of things.[28]

Space is One, Incorruptible, Eternal, Complete, Independent, Immense, Uncreated, Omnipresent, Incorporeal. Yet though

[28] *Enchiridion Metaphysicum* (London, 1671), ch. viii, sec. 8. The translation is that of Mary Whiton Calkins, quoted by John Tull Baker, *An Historical and Critical Examination of English Space and Time Theories* (Bronxville, 1930), p. 12.

More seemed to be approaching the identification of Space with God, he refused to go the whole way and declare, with some later philosophers, that Space *is* God. Space is divine, as the dwelling place of Deity. More might indeed have used the phrase of Newton, whose conception of space was so largely drawn from him, and said that Space is "the sensorium of Deity." But though Space was a way to God, it was not God. "The spiritual object that we call space," he wrote, "is only a passing shadow, which represents for us, in the weak light of our intellect, the true and universal nature of the continuous divine presence, till we are able to perceive it directly with open eyes and at a nearer distance."

In spite of his place in the history of metaphysics, More would not be so significant for our purposes if his feeling for the new space had not been basically that of a poet. As Wordsworth said,

> Oh! many are the Poets that are sown
> By Nature; men endowed with highest gifts,
> The vision and the faculty divine;
> Yet wanting the accomplishment of verse.[29]

The *Infinity of Worlds* was a song of praise to an infinite universe, created by an Infinite God, His nature such that He could never be satisfied with less than all. In contemplating Space as in contemplating God, the soul of man was elated; released from finite limitations, it stretched its wings and took off into a vast universe of which there was no end, to seek the inexhaustible Good, and experienced triumph rather than despair because its quest must always remain unfinished:

> Unseen, incomprehensible He moves
> About himself each seeking entity
> That never yet shall find that which it loves.
> No finite thing shall reach infinity,
> No thing dispers'd comprehend that Unity. . . .

[29] *The Excursion*, I, 77–80.

Still falling short they never fail to seek,
Nor find they nothing by their diligence;
They find repast, their lively longing eek
Rekindled still.[30]

Into the new universe of stars and suns and space, More sent
his ecstatic soul to rove and range and be filled with the "astonishment," "amazement," "rapture" that are reiterated strains in
his poetry and prose whenever he approaches the theme of the
vastness of the universe. Attempting to grasp the whole, imagination and spirit grow vast as they feed on vastness. "Then all
the works of God with close embrace," More wrote in a minor
poem,[31] "I dearly hug in my enlargéd arms"—arms of the spirit,
arms of the imagination, growing with the universe. In the new
philosophy More felt the "psychology of infinity," the insatiability of man, striving for what he can never reach, yet feeling
not failure but delight in the effort.

In the new philosophy More discovered, too, arguments for
variety and diversity more significant than those he had used
before. "If these globes be regions of life, And severall kinds
of plants therein do grow," what different varieties of "Grasse,
flowers, hearbs, trees" [32]—perhaps men—must exist even in this
one cosmic universe? How much more elsewhere, in worlds and
universes of the past and future, for "Long ago there Earths
have been, Peopled with men and beasts before this Earth . . .
and after this shall others be again, And still another in endless
repedation." The cosmos created to infinity and eternity by a
God of Plenitude must be infinitely filled with every sort of
variety and diversity. One world, one universe was not enough.
More felt as Thomas Traherne wrote in "Insatiableness":

'Tis mean Ambition to desire
A single World.
To many I aspire,

[30] *Psychatanasia*, III, iii, 13, 14. [31] "Cupid's Conflict," p. 171.
[32] *Infinity of Worlds*, stanza 31, p. 94.

The one upon another hurl'd,
Nor will they all, if they be all confin'd
      Delight my mind.

This busy, vast, enquiring Soul
      Brooks no Controul;
      'Tis very curious too,
Each one of all these Worlds must be
Enricht with infinite Variety
      And Worth; or 'twill not do.

The *Divine Dialogues,* More's wisest and most charming work, was written in full maturity, yet the reader feels much of the youthful exuberance and enthusiasm of the earlier poems. This was More's most complete reply to Hobbes and other "atheists"; it was also the finest expression of Cambridge Platonism. In the *Divine Dialogues* More not only "accepted the universe" but rejoiced in every aspect of its richness, fullness, diversity, variety. There was room in his universe for all possible things, even for those which narrow-minded men called "evils." The waste places of the world, the uninhabitability of torrid and frigid zones, the "morbidness" of extremes of climate, the occurrence of untimely death seem evils to man merely because of his limited point of view. Without them the scenery of the world would be languid and flat, unworthy of the dramatist who contrived it. Henry More's Great Dramatist—the figure is a favorite of his—was no classicist, following the rules and the unities, but a Shakespeare or a Marlowe, an Author who crowded into his "Tragick Comedy" beauty and ugliness, laughter and tears, birth and death, with overflowing bounty seeming to say, "Here is God's plenty!" Even such supposed distortions of Nature as mountains have become ornaments. More's Nature-vocabulary changed with the development of his ethics and aesthetics. A passage in the *Grand Mystery of Godliness,* published in 1660, still harks back to literary models, but Longinus seems to have replaced the Latin poets:

And therefore we look upon the vast Capacity of the Wide Universe as a most august and Sacred Temple of His Divine Majesty, who fills and possesses every Part thereof. . . . Whether therefore our Eyes be struck with that more radiant Lustre of the Sun, or whether we behold that more placid and calm Beauty of the Moon, or be refreshed with the sweet Breathings of the open Air, or be taken up with the Contemplation of those pure sparkling Lights of the Stars, or stand astonished at the gushing Down-falls of some mighty River, as that of Nile, or admire the Height of some insuperable and inaccessible Rock or Mountain, or with a pleasing Horror and Chilness look upon some silent Wood, or solemn shady Grove; . . . From whatever part of this magnificent Temple of his, the World, he shall send forth his Voice, our Hearts and Eyes are perfectly directed thitherward with Fear, Love, and Veneration.[33]

In one of his many visions of the paradisaical Utopia, More imagined the "airy, subtle bodies" of departed souls dispersed abroad in a countryside filled with the diversity of Nature. "There is nothing that we enjoy," he wrote in *The Immortality of the Soul,* "but they may have their fees out of it: fair fields, large and invious woods, pleasant gardens, high and healthful mountains, where the purest gusts of air are to be met with, crystal streams, mossy springs, solemnity of entertainments, theatrick pomps and shows." [34] Mountains that had once seemed "unnatural Protuberances upon the Face of the Earth" have become essential in a world as diverse and full as possible, a world metaphysically, ethically, and aesthetically "better" because of its variety and diversity than "a languid flat thing."

As Henry More's theater of the world seems to look back to the superabundance of the Elizabethans, so it looked forward to Shaftesbury's diverse and varied universe, to Leibniz' "best of all possible worlds." In an age when the shades of French

[33] *An Explanation of the Grand Mystery of Godliness,* in *Theological Works* (London, 1708), pp. 43-44.
[34] *The Immortality of the Soul,* in *A Collection of Several Philosophic Writings of Dr. Henry More* (London, 1712), p. 177.

classicism were closing around English literature, More was carrying on the native English romantic temperament. If he did not travel all the way, nevertheless in his mature works, most of all in the *Divine Dialogues*, he had cast aside his earlier belief in restraint and limitation and allowed full play to his natural enthusiasm, his love of variety, diversity, irregularity as principles of Nature.

V

We have found the beginning of "The Aesthetics of the Infinite." In a vastly expanded universe, men like Henry More discovered new powers in the human soul, new expansion of the imagination. Into an infinite universe, they read qualities of the Infinite who had created it, and in themselves, made in the image of the Creator, they found capacities they had not known before. More's "large-wing'd Muse" soared into the empyrean, upheld by "powerfull fire" that "made her soar so high that mortal wit" would "tire to trace her. . . . But now my beating veins new force again invades, and holy fury doth inspire." [35] Space-intoxicated, he had no vocabulary with which to express his new emotions and turned from the *furor poeticus* to a *furor astronomicus*. The combination of awe and delight that Christians had long felt when they worshiped God, More felt as he worshiped Space and Infinity.

During the Restoration, which carried the French spirit into England, such lyrical rhapsody over the *vast* was temporarily stilled among the poets. The true lyricists of that period were the scientists and philosophers who carried on the surging spirit of aspiration, the attempt to grasp in their "enlargéd arms" a universe infinitely full of all possible variety. The more there was to know, the more avidly man desired to know it. Knowledge, once finite, had grown beyond his power but not beyond his desire to comprehend. "We should be apt to think too meanly

[35] *Infinity of Worlds, passim.*

of those attributes of our Creator," wrote John Ray, "should we be able to come to an End of all his Works, even in this sublunary World; and therefore I believe that never Man did yet, never any Man shall so long as the World endures, by his utmost industry attain to the Knowledge of all the Species of Nature. . . . The World is so richly furnish'd and provided, that Man need not fear want of Employment should he live to the Age of Methuselah, or ten times as long." [36] If so in the sublunary world, how much more is an infinity of worlds?

Henry Power wrote to his contemporary scientists:

When I seriously contemplate the freedom of your Spirits, the excellency of your Principles, the vast Reach of your Designs, to unriddle all Nature, me-thinks you have done more than men already, and may be well placed in a rank Specifically different from the rest of groveling Humanity. And this is the Age wherein all mens Souls are in a kind of fermentation, and the spirit of Wisdom and Learning begins to mount and free itself from those drosses and terrene Impediments wherewith it hath so long been clogg'd. . . . This is the Age wherein (me-thinks) Philosophy comes in with a Spring-tide. . . . These are the days that must lay a new Foundation of a more magnificent Philosophy, never to be overthrown. [37]

Such was the mood of "Scientia" [38] in England during the pe-

---

[36] John Ray, *Wisdom of God*, pp. 25, 369.

[37] Henry Power, *Experimental Philosophy in Three Books* (London, 1664), pp. 122–123.

[38] Professor Lovejoy says in *The Great Chain of Being* (Cambridge, Mass., 1936), pp. 225–226: "Thus these subtle philosophers and grave divines, and the poets like Pope and Haller who popularized their reasonings, rested their assertion of the goodness of the universe ultimately upon the same ground as Stevenson's child in the nursery: 'The world is so full of a number of things.' This did not, it is true, necessarily make them 'as happy as kings.' That was a matter of individual temperament; and in point of fact most of them had not the child's robust delight in the sheer diversity and multiplicity of things. They were often men whose natural taste or training would have inclined them rather to prefer

riod we call "neoclassical" because a powerful group of poets and critics preached an old doctrine of limitation with new emphasis drawn from the French, who had as yet hardly felt the force of the whirlwind that was sweeping over English thought. If there was a temporary interruption to the naturally romantic development of English literature, there was none in English thought. The Battle of the Books had been won by the Moderns. *Ne Plus Ultra* had given way before *Plua Ultra*. The scientific temper of the day was unappeasable. Men had discovered so much in a few decades that there seemed no limit to discovery, invention, knowledge. Man's potentialities seemed as unlimited as Nature's. His world might have become a minor planet, a speck, an atom. He forgot its insignificance, conscious less of a finite world than of an indefinite and infinitely full universe. Finite in his body, man was infinite in his aspiration. Modern man was greater than Adam! He would go on from strength to strength, "and who can set a *non-ultra* to [his] endeavours?" [39]

"Had we but World enough and Time!" The old lament is gone. The universe has become so vast, so full, that "what we know at present . . . is so little in comparison of what we know not, that there remains a boundless Scope for our Enquiries and Discoveries" as long as we live. Even death is no longer a barrier. "What if this present were the world's last hour?" What, indeed? It is *not* too late to be ambitious. The Millennium is at hand when the world's great age will begin anew. On earth or in those happy

---

a somewhat thin, simple, and exclusive universe. The philosophers of optimism were not, in short, as a rule of a Romantic disposition." What Professor Lovejoy says is, of course, true of Pope and of such philosophers as Bolingbroke. It is certainly not true of the scientists and popularizers of science, who, as I have said, were lyrical on the subject of the fullness and diversity of the universe. Their "Prefaces" and "Conclusions" are often paeans of praise to the Infinite God of an infinitely full universe. Insofar as a "Romantic" disposition implies insatiability, striving for the unattainable, delight in diversity, the scientific writers of the late Restoration and the early eighteenth century out-romanticize the Romantics.

[39] Henry Power, *Experimental Philosophy*, Preface.

"middle regions" man will go on with new powers to new accomplishments.

It is too early to prove, though not too early to state, a major contention of this study. The sense of the "Sublime" in external Nature which, more than any other one attitude, marks the difference between seventeenth- and eighteenth-century landscape and aesthetics was not, as it has usually been interpreted, the result of a literary tradition stemming from the rediscovery of Longinus. The Sublime had come to England well before the rhetorical theories of Longinus began to interest Englishmen. Awe, compounded of mingled terror and exultation, once reserved for God, passed over in the seventeenth century first to an expanded cosmos, then from the macrocosm to the greatest objects in the geocosm—mountains, ocean, desert. "Mountains, who to your Makers view, seem less than mole-hills do to you" are only relatively *vast*, yet except for the heavens they are the grandest and most majestic objects known to man. Scientifically minded Platonists, reading their ideas of infinity into a God of Plenitude, then reading them out again, transferred from God to Space to Nature conceptions of majesty, grandeur, vastness in which both admiration and awe were combined. The seventeenth century discovered "The Aesthetics of the Infinite." It was less the metaphysics of infinity that liberated their imaginations than an aesthetic implicit in their response to grandeur, vastness, majesty, a gratification in the richness, fullness, vastness of a universe man might not intellectually comprehend, which yet satisfied his unquiet soul, fed his insatiability. In his divine discontent lay his greatness. He grew with that he attempted to comprehend. Mind and spirit released from finite bonds, he became in part the thing he sought. The basis of "The Aesthetics of the Infinite" was laid down by Englishmen who found themselves astounded yet enthralled by infinite space.

Chapter Four

The Geological Dilemma

"Hills Whose Heads Touch Heaven"

IN the "Digression of Air" Robert Burton sent the "long-winged hawk" of his imagination into space, "still soaring higher and higher till he be come to his full pitch." [1] For a time he wandered about the world, "mounted aloft to the ethereal orbs and celestial spheres," his inquiring mind intent upon the mysteries of interstellar space. Then he swooped down to earth to observe terrestrial phenomena. He wished to explore above, beneath, within the globe, to learn "whether the earth's superficies be bigger than the sea's" and "whether the theory of Blancanus was true, that in time the sea will wash away the land." He would determine to his own satisfaction the altitude of mountains, "whether Mount Athos, Pelion, Olympus, Ossa, Caucasus, Atlas be so high as Pliny, Solinus, Mela relate. . . . The pike of Teneriffe how high it is?" But he would not stop there:

I would have a convenient place to go down with Orpheus, Ulysses, Hercules, Lucian's Menippus . . . to descend and see what is

[1] "Digression of Air," in *Anatomy of Melancholy*, ed. by Floyd Dell and Paul Jordan-Smith (New York, 1927), pp. 407 ff., 412–413.

done in the bowels of the earth; do stones and metals grow there still? How come they to dig up fish-bones, shells, beams, iron-works, many fathoms under ground? . . . Came this from earthquake, or from Noah's flood, as Christians suppose, or is there a vicissitude of sea and land, as Anaximines held of old?

As usual Burton raised problems and offered no solutions. In turn he considered physical theories of many ages, balancing in a sentence the old and the new, Aristotle and Agricola, Pliny and Blancanus. Burton was characteristic of his age, torn by "vicissitudes" of ancient and modern geological theories. Again we shall find paradox and problems as a new earth struggles to emerge from the old.

I

There is nothing in the "geology" [2]—not yet so called—of the earlier seventeenth century so spectacular as the revolution in astronomy, no dramatic moment to be compared with the night in 1609 when Galileo saw through heaven, no one geological work that brought science home so abruptly to laymen as did Galileo's *Sidereus Nuncius*. Geology was still only a part

[2] The most valuable source book for early geological ideas is Frank Dawson Adams, *The Birth and Development of the Geological Sciences* (Baltimore, 1938). Mr. Adams, who has combed classical, medieval, and Renaissance literature, not only gives excellent résumés of the important thinkers, but quotes copiously, frequently giving English translations of important passages extant only in Latin. I have drawn upon his work, often without acknowledgment in footnotes. Another volume rich in bibliography is Katharine Brownell Collier, *Cosmogonies of Our Fathers* (New York, 1934). I have found another valuable source in the early chapters of Charles Lyell, *Principles of Geology* (London, 1830). Seventeenth-century encyclopedias have proved of assistance, particularly in connection with the interpretations laymen made of the new ideas. As Kester Svendsen has pointed out in "Milton and the Encyclopedias," *Studies in Philology*, XXXIX (1942), 303–327, the poets drew much of their scientific knowledge from these popular works. This was particularly true of geology, since there was no one treatment of the earth that attracted wide popular attention. It was less true in astronomy; the layman often read Kepler and Galileo, as well as the popularizations.

of "Natural Philosophy," and as yet not an important part. In 1712 Addison included "mineralogists" among the "authors of the new philosophy" who stimulated imagination, finding in their discoveries "something very engaging to the fancy as well as to the reason." [3] But in the earlier seventeenth century, although the realm of inorganic matter made some appeal to intellectual curiosity, it afforded no such impetus to literary imagination as did discoveries in the macrocosm. Compared with other branches of science, geology seemed to mark time. The reason is obvious. Almost alone among the sciences geology was retarded by Genesis, which taught not only the miraculous creation of the earth in time, but divine order in the creation of inorganic matter and organic species.

As we have reason to know, many of our forefathers were far from being "fundamentalists" in the modern sense of the term. There were literalists then as always, but even among churchmen who did not go so far as Mede and More, interpretation of the Bible was often extremely liberal. The Protestant spirit, which permitted man to read and interpret Scripture for himself, placed upon him a heavy responsibility that sometimes led to strict literalism, yet often to a breadth of interpretation more radical than we find in the nineteenth century. [4] That the simple should accept the Bible as statement of fact was generally agreed; but the learned man—and he was learned in that day as few of us are now—read the Bible in various languages, weighing interpretations of Hebrew and Christian Fathers, expounding the text by lessons drawn from divines past and present. For centuries the Bible had been interpreted ethically; there were also philosophical, cabbalistical, allegorical, analogical expositions. Even that

[3] *Spectator* 420.

[4] I was impressed by this fact when I was reading the manuscript of Alan Brown's *Metaphysical Society: Victorian Minds in Crisis* (New York, 1947) some years ago. Several of the issues that most disturbed members of the Metaphysical Society had not troubled seventeenth-century thinkers at all.

most sacred document, the Mosaic account of Creation, might be read in many ways. Yet the hard fact remained that to orthodoxy the world had been created in time and called into existence by miracle.

The chief basis of geological thinking had long been the *Meteorologica* of Aristotle, though, as we have seen, orthodox Christians of the seventeenth century did not accept the Aristotelian idea most important for the progress of geology—indefinite time. Inquiring minds had added much to Aristotle's knowledge of the external earth. History gave evidence of changes that had occurred since the period of Moses. Even if the earth had been created only in 4004 B.C., as standard chronologies taught, the chronicles of time afforded opportunity for comparison and contrast. Yet what are sparse records of less than six thousand years in comparison with what we now call "geological time"? Aristotle must be made to conform to Moses, and —with the exception of heretics such as Bruno and occasional free spirits such as Leonardo da Vinci—men continued to interpret their findings within a framework of miracle and Biblical time.

We have seen in George Hakewill a good example of a Renaissance mind groping its way toward sound geological conclusions, yet hampered in its progress by the necessity of keeping within the fold. The idea of the "decay of nature" hovered over geology almost as possessively as did Genesis. The world was growing old, and even men like Henry More who laid the basis for ideas of absolute space and time and the eternity of the universe still taught that this sublunary world would not continue indefinitely.

The dilemma may be seen in explanations offered for fossils in which Luther, Goodman, Hakewill, and Burton were interested, a problem closely connected with that of the origin of mountains. Marine fossils, deposited inland and at considerable elevation, had been familiar to the Greeks who, unhampered by any necessity of conforming to a specific date for creation, surmised that they were remains of once-living animals, exhibiting immense age and proving the vicissitude of sea and land. Medieval Fathers, more concerned with Genesis than geology, could accept no such explanation: land and sea had been separated on the third day of Creation, and animal life was not produced until the fourth. There seemed only two legitimate ways of meeting this paradox. The most customary practice was to deny that the remains were organic. Fossils were *lusus naturae*, sports of nature in a whimsical mood, or results of occult influences of the planets that had twisted stones into strange shapes. From its establishment by Avicenna and its adoption by Albertus Magnus, this conjecture remained the orthodox teaching of Rome. Indeed, as late as 1580 Bernard Palissy was denounced as a heretic for dissenting from it. Another way around the difficulty was to propose, as the cause of fossils, vicissitude of sea and land, posited by classicists, accepted as orthodox by many Fathers. Tertullian suggested that marine remains had been deposited by the Deluge as the waters receded from the hills; as much because of its accord with Scripture as for its apparently plausible explanation of physical facts, this theory gained prestige and was widely accepted, particularly during the Renaissance and Reformation. Luther took for granted that fossils were cast up by the Flood, as did Goodman a half-century later. Agricola did not deny that these strange formations might have been deposited by the Flood, though he believed that since that time they had developed in the earth, growing as some minerals were thought to grow. The heretic Giordano Bruno insisted that there had never been a Flood. But before and after Leonardo da Vinci and Hieronymus Frascastoro suggested the true explanation, most writers on the subject of fossils developed their hypotheses with reference to Mosaic accounts of either Creation or Deluge.

Among the traditional ideas accepted by most of our ancestors, none seems more remarkable to a modern reader than their conception of the size of mountains. "Philosophers have measured mountains," said Herbert. So they had, with surprising results. Athos, Pelion, Olympus, Caucasus, questioned Burton, "are they 1250 paces high, according to that measure of Dicearchus, or seventy-eight miles perpendicularly high, as Jacobus Mazonis . . . expounding that place of Aristotle about Caucasus?" [5] The names of Burton's mountains are familiar to most of us, as to him, only through books, yet our imaginations thrust them up to no such incredible heights. "It is found by experience and from sufficient witnesses proved true," noted John Swan in the *Speculum Mundi*, one of the many encyclopedias of the time, "that the tops of the highest mountains reach up unto that place which we call the middle region of the aire, being some of them more loftie than the clouds." [6] Seen through seventeenth-century eyes, terrestrial mountains seem as fantastic as lunar hills. Far more awe-

[5] This distortion of Aristotle was frequently repeated. On the subject of mountain altitudes in this period, see Lynn Thorndike, "Measurement of Mountain Altitudes," *Isis*, IX (1927), 425 ff.; Florian Cajori, "History of Determinations of the Heights of Mountains," *Isis*, XII (1929), 494 ff. Not until the latter part of the eighteenth century were the heights of mountains determined with any certainty, and in the meantime guesses continued and imagination was free to run riot.

[6] John Swan, *Speculum Mundi; or, A Glasse Representing the Face of the World* (2d ed.; Cambridge, Eng., 1643), pp. 61–62. Swan continued: "In Japan there is a mountain called Figeniana, which is some leagues higher then the clouds. And in Ternate among the Philippine islands there is a mountain, which (as Mr. Purchas in his pilgrimage relateth) is even angry with nature because it is fastned to the earth, and doth therefore not onely lift up his head above the middle Region of the aire, but endeavoureth also to conjoyn it self with the fierie Element. And of the mountain Athos between Macedon and Thrace, it is said to be so high, that it casteth shade more than thirty & seven miles. Also the mount of Olympus in Thessalie is said to be of that height, as neither the winds, clouds or rain do overtop it. And (although I omit others of exceeding height) it is also written of another mount so high above the clouds, that some who have seen it do witnesse that they have been on the top of it, and have had both a clear skie over their heads, and also clouds below them pouring down rain and breaking forth with thunder and lightning; at which those below have been terrified, but on the top of the hill there was no such matter."

some to them than the peaks of the Himalayas today, distant mountains in the seventeenth century offered imagination a terrestrial vastness we can hardly comprehend. If we try to imagine them as did they, we shall be better able to understand how the "Aesthetics of the Infinite" led men to transfer the immensity of interstellar space to the vastest terrestrial objects seen or imagined by man.

"The pike of Teneriffe, how high it is?" Burton wondered. Actually its highest peak rises 12,190 feet, but in the seventeenth century it was a hill whose head touched heaven. Milton used it for one of his grand figures to describe Satan who, "collecting all his might dilated stood, like Teneriffe or Atlas, unremoved." John Donne, we remember, thought it so high that "The floating Moone would shipwrack there, and sinke." Sir Walter Ralegh's *History of the World* shows how Pelion was piled on Ossa to make Teneriffe. Discussing a belief that Ararat was the highest mountain in the world, Ralegh wrote:

For the best cosmographers with others that have seen the mountains of Armenia, find them far inferior, and underset to divers other mountains even in that part of the world, and elsewhere; as the mountain Atlas between Macedon and Thrace, which Ptolemy calls Olympus . . . is far surmounting any mountain that hath ever been seen in Armenia; for it casteth shade three hundred furlongs, which is thirty-seven miles and upwards, of which Plutarch . . . "Athos shadoweth the cow of Lemnos." Also the mount of Olympus in Thessaly is said to be of that height, as neither the winds, clouds, or rain overtop it. . . . There are also in Mauritania, near the sea, the famous mountain of Atlas, of which Herodotus: . . . "Upon this coast there is a mountain called Atlas, whose height is said to be such as the eye of no mortal mind can discern the top thereof." And if we may believe Aristotle, then are all these inferior to Caucasus, which he maketh the most notorious for length and height. . . . But I cannot believe either; for the highest mountain of the world known is that of Teneriffe in the Canaries.[7]

[7] *The History of the World*, in Sir Walter Ralegh, *Works* (Oxford, 1829), II, 238–239. Ralegh was widely quoted throughout the century as

Marvell might flatter a patron by exaggerating the hill at Bill-borow:

> thus it all the field commands,
> And in unenvy'd greatness stands,
> Discerning further then the Cliff
> Of heaven-daring Teneriff.

But until well after the mid-century, "heaven-daring Teneriff," rising abruptly from sea level and startling mariners who first saw it, continued to dominate the hills of the world in most minds.

Discovery of mountains in the moon stimulated more accurate attempts at estimates of the altitudes of those on earth, though some astronomers thrust mountains up to still more awesome heights. Galileo and Kepler humbled terrestrial hills, insisting that earthly mountains were not more than a mile in height, while lunar mountains might be four times as high. John Wilkins wrote:

I affirm that there are very high mountains in the moon. Keplar and Galilaeus think that they are higher than any which are upon our earth. But I am not of their opinion in this, because I suppose they go upon a false ground, whilst they conceive that the highest mountain upon the earth is not above a mile perpendicular.

Whereas it is the common opinion, and found true enough by observation, that Olympus, Atlas, Taurus, and Emus, with many others, are much above this height. Tenariffa, in the Canary Islands, is commonly related to be above 8 miles perpendicular, and about this height (say some) is the mount Perjacca in America. . . . However, though these in the moon are not so high as some amongst us; yet certain it is that they are of a great height, and some of them at least four miles perpendicular.[8]

---

having said that the highest mountains reached thirty-seven miles. John Wilkins, attempting to correct this belief, based upon supposed ancient measurements, pointed out that the ancients had been speaking about the shadows, not about the true altitude of mountains. He said (*Mathematical and Philosophical Works* [London, 1802], I, 71): "You must consider the height of the mountains is but very little, if you compare them to the length of their shadows."

[8] *That the Moon May Be a World*, in *Mathematical and Philosophical Works* (London, 1708), I, 71-72.

Although the altitude of familiar mountains diminished somewhat during the seventeenth century as travelers brought back more accurate reports, remote peaks continued to tower to fantastic heights until well into the eighteenth century. Even Robert Boyle, who requested travelers to take the height of Teneriffe by the level of mercury in barometers, believed that the mountain was at least seven miles high and other mountains still loftier.

Why did mountains soar as they did in the imaginations of our ancestors, who lived after the great period of exploration and believed that the world was mapped and known? It was not all a matter of the tall tales of travelers about "antres vast and . . . rocks and hills whose heads touch heaven," though to be sure the Munchausens of the day did their part in carrying on old exaggerations, as Donne ironically suggested in "Upon Mr. Thomas Coryat's *Crudities*":

> Oh to what height will love of greatnesse drive
>   Thy leavened spirit, Sesqui-superlative?
>   Venice vast lake thou hadst seen, and would seek then
> Some vaster thing.

It was not the fault of Aristotle, for seventeenth-century men were aware that their own geographical knowledge was much more extensive than that of the Greeks, and they did not hesitate to take issue with Aristotle on matters which were far more important than this.

Milton's Adam, whose practical acquaintance with the world was limited to a small part of a small Garden of Eden, knew the reason that mountains rose above the clouds, taught as he was by an Angel who had been present at the Creation:

> Immediately the mountains huge appear
> Emergent, and their broad bare backs upheave
> Into the clouds; their tops ascend the sky.
> So high as heav'd the tumid hills, so low

> Down sunk a hollow bottom broad and deep,
> Capacious bed of waters.[9]

"Ye shall observe," Godfrey Goodman has said, "that the highest mountains upon earth, carrie some proportion to the lowest bottome at Sea . . . that God might observe some kind of proportion." We return, as so often, to ancient ideas of proportion and symmetry shown in the work of the Great Geometer who created the world with golden compasses. Ironically it was the more orthodox who encountered difficulty in discovering God's symmetry in the present structure of the earth. Those who asserted that the world was only a ruin could attribute to man's sin the extremes that "disproportion that fair forme." The traditionalists must interpret the original plan of God in another way, if they were to find in the earth the proportions of man who was "all symmetrie, Full of proportions, one limb to another."

There were two chief ways out of the dilemma. When Burton said that he wished to "examine that demonstration of Alexander Piccolominus, whether the earth's superficies be bigger than the sea's," his mind had gone back to a contention of many Fathers that the original areas of sea and land had been equal. On the third day, the land had been hollowed out to form beds for the waters. Great masses of earth were piled into mountains and hills, raised in exact proportion to the channels and abysses left in the bed of the sea. For every plain that had been humbled, a mountain had been exalted. Such had been the original state of things, and if Spenser's giant had had his way, nature would have returned to its primitive condition:

> Therefore I will throw down these mountains hie,
> And make them levell with the lowly plaine;
> These towring rockes, which reach unto the skie,

[9] *Paradise Lost*, VII, 285–290. The classical belief that the highest mountains were paralleled by the lowest depths of ocean was very common in the seventeenth century and continued into the eighteenth. This seems to have been Hakewill's position in the *Apologie*, II, 76; so too Blancanus in the *Sphaera Mundi* (Bologna, 1620), p. 108.

> I will thrust downe into the deepest maine,
> And as they were them equalize againe.[10]

The other way out of the difficulty has also been suggested by Burton. "Is there vicissitude of sea and land, as Anaximines of old?" Originally what we call land has been the bed of ocean and the bed of the sea had been the original land. In the course of time land and sea had changed places, but one still remained the exact duplicate of the other. The word of Jehovah, reported by Moses, was true, but so were the words of Plato and Pythagoras. Here again among Renaissance men who lived in two worlds, we find paradox and problem.

II

Yet although mountains continued to rise to fantastic heights and fossils remained rubbish cast up by the Deluge, Renaissance men were discovering much more about the crust of the earth and beginning to lay a new basis for consideration of mountains. Except in matters that presupposed the eternity of the world, they had been largely content to follow Aristotle and other classical authorities. This was a wise decision on the whole, since classical theories of epigene phenomena had been based upon careful observation, and explanation of the action of wind and rain in sculpturing the earth's surface, together with evidence of exposed strata in proving interaction of land and water, had been sound enough. Even unskilled observers could observe effects of wind, rain, and flood, as Agricola noted, discussing his theory that mountains had been produced over a period of time by the force of water and the strength of wind:

We can plainly see that a great abundance of water produces mountains, for the torrents first of all wash out the soft earth, next carry away the harder earth, and then roll down the rocks, and thus in a few years excavate the plains or slopes to a considerable depth; this may be noticed in mountainous regions even by unskilled ob-

[10] *Faerie Queene*, V, ii, 28, ll. 1–5.

servers. . . . The wind produces hills and mountains in two ways: either, when set loose and free from bonds, it violently moves and agitates the same, or else when, after having been driven into the hidden recesses of the Earth by cold, as into a prison, it struggles with a great effort to burst forth.[11]

Agricola was well acquainted with the surface of the earth, and because of his long experience as a physician in mining communities, he also knew regions immediately below the surface. His works on ores, minerals, and metals were the result of first-hand observation. Wherever he looked, he was impressed by changes going on about him. "All these varied and wonderful processes by which water destroying builds and building destroys, mightily altering the appearance of the earth's surface," he wrote, "have been in operation since the most remote antiquity, so far beyond the memory of man that none can tell when they had their beginning." As in the past, changes occur every day, though "the sharpest eye is not sensitive enough to follow the slow action of nature in her creative work." Scientist though he was, Agricola was often led by tradition to speak in terms of the "decay" and "mutability" of nature. He might have said, as did a minor seventeenth-century poet:

> 'Tis a strange thing, this world,
> Nothing but change I see. . . .
> All things below do change,
> The sea in rest ne'er lies;
> Plains up to mountains swell,
> While mountains do sink down.[12]

Observation continued until in 1669 the basic principles of modern stratigraphy were formulated by Nicolaus Steno,[13] who

[11] Georgius Agricola, *De Ortu et Causis Subterraneorum* (Basel, 1546). The translation is that of Herbert and Lou Henry Hoover in their edition of *De Re Metallica* (New York, 1950), pp. 595 ff.

[12] Patrick Carey, "Fallax et Instabilis," in *Minor Poets of the Caroline Period* (Oxford, 1906), II, 476–477.

[13] *Nicolai Stenonis de Solido intra Solidum naturaliter contento dis-*

showed that the earth's surface consists of strata, originally deposited from water horizontally, and that alteration of strata by subterraneous forces is the chief cause of superficial irregularities. Correlation of strata and their contents proved the order in deposition relative to creation. No matter what the appearance of the earth on the third day of creation, "all present mountains did not exist from the beginning," Steno insisted, since the earth's surface undergoes constant permutation by the action of superficial erosion and subterraneous eruption. Goodman had emphasized the "daily irrecoverable decay of mountaines and rockes"; Hakewill, while recognizing the decay, insisted that "'if any mountaines bee humbled into valleys, meanes are not wanting for the proportionable raising of valleys into mountaines." Steno, the father of modern stratigraphy, was no less susceptible than the Goodmans, the Hakewills, and the poets to dual moods of optimism and pessimism deeply imbedded in the thinking of his age. Scientifically his emphasis was upon development in the structure of the earth, yet he did not doubt that earth had been created less than six thousand years earlier, as he did not question that it would be destroyed by God. Throughout the *Prodromus* he vacillated between optimism and pessimism. Having published his major work, he turned from science to religion and found certainty in the Church of which he became a Bishop.

As the century advanced, ideas of change and development in mountain structure, suggested by Agricola, Leonardo, Steno, and others, began to complement, rather than to replace, belief in

---

sertationis prodromus (Florence, 1669). An English version was published by Henry Oldenburg, Secretary to the Royal Society, as *The Prodromus to a Dissertation concerning Solids Naturally Contained within Solids* (London, 1671). There is a modern translation by J. G. Winter (New York, 1916). Robert Hooke called attention of the Royal Society to Steno's theories. Hooke's mood is that of the optimistic modern. He emphasized Steno's observation of regenerative forces much more than the degenerative. See Robert Hooke, *Posthumous Works* (London, 1705), pp. 292 ff.

special creation or diluvian catastrophe. Mountains were studied in relation to wind and rain, to eruption and erosion, to springs and rivers, to strata, to minerals and metals. Italy and Germany led the way. England, in many fields the acknowledged leader of the scientific world, lagged behind the continent in geological theory until well after the Restoration. There is no English work to be compared in importance with the treatises of Agricola and Steno, no passing comments so suggestive as those of Leonardo or Fracastorio. English literary attitudes toward mountains continued to be dominated by the classics, the Bible, and inherited authority. The layman was quite willing to swallow the Deluge with Ralegh or to question idly with Burton. Among poets of the first half-century we look almost in vain for any indication of interest in geological ideas. After the invention of the telescope we find astronomy widespread in English prose and verse, as after the development of the microscope we find microbiology; but geology had as yet barely touched literary imagination.

There were various reasons why this was so; it was not entirely a matter of religious orthodoxy. Lay imagination, responsive to tragedy, spectacle, melodrama, demanded the dramatic and spectacular in science. Galileo had discovered a new cosmos, but geologists had not suddenly seen a new earth. "All these varied and wonderful processes" had been in operation since remote antiquity, "but the sharpest eye is not sensitive enough to follow the slow action of nature in her creative work." Imagination did not yet respond to the charm of long leisurely processes of development. History still lifted the world on pyramids that showed the "two tearmes and limits of Time's race":

> That, the Creation is; the Judgment, this;
> That, the World's Morning; this, her Midnight is.[14]

Time was finite, as space had been, and time must have a stop. But in the mid-century a revolution began in ideas of time, cor-

[14] Richard Crashaw, "Upon the Frontispiece of Mr. Isaacson's Chronologie."

responding to that we have already found in ideas of space. The new sense of time came from philosophers and scientists. Henry More laid the basis for a conception of absolute time that seemed a necessary corollary to his theory of the infinity of worlds. In the midst of his poetic proof in the early *Infinity of Worlds* that "long ago there earths have been . . . and after this shall others be again," he declared that, having proved

> That infinite space and infinite worlds there be:
> This load laid down, I'm freely now dispos'd
> A while to sing of times infinity.

Although More returned to the subject of time in a number of his prose works, it was less he than his Cambridge associate Isaac Barrow who formulated the theories of absolute time developed in varying ways by Newton, Locke, and Berkeley.[15] In the meanwhile, astronomers and physicists were making the layman aware of astronomical time. Poets like Young wrote, as seventeenth-century poets never did, of the immense distance of "nocturnal suns" and of the indefinite time required for the progress of light from distant stars:

> So distant (says the sage) 'twere not absurd
> To doubt if beams, sent out at Nature's birth,
> Are yet arrived at this so foreign world;
> Though nothing half so rapid as their flight.

Or they thought like Akenside of

> fields of radiance, whose unfading light
> Has travell'd the profound six thousand years,
> Nor yet arrives in sight of mortal things.[16]

[15] See John Tull Baker, *An Historical and Critical Examination of English Space and Time Theories from Henry More to Bishop Berkeley* (Bronxville, N.Y., 1930).

[16] Edward Young, *Night Thoughts* (London, 1793), IX, 1225–1228, p. 292; Mark Akenside, *The Pleasures of Imagination* (London, 1744), I, 204–206, p. 20.

With the dawning conception of indefinite time, we shall find a greater stirring of imagination about earth processes.

In the latter years of the seventeenth century, geology suddenly became dramatic and spectacular. Gentlemen of the late Restoration period read Burnet's *Sacred Theory of the Earth* as eagerly as their grandfathers had read Galileo's *Sidereus Nuncius* and followed the Burnet controversy as closely as did theologians and scientists. But until that time poets continued to turn back to the Bible for mountain drama. More melodramatic than any contemporary scientific account was the drama according to Moses or the Fathers: mountains had risen by miracle, making a joyful noise before the Lord; or they were the cataclysmic ruins of a world that had fallen with a universal groan when the sins of man culminated in the Deluge.

III

Genesis governed geology, yet we must not overstress the part played by Mosaic teaching to the exclusion of other ways of thought equally pervasive, as effectual as Scripture in retarding the advancement of earth science. Our seventeenth-century ancestors, as I have said elsewhere, were actually present at the death of the world, even though their world did not perish by the Conflagration and its end came in ways quite different from those anticipated by the prophets of doom. We are familiar with the spectacular revolution that changed the place of the earth from the "proud center" and made our globe only a lesser planet taking its way about the sun, responding to the natural laws that governed other planets. We know that, thanks to Galileo and Descartes, the earth became an ingenious machine made by the Great Artificer. But we do not always realize the extent to which "the death of a world" was involved in this change.[17]

[17] This section is a compression of ideas I have treated more fully in *The Breaking of the Circle*, where I have discussed the "death of a world"—the animate earth in which many men believed for centuries—

From Thales to Galileo, the world had been *animate*. It was permeated by mind, intelligent, alive. There was a world body and a world soul, since the universe, like man, was copy of God. Whether existing from eternity, as various Greek philosophers assumed, or created in time, as Christians believed, the world and the universe lived. The world and the universe lived as man lived; the world and even the universe, like man, was subject to decay and death. We dismiss this belief easily as a "hylozoistic fallacy," but it was no fallacy for many centuries. Between the great world of the earth and the greater world of the universe and the little world of man, many believed there was exact "correspondence," as we have seen upon more than one occasion. In the universe the elements existed in order and interdependence, as Milton's Angel taught Adam:

> For know, whatever was created, needs
> To be sustained and fed; of Elements
> The grosser feeds the purer, earth the sea,
> Earth and the Sea feed Air, the Air those Fires
> Ethereal.[18]

As the universe and the world were created of the four elements, so was man. "Fire, air, earth, water, all are at debate Which shall predominate." When man was at his best, the elements were in perfect balance and harmony, as they were in the universe at the time of Creation, for man was the "Microcosm, or complete abridgement of the Universe." If man *was*, in little, all the globe, he had every reason to expect to find in the globe and in the cosmos exact analogies for the structure, functions,

---

which was replaced by the mechanistic world of Galileo, Descartes, Harvey. I have also discussed in more detail the kind of analogical thinking widely accepted until the end of the Renaissance, with the belief in "correspondences," "signatures," etc.

[18] *Paradise Lost*, V, 414–418.

and processes of the human body, for as Donne said, "The whole world hath nothing, to which something in man doth not answere." Find "correspondences" man did, as Phineas Fletcher showed in *The Purple Island*, in which he described the repetition of the structure of the globe in the structure of man: bones, flesh, skin, cartilage, muscles and nerves, heart and liver, stomach, bladder, spleen—each had an exact analogy in the body of earth. *The Purple Island*, as I have said elsewhere, is negligible as poetry, though as a handbook of Elizabethan physiology it has a certain historical interest; as a handbook of geology, it is a warning of the dangers faced by men who, knowing little of the structure of either, read analogies from man's body into the earth and then back again.

In *The Breaking of the Circle* I have developed at length the kind of analogical thinking characteristic of the Renaissance, particularly the idea that the most perfect design of God had been the Circle of Perfection that He followed in creating the universe with its Ptolemaic spheres, the round globe of the world, the round head of man. I have attempted also to describe the breaking of the Circle which was shattered in the seventeenth century so far as the macrocosm was concerned, first by Kepler's discovery that the Copernican planets did not move in perfect circles, most of all by the idea of infinity that shattered the globes of the universe as it destroyed the *flammantia moenia mundi* and dissipated the once-finite universe into infinity that had no form or pattern. In *The Breaking of the Circle* I have tried, too, to describe the emotions of seventeenth-century men who were present at "The Death of a World"—the destruction of the old animate universe in which man had lived so long. With the death of an animate world and the breaking of the circles of the universe, old truths began to lose their force, gradually becoming the language of poets rather than of scientists.

But old habits die hard, and ways of thinking persistent for generations did not disappear rapidly as the new mechanical universe superseded the old animate one. If the metaphor of "the Divine Artist" tended to give way to that of "the Great Engineer," it did so gradually, and for many years scientists as well as poets based their hypotheses upon analogies between the body of man and the body of the world. The analogical way of thinking served for many years to retard the development of more modern attitudes in geology. Moses was less influential in that respect than were Plato and Pythagoras. The scientists were as confused in their thinking as were the divines and the poets. If they protested against "old" ways of thought that drew analogies between the living man and the living earth, they themselves were quick to carry over analogies from one science to another. When Steno in his *Prodromus* opposed the idea that mountains "grow"—a classical passage in histories of geology—he was not denying argument from analogy, which he frequently used, but merely saying that certain superficial resemblances long accepted were not correct. "There is no growing of mountains," he said. "Rocks and mountains have nothing in common with the bones of animals except a certain hardness." [19] But mountains continued to remain the "bones of the world" even among important scientists. And why not? Coral grows—at least many believed so; why not rocks? Were stones and minerals dead things, or were they, though lower in the hierarchy, something like vegetables? Minerals and stones were subject to decomposition and decay. There were many who held that they originated, like vegetables, in seeds, "petrific seeds" or "gorgonic seeds" since they turned to stone. [20] And the geologists turned to biology, a

[19] Marie-Pompée Colonée wrote in his *Histoire Naturelle de l'Univers* (Paris, 1734), I, 204: "Je suis porté à croire que les montagnes végétent et qu'une partie de celles que nous voyons à présent ont végéte sur la terre comme les arbres" (quoted in Adams, *Geological Sciences*, p. 363).

[20] There was, for instance, the theory of the "lapidifying juice" that converted porous bodies into stone; there were also theories of emana-

flourishing science, to find "analogies" to explain the nature of rocks and minerals, of which they knew little more than had remote ancestors.

Just at the time this kind of analogy might have died under the impact of the growing conception of a mechanical universe, a major scientific discovery in another field gave mineralogists reason to believe, even more than in the past, in a living earth in which all things were animate. Microbiology, discovering a new world of minute life, perceived "little animals" in stagnant water, in blood, in urine, in "the blue of plums," and in stones. Was there any point, asked an enthralled generation, at which life ceased? Might not supposed inorganic matter prove organic? "We see from the elephant just to the hand-worm," Fontenelle's Philosopher instructed his Marchioness; "here finishes our sight; but from the hand-worm begins an infinite multitude, to which that worm is as an elephant, and which our eyes cannot perceive without the assistance of art." Is there anything in the universe that is truly a solid? The Lady had begun to doubt it a short time before when she learned that the moon is not "a mass, all the parts of which are of an equal solidity." Her teacher declared, "We do not know any body of this nature, even marble is not; everything which is the most solid, is subject to change and alteration, either by some secret and invisible motion, which is, in itself, or by that which it receives from without." The microscope led to further question about the apparent solidity of inorganic matter:

A great many bodies which appear solid are scarce any thing, but a mass of those imperceptible animals. . . . A leaf of a tree is a little world, inhabited by invisible worms, who there know mountains and abysses. . . . We find even in some kinds of very hard

_____

tion or the "Tumultuous movements of terrestrial exhalations." Some writers suggested "a plastic virtue latent in the earth," transforming shells and bones into stony shapes. Lyell and Adams quote other ingenious theories.

stone, innumerable little worms which are there lodged in all parts in insensible voids, and who nourish themselves on these stones which they eat. . . . In short, all is full of life, all is animated.[21]

And so for a time mineralogists devoted themselves to attempts to discover in minerals and metals that "wondrous mass of Animals, or atoms organized" their fellow biologists were discovering in another nature once considered inanimate.

As there were sermons in stones, so there were books in the running brooks.[22] In spite of long debates of medieval and Renaissance Fathers, the seventeenth century had made little advance over the ancients in attempts to answer the question of the origin of springs and rivers and the perplexing difference between salt water and fresh. The Scriptures offered little help and some hindrance. If those original waters were salt, what was the origin of fresh water? If they were fresh, how did the the salt get into the sea? Ecclesiastes had declared: "All the rivers run into the sea; yet the sea is not full; unto the place from whence the rivers come, thither shall they return again." Aristotle had faced the issue more squarely: how did it happen that the great reservoir was never exhausted, when smaller ones on the earth's surface frequently dried and remained empty until rain fell? Certainly some water in rivers and springs must be derived from rain. He realized too that mountains played some part in the production of streams:

Just as above the earth, small drops form and these join others, till finally water descends in a body as rain, so too we must suppose that in the earth the water at first trickles together little by little, and

[21] *Conversations on the Plurality of Worlds . . . A New Translation . . . by a Gentleman of the Inner Temple* (London, 1760), pp. 159–160, 144.

[22] In *The Breaking of the Circle*, pp. 117 ff., I have discussed at more length seventeenth-century theories of the origin of fresh water, the analogies drawn between veins and arteries in man and streams and rivers on the body of the earth, and the effect of Harvey's discovery of the process of the circulation of the blood upon these ideas.

that the sources of rivers drop, as it were, out of the earth and then unite. Hence too the headwaters of rivers are found to flow from mountains and from the greatest mountains there flow the most numerous and greatest rivers. For mountains and high ground, suspended over the country like a saturated sponge, make the water ooze out and trickle together in minute quantities but in many places.[23]

But neither Aristotle nor any other thinker until close to the end of the seventeenth century believed that rainfall alone was responsible for all fresh water. During the earlier part of the century theories of the origin of streams and rivers were as confused as thēy had been among the Fathers.

We may let one mid-century encyclopedia speak for many and tell us some of the many ingenious processes by means of which "sea (through earth pipes distill'd) in cisterns shed, And power their liver springs in river veins," as Phineas Fletcher put it.[24] In the *Speculum Mundi,* Swan discussed first Aristotle's theory, then three other classical suggestions Aristotle had refuted:

One whereof is, that the waters overflowing the earth in the beginning of the world, were so dried up by the heat of the sunne, that not onely the drie-land appeared, but all those waters which

[23] *Meteorologica,* bk. I, ch. xiii. This was only one part of the Aristotelian theory; he also held that "air becomes water in the earth for the same reason that it does above it" and that mountains and higher lands cool the vapor that rises from land after rainfall and condense it back to water.

[24] Phineas Fletcher, *The Purple Island,* in *Poetical Works* (Cambridge, Eng., 1909), II, 27–28. *The Purple Island* deserves a place in the curiosa of mountain literature with Hobbes's "buttocks amply sticking up." For example, he describes the gall bladder (II, 38):

> Much like a mount it easily ascendeth;
> The upper part all smooth as slipperie glasse:
> But on the lower many a crag dependeth,
> Like to the hangings of some rockie masse.

remained (being the sea) were so sucked and robbed of their sweet savour, that they could not but be salt.

Another opinion agreeing to that of Plato, who generating the sea *ex tartaro,* or from great and deep gulfs in the earth, or (with others) drawing it through the bowels of the earth, gave occasion to think that the water in it self was sweet, and yet became salt by reason of the divers savours that it met withall in the ground or veins of the earth. . . .

A third was the opinion of Empedocles, who affirmed that the sea was but the sweat of the earth, being (as it were) rosted by the heat of the sunne; and was therefore salt, because all sweat is of such a savour.[25]

Swan dismissed these older theories yet considered seriously others suggested by later ingenious minds; his own choice was as "metaphysical" as Empedocles' "sweat of the earth" and based upon the same sort of analogical reasoning:

But beside these, there are other opinions also. Wherefore some again have attributed the cause to adust vapors, partly let fall on the sea, and partly raised from it to the brinks and face thereof; Others to the motion of the sea; Some to under-earth, or rather under-sea fires, of a bituminous nature, causing both drie aspera-tion exhaled out of the earth, and mixed with the water of the sea.

But that which followeth seemeth absolutely the best, namely that it is effected by the working of the sunne, which draweth out the purer and finer parts, leaving the grosser and more base behind; even as in this little world of our bodies, the purest part of our nourishment being employed in and on the bodie, the urine and other excrements remaining do retain a perfect saltnesse.

We have returned, as usual, to the analogy between microcosm and geocosm; so Empedocles had thought, so too the seventeenth-century John Swan.

Before Pierre Perrault measured the rainfall and drainage in the Seine basin and proved the earlier theory of Leonardo and

[25] *Speculum Mundi,* p. 195.

Palissy that rain and snow are the causes of rivers and springs, a major discovery in physiology had added to seventeenth-century confusion about the processes of waters. Both physiology and geology had long accepted as fact "correspondence" between rivers and streams in the earth and arteries and veins in the body of man. The "blew vaines" that spread through the body of earth, the "saphire streames which from great hills do spring" are "the Earths great duggs" from which issue "fresh moisture." To the pre-Harveian generation, the blood in the arteries differed from the blood in the veins as the waters in the sea differed from those on land. No one before Harvey had been able to solve the problem of its flow. When Harvey proved that arterial and venous blood are the same and that circulation is controlled by the action of the heart, his discoveries at first appealed even more to geology than to medicine. Here at last was an explanation for the circulation of waters on the earth entirely satisfactory to those who followed Ecclesiastes or Plato. The beating of the heart of the world sent on its way the "good fresh-water, the elixir of life." Thus analogy, whether drawn from the past or read into contemporary discoveries, sometimes aided and often retarded the developing earth science of the seventeenth century.

IV

Burton's long-winged hawk was not content with a mere flight around the world to determine the heights of mountains and the truth or falsity of such theories as those of Blancanus. He wished to "descend and see what is done in the bowels of the earth." So too did the seventeenth century, which was beginning to discover a subterranean world as strange, as romantic, as the new world in the moon. It seemed, Henry More said,[26] that "Nature kept House under Ground, and made several Hills her Chimneys." More was eager to know about forces and processes

[26] *Grand Mystery of Godliness*, bk. VI, ch. vii, sec. 4, in *Theological Works* (London, 1708), p. 160.

within the earth, that he might prove his theory that the Final Conflagration would be the result of natural forces within the earth itself. Within that earth were hidden cores of fire, which would burst forth in volcanic eruption on a universal scale. In their eagerness to understand these subterranean forces, geologists could find no such aid in Aristotle as they had found in their study of epigene phenomena. Classical theories of hypogene forces were inevitably the merest hypotheses. Man had not yet found "a convenient place to go down with Orpheus, Ulysses, Hercules, Lucian's Menippus . . . and see what is done in the bowels of the earth." Athanasius Kircher, however, had done his best.

No volume of the century did more to stimulate popular interest in a subterranean world than the *Mundus Subterraneus* [27] of Athanasius Kircher, Jesuit, traveler, and expert on volcanoes and earthquakes, who if he did not actually descend to the bowels of the earth had at least approached the jaws of Hell. After experiencing the great Calabrian earthquake of 1636, Kircher spent years of study and travel in an attempt to learn more about the causes of earthquake and volcano. He had watched Etna and Vesuvius in action and had been lowered into their craters. His *Mundus Subterraneus* stands between the old world of superstition and the new world of scientific observation. Kircher handed down to posterity much that was false and shrewdly surmised much that has proved true. Credulous, superstitious, deeply religious, he often repeated old legend and tradition. Yet

[27] The *Mundus Subterraneus* was published at Amsterdam in 1665; a second edition appeared in 1668, another in 1678. In the last year of the century some parts of the work were translated, or rather paraphrased, in *The Vulcanoes; or, Burning and Fire-vomiting Mountains, Famous in the World* (London, 1699). In the *Itinerarium Exstaticum* (Rome, 1656), Kircher wrote a cosmic voyage of a young couple with an angel guide, in which he largely discussed astronomy. Like Burton's hawk, however, Kircher's angel guide also descended to earth to teach his charges the elements of geology. Most of the geological ideas are more fully developed in the *Mundus Subterraneus*.

he was widely read in natural philosophy and he was a most acute observer, setting down observations and drawing diagrams as he stood on craters or investigated caverns. He has his niche in the history of science, since he was the first to prove by observation and experiment various facts about the subterranean earth which today we take for granted. Yet like his contemporaries he was conditioned by theology. He took frequent exception to Aristotle, but never to Moses.

Microcosmic-geocosmic analogy was central to Kircher's thought. Divine Wisdom showed the same expert craftsmanship in the structure of the internal earth as in the coiling intestines and intricate arteries of man. He developed, on what seemed sound scientific basis, analogies between earth and animal. Indeed Steno was referring particularly to Kircher when he devoted a section of the *Prodromus* to the contention that rocks and mountains have nothing in common with bones of animals save a certain resemblance in hardness. But for one Steno there were a dozen scientists and laymen who agreed with Kircher. Let the modern nonscientific reader turn to the compelling and often beautiful plates, charts, diagrams with which Kircher profusely illustrated his book and see whether he too is not persuaded that mountains are the bones of the world and rivers its arteries.

"All the rivers run into the sea; unto the place from whence the rivers come, thither they return again." Peering down into volcanic craters, making his way into caves where bellowing waters rushed and whirled, Kircher pondered the words of the Preacher and remembered Virgil as well. Kircher's journeys had led him into strange places; in echoing caverns he had heard reverberations of distant waters and had seen underground rivers that, like Alpheus, seemed to have lost their way. In the Alps he had watched streams that had "flowed without cessation since the beginning of the world to the present day," from which the Danube, the Rhine, the Rhone, and many others originated. The superficial earth showed a giant network of streams and rivers, innumerable and involved as the veins and arteries. He could not agree with Aristotle's simple explanation of the waters. "There is some hidden secret of nature which must here be brought to light." As in the Alps so in all other mountain ranges, "God decreed at the time of the Creation of the world that great *hydrophylacia* should be formed, from which in the various parts of the world rivers should flow."

Turn to Kircher's plates and see a cross section of a world laid bare: here in the ocean are whirlpools, each Charybdis indicating clefts in the bottom of the sea through which water is sucked down into a channel which in turn leads to a cavern under or in a mountain, from which again rivers carry water back to the sea in their swelling arteries. The sophisticated need not smile because water runs uphill on its journey to the mountains; [28] as blood flows up as well as down, so does water in the veins of earth. But water may be made to rise by artificial means as well —so Kircher proved in diagrams showing the devices he had invented for such processes. If man could do so by simple instruments, how much more may God make water flow in any direction, employing only natural causes.

Kircher presented ten different theories which had been suggested for the circulation of waters. Although he allowed other causes, he concentrated chiefly on his hydrophylacia and the central fires that raised vapors through the cracks of earth; sometimes the vapors emerged directly. Sometimes they were condensed in cold caverns near the surface of the earth. In the hydrophylacia and in those central fires burning eternally, Kircher found sufficient explanation for most hypogene phenomena— rivers and springs, volcanoes and earthquakes, fumaroles and mineral hot springs.

[28] Jean Baptist Van Helmont had developed at length similarities between the circulation of the blood and the upward direction of water flowing back from the sea by a "vitality of its own." See his *Opera Omnia* (Frankfurt, 1682), pt. II, secs. 7–8. Adams discusses Kircher's artificial devices for making water run uphill. Swift was probably satirizing this kind of invention in the third book of *Gulliver's Travels*.

In Kircher's plates we may see the central fires issuing forth here and there in volcanoes—delightful maps, one with the four winds in the corners, ships on the sea, trees on the land, all surrounding a volcano on whose slope, as Stevenson said, respectable married people with umbrellas might have sat placidly sipping tea. There is sublime terror in one of the most graphic pictures, a cross section of Vesuvius. Fire issues from subterraneous caverns; Vesuvius is a hollow shell which, when partially cut away, reveals a *mundus subterraneus*, another earth within the geocosm. In the diagrams of Etna drawn from Kircher's observations in 1637, we see huge rocks hurled forth by volcanic force. Did "the falcon's eye" of Samuel Taylor Coleridge, who knew a much less spectacular volume of Kircher's, fall upon this picture, and did it linger in his "deep well" when in "Kubla Khan" he dreamed the words that seem to describe Etna as Kircher saw it in the seventeenth century? [29]

> And from this chasm, with ceaseless turmoil seething,
> As if this earth in fast thick pants were breathing,
> A mighty fountain momently was forced:
> Amid whose swift half-intermitted burst
> Huge fragments vaulted like rebounding hail;
> Or chaffy grain beneath the thresher's flail;
> And 'mid these dancing rocks at once and ever
> It flung up momently the sacred river.

Kircher's *Mundus Subterraneus* is the richest and most vivid treatment of the hidden places of the internal earth and unquestionably the most influential upon the literary mind of the following period. Yet the growing interest in the irregularities of the earth's surface, fissures and chasms, mines and caves, volcanoes and earthquakes, is widely reflected in other works of the

[29] John Livingston Lowes in *The Road to Xanadu* (Boston and New York, 1927), *passim*, discusses Coleridge's use of Kircher's *Oedipus Aegyptiacus* and says, p. 389: "I must regretfully forego the opportunity . . . of dwelling on the astonishing Athanasius and his still more dumbfounding works."

same period. Many scientists of the late seventeenth century continued to think as Kircher thought. Edmund Halley's theory of the origin of waters seemed to mark a new epoch in geology, but we still hear old familiar ideas and phrases in a scientific paper [30] Halley read before the Royal Society:

This, if we may allow final Causes, seems to be the design of the Hills, that their Ridges being plac'd thro' the midst of the Continents, might serve, as it were, for Alembicks to distill fresh water for the use of Man and Beast, and their heights to give a descent to those Streams to run gently like so many Veins of the Macrocosm, to be the more beneficial to the Creation.

When Caspar Schott wrote a long and important treatise of the origin of rivers,[31] a work respectfully considered by historians of science, he still found his chief difficulty less in hydraulics than in Ecclesiastes. As earlier men had discovered a new heaven, gradually later men were discovering a new earth that had developed slowly from an older geocosm. But at its core still burned the central fire of ancient belief.

V

There was nothing in England to correspond to the first book exclusively devoted to mountains, the *De Montium Origine* [32] of

[30] Edmund Halley, "An Account of the Circulation of the Watry Vapours of the Sea and the Cause of Springs," published in the *Philosophical Transactions* for 1691, reprinted in Halley's *Miscellanea Curiosa* (London, 1705–1707).

[31] Gaspar Schott, *Anatomia Physico-Hydrostatica Fontium ac Fluminum Explicata* (Wurtzburg, 1663). On pp. 167–169, after discussion of various hypotheses suggested by others, Schott grapples with the familiar passage in Ecclesiastes. He does not doubt that the statement is true, but attempts to interpret it thus: "All enter it and all return to it, therefore all have issued from it."

[32] Frank Dawson Adams, in *The Birth and Development of the Geological Sciences*, pp. 344–357, has described this rare work. He has found record of three copies in Germany, one in Paris, and one in the Bodleian. He has given a translation of about one-half of the short work, naturally

Valerio Faenzi, published at the Aldine Press in 1561 by the short-lived Accademia Veneziana, in which we find both old and new mountain philosophies. Dedicated "from the lovely Ascanian Hills of Montegallium," this little book was written by a man who loved the romantic scenery of his native district. The scene was the shore of the Lake of Garda; the two speakers, Camillus and Rudolphus, were "struck by the wonderful beauty of the great stretch of water spread out before them, bounded in part by gentle slopes of verdure rising gradually from the waters but elsewhere by the frightful and forbidding mountains which ascend abruptly and whose summits tower above the lake. So seated, their minds turned to the question of how these mountains had come into being." In their dialogue we hear characteristic pondering of the Renaissance upon Scriptural, classical, and modern theories of mountains. "Atlas on account of his height is said to hold up the platform of heaven, Olympus is so sublime that he towers above the clouds, whereof saith Lucan 'He passeth beyond the clouds.'" These were mountains Camillus and Rudolphus knew only from books, but they themselves had seen the Alps, the Apennines, the Pyrenees. Sometimes such ranges seemed to "resemble waves of the sea, one crest following upon another in height, in arrangement and in position, just as if they had been set in due place by some marvellous artistry." Could this artistry be accidental? In turn they considered possible theories, Rudolphus, the chief speaker, showing wide knowledge of ancient and modern authorities. They discussed the possibility of an original smooth earth. "Some think," said Rudolphus, "that when the Supreme Architect created the world, it left His hands a smoothly rounded sphere, without mountains or valleys. These appeared in consequence of several distinct inundations at different times, so that before the first flood there were no mountains." Rudolphus believed that the earth was

selecting passages that deal with science. All the quotations below are taken from his pages.

spherical, but the idea that mountains were not in existence before the Deluge he found "repugnant both to reason and to inspiration."

Neither speaker doubted that "God the Supreme Architect" was originally responsible for many of the mountains they found so majestic. They did not deny Moses, but theirs was a Genesis interpreted by "Plato, Trismegistus, Orpheus and Hesiod." It was also a Genesis that must be made consistent with modern observation, for they had seen mountains thrown up by volcanic action and others whose size and position had been affected by earthquakes. As these had arisen or changed in a moment, so other mountains might have developed over long periods of time. In their conclusions, the two disputants combined Genesis with modern theories of development in mountains: "Some mountains arise directly at the command of God. Others through earthquakes, deluges, the stars (particularly the sun), by the force of winds, all of these, with the Mineral Virtue as a contributory factor."

Only much later in England do we find such comprehensive surveys of mountain attitudes, when the early arguments of Camillus and Rudolphus were repeated and carried further, combined with many later discoveries of the "new philosophy." Until the late seventeenth century most of the geological works widely read in England were continental. Let us look at one or two popular books of the mid-century to see how older theories were giving way to those more modern. *A Collection of Discourses of the Virtuosi of France*,[33] published in 1664 and 1665, was as popular in England as in France. In it we may see that "the Lord's Controversy" had become even more important than

[33] This work was published in two volumes, the first translated by G. Havers in 1664 under the above title; the second was called *Another Collection of Philosophical Conferences of the French Virtuosi upon Questions of All Sorts . . . Render'd into English by G. Havers and J. Davies* (London, 1665). All the quotations in this section are from Conference CLXXXIX, II, 310–313.

it had been among religious thinkers. Genesis and geology are coming face to face. Of the six speakers in the dialogue, two concerned themselves specifically with theological ideas when they approached the question of mountains, the first upholding the Mosaic account of Creation, the second attributing the emergence of mountains to the Flood. But the speaker who believed that mountains had been original based his belief less upon Moses than upon Galileo. "The discovery of the inequalities of the Celestial Bodies, observed in our dayes by Galileo's Tubes," proved that mountains existed in other worlds than ours. Such mountains as that "eminent one in Mars" could not "reasonably be attributed to any cause but his primary construction"; this must be equally true of terrestrial ranges. Although each of the first speakers turned back to the Bible, they were less concerned with the *metaphysics* of Genesis than with an implicit *aesthetic*. "God having created the world in perfection," said the first, "it was requisite that there should be Plains, Mountains, and Vallies upon the Earth, without which agreeable variety, there would be no proportion in its parts, wherein consists its principal ornament." The diluvian disputant was equally concerned with the aesthetics of Deity. The original earth, he believed, must have been a Circle of Perfection. "A craggy Earth" violated that "perfection which is found in the Spherical Figure, which God hath also pourtray'd in all his works, which observe the same exactly or come as near as their use will permit; as is seen particularly in the fabrick of Man's Body, his Master-piece, whereof all the original parts have somewhat of the Spherical or Cylindrical Figure, which is the production of a Circle. . . . 'Tis certain then that God gave the Earth that Spherical Form" and that it remained smooth and round until the Deluge.

All four later speakers agreed that "you cannot assign one certain or generall cause" for mountains. If some were produced at the time of Creation, others have arisen later, "partly by Rains and Torrents, partly by Winds and Earthquakes." The fourth and fifth speakers stressed ideas of "development," involved with waters around and within the earth. The final speaker suggested still another possibility. So long as man believed in the stability of earth, he had been able to explain the origin of mountains either by miracle or by Deluge. But our world, as we know, moves through space. "In pursuance of Copernicus' opinion which makes the Earth turn round the Sun," he concluded, "the several concussions it receives from that motion may possibly elevate one place and depress another."

A Collection of Discourses is indicative of the temper of the age that produced it. A shift is occurring from theology to "physico-theology." The sciences are aiding and abetting, sometimes retarding, each other. Physiology and microbiology are affecting geology. Geology is turning for ammunition to astronomy. Mountains in the moon afford evidence for theories of the mountains on earth; eclipses offer evidence not only for the "roundness" of the moon but for the form of earth as it would seem from the moon and planets. No matter how supernatural the origin of our earth, it is gradually becoming "mechanism" rather than "organism," responsive to natural law in all its parts. Newton had not yet given final expression to the law of gravitation, yet the speakers in this *Collection* were aware of discoveries of Kepler, Galileo, and Gilbert, with their laws of falling bodies, of motion, and of magnetism. Geogony, they had discovered with their century, was inevitably a part of cosmogony.

The *Geographia Generalis* of Bernhardus Varenius was the most popular treatment of physical geography in the seventeenth century, as it remained until well into the eighteenth. Published in England in 1650, it was widely read in that edition as well as in the edition of 1664. Revised and brought up to date by Newton in 1672, it appeared in still another guise in English in 1682 as *Cosmography and Geography*. For nearly a century it was read in both Latin and English and was frequently revised by experts, so that its science was always nearly up to date.[34] From Milton to Thomson, it was a handbook of poets. If we turn to either of the two editions available when the speakers of the *Collection* were discussing mountain theories, we shall find how science had been adapting to geology and cosmogony the old notion of the "Mundane Egg." Varenius, who did much to popularize the scientific conception of an original smooth world, had inherited his earth from many theological predecessors, but it was specifically the legacy from the *Sphaera Mundi* of Joseph Blancanus,[35] who like various other contemporaries attempted to reconcile a world of supernatural creation with an earth in which physical law was apparent. Seldom has a man been more consistent in his belief in the symmetry and proportion of the Great Geometer. Blancanus, as Burton has said, believed that the original areas of sea and land were equal; he was certain that the altitude of the highest mountain corresponded exactly to the depth of the sea at its lowest point. The world that had emerged on the third day was a perfect copy of the Circle of Deity, a smooth unblemished sphere. Blancanus the scientist was persuaded that within the original earth, submerged by the waters, existed the potentiality of natural laws according to which it operated for more than five thousand years; had it emerged from the waters only according to those laws, it would have been the smoothest of spheres. But Blancanus the Jesuit insisted that natural laws had not been permitted to perform their operation. On the third day the miraculous hand of God had scooped out the channel of the sea and deposited the soil on the site of the Alps. Left to its own nature, the world

---

[34] The Latin text was revised by Jurin in 1712 and again translated by Dugdale in the same year as *A Complete System of Geography*. It was further revised by Peter Shaw. Alan Dugald McKillop has discussed Thomson's use of Varenius in *The Background of Thomson's Seasons* (Minneapolis, 1942), pp. 78–81, 161–164, and *passim*.

[35] Joseph Blancanus (Guiseppe Biancani), *Sphaera Mundi* (Bologna, 1620). See particularly pp. 81–85, 94–99, 108–109.

would end as it began—overflowed with water, it would perish. But it would not perish by its own nature. Before its natural time, God would destroy it not by water but by fire. Vaguely conscious as he was of the orderly processes of nature, Blancanus was still more aware of the prophets of doom. Bruno had laughed at such a theory, but Bruno was a notorious heretic, Blancanus a believing Christian. "Whether that be true," Burton wondered, "which Jordanus Brunus scoffs at, that if God did not detain it, the Sea would overflow the earth by reason of his higher site, and which Josephus Blancanus the Jesuit, in his interpretation on those mathematical places in Aristotle, foolishly fears, and in a just tract proves by many circumstances, that in time the Sea will wash away the land, all the globe of the earth shall be covered with water." [36]

Varenius followed Blancanus in his theory of the original condition of the earth, though, writing thirty years later, he had the advantage of knowing more about natural law and natural processes and could offer more convincing proof for his theory. Still keeping within the fold, he stressed geology rather more than Genesis. Following in the train of such thinkers as Agricola and Leonardo, Varenius sought among the elements the chief cause of terrestrial mountains and found it in water—water from which the earth emerged, water that would ultimately destroy it.[37]

The *Geographia Generalis* led its author to study the whole known world; he paused for consideration of great ranges and peaks in every continent, calling the catalogue of the hills. Towering in imagination, hardly less grand and majestic than they had been to Ralegh, the ranges and peaks of the world were yet steadily being worn away by water; in a sense very different from that of Isaiah, in time every mountain *would* be laid low. In the ears of Varenius reverberated the words of the prophets

[36] "Digression of Air," in *Anatomy of Melancholy*, p. 412.
[37] *Geographia Generalis* (Amsterdam, 1664), pp. 289–319.

and of Moses, but the echoes were fainter; even the three decades that separated his work from that of Blancanus had changed the temper of the time. Geology, striving to emerge by natural principles, as the worlds of Blancanus and Varenius might have emerged, had found itself constantly repressed by the firm hand of authority, whether of Moses or of Aristotle. Yet in the seventeenth century a new world and a new universe were produced by a creator who feared the authority of neither Aristotle nor Moses.

VI

With characteristic impatience for indistinct ideas, especially those inherited from the past, René Descartes turned abruptly from the scheme of creation set forth in Genesis. "Having now ascertained certain principles of material things which were derived . . . from the light of reason, so that we cannot doubt of their truth, it is for us to examine whether from these alone we can explain all the phenomena of nature." [38] So begins the Cartesian cosmogony, which electrified its generation by abrupt departure from theories of Creation, Deluge, Conflagration, from the long hexaemeral tradition, and apparently from dependence on any creator save its author. To be sure, Descartes performed an ostensibly reverent genuflection: at least on paper God remained the First Cause. The mechanical universe presupposed a mechanic, manifestly an expert craftsman, if we may judge from the intricacy of his handiwork. Lip service paid, the Cartesian world scheme as conveniently forgot God as it forgot Moses.

[38] *The Principles of Philosophy*, in *Descartes, Philosophical Works*, trans. by Elizabeth Haldane and G. R. T. Ross (Cambridge, Eng., 1911), I, 270 ff. The origin of the cosmos is treated in book III of the *Principles*, the nature of the earth in book IV. Descartes is said to have developed his theory of the earth before the condemnation of Galileo in 1632 but, because of that event, to have withheld it until 1644. Contrary to his usual procedure, it was translated into Latin. It was published at Amsterdam and immediately condemned by the Sorbonne.

For the first time we see what Blancanus had vaguely surmised, a cosmos permitted to emerge by natural principles inherent in itself. Pondering the nature of matter and its disposition in chaos according to physical law, Descartes deduced from primeval chaos a theory of the origin of planets from fiery matter cast off by the sun, a universe of cosmical vortices.

"Ah! Madam," said Fontenelle's Philosopher, "if you knew what the Vortexes of Descartes are, these Vortexes, whose name is so terrible, and the idea of them so agreeable. . . . Must my head turn round, *said she* laughing. . . . Compleat my folly, I cannot longer forbear . . . let the whole World say what they please, I must be acquainted with these Vortexes." And the Philosopher continued:

That which is called a Vortex, is a great quantity of matter, the particles of which are detached from each other, and yet move all in one and the same sense; however, they are, at the same time, allowed to have some little particular motions, provided they always follow the general direction. . . . See therefore what this great Vortex is, of which the Sun is as master: but at the same time, the Planets compose little particular Vortexes, in imitation of that of the Sun. Each of them, in turning round the Sun do not withstanding turn round themselves, in the same sense, a certain quantity of this celestial matter. . . . If it happens, that there fall into this little Vortex any Planet less than that which there reigns, it will be carried away by the greater and indispensably forced to turn round it; and the whole together, the great Planet, the little one, and the Vortex which includes them, will nevertheless turn round the Sun. It was thus at the beginning of the world.[39]

As the other planets emerged, so did our earth. The particles of the "third element"—particles larger than the "luminous dust" of the "first element" forming the original chaos—acted upon by the heat and light of the "second element" were divided into earth particles and water particles until, with the cooling of the

[39] *Conversations on the Plurality of Worlds*, pp. 197–200, 214.

planet, a layer of liquid was contained within the harder crust, in which the elements were arranged in order of specific gravity. But under the influence of the sun's heat and the restlessness of the elements within the crust, the cracks in that crust became larger and the surface of the earth was ruptured and collapsed upon the inner globe still in the process of formation. Since there was much more matter in the outer sphere than room upon the inner, the collapse caused great irregularities, some matter rising above the level of the liquid through which it had descended, some falling below the level; hence arose hills and mountains, hence the hollows of the earth and the bed of ocean. The glowing central core still remained, a cause of volcanic eruptions, of earthquakes, and of other hypogene forces of nature.

Here was a complete and self-consistent theory of the earth, based upon neither the Greeks nor Moses. Here was a truly mechanistic universe, of which the mechanistic world was a part. It was a cosmos derived by the light of reason from a few general principles, the truth of which Descartes believed he had established. Here too was a vivid and dramatic world scheme, complex and intricate enough to satisfy physicists, astronomers, and mathematicians, yet so simple and graphic that it could be understood by Fontenelle's Marchioness, who, recovering from the initial shock of wild and whirling worlds, said piously: "My God! . . . permit me to be thankful for every thing, even for the Vortex in which I am placed."

Lucid and clear, like everything in the Cartesian reasoning, the scheme seemed to reduce complexity and multiplicity to simplicity. A mechanical cosmos, with a place for everything and everything in its place, it was also a spectacular universe, captivating the imagination that craved drama in its science. Now Nature had become, as the Philosopher said, "a great spectacle, which resembled that of an opera." Let the mathematicians, physicists, astronomers concern themselves with the machinery. Before the new spectacle the layman experienced the mingled astonishment and pleasure he felt at an elaborate play. "When you are at an opera," said Fontenelle's Philosopher, "you do not see the theatre as it is in reality made; they . . . dispose the decorations and machines, for causing, at a great distance, an agreeable effect; and they conceal from your view the springs, and wheels, which give motion to the whole machinery." For all the simplicity of the world machine, which seemed to bring complexity into order, harmony, and proportion, the Cartesian cosmos was not only a vast universe in itself but one into which might be read an infinity of worlds. Indeed it was to the Joshua trumpet of Descartes much more than to Galileo or Bruno that men of the later century attributed the fall of the *flammantia moenia mundi* which had confined man within a finite universe. The "Great Secretary of Nature," as Addison said, had "destroyed those orbs of glass which the whims of antiquity had fixed above," had "scorned to be any longer bounded within the straits and crystalline walls of an Aristotelic world." [40] "Nay, the noble and Elastical Soul of Descartes, that has stretch'd it self yet a pin higher," wrote Henry Power, "has done the Heavens and Upper World more right yet, as to the Magnificent vastness of its Expansion, and has shown us that every Fixed Star is a sun, and is set in the centre of a Vortex, or Planetary System . . . and that our whole Planetary Vortex shrinks almost into nothing, if compared to those innumerable Systems above us." [41]

Astronomy and geology have come together; geogony is now an integral part of cosmogony. Our earth has emerged not because of a miraculous Word or because of an ancient Deluge but by natural forces of physical law within macrocosm and geocosm. Descartes had cast aside authority of Scripture and classics, had rid himself and his universe of legend and tradition.

[40] Joseph Addison, "Oration in Praise of the New Philosophy," in *The Works of the Right Honourable Joseph Addison* (London, 1856), pp. 607–608.

[41] Henry Power, *Experimental Philosophy, in Three Books* (London, 1664), p. 162.

But had he? The "particles" of which his universe was made were descendants of the atoms of Democritus, Epicurus, Lucretius. In the Cartesian earth that emerged from particles cast off by the sun, were there not still reminiscences of that ancient belief, the "sense and language of all antiquity," the Mundane Egg? Jerome, Basil, and Abelard had no such complex idea of the structure of the egg; but if the smooth earth of Blancanus had emerged upon natural principles, it would more nearly have approached the Cartesian world. In this "modern" world, made by a master mechanic, were still the shell, with the elements arranged in order, the semiliquid "white," and the "core" corresponding vaguely to the yolk of the Mundane Egg. Even Descartes had not completely cast aside all elements of tradition, had not departed entirely from the faith of his fathers. Yet never since the days recounted by Moses had such an original earth arisen from chaos. Reason seemed to have triumphed over tradition and authority, geology over Genesis, man over God. A geocosm, developing from fiery matter cast off by the sun, had been called into existence by man and, operating smoothly, mechanically, efficiently, vied now for supremacy in a new War of the Worlds with the miraculous—if somewhat antiquated— earth that had emerged from the waters during the third day of the first week in 4004 B.C. Embedded within the Cartesian "hypothesis," as within the Cartesian world, burned a glowing central core, threatening eruption and earthquake to orthodoxy, presaging intellectual rupture as devastating as that caused in the beginning by natural forces when a once-smooth earth collapsed upon itself in wild irregularities.

Chapter Five

A Sacred Theory of the Earth

"The Ruins of a Broken World"

I

CURIOUSLY enough, three major crises in the long warfare of science and religion have been precipitated by three "doubting Thomases"—Thomas Huxley in the nineteenth, Tom Paine in the eighteenth, Thomas Burnet in the seventeenth century. The two later controversies are familiar today; the earlier one has been largely forgotten. Modern geologists tend to pass by Burnet and the "world-makers" with a shrug or a smile. Earlier historians were wiser, realizing that the amateur Burnet was more responsible than many whose names are honored in the history of science for the fact that geology began to emerge as a science in the last years of the seventeenth century.

In 1605 Francis Bacon had anticipated that the advancement of science would meet with opposition from the "divines." Yet for many years the lion and the lamb lay down quietly enough together in England. There were occasional flurries in the dovecote above, antiscientific voices raised in protest by the orthodox. Priests and bishops of the Anglican Church wrote important scientific treatises. Scientists prided themselves on being "Christian Virtuosi." Milton's Adam freely discussed with an Angel the new astronomy that had earlier called all in doubt. On the continent Galileo had been imprisoned for his astronomical hypotheses, Bruno burned at the stake for various heresies including his belief in a plurality of worlds. The banning, even the burning of books, was not unknown in the freer island, yet banned books in England were not those that taught the new science. In the Restoration period if any vestiges remained of earlier secret, mysterious, esoteric groups, on the whole the School of Night now operated openly in English daylight. The symbol of science had ceased to be the jealously guarded furnace of Dr. Faustus and had become the co-operative "Salomon's House" of the *New Atlantis*. The "Invisible College"—whatever it once was—had merged with the Royal Society, established under the patronage of His Majesty, who though he went to one meeting of the Society to scoff returned to praise. Before the Battle of the Books was fought, science had triumphed in England.

Indeed, as we look back from the periods of the two later Thomases, we feel that the English spirit in the seventeenth century was more liberal than it later became. There was no scientific idea raised by Tom Paine in the *Age of Reason* that had not been familiar in the seventeenth century. Members of the nineteenth-century "Metaphysical Society" boggled over questions which the early Royal Society had considered settled. When Burnet published the first edition of his *Telluris Theoria Sacra* [1]

---

[1] The first edition appeared as *Telluris Theoria Sacra: Orbis Nostri Originem et Mutationes Generalis, quas aut jam subiit, aut olim subiturus est, complectens; Libri duo priores de diluvio et paradiso* (London, 1681) and contained only two books. It was translated (somewhat enlarged and written in more popular style) as *The Sacred Theory of the Earth: Containing an Account of the Original of the Earth and of All the General Changes Which It Hath Already Undergone or Is to Undergo, till the Consummation of All Things* (London, 1684). In 1689 Burnet published a new edition of the Latin text, to which were added two more

in 1681, the discoveries of astronomy, physics, and microbiology were widely acclaimed by both scientists and laymen. God had grown with his universe: the Deity of the later seventeenth century was grander, vaster, more majestic than before, expressing Himself in unnumbered worlds.

It has become customary to say that in 1687 Newton brought order out of chaos. Yet we often overstress the chaos. Intelligent men of the Restoration years were not disturbed by the rapid increase of knowledge. Indeed, "progressivists" like Mede and More had taken as one of their mottoes the Scriptural words quoted by Bacon at the beginning of the *Novum Organum*, "Many shall run to and fro and knowledge shall be increased," insisting that the advancement of knowledge was inevitably bound up in God's plan for the world, a fulfillment of prophecy now understood for the first time. There seemed no necessary conflict between the Book of God's Works and the Book of God's Words. Indeed, there was no serious conflict so long as the chief theological problem lay in making certain sciences consistent with the teaching of Moses. Such consistency seemed possible, even plausible, because of the Protestant insistence that the Bible dealt with moral not scientific truth, and even more because of convenient lacunae in Genesis. All that Moses said about the two great lights, the sun and the moon, had been readily interpreted in terms of Copernicus and Galileo. Only in a vague way had Moses committed himself upon physics, and although unfortunately—from the point of view of biologists—he was specific about the order in production of plants and animals,

books, "De Conflagratione Mundi" and "De Novis Coelis et Nova Terra." All four books were translated into English and printed with Burnet's *Review of the Theory of the Earth* and his reply to Erasmus Warren in 1690–1691. There were various editions of the work during the eighteenth century and at least one in the nineteenth. I have purposely used the sixth edition of 1726, since I have found it readily available in libraries. It also contains Burnet's final position on certain matters on which his thinking had developed or changed.

nothing in his pronouncements forbade men to accept a world of microscopical life as much beyond the reach of Moses' eyes as was the new universe of cosmic space.

We know, however, that at least one modern science cannot ultimately be made consistent with Genesis. In our examination of the literary, theological, philosophical, and scientific heritages of the seventeenth century, we have faced many paradoxes, but until we reached problems involved with the geocosm, we have found our ancestors comfortably able to live in two worlds at once, accepting Moses and Plato, Augustine and Copernicus. We have known that this pleasant state of things could not continue indefinitely. Today we consider the *Principia* the most influential volume of the late seventeenth century. Six years earlier, however, another book appeared, publication of which precipitated the first major battle between science and religion. Much more than the *Principia*, which was widely acclaimed, Burnet's *Telluris Theoria Sacra* provoked reply, defense, attack. Theologians, scientists, and laymen were divided into warring camps, some accepting the book as a new Revelation, others condemning it as blasphemy. The Latin edition attracted so much attention that, at the request of the King, Burnet translated it into English in 1684. As the *Anatomy of Melancholy* to Burton, *The Sacred Theory of the Earth* became a life work to Burnet, who continued to add to it in both Latin and English. By 1691 it had grown to two Latin and two English volumes. Most of Burnet's later works stemmed from it, since he was forced to publish refutations, explications, interpretations. Even after the author's death in 1715, the popularity continued, and throughout the first half of the eighteenth century publishers continued to find the work a good investment.

Thomas Burnet,[2] Master of the Charterhouse and Chaplain to

[2] There is no authoritative life of Burnet, though a fairly lengthy one by Heathcote was added to later editions of the *Sacred Theory*. Because of disagreement among writers, I have largely followed the facts as

King William, would have objected to my grouping him among
the "doubting Thomases," for he considered himself first of all
a theologian. But he was also a man widely read in the new
science. His design in the *Sacred Theory* was less to reconcile
science and religion than to prove that science offered another
Revelation compatible with Scriptural accounts, implied, indeed,
in the prophetic books as they were interpreted by the Cambridge Platonists. However, during the very period when Newton seemed to be proving the final harmony of science and
religion, Burnet was unconsciously forcing recognition of the
cacophony. If Newton "put to rout all the error that oppressed
us, all the darkness and the doubt," as Halley said in the poem
he wrote for the *Principia*, Burnet caused confusion worse
confounded. Approaching his problem from a point of view
different from that of Tom Paine at the end of the century,
Burnet ultimately proved as decisively as Paine that there could
be no compromise. His subsequent career showed how impossible was the middle way he proposed. Attempting to save his
"sacred theory," he finally went so far in his Scriptural interpretations that he incurred the censure of the ecclesiastical
powers, was forced to resign the clerkship of the Closet, sacri-
ficed his ambitions for the primacy, and found himself dismissed
from consideration for any possible ecclesiastical preferment,
because he supposedly taught

> That all the books of Moses
> Were nothing but supposes. . . .
> That as for Father Adam
> And Mistress Eve, his Madam,
> And what the Devil spoke, sir,

given in the registers of Cambridge University and of Christ's College.
In references written after his death, I have found him referred to as a
physician and also as "Sir Thomas." This, I suspect, is the result of confusion with Thomas Burnet, brother of Gilbert Burnet, who was both
a physician and a knight.

'Twas nothing but a joke, Sir,
And well-invented flam.[3]

II

On June 8, 1684, John Evelyn returned to Samuel Pepys a copy of the first English version of *The Sacred Theory of the Earth*, which he had previously read in Latin. "With your excellent book," he wrote,[4] "I returne you likewise my most humble thanks for your inducement of me to reade it over again; finding in it severall things (as you told me) omitted in the Latine (which I had formerly read with great delight), still new, still surprizing and so rational, that I both admire and believe it at once." Evelyn was "infinitely pleased" with Burnet's "thoughts concerning the Universe." He was amazed that "some peevish and off Men" thought that the *Sacred Theory* "does in the least derogate from the Holy Scripture." "The gentleman," he felt, "has doubtlesse a noble and large soul, and one would wish to be acquainted with him." As the two diarists were enthusiastic about the book, so was Sir William Temple, until he came to one section. In 1690, he began his *Essay upon the Ancient and Modern Learning* with these words:

Two Pieces that have lately pleased me . . . are, one in English upon the *Antediluvian World*, and another in French upon the *Plurality of Worlds;* one Writ by a Divine, and the other by a Gentleman, but both very finely in their several Kinds and upon their several Subjects, which would have made very poor work in common hands. I was so pleased with the last (I mean the Fashion of it rather than the Matter, which is old and beaten) that I enquired for what else I could of the same hand, till I met with a small Piece concerning Poesy, which gave me the same exception

[3] "The Battle Royal" in William King, *Original Works* (London, 1776), I, 221–222. The "Battle" involved an argument between a Dean (Dr. William Sherlock) and a Deistic Prebendary (Dr. Smith) about the Trinity.

[4] Samuel Pepys, *Private Correspondence and Miscellaneous Papers*, ed. by J. R. Tanner (London, 1926), I, 23–24.

to both these Authors, whom I should otherwise have been very partial to. For the first could not end his Learned Treatise without a Panegyric of Modern Learning and Knowledge in comparison of the Ancient: And the other falls so grosly into the censure of the Old Poetry and preference of the New, that I could not read either of these Strains without some indignation.[5]

So began one of the most famous skirmishes in the war of Ancient versus Modern. From his reading of Burnet and Fontenelle, Temple turned to set down his own thoughts with results unfortunate for him personally, but fortunate for literature, since the writing of that treatise brought into the war its most famous single combatant and left us Swift's *Battle of the Books*.

A modern reader may glance through *The Sacred Theory of the Earth* [6] with some bewilderment, discovering two volumes

[5] *Critical Essays of the Seventeenth Century*, ed. by J. E. Spingarn (Oxford, 1908), III, 32–33. Clara Marburg, *Sir William Temple: A Seventeenth Century "Libertin"* (New Haven, 1932), says, p. 96: "In 1690 Temple published the four essays which make up the Second Part of the *Miscellanea*. . . . One can assume . . . with some assurance that 'An Essay upon the Ancient and Modern Learning' was not written before the year 1689, since in that year a complete edition of Thomas Burnet's *Sacred Theory of the Earth* was published for the first time in English, though it had appeared in Latin in 1686. But Temple refers to the English edition when he mentions the 'Two Pieces that have lately pleased me.' " I have found no edition of Burnet's work in either Latin or English in 1696. The 1689 edition was in Latin. That Temple was referring to the first English edition of 1684 seems clear from the fact that he speaks of the author as "concluding" his work with a panegyric on modern learning. The section Temple had in mind was Burnet's final chapter in the 1684 edition, bk. II, ch. ix, "A general Objection against this Theory, viz. That if there had been such a Primitive Earth, as we pretend, the fame of it would have sounded throughout all Antiquity. *The Eastern and Western Learning consider'd* . . ." This chapter does not *conclude* the later Latin and English editions, both of which contained two new books.

[6] The recent revival of interest in the *Sacred Theory* may be the result of the fact that Basil Willey devoted a long section to the work in his *Eighteenth Century Background* (London, 1940). Before that time, as I have suggested, the work had been noticed in detail only by Cecil

of a leisurely theological work which consists of "Two First Books Concerning the Deluge, and Concerning Paradise" and "Two Last Books Concerning the Burning of the World, and Concerning the New Heavens and the New Earth." But if he has patience to continue beyond the Table of Contents and if he reads *in* rather than *through* the volumes, he may share some part of the interest of his ancestors. Whatever its position in modern science, the *Sacred Theory* deserves a place in the history of literature. Buffon thought the book a fine historical romance,[7] as indeed it is, the work of a man whose real gifts were those of

---

Moore in the article mentioned above and by Robert A. Aubin in his "Grottoes, Geology, and the Gothic Revival," *S.P.*, xxi (1934), 408–416.

[7] George Louis Leclerc, Comte de Buffon, "Du Système de Mr. Burnet," in *Œuvres Philosophiques* (Paris, 1954), 83 B. Buffon discussed Burnet's style as well as his ideas in the *Histoire et Théorie de la Terre* (*ibid.*, 45 B). There is an interesting section in Burnet's Preface (pp. xxi–xxii) where he discusses the tendency of his time to dismiss such works as his as "philosophick Romances . . . pretty Amusements of the Mind, but without Truth or Reality." He continues: "Where there is Variety of Parts in a due Contexture, with something of surprizing Aptness in the Harmony and Correspondency of them, this they call a Romance; but such Romances must all Theories of Nature and of Providence be, and must have every Part of that Character with Advantage, if so they be well represented. There is in them, as I may say, a *Plot* or *Mystery* pursued thro' the whole Work, and certain grand Issues or Events upon which the rest depend, or to which they are subordinate; but these Things we do not make or contrive our selves, but find and discover them, being made already by the great Author and Governor of the Universe: And when they are clearly discover'd well digested, and well reason'd in every Part, there is, methinks, more of Beauty in such a Theory, at least a more masculine Beauty, than in any Poem or Romance; and that solid Truth that is at the Bottom gives a Satisfaction to the Mind, that it can never have from any Fiction how artificial soever it be."

As I have said, one of Burnet's limitations is that he could not handle character. His inability does not appear in the *Sacred Theory*—where his "characters" are the earth and generic man—but it shows clearly in the *Archaeologiae Philosophicae* published in 1692. Attempting to go further with his reinterpretation of Scripture, he treated Adam, Eve, Noah, and others with unfortunate results parodied by the doggerel writer quoted above.

a novelist or dramatist. Burnet could not handle human characters, but he could and did handle plot, he had an extraordinarily
vivid imagination, and he was a master of suspense. One must go
back to the Greeks or forward to Hardy to find a writer who
transmits to his readers such sense of impending doom as does
Burnet in his descriptions of the coming of the Deluge and
the approach of the Conflagration. In both these sections even
a sophisticated modern reader finds himself momentarily breath-
less as an artist compellingly reconstructs majestic scenes. We
are as persuaded that we were present when the heavens opened
and the rain descended, or that in some previous incarnation we
lived through awesome days when God destroyed a world with
fire, as we were when we saw Prometheus in his lonely agony in
the Caucasus or heard with the Trojan Women the noise of a
falling city.

Even if the reader is too impatient to read enough of the
Sacred Theory to follow its "plot," he may discover that Burnet
deserves a place in the history of English style—provided the
reader prefers the styles of the earlier seventeenth century to
those of the later. In some ways Burnet was born out of his due
time. Had he written a half-century earlier, some of his passages
would be familiar in modern anthologies. He was the last of the
seventeenth-century masters of sonorous prose poetry. Less consistent and less rhythmical than Sir Thomas Browne, Burnet at his
best is even more majestic, because his materials were more
sublime than Browne's. Burnet's prose is "baroque" [8]—in the
best sense of that abused term. His individual sentences do not
arrest us as do Browne's; he is much less quotable. His power
consists in his ability to sustain the organ voice for long periods.
His major fault lies in his verbosity. Having stated an idea or
evoked a mood, he continued to labor the idea and mood until the

[8] Burnet's style has been treated by Elisabeth Haller in *Die barocken
Stilmerkmade in der englischen, lateinischen und deutschen Fassung von
Dr. Thomas Burnets Theory of the Earth* (Bern, 1940).

reader tires. Today we have almost forgotten Burnet as a stylist, but he deserves to be rescued from oblivion. If to some of his contemporaries Burnet the thinker seemed to belong with Epicurus "deep in Dante's Hell," to many he was an artist second only to Milton.

> How strong each Line, each Thought how great,
> With what an Energy you rise!
> How shines each Fancy! with what Heat
> Does every glowing Page surprize?

This was Addison, who discovered Burnet in youth. Steele placed the author of the *Sacred Theory* in the company of such poet-philosophers as Plato. Joseph Warton classed him with Plato, Cicero, and Milton, among transcendent geniuses "who have at once enjoyed in full vigor a sublime and splendid imagination, a solid and profound understanding, an exact and tenacious memory." On another occasion, Warton spoke of him in a breath with Plato, Lucian, and Sidney, as one of those who, though not able "to express themselves with beauty and propriety in the letters of verse . . . have yet manifested the force, fertility and creative power of a most poetic genius in prose." Warton was not the only eighteenth-century critic who believed that Burnet "displayed an imagination very nearly equal to that of Milton." [9]

[9] Addison's poem, in Latin and English, was prefaced to the 1719 and later editions of Burnet's work. Steele devoted *Spectator* 146 to the *Sacred Theory*. He was lavish in his praise of the mountain scenes in the last book. Warton discussed him in his *Essay on the Genius and Writings of Pope* (London, 1806), I, 115, 266. Even Burnet's contemporary adversaries acknowledged that he was a master of style, sometimes using his rhetorical abilities against him. They implied that his readers were so carried away by rhetoric that they forgot logic. See, for a good example, John Keill, *An Examination of Dr. Burnet's Theory of the Earth* (London, 1734), p. 22. Burnet's own remarks on his style are very interesting, since he realized that he was using the older ornate rhetorical style in a period when the "new style" of clarity and plainness had conquered. In the Preface to his second volume, he said: "I always endeavour to express myself in a plain and perspicuous manner; that the Reader

Burnet's ideas about Genesis and geology were still lively in the nineteenth century, but the climax of enthusiasm for Burnet as a prose poet came with the Romanticists. Wordsworth read parts of the *Sacred Theory* after he completed the first book of *The Excursion* and copied out passages of Burnet's sonorous Latin to publish with his notes. That "small manuscript of ninety pages," Coleridge's Note Book [10] in the British Museum, offers evidence of the effect of Burnet's *Sacred Theory* upon the mind of a poet-philosopher. References to Burnet appear frequently in the Note Book. Coleridge proposed to turn *The Sacred Theory of the Earth* into poetry: "Burnet's theoria telluris translated into Blank Verse, the original at the bottom of the page." To be sure, Coleridge never produced that work, as he did not produce others he proposed, but he was right in feeling that the *Sacred Theory* had epic qualities. In his admiration for Burnet's "grand style," he went even further than earlier critics, classing Burnet and Plato together as evidence that "poetry of the highest kind may exist without metre." The "Tartarean fury and turbulence" of the *Sacred Theory* continued to echo in Coleridge's memory. Professor Lowes writes: "No one who knows Burnet's blending of imaginative splendours with a daringly impossible cosmogony (and the *Telluris Theoria Sacra* is well worth knowing) will wonder that Coleridge was stirred. Even Lucretius might have been, I think, could Burnet's grandiose cosmic drama have reached him beyond the *flammantia moenia mundi*." That Cole-

---

may not lose Time, nor wait too long to know my Meaning." But he added this apologia: "You must not think it strange, however, that the Author sometimes, in meditating upon this Subject, is warm in his Thoughts and Expressions. For to see a World perishing in Flames, Rocks melting, the Earth trembling, and an Host of Angels in the Clouds, one must be very much a Stoick, to be a cold and unconcern'd Spectator of all this."

[10] See John Livingston Lowes, *The Road to Xanadu* (Boston and New York, 1927), p. 17. See also pp. 98, 459, and *passim*. Professor George Meyer of Tulane University has written a paper, which I read in manuscript, on the possible influence of Burnet on Wordsworth.

ridge knew others of Burnet's later works is shown by the fact that the lines prefixed to the *Ancient Mariner* are quoted from the *Archaeologiae Philosophicae*. Of all sections of the *Sacred Theory* Coleridge remembered, there is no question which was most appealing to his imagination. "Burnet / de montibus in blank verse," he noted not long after the first Burnet entry. Like the Miltonic poets of the eighteenth century, Coleridge responded imaginatively both to the descriptions of mountains Burnet himself had seen and to the majestic catalogue of far-flung ranges, the last vestiges of our globe to perish in the Final Conflagration.

But we must come to the *Sacred Theory* itself, reading it less as did Coleridge than as it was read in the 1680's against a literary, theological, scientific background now familiar to us. All the paradoxes and dilemmas we have detected earlier appear in Burnet. The peculiar combination of Latin and Greek literatures, Old and New Testaments, the theological ideas of a smooth versus an irregular earth, "correspondences" between macrocosm and microcosm, astronomy and geology—all are there. As Burnet was born out of his due time stylistically, so he seems at first glance to belong somewhat earlier in the history of science than he lived. In an era of scientific invention and discovery Burnet discovered and invented nothing. But the bombardier who drops the bomb is not the man who invented it. Thomas Burnet lighted a spark that fired seventeenth-century gunpowder; he dropped a bomb that had been prepared by others. He was able to do so because he understood what theologians had been saying for centuries and scientists for decades and because he could use language so vividly that his words lingered in the minds of his contemporaries. If he retarded science, he also aided its progress.

III

The *Sacred Theory* was Burnet's Book of Revelation. Entirely in sympathy with the scientific discoveries of his century,

he realized that the prevailing enthusiasm for science might lead
to neglect of Scripture. In the *Sacred Theory* old theology and
new science are brought face to face. They should not struggle
as adversaries, Burnet declared. Science and Scripture are not
enemies but friends, one complementing the other. Burnet could
prove that, he believed, to the satisfaction of both scientists and
theologians, provided men would free themselves from prejudice
and preconception. The "Reader of this Theory," he said,
"should be of an ingenuous and unprejudic'd Temper." He need
not be learned, for it does not so much "require Book-learning
and Scholarship, as good natural Sense to distinguish True and
False." If at first we arbitrarily separate Burnet's theology from
his science and consider each separately, we do so without violence to Burnet himself. His own method was somewhat similar,
for he included in a discussion of a scientific idea a long historical excursus, seeking authorities among Hebrew and Christian
Fathers. Only after he had made his reader aware of theological
tradition did he attempt to interpret old ideas of Paradise, Deluge,
and Conflagration in terms of the new science. Burnet went back
to early theology to discover an orthodox account that might be
made consistent with the marked changes and mutabilities that
had occurred in the structure of the earth since Creation. He was
convinced that the terrestrial globe of the 1680's was not identical with the original world. Its gross irregularities and lack of
symmetry offended his sense of proportion; "there appearing
nothing of Order, or any regular Design in its Parts, it seems
reasonable to believe that it was not the Work of Nature, according to her first Intention, or according to the first Model
that was drawn in Measure and Proportion by the Line and by
the Plummet, but a secondary Work, and the best that could be
made of broken Materials." Everywhere in external Nature Burnet found broken arcs rather than the Circle of Perfection. Hand-
some and regular enough in some parts, "yet if we consider the
whole Surface of it, or the whole exterior Region, 'tis a broken

and confus'd Heap of Bodies, plac'd in no Order to one another, nor with any Correspondency or Regularity of Parts," a world that must look to men in the moon like the moon world seen through our glasses—"rude and ragged." Moon and earth, "they are both in my Judgment the Image or Picture of a great Ruin, and have the true aspect of a World lying in its Rubbish."[11]

"But keepes the earth her round Proportion still?" John Donne had asked in 1611. "What a rude Lump our World is that we are so apt to dote upon," pondered Thomas Burnet three-quarters of a century later. Three major "irregularities" offended Burnet's sense of decorum: the channel of the sea, the subterraneous caverns of the earth, the mountains and rocks he had seen on his Alpine travels:

Our Earth is first divided into Sea and Land, without any Regularity in the Portions, either of the one or of the other; in the Sea lie the Islands, scatter'd like Limbs torn from the rest of the Body; great Rocks stand rear'd up in the Waters; the Promontories and Capes shoot into the Sea, and the Sinus's and Creeks on the other hand run as much into the Land; and these without any Order or Uniformity. Upon the other Part of our Globe stand great Heaps of Earth or Stone, which we call Mountains; and if these were all plac'd together, they would take up a very considerable part of the dry Land: In the rest of it are lesser Hills, Valleys, Plains, Lakes and Marshes, Sands and Desarts, &c, and these also without any regular Disposition. Then the Inside of the Earth, or inward parts of it, are generally broken or hollow, especially about the Mountains and high Lands, as also towards the Shores of the Sea, and among the Rocks.[12]

"This is the Pourtraicture of our Earth, drawn without Flattery." The world Burnet saw could not be the world God had made.

As if he had been present at the Creation, Burnet proposed to show us that first world. "This is a bold Step," he acknowledged; "such a supposition carries us into another World, which we

[11] *Sacred Theory of the Earth,* I, 173–174, 147–148.
[12] *Ibid.,* I, 148–149.

have never seen, nor even yet heard relation of; and a World, it seems, of very different Scenes or Prospects from ours, or from any thing we have ever yet known." Here is Burnet's primitive earth:

The Face of the Earth before the Deluge was smooth, regular, and uniform; without Mountains, and without a Sea. . . . An Earth without a Sea, and plain as the Elysian Fields; if you travel it all over, you will not meet with a Mountain or a Rock, yet well provided of all requisite things for an habitable World. . . . And this is the great Thing that now comes into debate, the great Paradox which we offer to be examined, and which we affirm, That the Earth in its first Rise and Formation from a Chaos, was of the Form here described, and so continued for many hundreds of Years. . . .

In this smooth Earth were the first Scenes of the World, and the first Generations of Mankind; it had the Beauty of Youth and blooming Nature, fresh and fruitful, and not a Wrinkle, Scar or Fracture in all its Body; no Rocks nor Mountains, no hollow Caves, nor gaping Channels, but even and uniform all over. And the Smoothness of the Earth made the Face of the Heavens so too; the Air was calm and serene; none of those tumultuary Motions and Conflicts of Vapours, which the Mountains and the Winds cause in ours: 'Twas suited to a golden Age, and to the first innocency of Nature.[13]

In that smooth earth with the beauty of youth and blooming nature lived our Grandparents, Adam and Eve, perfect statues in a perfect setting.

"All this, you'll say, is well, we are got into a pleasant World indeed, but what's that to the Purpose?" This halcyon state of things did not continue indefinitely. Something occurred in human history and in earth history. Burnet seems to be echoing Luther, reading into the history of mankind a series of degenerations causing changes in the globe. Although his philosophy of

[13] *Ibid.*, I, 71–72, 89.

history was really very different from Luther's,[14] the sense of doom is often similar when Burnet treats the deteriorations of nature. The first great climax occurred in the period of Noah, when "Providence, that ruleth all things and all Ages, after the Earth had stood above sixteen hundred Years, thought fit to put a Period to that World." The smooth round globe, the "true Epitome" and "Model" of original beauty, perished. If ours is the same world, it is so changed that even God must recognize it only with difficulty.

As dramatist Burnet faced the problem of the Greek tragedians, since he was dealing with a story the end of which was known to all his readers. From the beginning Fate hangs heavy over the head of his chief character, the terrestrial globe. Like the Greeks, however, he somehow achieved suspense. "When the appointed Time was come" and "the Heavens began to melt, and the Rains to fall," even our sophisticated imaginations are spellbound. We feel the mounting intensity as the Flood begins, share the universal terror as the waters mount; we seem to ride the tumult in a small boat, freighted with the last vestiges of humanity, and watch the ebbing of the waters until we disembark to behold a grotesque caricature of the original world:

Thus the Flood came to its height; and 'tis not easy to represent to our selves this strange Scene of Things, when the Deluge was in its Fury and Extremity; when the Earth was broken and swallowed up in the Abyss, whose raging Waters rise higher than the Mountains, and fill'd the Air with broken Waves, with an universal Mist, and with thick Darkness, so as Nature seem'd to be in a second Chaos; and upon this Chaos rid the distress'd Ark, that bore the small Remains of Mankind. No Sea was ever so tumultuous as this, nor is there any thing in present Nature to be compar'd with the Disorder of these Waters; all the Poetry, and all the Hyperboles

[14] Ernest Lee Tuveson has shown in *Millennium and Utopia* (Berkeley and Los Angeles, 1949), chapter iv, Burnet's parallel "plot" of earth history and human history and his optimistic conclusion in regard to the future of man and the future of the world.

that are used in the Description of Storms and raging Seas, were literally true in this. . . . That Abyss which had devoured and swallow'd up whole Forests of Woods, Cities and Provinces, nay the whole Earth . . . could not destroy this single Ship. . . . A Ship, whose Cargo was no less than a whole World; that carry'd the Fortune and Hopes of all Posterity, and if this had perish'd, the Earth for any thing we know had been nothing but a Desart, a great Ruin, a dead heap of Rubbish, from the Deluge to the Conflagration. But Death and Hell, the Grave and Destruction have their Bounds.[15]

What of the world that emerged from the second Chaos? "God builds and unbuilds Worlds: and who shall build up that Arch that was broke down at the Deluge? Where shall they lay the Foundation, or how shall the Mountains be rear'd up again to make Part of the Roof? This is the Fabrick, which when God breaketh down, none can build up again." Adam's smooth, unblemished world was lying in its rubbish. Noah saw only a great ruin. His world, indeed, was much more piteous than ours, since, as Burnet says, Time's comforting hand gradually overlays with healing scars the "raw and ghastly" wounds of nature. When Noah descended from the ark, "the Sea reach'd much further inland, and clim'd higher upon the Sides of the Mountains" than it does today. For many years after the Deluge, ocean had "much larger Bounds" than before, and "the Land had a different Face in many Respects to what it hath now." There were lakes and pools, stagnant fens and bogs that remained "spungy" for generations "till the World begun to be pretty well stock'd with People, and human Industry cleansed and drained those unfruitful and unhabitable Places." Where once had lain "a wide and endless Plain, smooth as the calm sea" were now "wild, vast and indigested Heaps of Stone and Earth." [16] There stood our mountains as the Flood receded; there they stand today, the most spectacular "Ruins of a broken World."

[15] *Sacred Theory*, I, 131, 134–135.   [16] *Ibid.*, I, 123, 137–138.

IV

So Burnet "retriev'd a World that had been lost for some thousands of Years, out of the Memory of Man, and the Records of Time," and reintroduced into the thinking of a highly sophisticated generation, which had almost forgotten it, the tradition of the "Mundane Egg." Yet Burnet's egg was very different from that of the Fathers. His was a scientific globe, emerging from chaos by natural principles, as Blancanus and Varenius had implied, as Descartes had surmised. The wealth of his very real learning and erudition was of great advantage, for Burnet was able to show that his had indeed long been a "sacred theory." His science was even more influential than his theology. His book seemed to many who praised it exactly what its title implied: a theory of earth science consistent with Biblical teaching. Let us, then, reread the same sections in order to see how Burnet attempted to apply the science and philosophy of his day to Genesis.

The first problem was that of the emergence of the earth from chaos at the time of Creation. Burnet did not for a moment deny the efficacy of God's power in this process. Although God remained the First Cause, the God of science must have employed secondary causes consistent with modern laws of nature. "By the Chaos," wrote Burnet, "I understand the Matter of the Earth and Heavens, without Form or Order; reduc'd into a fluid Mass, wherein are the Materials and Ingredients of all Bodies, but mingled in Confusion one with another. . . . Mingled, I say, without any Order of higher or lower, heavier or lighter, solid or volatile, in such a kind of confus'd Mass as is here represented." Such was the original state of nature. When God said, "Let there be a firmament in the midst of the waters, and let it divide the waters from the waters," what actually happened?

The first Change that we should imagine to happen would be this, that the heaviest and grossest Parts would sink down towards the middle of it (for there we suppose the Center of its Gravity) and the rest would float above. These grosser Parts thus sunk down and compress'd more and more, would harden by degrees, and constitute the Interiour Parts of the Earth: The rest of the Mass, which swims above, would be also divided by the same Principle of Gravity into two Orders of Bodies, the one liquid like Water, the other volatile like Air. . . . And these first Separations being thus made, the Body of the Chaos would stand in that Form which is here represented.[17]

The next step, according to Burnet, depended upon "the liquid Mass which encircled the Earth," which was not "the mere Element of Water, but a Collection of all liquors that belong to the Earth." Of these "Terrestrial Liquors" there were two chief kinds, "those that are fat, oily and light; and those that are lean and more earthy, like common Water." Using homely metaphors, Burnet illustrated the process that must have taken place. As in "Cream, and thin Milk, Oil and Water and such like," the "more oily and light Part of this Mass would get above the other, and swim upon it." But this was not all. In a great mass of water, impurities inevitably existed; so too in the "Regions of the

[17] *Ibid.*, I, 74–75. The influence of Descartes on Burnet's world scheme was, of course, great. Burnet followed him almost step by step in his account of the emergence of the earth. But, jealously guarding his own originality—and wishing to free himself from association with one who was a heretic to many of the orthodox—he wrote (I, 153–154): "An eminent Philosopher of this Age, Monsieur des Cartes, hath made use of the like Hypothesis to explain the irregular Form of the present Earth; though he never dream'd of the Deluge, nor thought that first Orb, built over the Abyss, to have been any more than a transient Crust, and not a real habitable World that lasted for more than sixteen hundred Years, as we suppose it to have been. And though he hath, in my Opinion, in the Formation of that first Orb, and upon the Dissolution of it, committed some great Oversights . . . however he saw a Necessity of such a Thing, and of the Disruption of it, to bring the Earth into that Form and Posture wherein we now find it."

Burnet's book is lavishly illustrated with plates and diagrams which make his account of the creation and the destruction of the earth clear and graphic.

Air," for as yet the air was "thick, gross and dark, there being an abundance of little Terrestrial Particles swimming in it still." The heavier of these would descend more rapidly, the "lesser and lighter" more slowly, meeting, as they settled, with the "oily Liquor" of the watery mass. Mixing with "that unctuous Substance, they composed a certain Slime, or fat, soft, and light Earth, spread upon the Face of the Waters." What a soil this must have offered, reflected Burnet, for the original Garden. Granted his premises, Burnet continued, the earth as it first appeared must have been "smooth, regular and uniform, without Mountains and without a Sea." [18]

Interested though he was in the external figure of his Mundane Egg, Burnet was more concerned to explain its "inward Composition," upon which his theory depended. The egg consisted "of several Orbs, one including another, and in that Order, as to answer the several Elementary Regions of which the new-made Earth was constituted." The "Figure of the Earth" was not spherical but ovoid, "and a little extended toward the Poles." In the solid center—the yolk of the egg—burned the "central Fire." The "Membrane" lay above; "the exterior Region of the Earth is as the Shell of the Egg, and the Abyss under it is as the White that lies under the Shell." Burnet could not sufficiently praise the ingenuity and artistry of a Deity who had preconceived the intricate structure of the Mundane Egg. "This Structure," he wrote, "is so marvellous, that it ought rather to be consider'd as a particular Effect of the Divine Art, than as the Work of Nature. The whole Globe of the Water vaulted over, and the exterior Earth hanging above the Deep, sustain'd by nothing but its own Measures and Manner of Construction: A Building without Foundation or Corner-Stone. . . . A Piece of Divine Geometry or Architecture." [19]

Leaving Burnet's seventeenth-century terminology and rhetoric, let us see what he has said. Since chaos consisted of a fluid

---

[18] *Sacred Theory*, I, 75–76, 81–82.   [19] *Ibid.*, I, 85–87.

mass, by the action of surface tension it necessarily formed a smooth globe; by the action of gravity, the elements arranged themselves within the globe in concentric strata, in decreasing order of specific gravity. In the process of separation of liquid elements into heavy and light, an oily layer came to float upon the surface of the water, between water and air; as the dust settled, it was intercepted by this sphere of oil, with which it mixed to form a layer of fat, soft, and light earth upon the waters. "By Reason, the laws of Nature, and the Motions of the Chaos" emerged an earth "compacted out of Water and in Water."

As theologian, Burnet stressed Divine Wrath as the immediate cause of the Deluge. As scientist, however, he was insistent that the material cause of the Deluge—the collapse of earth's super-structure—had been inherent in earth itself and so closely derived from its structure as to seem at once inevitable and independent of God's decrees. Like the Church Fathers and hexaemeral com-mentators, Burnet was teased by the attempt to explain the origin of that vast flood of waters that inundated the world. He realized that his own hypothesis of an original smooth earth made the problem not simpler but more difficult:

What appearance of a Deluge here, where there is not so much as a Sea, nor half so much Water as we have in this Earth? Or what Appearance of Mountains or Caverns, or other Irregularities of the Earth, where all is level and united: So that instead of loosing the Knot, this ties it the harder. You pretend to shew us how the Deluge was made, and you lock up all the Waters within the Womb of the Earth, and set Bars and Doors, and a Wall of impenetrable Strength and Thickness to keep them there. And you pretend to shew us the Original of Rocks and Mountains, and Caverns of the Earth, and bring us to a wide and endless Plain, smooth as the calm Sea.[20]

[20] *Ibid.*, I, 90. Mr. Allen in *The Legend of Noah* (Urbana, 1949), has discussed Burnet's theories in relation to those of his predecessors, pp. 96 ff.

In turn Burnet considered many possibilities suggested by his predecessors. He rejected the theory that the Deluge had been localized, affecting only a small part of the earth, as he rejected the idea that the Flood was a miraculous intervention of God. Even forty days' rain was not sufficient explanation for a universal Deluge to a man who lived in a period when rainfall was being measured. As theologian, Burnet combed the Scriptures; there is no mysterious passage on "the waters" he did not quote. He knew all that could be known about the fountains of the deep, whether of Plato, Moses, or Ecclesiastes. Among the many Biblical passages was one which, he said, "could never be beaten out of my Head"—the words in II Peter: "There were heavens from of old; and an earth compacted of water and by water, by the word of God; by which means the world that then was, being overflowed with water, perished." To the "waters *above*" must be added those still imprisoned *within* the original smooth earth. When the deluge descended, the pressure of the waters above the earth became too great. "Suppose the great Frame of the exterior Earth to have broke at this time, or the Fountains of the great Abyss, as Moses saith, to have been then open'd." The shell of the Mundane Egg was cracked; the liquid within, pouring forth, inundated the world:

Let us then suppose, that at a Time appointed by Divine Providence, and from Causes made ready to do that great Execution upon a sinful World, that this Abyss was open'd, or that the Frame of the Earth broke and fell down into the great Abyss. At this one stroke all Nature would be chang'd, and this single Action would have two great and visible Effects: The one Transient, and the other Permanent. First, an Universal Deluge would overflow all the Parts and Regions of the broken Earth during the great Commotion and Agitation of the Abyss, by the violent Fall of the Earth into it. This would be the first and unquestionable Effect of this Dissolution, and all that World would be destroy'd. Then when the Agitation of the Abyss was asswag'd . . . you would see the true image of the present Earth in the ruins of the first. The Surface of the

Globe would be divided into Land and Sea; the Land would consist
of Plains and Valleys and Mountains, according as the Pieces of
this Ruin were plac'd and dispos'd: Upon the Banks of the Sea
would stand the Rocks, and near the Shore would be the Islands, or
lesser Fragments of Earth compass'd round by Water. Then as to
subterraneous Waters, and all subterraneous Caverns and Hollownesses, upon this Supposition those things cou'd not be otherwise
for the Parts would fall hollow in many Places in this, as in all other
Ruins.[21]

"The Ruins of a broken World"—this is a persistent refrain
of the "Two First Books Concerning the Deluge." It is somber
music, as if it were the lament of Noah over the world he saw as
he emerged wearily from the ark. "What can have more the
Figure and Mien of a Ruin, than Crags, and Rocks, and Cliffs?"
"That hollow and broken Posture of Things under Ground, all
these Caves and Holes, and blind Recesses. . . . say but they
are a Ruin, and you have in one Word explain'd them all." "Our
Cities are built upon Ruins, and our Fields and Countries stand
upon broken Arches and Vaults, and so does the greatest Part of
the outward Frame of the Earth." [22] As we read the Deluge
passages in the *Sacred Theory*, we forget Burnet the scientist
and the progressivist and remember a man who should have been
born a poet in the earlier age of melancholy. The more we listen
to his passages of doom and ruin, the better we understand his
poetic influence in the eighteenth century that merged with
Milton's, one organ voice replying antiphonally to another. The
"white melancholy" of the eighteenth century was usually that
of "Il Penseroso"; the "black melancholy" of the graveyard
school, the poets of Judgment, and the thinkers of night thoughts
was more often that of Burnet, living on a "rude lump," the ruins
of a broken world.

[21] *Sacred Theory*, I, 90–91.   [22] *Ibid.*, I, 51, 43, 171, 164.

V

Burnet was peculiarly a product of the paradoxical age that produced him. Now gloomy, now triumphant, he brings sharply into focus the conflicts and paradoxes we have found. It is not alone because of his resurrection of the old theological idea of a smooth earth or because of his attempt to explain scientifically the present earth's irregularities that he legitimately occupies a central position in this study. As in his science and theology, so in his aesthetic response to the vast and grand in external Nature, he was a "true amphibian." We have hitherto encountered many men who were uninterested in grand Nature, some who actively disliked hills, a few who felt a momentary dawning of the "Mountain Glory." But we have found nothing like the contradictions of Thomas Burnet. Among earlier English writers, interest in mountains has been secondary. To Burnet the existence of mountains was of primary importance. His "sacred theory" developed from his engrossing interest in these phenomena.

In 1671 Burnet had made the Grand Tour with the Earl of Wiltshire, later Duke of Bolton, to whom he dedicated the Latin edition of the work. He suggests that he began to write the book while he was on his travels, in an attempt to explain to himself the extraordinary impression mountains had made upon him:

There is nothing doth more awaken our Thoughts, or excite our Minds to enquire into the Causes of such Things, than the actual View of them; as I have had Experience my self, when it was my Fortune to cross the Alps and Apennine Mountains; for the Sight of those wild, vast, and indigested Heaps of Stones and Earth did so deeply stir my Fancy, that I was not easy till I could give my self some tolerable Account how that Confusion came in Nature.

Burnet had gone abroad, as had Coryat, Howell, and Evelyn, conditioned by acquired "idols." Among his books, he had responded to the dual literary traditions we have found. If he felt the Latin and Christian withdrawal from that which is high, nevertheless Sinai and Olympus were one to him, as to Milton, and mortals talked with gods on both. Burnet had taken for granted doctrines of correspondence, proportion, symmetry. "We are assured," he wrote, "that all Things were made at first in Beauty and Proportion." But until he went to the continent, he had had no conception how broken was the earthly arc that should have been a perfect round. It was easy for men in their studies in Cambridge to talk about the "regular figure of the earth" and believe in proportion and symmetry in the geocosm:

'Tis certain that we naturally imagine the Surface of the Earth much more regular than it is; for unless we be in some mountainous Parts, there seldom occur any great Inequalities within so much Compass of Ground as we can at once reach with our Eye; and to conceive the Rest, we multiply the same Idea, and extend it to those Parts of the Earth that we do not see, and so fancy the whole Globe much more smooth and uniform than it is.[23]

Before 1671 Burnet's travels had been only in books. In his atlas, mountain ranges seemed neat and pleasing to decorum, like those in Calvin's map of Eden. The "Geographers," Burnet said, were careful enough in their "Civil Maps"; they "note the Distinction of Countries and of Cities." But their globes were as smooth as the "Mundane Egg." Burnet felt that, had he been familiar with raised maps and globes, his experience in the Alps and Apennines might not have come as such a shock; in youth he would have looked "upon such bare Draughts as show us Nature undrest;

[23] This and the preceding quotation may be found in *ibid.*, I, 190–191. Burnet frequently mentions the fact that the flat maps in atlases gave a misleading impression of the topography of the earth. He praised "Cluverius, [who] in his Description of Ancient Germany, Switzerland, and Italy hath given Maps of those Countries more approaching to the natural Face of them." Burnet illustrated his own thesis by drawing "natural" maps "without marking Countries or Towns, or any such artificial Things, distinguishing only Land and Sea, Islands and Continents, Mountains and not Mountains" (I, 190–191).

for then we are best able to judge what her true Shapes and Proportions are."

When he saw the Alps from a distance, Burnet could still believe in proportion and symmetry. It is not until he made the first ascent that he was impressed by the confusion of "indigested Nature":

But suppose a Man was carried asleep out of a plain Country amongst the Alps, and left there upon the Top of one of the highest Mountains, when he wak'd and look'd about him, he wou'd think himself in an inchanted Country, or carried into another World; every Thing wou'd appear to him so different to what he had ever seen or imagin'd before. To see on every Hand of him a Multitude of vast Bodies thrown together in Confusion, as those Mountains are; Rocks standing naked round about him; and the hollow Valleys gaping under him; and at his Feet, it may be, an Heap of Frozen Snow in the midst of summer. He would hear the Thunder come from below, and see the black Clouds hanging beneath him; upon such a Prospect it would not be easy to him to persuade himself that he was still upon the same Earth; but if he did, he would be convinc'd, at least, that there are some Regions of it strangely rude, and ruin-like, and very different from what he had ever thought of before.[24]

This is not rhetoric; it is straightforward reporting on the part of a man who thought he knew all about mountains, yet found himself completely unprepared for the actual experience of crossing the Alps. Burnet's repulsion was not, like Coryat's, the instinctive fear of a man who has no head for heights. He was less frightened than he was appalled by the "incredible Confusion" of passes and summits. All his idols of proportion, symmetry, and decorum in Nature were suddenly shattered by Nature herself. Like the rude rocks, his ideals lay before him, ruins of a broken world:

[24] *Sacred Theory*, I, 191–192. Some of Burnet's mountain passages have been considered by H. V. S. Ogden in "Thomas Burnet's *Telluris Theoria Sacra* and Mountain-Scenery," *E.L.H.*, XIV (1947), 139 ff.

These Mountains are plac'd in no Order one with another, that can either respect Use or Beauty; and if you consider them singly, they do not consist of any Proportion of Parts that is referable to any Design, or that hath the least Footsteps of Art or Counsel. There is nothing in Nature more shapeless and ill-figur'd than an old Rock or Mountain, and all that Variety that is among them, is but the many various Modes of Irregularity; so as you can not make a better Character of them, in short, than to say they are of all Forms and Figures except regular. . . . And lastly, if you look upon an Heap of them together, or a mountainous Country, they are the greatest Examples of Confusion that we know in Nature; no Tempest or Earthquake puts Things into more Disorder. 'Tis true they cannot look so ill now as they did at first; a Ruin that is fresh, looks much worse than afterwards, when the Earth grows discolour'd and skinn'd over. But I fancy, if we had seen the Mountains when they were new born and raw, when the Earth was fresh broken, and the Waters of the Deluge newly retir'd, the Fractions and Confusions of them would have appear'd very ghastly and frightful.[25]

"Chaos is come again"; nor was chaos limited to one small part of earth, where it might be explained by local tempest or earthquake. Mountains were everywhere. "They are in the New World as well as the Old; and if they could discover two or three New Worlds or Continents more, they would still find them there. Neither is there any Original Island upon the Earth, but is either all a Rock, or hath Rocks or Mountains in it. And all the dry Land, and every Continent, is but a kind of Mountain." [26]

Mountains were bad enough, but apparently confusion and irregularity were universal. On his travels Burnet had seen dens and caverns and caught glimpses of the fantastic shapes of the earth's entrails; he learned from experience much more than books had taught him about the violence of volcano and earthquake:

If we now could open the Earth . . . and go down into the Bosom of it; see all the dark Chambers and Apartments there, how ill

[25] *Sacred Theory*, I, 195–196.   [26] *Ibid.*, I, 193.

contriv'd, and how ill kept; so many Holes and Corners, some fill'd with Smoak and Fire, some with Water, and some with Vapours and mouldy Air; how like a Ruin it lies, gaping and torn in the Parts of it.[27]

Most appalling of all, because man could not see but must imagine it, was the channel of the sea:

The Inside of a Cave is rough and unsightly; the Beds of great Rivers and great Lakes, when they are laid dry, look very raw and rude, the Valleys of the Earth, if they were naked, without Trees and without Grass, nothing but bare Ground and bare Stones, from the tops of their Mountains, would have a ghastly Aspect; but the Sea-Channel is the complex of all these; here Caves, empty Lakes, naked Valleys are represented as in their Original, or rather far exceeded and out-done as to all their Irregularities; for the Cavity of the Ocean is universally irregular, both as to the Shores and Borders of it. . . . If the Sea had been drawn round the Earth in regular Figures and Borders, it might have been a great Beauty to our Globe.

If we could descend to the bottom of the sea or by some power behold the bed of ocean drained of its waters, "how horribly and barbarously would it look? And with what Amazement should we see it lie under us like an open Hell, or a wide bottomless Pit? So deep and hollow and vast, so broken and confus'd, so every where deform'd and monstrous." Not even the army of Xerxes, had it been at work since the beginning of the world, could have made "a Ditch of this Greatness," produced anything to correspond to "that vast and prodigious Cavity that runs quite round the Globe, and reacheth, for ought we know, from Pole to Pole, and in many Places is unsearchably deep: When I present this great Gulf to my Imagination, emptied of all its Waters, naked and gaping at the Sun, stretching its Jaws from one End of the Earth to another, it appears to me the most ghastly thing in Nature." [28]

[27] *Ibid.*, I, 169–170.   [28] *Ibid.*, I, 173–175.

What can man say when he considers this chaos, without proportion, without restraint or symmetry? Can he look upon such wild irregularity and still believe that Nature is the Art of God? On his Alpine journey Burnet faced what he believed was a religious crisis. It was less his theology than his aesthetics that was threatened. When he began to write the *Telluris Theoria Sacra*, Burnet was not so much trying to justify Genesis as attempting to save for himself Plato and Augustine, Ficino and Kepler. "Assured that all Things were made at first in Beauty and Proportion," he stubbornly asserted, it was impossible to believe that the world as he had seen it on his travels was the work of the Great Architect. "There appearing nothing of Order, or any regular Design in its Parts, it seems reasonable to believe that it was not the Work of Nature, according to her first Intention, or according to the first Model that was drawn in Measure and Proportion by the Line and by the Plummet, but a secondary Work, and the best that could be made of broken Materials." This "Wild and multifarious Confusion . . . strange and unaccountable" was not God's creation, but "another Chaos in its kind; who can paint the Scenes of it? Gulphs, and Precipices, and Cataracts; Pits within Pits, and Rocks under Rocks, broken Mountains and ragged Islands, that look as if they had been Countries pull'd up by the Roots, and planted in the Sea." [29] The Burnet who returned to England after three years' travel was a different man. He came back to finish the book he had begun among the Alps, to propound a "sacred theory" that would justify God and Nature but even more save his own aesthetic and ethical ideals.

VI

I have said that Burnet was a paradoxical son of a paradoxical century, but so far I have deliberately quoted him in such a way that he seems the most consistent of all writers we have con-

[29] *Ibid.*, I, 179, 173-174.

sidered in his condemnation of the monstrosities of Nature. Like Luther he beat his breast when he looked on the ruins caused by man's sin. Theologically Burnet condemned mountains; actually he was obsessed by them. He believed himself an apostle of decorum and proportion, but he was so strongly attracted by the grandeur of external Nature that he persistently fought the attraction. I have done him no injustice in isolating his vehemence and violence against mountains, for this was the impression he intended to produce. Wherever we look among his passages on wild nature, we find conflict between intellectual condemnation of asymmetry and emotional response to the attraction of the vast.

In the midst of a condemnation of the uncouth holes and hollows of a broken world, we hear Burnet saying: "Places that are strange and solemn strike an Awe into us and incline us to a kind of superstitious Timidity and Veneration." He let his fancy roam over the subterraneous world, finding delight as well as terror in grottoes, caves, dens, and hollows. "It would be very pleasant," he wrote, "to read good Descriptions of these subterraneous Places, and of all the strange Works of Nature there; how she furnisheth forth these dark neglected Grotto's." [30] When Burnet first saw mountains, he had thought of clouds, but upon that occasion clouds, mountains, and rocks seemed alike amorphous and offensive to decorum: "In what Confusion do they lie? They have neither Form, nor Beauty, nor Shape, nor Order, no more than the Clouds in the Air." Yet Burnet's Fancy found pleasure in the sea caves, where the waves roll underground "and wear the hard Rock into as many odd Shapes and Figures as we see in the Clouds." Intellectually Burnet was persuaded that "if the Sea had been drawn round the Earth in regular Figures and Borders, it might have been a great Beauty to our Globe." Emotionally he felt the vastness and majesty of oceans as few English travelers before his time.

Let us try Burnet upon another issue—his response to the

[30] *Ibid.*, I, 155–156.

night skies. Burnet's sense of symmetry was as offended when he surveyed the stars as when he stood among the hills:

They lie carelessly scatter'd, as if they had been sown in the Heaven, like seeds, by handfuls; and not by a skilful Hand neither. What a beautiful Hemisphere they would have made, if they had been plac'd in Rank and Order; if they had been all dispos'd into regular Figures, and the little ones set with due Regard to the greater, than all finish'd and made up into one Symmetry; what a surprizing Beauty this would have been to the Inhabitants of the Earth? What a lovely Roof to our little World? [31]

Stars, mountain, clouds—they are all "plac'd in no Order one with another, that could either respect Use or Beauty. . . . They do not consist of any Proportion of Parts that is referable to any Design, or that hath the least Footsteps of Art or Counsel." It would have "cost no more"—this is one of Burnet's persistent refrains—to have made all things in "better Order." "All that variety that is among them, is but the various Modes of Irregularity; so as you cannot make a better Character of them, in short, than to say they are of all Forms and Figures except regular."

The chapter in which Burnet most drastically condemned the gross disproportion and irregularity of mountains began with a tribute to their majesty:

The greatest Objects of Nature are, methinks, the most pleasing to behold; and next to the Great Concave of the Heavens, and those boundless Regions where the Stars inhabit, there is nothing that I look upon with more Pleasure than the wide Sea and the Mountains of the Earth. There is something august and stately in the Air of these things, that inspires the Mind with great Thoughts and Passions; we do naturally, upon such Occasions, think of God and his Greatness: And whatsover hath but the Shadow and Appearance of INFINITE, as all Things have that are too big for our Comprehension, they fill and overbear the Mind with their Excess, and cast it into a pleasing kind of Stupor and Admiration.[32]

[31] *Ibid.*, vol. II, bk. IV, ch. xi, pp. 312–313.   [32] *Ibid.*, I, 188–189.

This is the same Burnet; these are the same night skies and the same mountains "plac'd in no Order one with another that can either respect Use or Beauty." If Burnet could not forgive Nature for her confusion, he could not deny the effect of her vastness. "These Mountains . . . are nothing but great Ruins; but such as shew a certain Magnificence in Nature." So too when he "presented" to his "Imagination" that vast and prodigious cavity of ocean: it seemed to him "the most ghastly Thing in Nature." Its vastness, however, impressed his Fancy at the same time that it appalled his Reason. "We justly admire its Greatness," though "we cannot at all admire its Beauty or Elegancy, for 'tis as deformed and irregular as it is great."

Burnet was "rapt" and "ravished" by the vast, the grand, the majestic. Before vastness he experienced the awe and wonder he had associated with God. But he could not understand his own emotions. He knew that his response was not to "Beauty." On every possible occasion, he sharply differentiated between response to Beauty and the new emotions inspired by the grandeur of Nature. Vast and irregular mountains were not beautiful, but, except for the vast and irregular night skies, nothing had ever moved Burnet to such awe or so led his mind to thoughts of God and infinity as did the mountains and the sea.

Cowley, we remember, had loved "littleness" and had hoped that if he fell in love again it would be with "prettiness," not with "Majestical Beauty." Fontenelle's Lady in the *Plurality of Worlds* shrank back from vastness. "I protest it is dreadful," she declared. But Fontenelle's Philosopher "began to breathe with more freedom and think the Earth to be incomparably more magnificent than it was before." Yet even the Philosopher differentiated between the "magnificent" and the "beautiful," the latter associated in his mind with "prettiness":

I confess, I am guilty of so much weakness, as to be in love with what is beautiful; that's my distemper, and I am confident, the Vortex's will never cure it. What if the other Worlds render ours so very little? They cannot spoil fine Eyes, or a pretty Mouth; their value is still the same, in spite of all the Worlds that can possibly exist.[33]

Burnet had believed that the essence of beauty lay in limitation and restraint rather than in grandeur. He thought that he agreed with Saint-Evremond: "*Vastness* signifies an excessive Greatness. Vast Things differ mightily from those that make an agreeable Impression upon us." But Burnet was English, not French. In spite of his acquired idols, he was emotionally moved by vastness, though the pleasure he felt was a mixture of attraction and repulsion, distaste and exultation. It was a response not of the "Understanding" but of "phansy," of imagination that expanded in the presence of "wild, vast, and indigested Nature." In a later section of the *Sacred Theory* [34] he made a distinction which may not unfairly be applied to Burnet himself. "For my Part," he said, "I do generally distinguish of two Sorts of Opinions in all Men, *Inclination-opinions*, and *Reason'd-opinions*; Opinions that grow upon Mens Complexions, and Opinions that are the results of their Reason; and I meet with very few that are of a Temperament so equal, or a Constitution so even pois'd, but they incline to one set of Opinions rather than another." Burnet's conflict in the Alps was between the "Reason'd-opinions" with which he had gone abroad and his "Inclination-opinions," deep-seated in a native "Complexion" of "Enthusiasm." He went on to say that one may distinguish the "Inclination" from the "Reason'd opinions" because the first are usually "accompanied with more Heat than Light, a great deal of Eagerness and Impatience in defending of them, and but slender Arguments." So it was to prove in his own case when he attempted to defend the "Inclination" that, against all argument and "Reason'd-opinion," led him to respond imaginatively to the Sublime in Nature.

[33] Fontenelle, *A Plurality of Worlds, Translated into English by Mr. Glanvill* (London, 1702), pp. 128–129.

[34] *Sacred Theory*, I, 412–413.

VII

Burnet was characteristic of his age. Except for his rhetorical gifts, he was in no way remarkable. Therefore if we can disentangle some of the various strands of influence under which he had developed the ideals that were challenged by his Alpine experience, we may be better able to understand his age and its place in the history of aesthetics, for this is a generation over which historians of aesthetics pass too easily.

Burnet was born, of Scottish ancestry, at Croft, near Darlington in Durham. He was educated at Northallerton across the Yorkshire border. Earth's minor irregularities had been familiar to him in youth, as later to Wordsworth in Cumberland. He is said to have entered the university when he was older than the average matriculant. Officially he was a student of Owtram's at Clare Hall, but he seems to have spent more time under Tillotson,[35] whom, ironically, Burnet would probably have succeeded as Archbishop of Canterbury had he not written *The Sacred Theory of the Earth*. At Clare Hall, however, Burnet's

---

[35] Burnet received the Bachelor's degree in 1655 and apparently migrated to Christ's the next year. He seems to have remained at Christ's until 1670, after which date the registers indicate complaints because of his "long absences." (See John Peile, *Biographical Registers of Christ's College* [Cambridge, Eng., 1900].) That Burnet was a privileged character at Christ's is suggested by the fact that among the charges hurled at Cudworth and the "latitude-men" was the fact that Cudworth showed favoritism; Burnet is specifically mentioned as one whom Cudworth permitted to be absent for longer than statutory periods. Burnet seems to have had royal privilege, since Cudworth replied on one occasion that a royal order had been responsible for one of Burnet's longest absences.

Some accounts of Burnet imply that he had difficulty with Tillotson while a student at Clare Hall. Mr. Tuveson, however, calls my attention to two comments that contradict that tradition. Dr. Ralph Heathcote in his "Life of Burnet," prefixed to the seventh edition of the *Sacred Theory* (London, 1759), says that Tillotson recommended Burnet to the post of Clerk of the Closet. Thomas Birch in Tillotson, *Works* (London, 1752), I, lxxvii, says that Tillotson was "desirous to promote" Burnet.

first allegiance was to Ralph Cudworth, whom he followed to Christ's College when Cudworth became Master of Christ's. Cudworth had not been happy at Clare Hall. Tillotson had little sympathy with the growing Platonist movement and on more than one occasion openly attacked the Cambridge Platonists. At Christ's College both Cudworth and Burnet found a congenial atmosphere. It was during this period that Christ's rather than Emmanuel became the center of the new movement, and it was of this period that Joseph Glanvill spoke, regretting that he had spent barren years at Oxford when the spirit of a new philosophy was abroad at Cambridge. Cudworth had satisfied Burnet's intellect, but at Christ's he found an even more congenial master. Henry More fed both his mind and his emotions.

When Burnet entered Christ's College, More was becoming the leading spirit of the Platonists. He was now in his early forties, in the prime of life and vigor. His "Platonic Poems" were eagerly read by the younger generation. Joseph Mede's great apocalyptical studies were widely acclaimed,[36] and More was following him in attempts to decode Daniel, Revelation, and other cryptic passages. He was enthusiastically preaching the gospel of a new "progressive" dispensation. Burnet found More in the period of his greatest productivity, when book after book was coming from the press, when, indeed, More was publishing not only his own ideas but possibly some of Cudworth's, who was always slow to write and slower to print.[37] Of the various works

[36] Mede's *Key to the Revelation*, translated by Richard Moore, appeared in London in 1643. His *Clavis Apocalyptica* appeared in three editions, 1627, 1632, and 1642. Mr. Tuveson (p. 229) says: "Its translation was ordered by Parliament in 1643, and it is easy to see that Mede's work was a propaganda document of considerable value in the contemporaneous situation."

[37] The only shadow on the relationship of More and Cudworth occurred shortly after Burnet migrated to Christ's College. Cudworth felt that More was publishing some of his ideas in the works that were appearing so rapidly. There was probably truth in Cudworth's belief, since More was very susceptible to the ideas of others and often made them his own.

published by More in the early years of Burnet's residence in Cambridge, two are of particular importance in understanding the later Burnet. In 1653 More wrote his *Conjectura Cabbalistica*, a small volume in which, following a long train of interpreters and expositors, he reinterpreted the first chapter of Genesis. Moses had written, he said, in such a way that his words were to be understood literally by the simple and unlearned who should not concern themselves with hidden meaning. But Moses was also speaking ethically and metaphysically; the language of Genesis was deliberately symbolic. When Burnet wrote the *Sacred Theory*, and even more when he added the *Archaeologiae Philosophicae*, he considered that he was following in More's steps. In 1656, when Cudworth became Master of Christ's, More published *Enthusiasmus Triumphatus*, one of his most paradoxical works, an attack upon growing tendencies toward "Enthusiasm" in religion and a defense of true "Enthusiasm," of which we shall hear more.

Burnet had been under the influence of the Cambridge Platonists for sixteen years before he went to the continent. From both More and Cudworth he drew in Neoplatonic ideas of "the true intellectual system of the universe," "the eternal and immutable morality." He was taught that the external world reflects some shadow of the first Beauty, that all things in Nature exhibit design and plan, that proportion, relation, correspondence, symmetry are repeated in macrocosm, geocosm, microcosm, that Beauty is consonant with Reason, to be apprehended by the

---

In More's defense it may be said that Cudworth was the type of academic scholar so slow to write and publish that a generation of his students were teaching and writing according to his doctrines before Cudworth published any major work. The *True Intellectual System of the Universe* did not appear until 1678, though its ideas were widely known before that time. The *Treatise concerning the Eternal and Immutable Morality* was left in manuscript and did not appear until Cudworth had been dead for many years. In the *Divine Dialogues*, as I have said in the *Conway Letters*, More made his apology, indicating clearly that Cudworth had been his master and the chief intellect among the Cambridge Platonists.

rational faculty. Old mathematics had taught that the compass of the Geometer repeated the Circle of Perfection; the newer mathematics laid still more stress upon "geometrical accuracy" in nature. Yet at the same time that Burnet was developing his belief in order, restraint, limitation, and harmony, he was responsive to that other Platonism of "infinite worlds in infinite aether," to conceptions of the new philosophy that were breaking down restraint and limitation and exalting above Reason an insatiable Imagination that sought "more beyond."

Burnet went abroad in 1671 with his head filled with contradictions, with a classical training rich in paradoxes, with belief in the Old and New Testaments and in the truth of both Moses and Plato. Suddenly he was face to face with a Nature unfamiliar to English university men. On "Nature's Alps" Burnet found himself both shocked and enthralled, torn between the responses of "Reason" and "Phansy." To Burnet both Reason and Fancy were innate. Reason, while inborn, must be developed and trained by study; the extent to which Fancy or Imagination, too, might be cultivated Burnet's generation did not consider as curiously as Addison's. Burnet had been trained to be suspicious of "Phansy," to distrust "that Temper that disposes a man to listen to the Magisterial Dictates of an over-bearing Phansy, more then to calm and cautious insinuations of free Reason." It was this temper, said More, that led men to Enthusiasm. Burnet was afraid of Enthusiasm, suspicious of anything "that captivates our Imagination, and carries it wide away out of the reach of hearing of that more free and superiour Faculty of Reason." [38] The emotions he felt among the Alps were enthusiastic, primitive, and violent and as such repellent to a disciple of Reason.

Thomas Burnet possessed native "Phansy" to a degree we have not encountered among earlier English travelers. When he stood

[38] Henry More, *Enthusiasmus Triumphatus* (London, 1712), pp. 2–3. In this edition the *Enthusiasmus* appeared with More's *Immortality of the Soul* and other theological works.

amid the ruins of a broken world, he could not be content merely to mention the blisters and imposthumes of the earth, as did Howell, to draw a breath of relief and forget the "Sesqui-Superlatives," like Coryat, or to sweep aside the rubbish of the world in a metaphor with Evelyn. The "multifarious Confusion" of Nature shocked Reason. Yet Burnet was moved by the vast as never before. A generation later, he was repeating the experience of Henry More who had first denied, then triumphantly affirmed the vastness of space, whose spirits moved with "pleasant trembeling" when he surveyed the new heavens, who read over into Space epithets and emotions once reserved for Deity. "Things that are great or vehement," More wrote in the *Enthusiasmus Triumphatus*, "People are subject to suspect that they rise from some supernatural Cause. . . . So rude Antiquity conceiv'd a kind of Divinity in almost any thing that was extraordinarily great. Whence some have worshipped very tall Trees, others large Rivers, some a great Stone or Rock, others some high and vast Mountains." [39] But these were primitive men "of rude Antiquity." The learned Burnet should not have felt such emotions as he did toward mountains. But like More himself Burnet was a native "Enthusiast." As More before Space, so Burnet before mountains was seized by "the God within," his "Phansy" ravished by a power greater than he. The adjectives and epithets that came to his mind were words that had always been legitimate when applied to God. Henry More might have had the same experience as did Burnet had he ever seen a mountain. But neither More nor any other teacher had prepared Burnet for his experience in a place of seeming chaos and confusion, when he felt before the monstrosities of Nature emotions he had believed legitimate only in the contemplation of God. God, stars and planets, the vastness of interstellar space, the mountains and the sea were one in their effect upon imagination.

As with Petrarch on Mount Ventoux, training conquered

[39] *Ibid.*, p. 11.

instinct in Burnet. Across Petrarch's momentary "Mountain Glory" fell the shadow of St. Augustine. The shadow of the same saint, with other classical and medieval memories, clouded Burnet's eyes. Even while he felt their sublimity, he denied that mountains were beautiful. Mountains became Burnet's "King Charles' head." He could not forgive them but he could not forget them. He tried them against all his aesthetic standards and found them guilty. But in their presence he had been moved to emotions he had never experienced before. He returned to England to write the book that might explain his own dilemma, turning to old theology and new science to discover a cosmogony that might explain the origin of mountains.

Burnet intended his *Sacred Theory* as a contribution to both theology and science. It never occurred to him that it might find a place in the history of aesthetics. Here, however, for the first time in England we find a sharp distinction between the emotional effects of the *sublime* and the *beautiful* in external Nature and find, too, awareness of a conflict between old ideas that such qualities as *beauty* exist in objects and a growing realization that they are subjective, residing not in the object but in the "soul" of the man perceiving the object.

Burnet showed his mountain obsession in the many "animadversions" he wrote in reply to attacks upon his "sacred theory." He could reply logically when his theology was under attack, even when his science was discredited. But he could not restrain his emotions when his detractors took their departure from his apparently dualistic aesthetics and stressed the inconsistency between his condemnation and praise of mountains. The lasting effect of mountains upon his imagination is shown, too, in the growth of the *Sacred Theory* in his mind. When he added the second volume dealing with the Conflagration, memories of "something august and stately" in mountains still inspired him with "great Thoughts and Passions." He never wrote more majestically than in those chapters in which he described the burning of the globe. One by one the familiar places of the world disappeared:

All the Varieties of Nature, all the Works of Art, all the Labours of Men, are reduc'd to nothing; all that we admir'd and ador'd before, as great and magnificent, is obliterated and vanish'd; and another Form and Face of Things, plain, simple, and every where the same, overspreads the whole Earth. Where are now the great Empires of the World, and their chief imperial Cities? Their Pillars, Trophies, and Monuments of Glory? Shew me where they stood, read the Inscription, tell me the Victor's name. . . . Rome itself, eternal Rome, the great City, the Empress of the World . . . what is become of her now? She laid her Foundations deep, and her Palaces were strong and sumptuous. . . . But her Hour is come, she is wip'd away from the Face of the Earth, and buried in perpetual Oblivion.[40]

"My name is Ozymandias, King of Kings"; but "nothing beside remains." Rome fell, and its ruins were mingled with the ruins of a broken world. Until the last moment, when "the Exterior Region of the Earth [was] melted into a Fluour, like molten Glass, or running Metal," Burnet's mountains stood, vast and majestic even in the hour of destruction. Only when the world ended did the mountains finally disappear. Burnet spoke their epitaph:

The everlasting Hills, the Mountains and Rocks of the Earth, are melted as Wax before the Sun; and their Place is nowhere found. Here stood the Alps, a prodigious Range of Stone, the Load of the Earth, that cover'd many Countries, and reach'd their Armes from the Ocean to the Black Sea; this huge Mass of Stone is soften'd and dissolv'd as a tender Cloud into Rain. Here stood the African Mountains, and Atlas with his Top above the Clouds. There was frozen Caucasus, and Taurus, and Imaus, and Mountains of Asia. And yonder, toward the North, stood the Riphaean Hills, cloath'd in

---

[40] *Sacred Theory*, II, 159. The description of the Fire is in bk. III, ch. xii.

Ice and Snow. All these are vanish'd, dropt away as the Snow upon their Heads, and swallow'd up in a red Sea of Fire.[41]

From the time of the publication of *The Sacred Theory of the Earth*, the mountains were in labor. Volcanic forces, working within the monstrous excrescences, like cores of fire burning at the center of other theories of the earth, caused intellectual eruptions, and in a tumultuous period arrayed thinkers of the late seventeenth century on either side of an apparently impassable abyss. The years that followed were important in the history of theology, important too in the history of geology. They were equally important in the history of aesthetics. Other men like Burnet, conditioned by the same paradoxes, were to have similar experiences when they ascended the Alps and Apennines to experience conflict between their classical idols and aesthetic feelings born of the new philosophy. Like Burnet they read into mountains emotions once reserved for God and then transferred in the earlier seventeenth century to interstellar space. They gradually found a vocabulary in which to express their emotions. Mountains were not yet "beautiful," but even in Burnet's lifetime they became "sublime."

[41] *Ibid.*, II, 159–160.

Chapter Six

The Burnet Controversy

"The Mountains in Labor"

"THE Mountain begins to roar and bellow in its hollow Caverns; cries out, as it were, in Pain to be deliver'd of some Burthen too heavy to be born, and too big to be easily discharg'd." [1] The rumbling of Burnet's volcanic mountain was a presage to the Conflagration, but his words may be taken symbolically as a prophecy of the intellectual upheaval that occurred during the last years of the seventeenth century. The mountains were in labor: mountains of Augustine and Bede, of Luther and Calvin, of Goodman and Hakewill. Intellectual forces, long imprisoned in the earth, strove to burst their barriers. Although the mountain travail produced more than one ridiculous mouse, the final result was the birth of a new geology and a new aesthetics.

I

For many years Thomas Burnet's "ingenious Theorie" lingered in the minds of English travelers and poets. Gilbert Burnet, crossing the Alps shortly after the first Latin and Eng-

[1] *Sacred Theory*, II, 79.

lish editions of the *Sacred Theory* had appeared, remembered
Burnet's graphic picture of the postdiluvian world. He said in
his account of his travels:

> When one considers the height of those Hills, the chain of so
> many of them together, their extent both in length and breadth:
> If at first he thinks of the old Fables of laying one Hill upon the
> top of another, he will be afterwards apt to imagine them according
> to the ingenious conjecture of one that travelled over them more
> than once. That they cannot be the primary Productions of the
> Author of Nature: But are the vast Ruines of the first World,
> which at the Deluge broke here into many inequalities.[2]

On the other hand, John Jackson, Pepys's nephew, wrote to his
uncle of his admiration for the plains of Lombardy, which he
found "as even as a bowling-green from one end to t'other;
with roads like avenues sett with trees and strait as an arrow
for miles together; . . . in a word, with such a concurrence of
all that's beautifull and usefull in Nature that I could not but
fancy it an undisturbed reminder of Dr. Burnet's primitive
earth." [3] James Thomson echoed Burnet when he wrote of "the
scattered spots Which nature left in her destroying rage"; [4]
when he first saw "the cloudy Apennines, capt with gray mists
and everlasting snows," he agreed with Burnet that "nature in
stupendous ruin lies." Before he went abroad, Thomson had
versified the thesis of the *Sacred Theory* in lines that modern
critics have made increasingly familiar. Before the Deluge,
"great Spring . . . greened all the year," but now

Nature disturbed

Is deemed, vindictive, to have changed her course.

[2] Gilbert Burnet, *Travels* (Amsterdam, 1687), p. 11.

[3] Pepys, *Private Correspondence*, ed. by J. R. Tanner (London, 1926),
II, 6. Jackson's letter was written in July, 1700.

[4] *Liberty*, IV, 273–284. Thomson added a note: "According to Dr.
Burnet's System of the Deluge." See James Thomson, *Complete Poetical
Works*, ed. by J. L. Robertson (Oxford, 1908), p. 365. All references to
Thomson are to this variorum edition.

Hence in old dusky time, a deluge came,
When the deep-cleft disparting orb, that arched
The central waters round, impetuous rushed
With universal burst into the gulf,
And o'er the high-piled hills of fractured earth
Wide-dashed the waves in undulation vast,
Till, from the centre to the streaming clouds,
A shoreless ocean tumbled round the globe.[5]

It was not necessary to travel to the Alps in order to see the world through Burnet spectacles. Men and women, exchanging one literary tradition for another, were quite capable of exaggerating British hills into Burnet mountains. Samuel Bowden, describing the Cheddar cliffs and Mendip hills,[6] was impressed by the contrast between sunny spots of greenery and bleak hills. "The nodding arches big with ruin show And prominent still frown with ponderous woe." "In each Shire, deformed Prospects rise," and "ruin'd Rocks and frightful Forms surprize," less because of Bowden's own observation than because of the *Sacred Theory*:

In lawless sway despotic Chaos reigns,
And dreary Ruin desolates the Plains;

[5] "Spring," ll. 307–316. Alan McKillop in *The Background of Thomson's Seasons* (Minneapolis, 1942), pp. 97 ff., summarizes the various versions of the passage as it grew in the different editions of the *Seasons*.

[6] Samuel Bowden, "A Description of Chedder-Cliffs and Part of Mendip-Hills near Wells," in *Poems on Various Subjects* (Bath, 1754), pp. 43, 56. Allusions to Burnet's various theories are so persistent in the literature of the eighteenth century that I give only a sampling. Robert A. Aubin collected some in his early "Grottoes, Geology, and the Gothic Revival," *S.P.*, XXXI (1934), 408–416, and added others in his *Topographical Poetry in XVIII-Century England* (New York, 1936). Margaret Fitzgerald, a former Columbia student of mine, who made a study of English poetry from 1725 to 1750 for her book, *First Follow Nature* (New York, 1947), collected a sheaf of references for me, particularly in periodical literature. The passages are so repetitious that I have used only a few.

> While Nature takes a pleasure to be odd,
> And wears the ancient Spoils of Noah's Flood.

Mrs. Mary Chandler, looking with affection upon the "friendly hills of England" near Bath, nevertheless pondered:

> Thence view the pendant Rocks majestic Shade,
> That speaks the Ruins conqu'ring Time has made.
> Whether the Egg was by the Deluge broke,
> Or Nature since has felt some other Shock;
> Ingenious Burnet, thine's a pleasing Scheme,
> A gay Delusion, if it be a Dream.
> The shatter'd Rocks and Strata seem to say,
> Nature is old, and tends to her Decay.[7]

Later in the century, Mrs. Elizabeth Carter, taking a "ramble into the wildest and most unfrequented parts of the country," wrote from Deal to Miss Catherine Talbot that she had ascended a cliff "where all was uninhabited waste around me, and all blank ocean below." Her thoughts too turned to the *Sacred Theory*:

The broken irregular scene around us, the tide rolling beneath, and the coast of the opposite kingdom, which was full in our view, led us to converse on that tremendous transformation of the deluged world, when the fountains of the great deep burst their inclosures, and probably disjointed the solid continent.[8]

Burnet's ruins became a persistent motif among minor poets of the eighteenth century, many of whom inquired:

> What caus'd the Mountains? whence, and when their birth?
> Are they indeed coeval with the Earth?
> Or, as some learned Theorists declare,
> The rugged Ruins of a delug'd Sphere?[9]

[7] Mary Chandler, *A Description of Bath* (1st ed., 1734; London, 1743), p. 8.

[8] *A Series of Letters between Mrs. Elizabeth Carter and Miss Catherine Talbot* (London, 1809), III, 288–289.

[9] James Kirkpatrick, *The Sea-Piece: A Narrative, Philosophical, and Descriptive Poem* (first pub., 1749; London, 1750), p. 17.

Bevil Higgons, in a poem written in imitation of Lucretius, grouped Burnet with "impious Atheists." Opposing the Epicurean theory, he wrote:

> But where by Chance the taller Columns fell,
> Above the Convex rising Mountains swell;
> Although their Use the Theorist deny'd
> (Cartesian Burnet) with dogmatic Pride;
> These Heaps of Ruin we shall wisely find
> To noble Ends by Providence assign'd.[10]

Moses Brown, too, took exception to any who denied the power and providence of God in Creation:

> Some think ere this nor Sea nor Hill was found,
> But a smooth Surface cloath'd our Planet round,
> Till torn by Earthquakes its convexive Shell,
> Sapp'd by th' unbosomed Waters, inward fell;
> When strait th' unbroken Fountains pour'd their Stores;
> Relicts of Ruin and deforming Woe.[11]

John Ogilvie, in his allegorical poem *Providence*, described the effect upon a young poet of his first view of mountains.[12] Overcome by new sensations and torn between divided emotions, this later youthful Burnet could not decide what he really felt about mountains, until his tutor advised him not to think of them as a "pile of ruins," but to realize that Beauty demands "variety in all." Mountains are not the result of a "casual Fault of Nature," but an integral part of God's plan, displaying "the romantic wild, solemn and vast."

If some poets saw in Burnet's mountains "Relicts of Ruin and deforming Woe," others were filled with Burnet's awe, as was an unknown poet of the mid-century:

[10] Bevil Higgons, *A Poem on Nature: In Imitation of Lucretius* (London, 1736), p. 6.

[11] Moses Browne, "Essay on the Universe," in *Poems* (London, 1739), p. 307.

[12] John Ogilvie, *Providence: An Allegorical Poem* (London, 1764), p. 39.

Trembling, I ask, what mighty arm could raise
Those spiring summits from their rooted base?
Whose cloudless points as high in Aether glow,
As sink the caverns of the deep below;
What awe, what thoughts these pathless wilds impart?
They whisper omnipresence to the heart! . . .
I wonder not the bards of old inspir'd,
Or prophets by celestial visions fir'd,
To unfrequented scenes like these retir'd;
On Sinai's top, possess'd with pious awe,
Moses received the heav'n-descended law; . . .
See what romantic views surprise around;
Where'er I tread seems visionary ground.[13]

In 1691 Thomas Heyrick published his *Submarine Voyage*.[14]
Through "Fancy" he followed Burnet into the subterraneous
world. In the depths of ocean he found evidence of the vast
cataclysm that had once changed the face of nature, "lowly
Valleys into Mountains rais'd." Everywhere on his journey he
saw the result of the destructive work of the Flood, "Where
Hills were by the Deluge made, Where Continents broke, and
Isles spread." Visiting "the bottom of a monstrous world," he
journeyed underneath the mountains at which he seemed to
peer, as through an early periscope, to conclude that they "do
not seem the Work of Nature's Hand, But broken Ruines of
the former World":

Now I in Switzerland uplift my Head,
          And trembling and agast,
The barren Rocks and threatening Mountains dread:
Where Nature shows but a Step-Mother's Love.

Following Burnet, eighteenth-century poets dived to the bottom of the sea, rose to the summits of mountains, recalled

[13] Anon., "The Prospect," in *Gentleman's Magazine*, XIII (1743), 608.
[14] Thomas Heyrick, *The Submarine Voyage: A Pindarick Poem in
Four Parts* (Cambridge, Eng., 1691), pp. 21–23, 50.

a primitive smooth earth, condemned or praised the form of our
present globe. It is difficult to say which of Burnet's many
themes was the most popular, but certainly "ruin" held a leading
place during the earlier years:

> Hills pil'd on hills, and rocks together hurl'd;
> Sure, Burnet, these the ruins of thy world.[15]

Burnet's Deluge became one of the "sublime" themes of an era
that went mad over sublimity. When Thomson's friend, David
Mallet, was writing *The Excursion*, he found among notes
Thomson sent him the suggestion: "Here, if you could insert
a sketch of the Deluge, what more affecting and noble?" [16]
Young felt a gloomy satisfaction in remembering the destruction
of an early world through Deluge:

> But, O Lorenzo! far the rest above,
> Of ghastly nature, and enormous size,
> One form assaults my sight, and chills my blood,
> And shakes my frame. Of one departed world
> I see the mighty shadow: Oozy wreath
> And dismal sea-weed crown her; o'er her urn
> Reclin'd, she weeps her desolated realms
> And bloated sons; and, weeping, prophesies
> Another's dissolution, soon in flames. . . .
> Deluge and Conflagration, dreadful pow'rs!

His prophecy of the final dissolution of the hills echoed Burnet's:

> Amazing period! when each mountain-height
> Outburns Vesuvius; rocks eternal pour
> Their melted mass, as rivers once they poured;
> Stars rush; and final ruin fiercely drives
> Her ploughshare o'er Creation. . . .
> Terror and glory join'd in their extremes!

[15] "The Prospect," p. 608.
[16] Thomson's letters to Mallet, dated August 2, 1726, published in *Miscellanies of the Philobiblon Society*, IV (1857-1858), 30.

> Our God in grandeur, and our world on fire!
> All nature struggling in the pangs of death! [17]

From Young's early poem on the "last Judgment" through the Ninth Night of the *Night Thoughts*, Burnet's influence was second only to that of Milton.

The "Doomsday" and "Judgment" poems of the eighteenth century differ in many ways from their antecedents, in part because the later poets followed Burnet's graphic and realistic pictures of a world on fire and in part because, as we shall see, the authors were geology conscious. Description of the last days impressed Steele, who devoted a number of the *Spectator* [18] to the *Sacred Theory*, first quoting Cicero's version of the speech of Socrates to his judges, then passages from Burnet. "Oh, how glorious is the old age of that great Man," he wrote of Burnet, who has "with a Celestial Ambition, as far as it is consistent with Humility and Devotion, examin'd the Ways of Providence, from the Creation to the Dissolution of the visible World." In conclusion Steele quoted Burnet's "funeral Oration over this Globe," his farewell to the "Mountains and Rocks of the Earth [which] are melted as Wax before the Sun, and their place is no where found. . . . Great and Marvellous are thy Works, just and true thy ways, thou King of Saints!" Burnet's mountain catalogue recurred, too, among poets, particularly Blackmore and Thomson, who with a new feeling for the majesty of the far-flung ranges called the roll of mountains throughout the earth.[19]

[17] Edward Young, *Night Thoughts*, IX, 127–131, 164–207.
[18] *Spectator* 146.
[19] Mr. McKillop in *The Background of Thomson's Seasons*, pp. 85–91, suggests various sources for Thomson's catalogue, pointing out similarities with the *Geographia Generalis* of Varenius. As he himself says in another connection, however, none of the sources suggests the poetic sweep of Thomson's passage, which to me is more reminiscent of Burnet.

II

Casual references to the *Sacred Theory* are significant only in suggesting the widespread interest in Burnet's work. More important were books and pamphlets that poured from the press attacking, defending, amplifying Burnet's theories. The documents in the Burnet controversy were almost as numerous as the replies to Hobbes a few years earlier and were a close second to the attacks and defenses provoked by Tom Paine's *Age of Reason* a century later.[20] On the continent Burnet was considered by many one of the most important thinkers of his generation, in spite of Voltaire, who satirized his "strange ideas" of the Deluge and of the configuration of the globe and declared that Burnet and other theorists were as fond of changes of scene on the face of the globe as spectators at a play. "Every one of them destroys and renovates the earth after his own fashion, as Descartes framed it; for philosophers put themselves without ceremony in the place of God, and think to create a universe with a word." [21]

The Encyclopedists, however, took Burnet seriously. A modern critic finds that of all English writers of the period, Burnet is most frequently quoted by Diderot, Boulanger, Formey, and

[20] There is no bibliography of the Burnet controversy. Katharine Brownell Collier mentions a number of the defenses and attacks in *Cosmogonies of Our Fathers* (New York, 1934). Don Cameron Allen discusses some of Burnet's opponents and defenders in *The Legend of Noah* (Urbana, 1949). Mr. Allen pays particular attention to writers on fossils and on the source and volume of the waters of the Flood. A complete critical bibliography of all the books and pamphlets in the controversy would, I think, be a real contribution to intellectual history, since there is no aspect of current scientific and theological thinking that did not show itself in one way or another.

[21] Voltaire's references to Burnet's "strange ideas" may be found in *Œuvres Complètes* (Paris, 1885), XXII, 549; X, 206. The quotation is from "Dissertation envoyée à l'Academie de Bologne, sur les changements arrivés dans notre globe," quoted in Charles Lyell, *Principles of Geology*.

Jaucourt, who placed him with Descartes and Newton.[22] The *Sacred Theory* was consistently treated with respect in the *Encyclopédie*. The later Burnet of the *Archaeologiae*, however, was suspect, if we may trust the article "Unitaires," in which Burnet was classed with Socinians. Later Buffon followed the *Sacred Theory* in several important points. Burnet's influence in Germany was great,[23] thanks in large part to Johann Gottsched who from his powerful seat at Leipzig not only endorsed Burnet's theory, but wrote two works in which he took much the same position in connection with the effects of the Deluge. Unfortunately for Burnet the work of the greatest philosopher among his disciples appeared posthumously, when, the tumult over, it caused little more than a ripple of interest. Even today the *Protogaea*, written in 1690, remains one of the lesser known works of Leibniz. During the author's lifetime only a brief

[22] Louis S. Gaudin, *Les Lettres Anglaises dans l'Encyclopédie* (New York, 1942), pp. 154–155. Cf. also D. Mornet, *Les Sciences de la Nature en France au XVIIIᵉ Siècle* (Paris, 1911), pp. 29 ff.; Ira Wade, *The Clandestine Organizations and Diffusion of Philosophic Ideas in France from 1700–1720* (Princeton, 1938), pp. 244 ff.

[23] In Germany, C. Wagner replied to Burnet in *Animadversions in T. Burnetii Telluris Theorem Sacram* (Leipzig, 1685); Caspar Bussinger in *De Situ Telluris Paradisiacae et Chiliasticae Burnetiano* (Hamburg, 1695). These works, however, were concerned with Burnet's theology rather than his science. Andrew D. White, in *History of the Warfare of Science with Theology in Christendom* (New York and London, 1910), I, 206, said: "The theories of Whiston and Burnet found wide acceptance in Germany, mainly through the all-powerful mediation of Gottsched, so long, from his professor's chair at Leipsic, the dictator of orthodox thought, who not only wrote a brief tractate of his own upon the subject, but furnished a voluminous historical introduction to the more elaborate treatise of Heyn. In this book, which appeared at Leipsic in 1742, the agency of comets in the creation, the flood, and the final destruction of the world is fully proved." The *Protogaea* of Leibniz remained unpublished until 1749, when Christian Ludovic Scheidt prepared it for the press, with a preface in which he discussed Leibniz's theories of the Deluge and of fossils. It may be found in the *Opera Omnia* of Leibniz (Geneva, 1768), II, 201–240.

summary of the work appeared in the *Acta Eruditorum*, a statement so brief that the similarities to Burnet escaped notice. In the complete work, however, the resemblances are striking, particularly in the sections on the Deluge and its effect on the formation of mountains.

In England the list of those who expressed themselves on Burnet's theories is an imposing one, including in the period from 1685 to 1715 the names of nearly all men now remembered in the history of science and theology as well as those of many who have been forgotten. Newton was one of the few scientists who took no public part in the controversy, though William Whiston's reply to Burnet was dedicated to Newton and sent him before publication and Newton set down his opinions in a long letter to Burnet.[24] During the decade after the publication

[24] Newton's letter to Burnet is given by Sir David Brewster in his *Memoirs of the Life, Writings, and Discoveries of Sir Isaac Newton* (Edinburgh, 1855), II, 447 ff. The letter is unsigned, but Brewster states that the handwriting is Newton's. Brewster says (II, 99) that Burnet sent an advance copy of the *Theoria* to Newton, asking for his comments. Newton took exception to some passages. Burnet replied in a long letter, and Newton answered with one nearly as long, which is that published in the Brewster volume. Newton began with a discussion of the shape of the world, opposing Burnet's theory that it is oval, insisting—on the basis of the shape of other heavenly bodies seen through the telescope—that it is spherical. Of the appearance of earth he wrote, "Of our present seas, rocks, mountains etc., I think you have given the most plausible account." Although he suggested an alternative theory, he added: "All this I write not to oppose you, for I think the main part of your hypothesis as probable as that I have written, if not in some respects more probable." Newton discussed at length the Mosaic account of Creation, saying that Moses described reality "in a language artificially adapted to the sense of the vulgar." He suggested an alternative theory of the origin of mountains, adding still another homely household figure of speech to the figures of eggs, yeast, and bread that are to be found: "As I am writing, another illustration of the generation of hills, proposed above, comes into my mind. Milk is as uniform a liquor as the chaos was. If beer be poured into it, and the mixture let stand till it be dry, the surface of the curdled substance will appear as rugged and mountainous as the earth in any place."

of the first edition of the *Telluris Theoria Sacra* Burnet was widely acclaimed. If some few "peevish and off men" protested Burnet's liberalism, the attitude of most early readers was similar to that in the correspondence between Pepys and Evelyn. The King had urged translation of the Latin work and amplification of the English. One preferment after another came to Burnet: in 1685 he became Master of the Charterhouse; shortly after the Revolution, he was appointed Chaplain in Ordinary and Clerk of the Closet to King William. In view of His Majesty's patronage and the great popular interest in the *Sacred Theory*, it seemed probable that Burnet would succeed Tillotson as Primate of all England.

But as Burnet said of the Garden of Eden, this happy state of things was not to last. During the 1690's, opposition to Burnet became vocal and vehement, and England was torn between defense and attack. The "divines," the "politiques," and the "learned men," whose objections Bacon had anticipated, united against Bacon's followers. In part the opposition was deliberately fomented by clergy, sometimes suspicious of Burnet's orthodoxy, often jealous of his growing prestige. In part it was the result of Burnet's own tendency to say too much and go too far in attempts to bolster up his "ingenious Hypothesis." During the eighties, he confined himself to amplifications of the two volumes of the *Sacred Theory*, but from 1690 on he began to enter into open controversy with his opponents.

So far as published record shows, Burnet paid no attention

The satirists were quick to seize upon this kind of imagery. In a "Letter to the·Students of Both Universities, Relating to the New Discoveries in Religion and the Sciences," attributed to Swift but probably the work of one of his many imitators, we find: "to discover the Globe of the Earth to be only a large Work of a kind of Pastry, and that the Crust parting by excess of Heat, and dropping Piecemeal into the Liquor enclos'd occasion'd the Deluge" ("A Supplement to Dean Sw . . . t's Miscellanies," in *Miscellaneous Works of the Late Dr. Arbuthnot* [Glasgow, 1751], II, 108).

to an answer of Herbert Croft, Bishop of Hereford, and issued
no reply to any other early document in which his theory may
have been challenged. In 1690, however, Erasmus Warren published his *Geologia*. Stung as he had not been before, Burnet
replied, and when Warren answered Burnet wrote again. This
was the real beginning of the Burnet controversy, which was
later made more acute by John Keill, the mathematician, whose
Examination of Dr. Burnet's Theory of the Earth [25] remains important in the history of science. Other antagonists aroused
Burnet's logic; Warren and Keill affected him emotionally. As
we shall see, Warren attacked his aesthetics, whereas Keill not
only deftly found every weak place in Burnet's scientific armor,
but in cavalier fashion dismissed Burnet as a mere "poet," as he
dismissed the philosophers to whom Burnet's deepest allegiance
had been given, the Platonists and Pythagoreans of the past and
the Platonists of his own century. All of them, declared Keill,
were victims of excessive imagination. Their cosmological theories were only fantasies of poets. Even Descartes and Hobbes
were condemned by Keill as victims of imagination. Burnet
was another poet; never was there a more "plausible" piece of
supposed philosophical writing, and never (we surmise) one
more absurd. Burnet was a "rhetorician"—a dangerous sort of
rhetorician—whose music charmed logic to sleep. But Keill did

---

[25] Croft's and Warren's replies will be considered later. John Keill's
attack appeared as *An Examination of Dr. Burnet's Theory of the Earth*
(London, 1698). My references are to a second edition of 1734, pp. 44,
198–199. I single out Keill's book for comment because it seems to me
the ablest scientific refutation of Burnet's theories and also because
Keill realized the extent to which Burnet was carrying on traditions of
the Cambridge Platonists. Robert Hooke took exception to Burnet's
theory and proposed a general transformation of the earth's surface by
"a raising . . . of those parts that were before sunk to receive the Sea;
and a Consequent . . . sinking of that which was the dry Land," though
he ascribed the changes only to "a preternatural *digitus Dei*" (Robert
Hooke, *Posthumous Works* [London, 1705], p. 412). Hooke's lecture, in
which he made these points, was read in February, 1688.

not stop here. Unfortunately for Burnet, he was an exper mathematician and an able scientist who could use against Bur net various kinds of proof. One by one he grimly pointed ou Burnet's errors in science, his mistakes in mathematical com putation, until he reduced the precious theory to the imagina tive poetry it was.

Attempting to save his *Sacred Theory*, Burnet departed fur ther and further from literal acceptance of Scripture, until th time came when he could no longer keep the middle way h had once believed possible. There could be no doubt of hi heterodoxy in the minds of most theologians after the publica tion of the *Archaeologiae Philosophicae* in 1692. By the end o the century, the man who had sincerely tried to combine Gene sis and geology into a new Revelation found himself hailed a a master by the freethinkers, damned by the orthodox, and ou of favor with the Church and with royalty. Nearly every heresy known to the day was read into him. He had mentioned Lucre tius and Epicurus to criticize them, but he became a suppose leader of the "impious atomists." He had opposed Hobbes only to become a disciple of that archfiend in the popular mind. Be cause he had adapted the Cartesian world scheme, he was a fol lower of the "heretic" Descartes, who had no place for God i his universe. "Blind mechanism and blinder chance," as Bentley declared, were considered to be Burnet's principles. Burnet pro tested in vain. Like Milton's Satan he found himself enmeshe in bonds made by his own ingenuity.

We need not enter into the charges against Burnet's liberalism in Scripture. One widespread belief of the day cannot be passed over, however, since it explains attacks other than those upor his theology. Many in the early eighteenth century considere Burnet the father of English Deism. Anthony Collins, in th work that preceded his suicide, took off from Burnet's *Ar chaeologiae;* so did Charles Blount, who transplanted a section i his *Oracles of Reason*. The basic conceptions of Deism were then read back by Burnet's antagonists into the *Sacred Theory*. Burnet's use of the term *Deist* and his distinction between *Deist* and *Atheist* [26] were not the first instances of such antithesis, but his implications seemed clear to the orthodox.

Certainly many passages and ideas in the *Sacred Theory*, taken from their context, read as if they had come from a Deist's handbook. Religion, Burnet said, does not depend upon revelation given to a small group of men at a particular time. It is "that universal Consent of Mankind, or natural Instinct of Religion, which we see, more or less, throughout all Nations, barbarous or civil." [27] He opposed superstition energetically. " 'Tis full time now to sweep away these Cobwebs of Superstition, these Relicks of Paganism," he said in effect again and again. Throughout the *Sacred Theory* he urged man to follow Reason: "Reason is to be our first Guide; and where that falls short, or any other just Occasion offers it self, we may receive further Light and Confirmation from the Sacred Writings." [28] If Burnet became the Father of English Deism, he had no such intention when he wrote the *Sacred Theory*. To isolate individual sentences, as did men like Collins and Blount, is to do Burnet grave injustice and miss the central idea he shared with the Cambridge Platonists. Religion, Burnet believed, is progressive, Revelation one stage in man's advance to perfection. Like Mede and More, he was less concerned with individual salvation—the old theme of the Fathers—than with the ultimate salvation of all men, a climax in the great "Plot" of God for humanity. But we cannot linger over Burnet's theology,

[26] *Sacred Theory*, I, 430–431. Archibald Lovell, in *A Summary of Material Heads Which May Be Enlarged and Improved into a Compleat Answer to Dr. Burnet's Theory of the Earth* (London, 1696), asserted that Burnet was a freethinker; he was particularly concerned over the probable effect of Burnet upon the younger generation.

[27] *Sacred Theory*, I, 429.   [28] *Ibid.*, II, 40; I, 8.

since it was rather his science that led to a new conception of external Nature.

Scientists were as vocal as theologians in their attack upon the author of the *Sacred Theory*.[29] Earlier argument on the emergence of mountains, as we have seen, had been largely theological, involved with problems of man's sin and God's punishment. It now became scientific, a matter of geogony and cosmogony. Curious hypotheses were proposed in answer to Burnet's theory of mountain origin. Those offered by laymen are not surprising, for as Burnet himself said impatiently:

The Generality of People have not Sense and Curiosity enough to raise a Question concerning these things or concerning the Original of them; You may tell them that Mountains grow out of the Earth like Fuzz-balls, or that there are Monsters under Ground, that throw up Mountains as Moles do Mole-hills. . . . Or if you would appear more learned, tell them that the Earth is a great Animal, and these are Wens that grow upon its Body; this would pass current for Philosophy.[30]

Some of the hypotheses of reputable scientists of Burnet's period sound as strange to modern ears. The literary student may be interested to read them as they were versified in Jago's *Edge-Hill*.[31] Taking his point of departure from Burnet, Jago declared that his "daring song"

> unfolds the cause, whence rose
> This various face of things—of high, of low—
> Of rough and smooth. For with its parent Earth
> Coeval not prevailed what now appears
> Of hill and dale.

[29] See E. G. R. Taylor, "English Worldmakers of the Seventeenth Century and Their Influence on the Earth Sciences," *Geographical Review*, XXXVIII (1948), 104–112.

[30] *Sacred Theory*, I, 189.

[31] Richard Jago, *Edge-Hill*, in Alexander Chalmers, *Works of the English Poets* (London, 1810), XVII, 288–289. This is the most extensive versification of the Burnet controversy I have found.

Although he agreed with Burnet that the original face of nature
was not as we see it, he did not follow Burnet all the way:

> nor was its new-formed shape,
> Like a new polish'd orb, a surface plain,
> Wanting the sweet variety of change,
> Concave, convex, the deep, and the sublime;
> Nor from old Ocean's watery bed, were scoop'd
> Its neighb'ring shores; nor were they now depress'd,
> Now rais'd by sudden shocks; but fashion'd all
> In perfect harmony by laws divine,
> On passive matter, at its birth impress'd.

As if he were writing—as he probably was—with several volumes of the Burnet controversy before him, Jago versified one
after another of the theories proposed by Burnet's followers
and opponents. Jago did not versify, though he discussed in his
notes, the ingenious theory of John Beaumont [32] who "supposed
that hills and mountains might be occasion'd by fermentation,
after the manner of leaven in dough." In the chaos, Beaumont
suggested, was contained an "infinite variety of seminal Principles, from which the hills became elevated as the leaven acted
within the dough of the earth." A strange "little world," indeed,
which suggested an egg to some men, a loaf of bread to others,
and beer to Isaac Newton! Jago himself followed the theory of
Erasmus Warren who stated in the *Geologia* [33] that much of the
present irregularity of the earth was caused on the third day of
Creation when the sea was hollowed out and the waters rushed

[32] John Beaumont, *Considerations on a Book entituled The Theory of
the Earth, Publisht Some Years Since by the Learned Dr. Burnet* (London, 1692–1693), pp. 25–30.

[33] Warren discussed his theory in *Geologia* (London, 1690), pp. 209–
214, and further developed it in *A Defence of the Discourse concerning
the Earth before the Flood* (London, 1691), pp. 90–101. He returned to
the problem again in *Some Reflections upon the Short Consideration of
the Defence of the Exceptions against the Theory of the Earth* (London,
1692), pp. 5–6.

down. Under the heat of the sun, the vapors within the crust of the newly created earth struggled to arise; with the ascent of those vapors rose also "rugosities" which then hardened in the heat.

"Nor were [the mountains] now depress'd, Now rais'd by sudden shock," said Jago. Many of Burnet's contemporaries did not agree. Of all the theories of mountain origin proposed in the period, that of "sudden shock" of one sort or another was the most persistent. Had not the Psalmist implied such "shocks" when he said that "a great noise" accompanied the emergence of mountains? Men like Henry More believed that there were forces imprisoned within the earth sufficient to cause the Conflagration. Even the layman knew a good deal about gunpowder, as used in war and for blasting in mines and quarries. John Woodward declared that both at Creation and after the Deluge mountains were elevated by natural explosive forces within the earth.[34] John Ray found in such subterraneous forces a secondary agent of God in Creation. After describing Monte Nuovo as he had seen it, he said: "If such Hills, I say, as these, may be, and have been elevated by subterraneous Wild-fire, Flatus, or Earthquakes, *si parvis liceat componere magna*, if we may compare great things with small, why may not the greatest and highest Mountains in the World be raised up in like Manner by a subterraneous Flatus or Wild-fire, of Quantity and Force sufficient to work such an effect?"[35]

III

"Shock" of a different sort was proposed by one of Burnet's followers, who precipitated still another chapter in the Burnet

[34] John Woodward, *An Essay toward a Natural History of the Earth* (London, 1693), pp. 110–112 and *passim*.

[35] John Ray, *Three Physico-Theological Discourses, concerning I. The Primitive Chaos and Creation of the World; II. The General Deluge, Its Causes and Effects; III. The Dissolution of the World and Future Conflagration, Wherein Are Largely Discussed the Production and Use of Mountains* (London, 1693), p. 13.

controversy and brought into the fray men whose names are familiar in the history of science and literature. Edmund Halley, who had come into prominence through his part in preparing Newton's *Principia* for publication, was greatly impressed by the *Sacred Theory*. He was persuaded of the soundness of Burnet's conclusions about the effects of the Flood, though not satisfied with Burnet's hypothesis about its cause. Halley had already gone far in his study of the periodicity of comets, based particularly upon the comet of 1682. In December, 1694, he read before the Royal Society two papers in which he posited a natural rather than supernatural cause for the Deluge, which he found in "the casual Choc of a Comet." In language reminiscent of Burnet he discussed the agitation such a "Choc" must have caused in the seas, sufficient

to answer for all those strange Appearances of heaping vast quantities of Earth and high Cliffs upon Beds of Shells, which were once the Bottom of the Seas; and raising up Mountains where none were before, mixing the Elements into such an Heap as the Poets describe the old Chaos; for such a Choc impelling the solid Parts would occasion the Waters, and all fluid Substances that were unconfined, as the Sea, is, with one Impetus to run violently toward Part of the Globe were [*sic*] the Blow was received; and that with Force sufficient to rake with it the whole Bottom of the Ocean, and to carry it upon the Land; heaping up into Mountains those earthy Parts it had born away with it, in those Places where the opposite Waves balance each other, *miscens ima sumis*, which may account for those long continued Ridges of Mountains.

Despite the brilliance of the hypothesis, which greatly impressed the hearers, Halley, "apprehensive [lest] . . . he might incur the Censure of the Sacred Order" by the disregard of Scripture implied in his theory, refused to permit the publication of his papers. Thirty years later, however, when he was firmly established as one of the leading scientists of the period and when the world was eagerly awaiting the return of the comet "faithful to his time," predicted for 1726, Halley permitted the publication of his earlier papers in the *Philosophical Transactions of the Royal Society.*[36]

William Whiston showed no such restraint.[37] It was unfortunate for Burnet's reputation among the neoclassicists that Whiston should have been one of his most ardent followers. It was unfortunate for Whiston that a man of such great learning, successor to Isaac Newton at Cambridge, should have been brought into popular disrepute by the laughter of the Scriblerians. In his *New Theory of the Earth,*[38] written in his first flush of enthusiasm for the *Sacred Theory,* Whiston proposed a diluvian

---

[36] In my earlier paper on Swift, republished in *Science and Imagination* (Great Seal Books; Ithaca, 1956), p. 131, note 43, I stated that Halley read one paper before the Royal Society in December, 1694, and delivered a later version in 1724. Further study of the evidence leads me to the conclusion that both papers were read in 1694, though not published at that time. In *Philosophical Transactions from the Year 1719, to the Year 1733, Abridged* (London, 1734), two papers appear, under the general title "Some Considerations about the Cause of the Universal Deluge." The statement after the title on p. 1 is "laid before the Royal Society on the 12th of Dec. 1694, by Dr. Edmond Halley, RSS No. 383, p. 118." This is followed, p. 4, by "Some farther Thoughts about the same Subject delivered on the 19th of the same Month, by the same. Ibid., p. 123." The Table of Contents of *Phil. Trans. Abridged* (London, 1734) gives the date of no. 383 as "May, June 1724," from which I had surmised that Halley delivered a second paper at that time. Apparently, however, the papers were merely published at the later date. Following the two papers is this note: "N.B. The foregoing Papers having been read before the Society thirty years since, were then deposited by the Author in their Archives, and not published; he being sensible that he might have ventured *ultra crepidam:* and apprehensive least [*sic*] by some unguarded Expression he might incur the Censure of the Sacred Order. Nor had they now been printed, but at the Desire of a late Committee of the Society, who were pleased to think them not unworthy of the Press."

[37] Appended to the comments of Halley or his editors, referred to in the preceding note, is this statement: "Here the Reader is desired to observe, that Mr. William Whiston's Book, entitled, *A New Theory of the Earth,* was not published till about a Year and a half after the Date hereof, and was not presented before June 24, 1696, to the Royal Society."

[38] William Whiston, *A New Theory of the Earth, from Its Original, to the Consummation of All Things* (London, 1696). This was followed by *A Vindication of the New Theory of the Earth from the Exceptions*

theory almost identical with Halley's, suggested two years earlier. "On the first Day of the Deluge," he declared, a comet "pass'd before the Body of our Earth." Following theories adapted from Halley and Newton, Whiston asserted that this was the "Comet of 1680" which, with a period of 575 years, would have appeared in 1770 B.C., a date sometimes given as that of the Deluge. The "Choc" of this comet, for the appearance of which Whiston found authority in "Proofs from ancient Tradition," would have been sufficient to account for all the phenomena of the Deluge as described by Burnet. As a comet had brought about the first great terrestrial catastrophe in the Deluge, so a comet would bring about the last, the final destruction of our Mundane Egg. Perhaps it might draw the earth so far out of its orbit that earth would be parched by the sun. Certainly it would provoke enormous tides that in their turn would cause fissures and abysses from which all water would be drained. Devoid of life, the earth would return to its original state without oceans or lakes. Its orbit changed, it would cease to be a planet and would take its place in the firmament as a star or a comet threatening destruction to other earths.

A year before Whiston's *New Theory of the Earth* appeared, John Woodward published his *Essay toward a Natural History*

---

of *Mr. Keill and Others* (London, 1698). Opinion was much divided on Whiston. Ray called his theory "pretty odd and extravagant" and charged that Whiston had "borrowed of Mr. Newton in great part" (*Further Correspondence*, ed. by R. T. Gunther [London, 1928], p. 301). Locke, on the contrary, treated him with respect. Writing to Molyneux in answer to an inquiry about Whiston's theory, he said: "I have not heard any one of my acquaintance speak of it, but with great commendation, as I think it deserves." He stressed the originality of Whiston's theory, which he found illuminating, and implied that he was being attacked by conservatives adverse to the new. Locke says of himself: "I am always for the builders, who find some addition to our knowledge" (*Works* [London, 1751], III, 534).

The widespread interest in these theories of "shock" and the possibility of the destruction of earth by a comet should not seem surprising to our own generation, in which *Worlds in Collision* became a best seller, praised by laymen and some theologians, attacked by many scientists.

of the Earth,[39] in part a sequel to Burnet's work, in part a reply
to some of his arguments, in which Woodward believed that
Burnet had not gone far enough. Woodward was a passionate
collector of fossils. Although his own observations had been
confined to England, he had compared his data with that of
collectors in other countries—indeed, he mentioned two dozen
such countries. He dismissed impatiently the old idea of fossils as *lusus naturae.* His theory that they were petrified shells
shows us how far we have proceeded from theological to scientific explanations of these mysterious "remains," for Woodward's
proof was based upon studies of the similar specific gravity and
chemical properties of fossils and the shells he picked up on
English shores. Burnet's theory of the Deluge offered fresh
ammunition for Woodward's beliefs. Straining at Burnet's fossils, he swallowed his Deluge, and indeed went farther than
Burnet in his *Account of the Universal Deluge and of the Effects That It Had upon the Earth,* which he appended to his
Essay. So obsessed was Woodward with the Deluge that that
cataclysm, usually associated in the popular mind with Burnet,
became to Swift and his friends Woodward's "great beloved
Catastrophe." Unfortunately for Woodward, the Scriblerians'
scientific adviser, Dr. John Arbuthnot, was also a collector
of fossils. His *Examination of Dr. Woodward's Account of the
Deluge,*[40] published in 1697, was only one of many pamphlets

[39] John Woodward, *An Essay toward a Natural History of the Earth
and Terrestrial Bodies, Especially Minerals, as Also of the Sea, Rivers,
and Springs, with an Account of the Universal Deluge and of the Effects
That It Had upon the Earth* (London, 1693). Woodward constantly said
that he was planning a *magnum opus* on the subject of the Flood, but
that work never appeared. Charles Richard Weld in the *History of the
Royal Society* (London, 1848), I, 352–353, says that as a result of the
arrogance shown in this book and in his general attitude Woodward was
expelled from the Royal Society.

[40] Woodward's book provoked a controversy between Arbuthnot and
John Harris, the substance of which appeared in Arbuthnot's *Examination of Dr. Woodward's Account of the Deluge* (London, 1697). The

written in reply to Burnet and Woodward and scientifically not the most important one. But from the point of view of literary history, it proved the most troublesome, since it brought the Scriblerians, Swift, Pope, and Gay, into the Burnet controversy.

Burnet's early edition of the *Sacred Theory* had obliquely helped Swift to his early fame, as we have noted. When the Scriblerus Club was meeting in London, the members undertook the writing of *The Memoirs of Martinus Scriblerus*,[41] both a sequel to Swift's satire in *A Tale of a Tub* and an anticipation of *Gullivers's Travels* and of the *Dunciad* and various of Pope's lesser parodies and satires. Young Martinus Scriblerus, that "Prodigy of the Age," was to be "The Philosopher of Ultimate Causes," who without any need of "trivial helps of Experiments, or Observations" would be "the Inventor of most of the modern Systems and Hypotheses." Among the discoveries that would make Martinus famous were "all the new Theories of the Deluge." Like Descartes and Burnet he would propound "A Mechanical Explication of the Formation of the Universe, according to the Epicurean Hypothesis." Like Halley and Whiston he would draw up "Tide-Tables for a Comet, that is to approximate toward the Earth," and discover a "Menstruum to dissolve the Stone, made of Dr. Woodward's Universal Deluge-Water."

Whiston was the villain of Swift's *True and Faithful Narrative of What Passsed in London.* "Friends and Fellow-Citizens," said Whiston to the "Audience of Fourteen worthy Citizens," made up of butcher, baker, candlestick maker, "all speculative Science is at an end; the Period of all things is at Hand; on Friday next this

controversy was discussed by Lester Beattie in *John Arbuthnot: Mathematician and Satirist* (Cambridge, Mass., 1935), ch. iii. There is further material in Ernest Lee Tuveson, "Swift and the World-Makers," *Journal of the History of Ideas*, XI (1950), 54–74.

[41] The allusions in the *Memoirs of Martinus Scriblerus* have been decoded and documented by Charles Kerby-Miller in his admirable edition of the *Memoirs* (New Haven, 1950).

World shall be no more. . . . Tomorrow Morning five Minutes after Five the Truth will be Evident; in that instant the Comet shall appear, of which I have heretofore warn'd you. As ye have heard, believe. Go hence, and prepare your Wives, your Families and Friends, for the universal Change." The prophet proved without honor; the world continued on its orderly way.

Still more drastic was the parody of the "diluvists" in Pope's and Gay's *Three Hours after Marriage*,[42] in which Woodward was "Fossile," the antiquary and collector, and John Dennis, with his enthusiasm for the "vast" in nature, became "Sir Tremendous Longinus." Phoebe Clinket, the poetess-niece of Fossile-Woodward, inspired by her uncle's "great beloved Catastrophe," had written a drama called *The Universal Deluge*, though her Deluge was classical, not Scriptural. "I chose that of Deucalion and Pyrrha," [43] she said, "because neither our Stage nor Actors are hallow'd enough for Sacred Story." But the waters that threatened to overwhelm the eighteenth-century stage as they had inundated the globe were the waters of Burnet, Woodward, Whiston. The Deluge, declared Phoebe, was a subject "beyond every Thing. So adapted for tragical Machines! So proper to excite the Passions!

[42] *Three Hours after Marriage: A Comedy as It Is Acted at the Theatre Royal* (London, 1717), pp. 5, 21.

[43] I suspect that the authors intended a double barb in this insistence upon Deucalion's Flood. As Mr. Allen has shown in his *Legend of Noah*, pagans long insisted that the Hebraic tradition of Noah was merely a variant upon old classical legends of the Flood. During the Renaissance, the matter was widely discussed, Christians insisting that the classical version was only a result of memories of the true Flood. The problem became more acute during the seventeenth century in connection with the argument over the universality of the Deluge. Woodward refused to accept Deucalion's Flood as an explanation of fossils, though he accepted the Hebraic Flood. Pope and Gay may also have had reference to the literary controversy over the propriety of classical versus Biblical themes in the epic, which had been precipitated by Hobbes and Davenant in the "Gondibert Papers." Cowley said in his Preface to his *Poems*: "What can we imagine more proper for the ornaments of Wit or Learning in the story of Deucalion, then in that of Noah?"

Not in the least encumber'd with Episodes! The *Vray-semblance* and the Miraculous are linkt together with such Propriety." Phoebe's was a drama "in which are Terror and Pity in Perfection," as even the stage setting shows:

The Scene opens, and discovers the Heavens cloudy. A prodigous shower of Rain, at a distance appears the Top of the Mountain Parnassus. All the Fields beneath are over-flowed, there are seen Cattle and Men swimming. The Tops of Steeples rise above the Floud, with Men and Women perching on their Weather-Cocks.

Sublime in theme, Phobe Clinket's *Universal Deluge* was equally sublime in style, if we may judge by an extant fragment, read aloud painfully by Phoebe's maid:

> Swell'd with a Dropsy, sickly Nature lies,
> And melting in a Diabetes, dies. . . .
> The roaring Seas o'er the tall Woods have broke,
> Now perch, thou Whale, upon the sturdy Oak.

In the third book of *Gulliver's Travels* Swift had his fun with Halley, Whiston, and the other comet prophets. Confirmed pessimists as they were, the Laputans were so conscious of the probable end of their world through natural causes that their first question on meeting an acquaintance in the morning was "about the sun's health, how he looked at his setting and rising, and what hopes they have to avoid the stroke of the approaching comet." They were persuaded "that the earth very narrowly escaped a brush from the tail of the last comet, which would have infallibly have reduced it to ashes; and that the next, which they have calculated for one and thirty years hence, will probably destroy us." [44]

[44] See Marjorie Hope Nicolson and Nora M. Mohler, "The Scientific Background of Swift's *Voyage to Laputa*," *Annals of Science*, II (1937), 299–334; reprinted in *Science and Imagination*, pp. 110–154.

IV

The Scriblerians laughed, and London laughed with them. But a new geology was emerging from the ruins of a broken world. All the dilemmas we have encountered in the earlier period were resurrected or continued, to be debated at length during the period of the Burnet controversy. In view of the state of earth science at this period, many of Burnet's conclusions seemed so sound that refutation of his work led his adversaries to consider his evidence carefully. New hypotheses of the origin of waters, of fossils, of mountains, poured forth. Most important for the development of geology was a growing interest in the possibility of indefinite time for the development of the earth.[45]

Aristotle's theory of the eternity of the world was still heterodox to men like Burnet who were endeavoring to save Scripture. Indeed, the fourth chapter of the first book of Burnet's *Sacred Theory* was devoted to the thesis "That the Earth and Mankind had an Original, and were not from Eternity: Prov'd against Aristotle." Other writers in the Burnet controversy were more interested than Burnet himself in the length of the "Divine Week." One way around the theological dilemma was to assert that before the creation of man, *time* was not. Milton's Angel had faced that problem when he attempted to explain to Adam's finite mind the mystery of Creation, and he used analogies, "likening spiritual to corporal forms." Raphael began his account of the Creation with a discourse on time:

> As yet this world was not, and Chaos wild
> Reign'd where these Heavens now roll, where Earth
> now rests
> Upon her center pois'd, when on a day

[45] Some of the theories of time that developed in this period are discussed by John Tull Baker, *English Space and Time Theories*, mentioned in Chapter Four, note 15. Katharine Collier has discussed several scientific hypotheses in *Cosmogonies of Our Fathers*.

> (For Time, though in Eternity applied
> To motion, measures all things durable
> By present, past, and future) . . .

Milton himself included the period of the creation of the earth within the orthodox six thousand years. The physicotheologists, however, more often numbered those years from the date of the creation of *man*, thereby allowing themselves much more scope. Old theological interpretations came back with new meaning, since the writers of analogical, anagogical, cabbalistical interpretations of Scripture had paved the way. The Psalmist had afforded opportunity for reinterpretation of Moses' literal account: "A thousand years in Thy sight are but as yesterday when it is past, and as a watch in the night." The "six days" of Moses were intended to be taken literally only by simple men. The "days" of Creation were not lunar or solar days but "God's days," each one a millennium. To the modern geologist, of course, a span of six thousand years is an absurdly short period to explain the changes and developments in earth's structure, yet it seemed a possible extent to many intelligent men in the seventeenth century. But disciples of the "new philosophy" went much further.

The Cartesian exponents of a mechanistic universe had less difficulty than those hylozoistically inclined, who still thought of the earth as organism, growing and degenerating like man and animal. If the earth was mechanism governed by natural law, it need experience no organic decay. "Now in all likelihood," said Henry Power, "he that made this great Automaton of the world, will not destroy it, till the slowest Motion therein has made one Revolution." An Hebraic God of justice might destroy his creation; the God of the mechanists was more careful of his great clock. Such is the impression given by Power in his "Essay, to prove the World's Duration, from the slow motion of the Sun's Apogaeum, or the Earth's Aphelion":

For would it not even in a common Watchmaker (that has made a curious Watch for some Gentleman or other, to shew him the rarity of his Art) be great indiscretion, and a most imprudent act, and argue also a dislike of his own work, to pluck the said Watch in pieces before every wheel therein had made one revolution at least? Now the Apogaeum (if it move equally, as it hath hitherto done) will not perfect one Revolution under 20000 years, whereof there is but one Quadrant yet spent, and 15000 years are yet to come.[46]

The optimistic sons of Scientia were pushing time back and extending it forward. If even a mechanical world must end by fiat of God, there was reason to believe that the end would come not in two hundred but after fifteen thousand years. The Cambridge divines read a lesson of new hope from Daniel and the Apocalypse; the scientists read it from mathematics, physics, and astronomy; together they were tending toward an indefinite past and future long denied by the orthodox.

As the concept of indefinite space had affected the thinking of the later seventeenth century, the concept of indefinite time was to capture the imagination of the eighteenth. Except to such philosophers as Barrow and More, time was not yet infinite, but the extent to which "geological time" developed during the early part of the eighteenth century may be seen in Buffon's *Théorie de la Terre*, published in 1744. Having experimented for a long period with molten metals, Buffon was persuaded that the first "day" of Creation, during which the body of the earth could have cooled to such a point that water could settle upon it, must have been at least twenty-five thousand years. The second "day," during which the waters were precipitated upon earth, must have lasted ten thousand years. During another "day," of fifteen to twenty thousand years, the waters stood above the earth, and the tops of the mountains were covered. Still another "day" of ten thousand years was necessary for the subsidence of the waters because of violent upheavals caused by earthquakes and volcanic

[46] Henry Power, *Experimental Philosophy* (London, 1664), pp. 189–190. The "Essay" is contained within the larger work, pp. 188–193.

action. During the fifth era of perhaps five thousand years, the first terrestrial animals appeared. Another era of the same length must have passed before man finally appeared on earth, where he had spent at least five thousand years—a total time of seventy-five thousand years since the beginning of Creation.[47] "Had we but World enough and Time!" World enough men possessed; a new universe of space was already theirs. The eighteenth century was discovering indefinite time, sufficient for the leisurely processes of earth science.

V

Let us return from these broader issues to the effect of the Burnet controversy upon our lesser problem of the orgin of mountains. If Burnet did nothing else, he made his generation "mountain conscious" to an extent never before known in England. Both his followers and his antagonists found it necessary to enter into the mountain controversy, theologically, scientifically, or aesthetically. From the time of the publication of *The Sacred Theory of the Earth*, the battle of the mountains ceased to be a minor skirmish and became a major engagement. Book after book, pamphlet after pamphlet poured forth from the press, attacking, defending, amplifying Burnet's contentions.

The model for most of the later physicotheological treatises was *The Wisdom of God*, published in 1691 by John Ray, the father of English natural history. Ray was at this time sixty-four years of age. He had written his important *opera* on birds and fishes and plants and had laid the basis on which future study of

[47] Buffon's theories are to be found not only in the *Théorie* but scattered through his works. My colleague Professor Otis Fellows, who has had access to Buffon manuscripts, as well as to all versions of the published works, tells me that Buffon's estimate of the period of time required for the emergence of the earth increased markedly in each variant text. Estimates in the manuscript versions became so spectacularly large that Buffon obviously found it necessary to tone them down in the printed versions.

flora and fauna proceeded in England for many years. He had enriched British collections of natural history through his own travels and those of his assistant and colleague, Francis Willughby, the ornithologist. In the Preface to *The Wisdom of God*, Ray stated his purpose modestly: "By Virtue of my Function, I suspect my self to be oblig'd to write something in Divinity, having written so much on other Subjects; for not being permitted to serve the Church with my Tongue in Preaching, I know not but it may be my Duty to serve it with my Hand by Writing." He was, he said, doing nothing that his predecessors had not done better. His masters in this kind of writing had been Henry More, Edward Stillingfleet, Ralph Cudworth, and Robert Boyle. More's *Antidote against Atheism* was clearly his model; *The Wisdom of God* went through at least twelve editions within a few years and was so widely used by the later physicotheologists that it was constantly quoted, often without acknowledgment.[48]

Ray was replying to Lucretius, who had denied the design and plan of God in the universe, but he had in mind specifically Burnet's *Sacred Theory*. All that he had to say about the "figure of the earth" was written with Burnet in mind. He opposed Burnet still more directly in a companion volume on which he was working at the time af his death, the long title of which shows its close relation to Burnet's book: *Three Physico-Theological Discourses, concerning I. The Primitive Chaos and Creation of the World; II. The General Deluge, Its Causes and Effects; III. The*

---

[48] John Ray, *The Wisdom of God Manifested in the Works of the Creation* (London, 1691). My references are to the tenth edition (London, 1735). The parallels with More's *Antidote against Atheism*, which appeared in 1653, may have been a result of the fact that Ray used as the basis of his *Wisdom of God* a series of sermons he had delivered much earlier, evidently before 1660. The similarities may also have gone back to the fact that both More and Ray seem to have been much influenced by a work of Kepler's which was apparently called *The Wisdom of God in the Creation*. I have not been able to locate that work. It does not appear under any such title in the *Opera Omnia*, nor have I found it in the volumes of Kepler's *Gesammelte Werke* so far available.

Dissolution of the World and Future Conflagration, Wherein Are Largely Discussed the Production and Use of Mountains. In turn Ray took up arguments of Aristotle, of Descartes, of Hobbes and his supposed followers. Among all the atheists, a special place in Ray's Hell was reserved for Hobbes's followers, who attempted to prove that the "uses" of natural objects "were not designed by Nature in the Formation of things, but that the Things were by the Wit of Man accommodated to those Uses." In both volumes, mountains afforded Ray one of his most important arguments for design and plan and the wisdom of God.

Ray's mountain defense was largely the old pragmatic and utilitarian argument. He took his point of departure from a classic passage in the second book of Cicero's *De Natura Deorum,* in which Cicero, opposing the atomical hypothesis, argued that "this most beautiful and adorn'd World" could not have been produced by a fortuitous concourse of atoms.[49] "Because Mountains have been look'd upon by some as Warts and superfluous Excrescences, of no Use or Benefit, nay, rather as Signs and Proofs that the present Earth is nothing else but a Heap of Rubbish and Ruins," said Ray, "I shall reduce and demonstrate Par-

[49] Hakewill, More, and many others also quoted the Ciceronian passage, which had become a *locus classicus.* Ray gives it thus (*Wisdom of God,* pp. 35–36): "If the Works of Nature are better, more exact and perfect, than the Works of Art, and Art effects nothing without Reason, neither can the Works of Nature be thought to be effected with Reason; for, is it not absurd and incongruous, that when thou beholdest a Statue or curious Picture, thou shoulds't acknowledge that Art was us'd in the making of it; or when thou seest the Course of a Ship upon the Waters, thou should'st not doubt but the Motion of it is regular and directed by Reason and Art; or when thou considerest a Sun-Dyal or Clock, thou should'st understand presently, that the Hours are shewn by Art, and not by Chance; and yet imagine or believe, that the World, which comprehends all these Arts and Artificers, was made without Counsel or Reason? . . . A Wonder then it needs must be, that there should be any Man found so stupid and Forsaken of Reason, as to persuade himself, that this most beautiful and adorn'd World was, or could be, produced by the fortuitous Concourse of Atoms."

ticularly the great Use, Benefit and Necessity of them." There followed the imposing list of the "uses" of mountains, in which Ray was slavishly followed for many years. Pliny, Hakewill, and others, as we know, had said much of this before, but there were two significant differences in Ray's treatment. Clearly the influence of the "Lucretian atheists" had grown increasingly with the success of scientific atomism and the infiltration into England of French enthusiasm for Lucretius. In the early chapters of *The Wisdom of God*, Ray devoted a lengthy section to "The Epicurean Hypothesis rejected." His extensive table of the "uses" of mountains was intended as a direct reply to the followers of Lucretius, including Hobbes. In addition, Ray was developing the principle of plenitude. In earlier works, with the exception of Hakewill's argument from mountains had been incidental. To Ray mountains were significant and essential in a diversified universe created by a God of overflowing benignity, expressing Himself in an infinity of worlds and in the fullest possible diversity in each of those worlds.

Ray's *Wisdom of God* appeared during the year of Robert Boyle's death. Boyle's will contained a codicil arranging for the publication of what came to be known, for two centuries, as the "Boyle Lectures," the purpose of which Boyle stated as "The Proof of the Christion Religion against Notorious Infidels; viz., Atheists, Pagans, Jews, and Mahometants." [50] The first "Boyle Lecturer," Richard Bentley, selected by the trustees of the foundation, was surprisingly young for such an important assignment, since he was still under thirty. His qualifications for the post seem

---

[50] William Derham in his *Physico-Theology* (see below, note 54), the "Boyle Lectures" for 1711 and 1712, published in 1713, gives considerable information about the establishment of the lectures and the difficulties faced by the trustees. He says (12th ed. [London, 1754], Preface, p. v): "The Business he appointed those Lectures for was, among others, To be ready to satisfy real Scruples, and to answer such new Objections and Difficulties as might be stated, to which good Answers had not been made."

to have been chiefly that he had been tutor to the son of Edward Stillingfleet, author of *Origines Sacrae*, and that he had recently been appointed Keeper of the King's Library at Oxford. Later Bentley's name was to be associated with that of Boyle in a different way, because of his bitter antagonism to Robert Boyle's Kinsman, Charles Boyle, fourth Earl of Orrery, who edited *The Epistles of Phalaris* and expressed himself too vigorously upon a lack of courtesy he had met with in the King's Librarian, with results familiar in Swift's *Battle of the Books*. But these were still matters for the future when Bentley delivered the "Boyle Lectures" in 1692.

Unlike Ray, Bentley was a fighter. The title of his series of lectures suggested belligerence: *The Folly and Unreasonableness of Atheism Demonstrated from the Origin and Frame of the World*. Like Ray, he opposed all prevailing "heresies," but in the sections [51] on Burnet he exhibited his characteristic temper. "Some men," he began abruptly,

are out of love with the features and mien of our earth; they do not like this rugged and irregular surface, these precipices and valleys, and the gaping channel of the ocean. This with them is deformity, and rather carries the face of a ruin, or a rude and indigested lump of atoms that casually convened so, then a work of divine artifice. They would have the vast body of a planet to be as elegant and round as a factitious globe represents it; to be every where smooth and equable, and as plain as the Elysian fields.

Point by point he replied to Burnet. His chief weapon was still the pragmatic argument: "Would not this be a fine bargain, indeed? to part with all our commodious ports and harbours, which, the greater the inlet is, are so much the better, for the imaginary pleasure of an open and straight shore, without any retreat or shelter from the winds?"

[51] Richard Bentley, *The Folly and Unreasonableness of Atheism Demonstrated from the Origin and Frame of the World* (London, 1693), pp. 32–41.

So repetitious were the pragmatic defenses of mountains, most of which merely echoed Ray's arguments, that Daniel Defoe's development of this last point makes a pleasant diversion.[52] Concerned as usual with economic theories of trade, Defoe found a new point of departure in Burnet's *Sacred Theory*. In a preceding number of the *Review* he had been discussing the fact that "Providence concurs in, and seems to have prepared the World for Commerce." When he returned to the theme on February 5, 1713, Burnet's theory suggested an interesting argument. "In my last," Defoe noted, "I said something about the Harmony of the Creation, and the Beauty and Concern of Providence, in preparing the World for Trade." Then he turned to Burnet:

He thinks this World in Ruines, as he calls it, less beautiful than the Antidiluvian Earth; yet, this must be said to the Glory of him that brings the Grateful Order out of the Greatest Confusion, that this irregular Earth, this Rupture, and Dislocation of the Parts of the Earth, this intervention of Waters, and the whole Distortion of Parts which he speaks of, are the First moving causes, as well as the subsequent Assistants to Commerce in the World.

It was well for the future state of the world, Defoe said in effect, that the shock of the Deluge should heve separated continent from continent, island from island, spurring man on to trade, that it should have caused the rough and ragged coastline, affording excellent harbors for ships. As the sin of man once separated nations, Commerce may bring nations more closely together and make man realize the interdependence of one upon another. "No man is an island," John Donne wrote. "Every man is a piece of the continent, a part of the main." So, if less poetically and religiously, Defoe believed. The English lived on an island, even though it seemed to them the mainland.

[52] Defoe's first notation was for February, 1713. His review of Burnet's book may be found in the edition of the *Review* published by the Facsimile Text Society (New York, 1938), IX, 109. There were suggestions of this approach in Bentley, Warren, and Ray, but Defoe carried the economic argument farther than any of his predecessors.

VI

For two decades after the first complete edition of the *Sacred Theory*, the pragmatic argument seemed the most important "defense" of mountains to men who were replying not only to Burnet but to Lucretius. Derham could still say in 1713: "Be the Case as it will as to *Beauty, which is the least valuable Consideration*, we shall find as to Convenience, this Configuration of Earth far the most Commodious on several Accounts." [53] However, Derham, who had little aesthetic feeling, added: "As to the Business of Ornament, Beauty and Pleasure, I may appeal to all Men's Senses, whether the grateful Variety of Hills and Dales, be not more pleasing then the largest continued Planes." To other writers in the controversy, however, Beauty was not "the least valuable Consideration."

The earliest reply to Burnet was the *Animadversions* published in 1685 by Herbert Croft, Bishop of Hereford. There is nothing original in the general argument: the orthodox churchman opposed to Burnet's liberal science his own belief in miracle and disputed Burnet's learning by insisting on a more literal interpretation of Genesis. But Croft's one slight sally into aesthetics is amusing in its homely terminology and invective against the man who has dared to accuse God of ugliness in His Creation:

I desire him to give me leave to set forth our *Microcosm*, Man, in some such deformed way, as he doth the *Megacosm*, or great World. I might affirm him to be a most misshapen creature also; and his Head to be like a Jug or Bottle with the neck turned downwards, much deformed in it self, one side all rough and hairy, the other

---

[53] *Physico-Theology; or, A Demonstration of the Being and Attributes of God, from the Works of His Creation, Being the Substance of Sixteen Sermons Preached in St. Mary-le-Bow Church, London, at the Honourable Mr. Boyle's Lectures, in the Years 1711 and 1712* (London, 1713), book III, chapter iv, was devoted to discussion "Of Mountains and Valleys." My passage is quoted from the twelfth edition (London, 1754), p. 71.

bald, as it were, all battered and broken. Yet we believe this mis-
shapen Body was framed by God himself . . . and much admire
the wonderful structure and usefulness of every part. . . . And so
this great body of the Earth taken altogether hath such a wonderful beauty and admirable structure, even in those parts which
he sets forth as most disagreeing and deformed. The high and rocky
Mountains immediately adjoyning to the boundless Seas, quite of
another nature, represent unto us the infinite Power and Majesty
of God.[54]

John Ray might well have called his book not "The *Wisdom*
of God" but "The *Goodness* of God in the Works of the Creation," for his survey of the world and the universe was a song of
praise to the overflowing benignity of a Creator whose nature
was to create to profusion: "All the Earth is full of thy Riches"
was his theme. Scientist and collector, Ray was familiar with the
profusion of Nature shown in plants, in animals, in birds, in insects. Although he made use of every argument familiar to theologians and scientists, his basic emphasis was upon variety and
diversity in the richness of the world. This earth as he had found
it was better in every way than an earth less diverse and various,
filled as it was with everything not only for man's use but also for
his pleasure. Without diversification of land and sea,

all the Beauty, Glory, and Variety of this inferior World had been
gone. . . . That therefore the Earth should be made thus, and not
only so, but with so great a Variety of Parts, as Mountains, Plains,
Vallies, etc . . . which are so delectable and pleasant, and likewise
so useful . . . these things, I say, must needs be the Result of
Counsel, Wisdom and Design.

He replied to Burnet's contention that "the present Earth looks
like a Heap of Rubbish and Ruins":

[54] Herbert [Croft], Lord Bishop of Hereford, *Some Animadversions
upon a Book Intituled the Theory of the Earth* (London, 1685), pp. 140–
141.

I answer, That the present Face of the Earth, with all its Mountains and Hills, its Promontories and Rockes, so rude and deformed as they appear, seem to me a beautiful and pleasant Object, and with all that Variety of Hills, and Valleys, and Inequalities, far more grateful to behold, than a perfectly level Country without any Rising or Protuberancy to terminate the Sight.

Ray devoted a section of his pragmatic defense of hills to the thesis that "they are very ornamental to the Earth, affording pleasant and delightful Prospects, both to them that look downwards from them upon the adjacent Countries . . . and to those that look upwards, and behold them from the Plains and low Grounds. . . . What a Refreshing and Pleasure it is to the Eye." His illustrations were not drawn only from books. He himself had looked up to ruggedness and down to beauty. He remembered experiences in the Isle of Ely and on the Sussex downs, where he "enjoy'd that ravishing Prospect of the Sea on one hand, and the Country far and wide on the other." His favorite landscape was characteristically English, a scene diversified with hills and valleys, the earth "cover'd over with a lovely Carpet of green Grass, and other Herbs, of a Colour not onely most grateful and agreeable, but most useful and salutary to the Eye; . . . for the Refreshment of our Spirits and our innocent Delight." Various passages show his "innocent Delight" in his native landscape and suggest as well his interest in the kind of landscape painting that was becoming steadily more popular in England, whether imported from abroad or produced at home. "That the Mountains are pleasant Objects to behold," he wrote, "appears in that the very Images of them, their Draughts and Landskips, are so much esteem'd." [55]

We have already heard Richard Bentley's pragmatic defense of mountains in his "Boyle Lectures." By nature as well as by profession Bentley lived among books. He was one of the last of our writers who in a "defense" of mountains still used the old

[55] *Wisdom of God*, pp. 206–207.

vocabulary, "Warts and superfluous Excrescences." His Biblical heritage echoes in his defense: "Are there then such ravishing charms in a dull, unvaried flat, to make sufficient compensation for *the chief things of the ancient mountains and for the precious things of the everlasting hills?*" There were echoes, too, of the classical heritage: "What were the Tempe of Thessaly, so celebrated in ancient story, for their unparalleled pleasantness, but a vale divided with a river, and terminated with hills? Are not all the descriptions of poets embellished with such ideas, when they would represent any sacred habitation of gods or goddesses?" The landscape Bentley defended was not English but classical and Scriptural, a landscape as literary as his allusions. Burnet had not led Bentley to look at Nature with new eyes. He disposed of Burnet's vision of a primitive smooth and beautiful world in one sentence: "We have but one general and sufficient answer for all seeming defects . . . that we do not contend to have earth pass for a Paradise." [56]

In answer to Henry More, whose passage on "regular solids" he quoted, Bentley introduced into his defense one idea we have not found before. "There is no Universal Reason," he said, "that a Figure by us called Regular, which hath equal Sides and Angles, is absolutely more beautiful than any irregular one." Bentley was denying the appeal to Reason of geometrical beauty as he was denying old absolute standards of beauty and truth. "All Pulchritude is Relative," said Bentley, and he carried his attack on absolute standards into issues concerning irregularity

[56] *The Folly and Unreasonableness of Atheism*, pp. 35–39. Francis Litz reprinted Bentley's passage, with a brief discussion, in *E.L.H.*, XII (1945), 327–332. The passage on regular figures, which Mr. Litz attributes (in his note 19) to Ray, was not Ray's but was Henry More's passage, quoted above. Ray drew many of his illustrations from More and did not always acknowledge his sources. The extent to which later authors repeated earlier writers may be seen by comparing with Bentley's words here their later adaptation in Derham's *Physico-Theology*, words which have been sometimes considered by scholars as if they had been original with Derham in 1713.

in the terrestrial world. "We ought not then to believe," he wrote, "that the banks of Ocean are *really* deformed, because they have not the form of a regular pyramid; nor that the mountains are out of shape, because they were not exact pyramids or cones; nor that the stars are unskilfully placed, because they are not all situated at uniform distance." The supposed "deformity" is not in *Nature,* as men had so long insisted. It has been read into Nature by men who, trying her against their self-imposed standards of symmetry, regularity, and proportion, have found her guilty. "*This objected Deformity,*" said Bentley, "*is in our Imaginations only, and not really in the things themselves.*" [57] Richard Bentley is the first English "subjectivist" we have found among the mountain controversialists, as well as the first "relativist." He insisted that the supposed limitations of Nature were not in Nature, but in the *thinking mind* that had read into Nature "supposed deformities," applying to Nature artificial standards of beauty, made in the image of their own "Reason." With Bentley's passage, we are standing at the crossroads. The "new aesthetics" will lead in two directions: the "relativism" of Hobbes versus the "absolutism" of the Cambridge Platonists; the old belief that defects or beauties of Nature existed in Nature herself versus the drastic separation of mind from Nature by the Cartesian shears. Bentley's sentences remain only sentences; their development into a full-fledged aesthetic occurred in the eighteenth century.

Three years before Ray and Bentley published their lectures, the issue of the "Comeliness" of mountains had been faced by an Englishman more sensitive to the beauty of English landscape than any other writer in the Burnet controversy. Erasmus Warren, Rector of Worlington in Suffolk, has found no place in

---

[57] *The Folly and Unreasonableness of Atheism*, pp. 35–38. The italics are mine. Bentley, of course, knew Descartes and Hobbes; but I am inclined to think that it was Locke's *Essay*, recently published in 1690 and already widely read, that made him realize these implications. I have discussed the attitude of Addison and some of the later poets to this problem in *Newton Demands the Muse* (Princeton, 1946), chapter vi.

either literary or intellectual histories, yet he deserves a niche in both. His *Geologia*,[58] published in 1690, really precipitated the Burnet controversy, provoking Burnet to his first reply, forcing him further upon the road that led to Deism. Warren was able to oppose Burnet's theology because he too was a well-trained theologian. He was well read enough in science to see the weaknesses of some of Burnet's hypotheses. But Warren was not primarily concerned with Burnet's liberalism in Scripture or with his scientific inconsistencies. The two men stood opposed on what seemed to Warren a more fundamental issue—the relation of God to His universe. Was He, as Burnet seemed to imply, a powerful but unforgiving Judge, willing to permit the deformity of mountains in an originally beautiful earth in order that they might serve as reminders to man of the sins of his ancestors? Was He a Cartesian mechanic who, having set his machine in motion, remained apart from it, idly watching its revolutions? Warren's God was "Wise and Powerful," but he was also a kindly and interested participant in every event in the world, a God who numbered the sparrows and was as concerned with the fall of a feather as with the courses of the planets. Moreover, he was a Divine Artist.

Warren's was a God of Beauty. "The first Notion men had of him," he wrote, "they took from the beauty of aspectable things." Any attack upon the beauty of Nature was an attack on God. The forgotten clergyman of the late seventeenth century possessed a feeling for the beauty of earth that we shall not find

[58] Erasmus Warren, *Geologia; or, A Discourse concerning the Earth before the Deluge, Wherein the Form and Properties Ascribed to It, in a Book Intituled The Theory of the Earth, Are Excepted Against, and It Is Made to Appear That the Dissolution of That Earth Was Not the Cause of the Universal Flood* (London, 1690). Warren returned to the attack in *Some Reflections upon the Short Considerations of the Defence of the Exceptions against the Theory of the Earth* (London, 1692). Burnet's reply to Warren, with a second paper on the subject, *Reflections upon the Theory of the Earth Occasion'd by a Late Examination of It, in a Letter to a Friend*, was published with several of the editions of the *Sacred Theory*. The passages I use are on pp. 121-122.

surpassed for some years. Burnet might consider this "World on which men doted" a "rude Lump," but as the Rector of Worlington walked abroad in the English countryside, he did not need to presuppose a primitive paradisaical state of the earth. England was beautiful enough for him. His was the timeless feeling of English poets, of Shakespeare's "other Eden, demi-Paradise. . . . This blessed plot, this earth," of Rupert Brooke, to whom "a pulse in the eternal mind. . . . Gives back somewhere the thoughts by England given." Warren's vocabulary was different from Brooke's, different too from Shakespeare's, yet his emotions were similar when he defended his native landscape from charges Burnet had brought against the ugliness of earth:

And may not this Earth, in those regards, be allowed to vie with that supposititious one under debate? Yes, does it not in some things excel it? For though it has not the very same Elegancies, which that Earth had; yet it has other Embellishments equal to them, if not beyond them. Indeed it does not have that smoothness and entireness, which is pretended to have been in the first Earth. But then (which is more considerable): it has the raised Work, of Hills; the Embossings, of Mountains; the Ænamellings, of lesser Seas; the Open-Work, of vast Oceans; and the Fret-Work of Rocks. To say nothing of those stately Curtains over-head (wanting heretofore) which are frequently drawn and flung open upon occasion; and sometimes curiously wrought and most richly gilt, even to admiration; far surpassing the goodliest Landskips, that ever were or can be painted: I mean the Clouds.[59]

We have returned to old aesthetic conflicts apparently deeply embedded in human thinking, to attitudes implied and sometimes expressed by the Greeks and by the Christian Fathers. Plato and Aristotle, in varying ways, had stressed symmetry and regularity, as did Augustine after them. Beauty was a principle apprehended by Reason, upon which rational men must agree. But Plotinus had felt differently. "The same bodies," he had said, "appear

[59] The passages I quote from Warren's *Geologia* are on pp. 121–122.

sometimes beautiful, sometimes not; so that there is a good deal between being *body* and being *beautiful*." Response to beauty is not a matter of logical agreement of rational men; it is emotional. Beauty in an object "is something perceived . . . at the first glance, something the soul names as from an ancient knowledge and, recognizing, welcomes it, and enters into unison with it." Whether or not the Rector of Worlington had read Plotinus, he felt as Plotinus felt and in effect said with him, "We mean by beauty *what we love*." If Warren was thinking of any specific source when he wrote the passage in the *Geologia*, he may have remembered the *De Venustate Mundi et Pulchritudine Dei* of Denis the Carthusian. His last sentence implies a distinction Denis was fond of making, though Warren has reversed the emphasis. True *Beauty*, said Denis, belongs to God; things of this earth possess *Prettiness*. Warren agreed that the highest beauty was God's, but he was sure that the world was as "pretty" as any lesser nature could be. There is one glory of the sun and another of the moon:

So is this Earth, though it has not the beauty of finer things in it, but only that which is peculiar to it self. For as the beauty of the Sun, lies in brightness and glory; and the beauty of the Sky, in clearness and serenity; so the beauty of the Earth, which is a different thing, does and needs must lie in very different instances, namely, in Seas and Lakes, and Islands and Continents; in Flats and Prominencies, and Plains and Protuberances, and Hollownesses and Convexities; in smooth and spacious Levels in some places, and Hills and Mountainous Roughnesses in others. Whose careless diversifications, and interchangeable mixtures, as they mutually set off one another; so they all conspire to adorn the Earth; Insomuch that to suppose it of the prediluvian Form, would be rather to detract from its measures, than improve them. Yea, it would be in a manner to make it no Earth, or at least not so perfect a one as it is. For as we can have no Camels without Bunches; nor Mules without Hairs; nor Fowls without Feathers; or if we could, they would be but the more imperfect; so were the Earth abstracted from its aforesaid appendages, however it might have the more uniformity in it, yet as an Earth, it would have the less Comeliness.

Spenser's "E. K." and other writers of the earlier seventeenth century had made a point of "disorderly order" in landscape, but their "rude" background was there only for contrast, as the ugliness of the "Peak" district served to enhance the beauty of Chatsworth. Warren felt that the irregularities of earth were not mere contrast to its regularity but an integral element in its beauty. Sir Thomas Browne had justified the apparent ugliness of the toad, the bear, and the elephant on grounds of their adaptation to their use, as had Denis the Carthusian, from whom Warren may have picked up his camel and his mule; but in Warren's mind the bunches on the camel, the hair on the mule, the feathers on the fowl were more than merely justifiable. They were essential. Without them camel, mule, and fowl "would be the more imperfect." Without its irregularities, ruggednesses, and inequalities, the earth would be not only less useful and less diverse but less comely. "Art" might call them "rudenesses," but Warren believed that Nature, as created by God, "consists in asymetries and a wild variety."

His earlier vocabulary has indicated that Warren was interested in painting and in architecture. On another occasion he wrote: "And truly that roughness, brokenness, and multiform confusion in the surface of the Earth; which to the inadvertent may seem to be nothing but inelegancies or frightful Disfigurements, to thinking Men will appear to be as the Tornings [*sic*] and Carvings, and ornamental Sculptures; that make up the Lineaments and Features of Nature, not to say her Braveries." He carried over his defense of asymmetry and irregularity in Nature to prospect in landscape painting:

Were a Man to contrive a Prospect for himself, we may be sure he would not have it all of a piece, or alike throughout: but would have it cast into Swamps and Hillocks, Bottoms and Gibbosities, Evenness and Asperities; yea, into Seas and Ilets, and Rocks, if it could be; and so it would be an Image not of the primitive, but present Earth. A pretty Argument to prove, that there is something of perfection, or at least of pleasingness, in this Earths disorder (if we may call it so) and that it is fitter to gratifie its principal Inhabitants (and so far) better in itself, than if it had been regular and undiversified. And the truth is, several of these appearances, which we are apt to call *rude, confused,* and *uncouth;* and to count but Blemishes, Scars, and Deformities; are commonly so well plac'd and suited to one another, as to become very taking in artificial Draughts, and a kind of natural Landskips.

To Warren, in other words, the English landscape was "pretty as a picture."

The early replies to Burnet had certain immediate effects. If Keill forced Burnet to a reluctant decision for science over Revelation, Warren faced him with as difficult a choice between his emotional response to mountains and his intellectual condemnation of the ruins of Nature. Burnet's apparent vacillation was noted by many of his critics, but it was Warren, more than any other antagonist, who caused him to reconsider his aesthetics. To Burnet's credit as logician if not as aesthetician, it may be said that Burnet finally chose "Reason" rather than "Phansy." Memories of his experience in the Alps lingered for many years. The mountain passages in the later versions of the *Sacred Theory* contained details absent from the first Latin edition. But his later works show nothing of the fervor and rapture he had once experienced.

In answer to Warren's passage on the "Embossings of Mountains" and the "Fret-Work of Rocks" and his insistence that "natural pulchritude is made up of such things as Art would call rudenesses," Burnet replied in his *Answer to the Exceptions:* [60] "These make a great noise, but they might all be apply'd to the

---

[60] Burnet's first reply to Warren appeared in the 1690 edition of the *Sacred Theory*. "A Short Consideration of Mr. Erasmus Warren's Defence" was in the edition of 1691.

ruins of an old Bridge, fallen into the Water." So indeed they might, and so they were to be applied. Burnet could not anticipate the extent to which admiration for "ruins" was to grow in England, ironically enough in large part because of his own graphic descriptions of the "Ruins of a broken World." "We are pleas'd, he wrote, "in looking upon the Ruins of a Roman Amphitheatre; or a Triumphal Arch, tho' time have defaced its beauty. A man may be pleas'd in looking upon a Monster, will you conclude therefore that he takes it for a Beauty?" Burnet has departed sharply here from the tradition that justified "Monsters" because of their functional adaptation. The ruins of the amphitheater are not beautiful, nor is the triumphal arch, defaced by time. A man may be "pleas'd" in looking upon them, but the "pleasure of the imagination" he receives has nothing to do with beauty.

Twenty years elapsed between the publication of Burnet's *Answer* and that of Addison's *Pleasures of the Imagination*, yet the Addisonian categories of the "great," the "uncommon," and the "beautiful" are all here, as indeed they were all implicit in Longinus. Monsters or the ruins of an amphitheater, devoid of beauty though they were, please imagination because they are strange and unfamiliar.[61] Burnet did not go far in the development of the third category, though he implied it on a number of occasions. His chief distinction was always between the beautiful and the vast.

Burnet's *Sacred Theory* led to a new interest in geology. The layman and the poet in the eighteenth century were "geology conscious," as laymen and poets had not been in the seventeenth century. The *Sacred Theory* led also to a new aesthetics. It precipitated arguments between notions of regularity, derived from classical and medieval thinkers, and native English feeling

[61] To Burnet the "strange" did not enhance beauty, as it sometimes did to Addison. Strangeness was distinct from either the beautiful or the great; it appealed to the intellect rather than the emotion.

for irregularity, as an aesthetic norm. It led men to consider more carefully "absolute" and "relative" standards of Beauty, to question also whether such standards were inherent in nature or in their own minds. It led them also to consider, more than man had considered before, similarities and differences between Beauty and Sublimity. The new aesthetics is still embryonic, but its origin is clear. From the discovery of the new cosmic heavens, vastness and irregularity passed to terrestrial Nature. In the wide seas and the mountains of the earth, men were discovering a new "Magnificence of Nature," finding that their "elastical souls" expanded with the vastness and expansiveness of Nature. It remained for the next generation to analyze "the Aesthetics of the Infinite."

Chapter Seven

The Aesthetics of the Infinite

"Alps on Alps Arise"

AS intellectual forces, imprisoned in the earth, strove to burst old theological and scientific barriers, so aesthetic emotions, long felt but never clearly defined, were struggling for utterance. Later travelers experienced Burnet's dilemma. On their travels a generation of men, trained in the classics, the Bible, the Church Fathers, sought a vocabulary to express an experience unknown to their ancestors, a paradoxical response at once to old criteria of Beauty and new emotions aroused by the Sublime.

Among neoclassical writers, the concept of Beauty remained identical with that which we found in the classical and medieval thinkers. As it had been for centuries, it was a principle recognized by Reason. Proof was drawn from the Art of God in the world and the universe. The appeal to Nature for standards in ethics and aesthetics was as clear as in the past. But the eighteenth-century writers were in a more strategic position than their predecessors, no longer so dependent upon Plato and Aristotle, Augustine and Aquinas. In 1611 John Donne had been appalled at the destruction of order in a universe from which all coherence was gone, from which Beauty had fled with the loss of "proportion." But by the time of Pope, order in the cosmos was more immediately apparent even to the layman than it had formerly been to philosophers. As Pope said:

> Nature and Nature's laws lay hid in night;
> God said, "Let Newton be!" and all was light.

The *Principia* offered climactic proof that order, proportion, regularity were universal principles, comprising the harmony of the universe. More than ever before, man could turn to the cosmos for his ethics of limitation, his aesthetics of order and proportion. Evidence drawn from Newton that Beauty existed in the universe was a constant refrain of the physicotheologists, a clinching proof against the "impious Atheists" that the universe arose not by chance but by the deliberate design of a Great Architect. From another point of view Newton's *Opticks* offered new evidence for Beauty.[1] In the dedicatory poems written at the time of Newton's death, the poets were unanimous in their praise for Newton who had proved equally the "simplicity" and the "beauty" of laws that governed heavens and earth. Indeed, the apparently indisputable proof drawn from Newton's laws that Beauty consisted in limitation and proportion was in part responsible for the fact that theories of Beauty remained as static as they did during the neoclassical period and that critics and aestheticians experienced difficulty in attempting to explain their new feeling for the Sublime against their heritage of the Beautiful.

"Great objects make great minds," Young wrote in the *Night Thoughts*. The physicotheologists, the Christian philosphers, the poets who refused to be hemmed in by limitation—these were the "Elastical Souls of the Universe" who, as they read attributes of Deity into Space, discovered in their souls potentialities and capacities they had not recognized. As yet they had no language in which to express their emotions, and we shall hear them strug-

---

[1] I have discussed some of these matters in *Newton Demands the Muse*.

gling for a vocabulary, which ranged from the *furor astronomicus* to a language of "enthusiasm." For a time the rhetorical and the natural Sublimes ran parallel courses. They will be found clearly distinguished in Addison's *Pleasures of the Imagination*, but before that time we may observe the "transfer" of the vastness of Space to terrestrial grandeur in a great poet and two important critics, who will show the gradual development of a threefold "Aesthetics of the Infinite."

I

More than a decade before the first edition of Burnet's work, another "sacred theory" had been published. *Paradise Lost* and *The Sacred Theory of the Earth* were the two most widely read theodicies of the earlier eighteenth century. Theologically and scientifically the authors stood at opposite poles, so that their works both contradicted and supplemented. As we have noted, Burnet's style seemed no less sublime than Milton's, and the two were more responsible than any other English writers for the cult of literary sublimity that towered to such heights. Since Milton left little literary criticism, we cannot tell whether he was conscious of the fact that in *Paradise Lost* he was writing in the style advocated by Longinus, though he knew the rhetorician's work. Nor can we tell whether in his two great epics he was aware that he was the first English poet to practice the "Aesthetics of the Infinite," the transfer of vastness from God to interstellar space, then to terrestrial mountains.

What Milton felt when he crossed the Alps we do not know, since he left no comment upon the experience. But that his imagination was stirred by the vastness of the new cosmos *Paradise Lost* gives evidence in every part of the canvas of interstellar space against which Milton's drama was played. His great scenes of cosmic perspective were his heritage from the telescope. God from his heavenly throne, Satan from the lowest stair of the celestial ladder "look down with wonder to behold" the vastest panorama ever described by an English poet. Ethically the Angel warned Adam against considering too curiously the new astronomy; emotionally the Angel was as much impressed by it as Adam. Philosophically Milton denied the idea of infinity, as theologically he denied the God of Plenitude. But aesthetically Milton was as responsive as Henry More to the vastness of a universe in which Infinite God was reflected in Infinite Space.[2]

In *Paradise Regained* the blind Milton's imagination carried over to earth the sense of vastness he had felt in the cosmos. The most extensive terrestrial panoramas of the seventeenth century are those Satan showed Christ from a mountaintop. There were literary memories here, of course—Aeneas' prospect of Carthage, Moses' of Pisgah—as there were reminiscences of Milton's own experiences in Italy.[3] Milton knew "the Imperial City . . . with towers and temples proudly elevate On seven small hills." He had seen such prospects as he described at the beginning of the temptation:

> It was a mountain at whose verdant feet
> A spacious plain outstretched in circuit wide
> Lay pleasant; from his side two rivers flowed. . . .
> Fertile of corn the glebe, of oil, and wine;
> With herds the pastures thronged, with flocks the hills.[4]

But literary and personal reminiscence ceased as Milton's panorama widened to include vistas impossible to be seen by human eye:

[2] This was my contention in "Milton and the Telescope," *E.L.H.*, II (1935), 1–32. The essay has been reprinted in *Science and Imagination* (Great Seal Books; Ithaca, 1956), pp. 80–109. I have discussed Milton's vacillation between limitation and superabundance in *The Breaking of the Circle*, pp. 160–166.

[3] Rebecca W. Smith in "The Source of Milton's Pandemonium," *Modern Philology*, XXIX (1931), 187–198, has shown the reminiscences of St. Peter's in Milton's Pandemonium. I have suggested that a source of Milton's first Hell was the Phlegraean Fields; see "Milton's Hell and the Phlegraean Fields," *University of Toronto Quarterly*, VII (1938), 500–513.

[4] *Paradise Regained*, III, 253–260.

> so large
> The prospect was, that here and there was room
> For barren desert, fountainless and dry. . . .
>   Here thou behold'st
> Assyria, and her empire's ancient bounds,
> Araxes, and the Caspian lake; whence on
> As far as Indus east, Euphrates west,
> And oft beyond; to south the Persian bay,
> And inaccessible, the Arabian drouth.[5]

This is only the beginning. "Turning with easy eye," Christ beholds Nineveh and Babylon, Persepolis, Bactra, Araxata, Teredon, Ctesiphon—the succession of names overwhelms, as we survey the pageant of Biblical history Milton welded into one vast landscape.

The writers of the Gospels had gone into no such detail, nor were they curious about the means by which Satan showed Christ all the kingdoms of the world. But Milton's generation had tasted of another dispensation. He himself implied that imaginatively he was using the telescope as Galileo had first used it, for terrestrial observation. On two occasions he mentioned an "optick glass" in connection with the vision from the mount.[6] "So well have I disposed my aerie microscope," Satan said to Christ, "thou mayst behold Outside and inside both." When he described the scene from the "specular mount," Milton added:

> By what strange parallax, or optic skill
> Of vision, multiplied through air, or glass
> Of telescope, were curious to inquire.

Not only in his deliberate association of astronomical instruments with earthly panoramas, but even more in carrying over to earth the sense of cosmic vastness that he had made peculiarly his own in the cosmic perspectives of *Paradise Lost*, Milton made the "transfer" that was to become increasingly familiar: from God,

---

[5] *Ibid.*, III, 262–274.   [6] *Ibid.*, IV, 40–42, 56–58.

to Space, to vast scenes in the terrestrial globe. The "natural Sublime" had come to England in the works of philosophers and physicotheologists and of at least one poet,[7] before a group of critics, analyzing their experience in the presence of grand nature, began to develop a critical theory by which to explain their peculiar responses.

II

In 1688 John Dennis, following the same route over the Alps as Thomas Coryat three-quarters of a century before, wrote to an untraveled English friend who had "earnestly desired . . . an account of the Alpes." " 'Tis an easy thing," he began, "to describe Rome or Naples to you, because you have seen something yourself that holds at least some resemblance with them; but impossible to set a Mountain before your Eyes, that is inaccessible almost to the sight, and wearies the very Eye to climb

---

[7] I have not treated in the text the most extreme example I have found of this kind of transfer, since to descend from *Paradise Regained* to *Belvoir Castle* would be to fall from the sublime to the ridiculous. Because the author was a third-rate poet, the device is much more self-conscious and obvious than in Milton. *Belvoir: Being a Pindarick Ode upon Belvoir Castle* is included in the *Harleian Miscellany* (1743), IV, 526 ff.; it is dated 1679. Like Marvell the unknown poet was flattering a patron whose castle was situated on a hill. He did so by obviously gross exaggeration of both hill and castle. "Belvoir's a subject high and great," we are told. It has "a glory of its own, a genuine worth not borrowed from [though the reader may doubt it] the daub of rhetorick, or scum Of heated brain and lavish tongue." Belvoir Hill towers so high that it is literally a hill whose top touches heaven. In the curious cosmography of this celestial castle, the rooms become as vast as planets and the Countess of Rutland the central sun around whom the family take their planetary way. We follow the guide through endless rooms in an apparently infinite castle and ascend to the roof for a final series of vast terrestrial panoramas, as we wait for a Pindaric steed with whom we are presumably to visit still other castles in the air. *Belvoir Castle* is a good example of the "debased Longinianism" against which Samuel Monk and Ronald Crane rightly protest; the language is a pastiche of Longinian clichés.

it." [8] If Dennis did not succeed in making his friend *see* mountains, he may have made him *feel* them:

We entered into Savoy in the Morning, and past over Mount Aiguebellette. The ascent was the more easie, because it wound about the Mountain. But as soon as we had conquer'd one half of it, the unusual heighth in which we found our selves, the impending Rock that hung over us, the dreadful Depth of the Precipice, and the Torrent that roar'd at the bottom, gave us such a view as was altogether new and amazing. On the other side of the Torrent, was a Mountain that equall'd ours, about the distance of thirty Yards from us. Its craggy Clifts, which we half discern'd thro the misty gloom of the Clouds that surrounded them, sometimes gave us a horrid Prospect. And sometimes its face appear'd Smooth and Beautiful as the most even and fruitful Vallies. So different from themselves were the different parts of it: In the very same place Nature was seen Severe and Wanton. In the mean time we walk'd upon the very brink, in a literal sense, of Destruction; one Stumble, and both Life and Carcass had been at once destroy'd. The sense of all this produc'd different motions in me, viz., a delightful Horrour, a terrible Joy, and at the same time, that I was infinitely pleas'd, I trembled.

Coming at last to Mont Cenis, "we sent our Horses about, and getting up on Mules began to ascend the Mountain." A hundred yards from the summit, they discerned "another vast Mountain still upon that." Dennis lost himself for a time in one of the "meditations" that became important in his later critical theory:

If these Hills were first made with the World, as has been a long time thought, and Nature design'd them only as a Mound to inclose

---

[8] John Dennis, *Miscellanies in Verse and Prose* (London, 1693). All the quotations about Dennis' Alpine experience are from the journal-letter he wrote immediately after his experience. It may be found more conveniently in the Appendix to John Dennis, *Critical Works*, edited by Edward Niles Hooker (Baltimore, 1939–1943), II, 380 ff. The mountain experience of Dennis and Addison has been discussed by Clarence D. Thorpe, "Two Augustans Cross the Alps," *Studies in Philology*, XXXII (1935), 463–482.

her garden Italy; Then we may well say of her what some affirm of great Wits, that her careless, irregular and boldest Strokes are most admirable. For the Alps are works which she seems to have design'd, and execut'd too in Fury. Yet she moves us less, when she studies to please us more. I am delighted, 'tis true at the prospect of Hills and Valleys, of flowry Meads, and murmuring Streams, yet it is a delight that is consistent with Reason, a delight that creates or improves Meditation. But transporting Pleasures follow'd the sight of the Alpes, and what unusual Transports think you were those, that were mingled with horrours, and sometimes almost with despair?

Trained to seek authority in books, Dennis' mind turned to Longinus, whom he was paraphrasing in the passage on "great Wits" and the "careless, irregular and boldest Strokes" of Nature. But Longinus was not enough, nor was the old commonplace that the rude surroundings were intended by Nature only to enhance the beauty of "her garden Italy." Dennis found a more satisfying explanation in Burnet's *Sacred Theory of the Earth:*

But if these Mountains were not a Creation, but form'd by universal Destruction, when the Arch with a mighty flaw dissolv'd and fell into the vast Abyss (which surely is the best opinion) then are these Ruines of the old World the greatest wonders of the New. For they are not only vast, but horrid, hideous, ghastly Ruins. After we had gallop'd a League over the Plain, and came at last to descend, to descend thro the very Bowels as it were of the Mountain, for we seem'd to be enclos'd on all sides: What an astonishing Prospect was there? Ruins upon Ruins in monstrous Heaps, and Heaven and Earth confounded. The uncouth Rocks that were above us, Rocks that were void of all form, but what they had receiv'd from Ruine; the frightful view of the Precipices, and the foaming Waters that threw themselves headlong down them, made all such a Consort up for the Eye, as that sort of Musick does for the Ear, in which Horrour can be joyn'd with Harmony. I am afraid you will think that I have said too much. Yet if you had but seen what I have done, you would surely think that I have said too little. However Hyperboles might easily here be forgiven. The Alpes appear to be Nature's extravagancies, and who should blush to be guilty of Extravagancies, in words that make mention of her's?

Looking back to the travelers of the earlier seventeenth century, we see that a change has occurred. Mountain travel was no safer than it had been, and Dennis faced as much physical danger as had Coryat. But in addition to natural fright, Dennis experienced "delightful Horrour" and "terrible Joy." He had had an experience for which nothing in his training had prepared him. Among the "horrid, hideous, ghastly Ruins," Dennis, like Burnet, experienced emotions strange to him. At the same moment that his Reason condemned the shapelessness and confusion, he felt an enlargement of spirit Beauty had never produced and, responding to the "extravagancies" of Nature, expressed his sensations in a language of extravagance and hyperbole.

When Burnet returned from his travels to write a book in which he attempted to explain his experience, he turned to theology and science. Dennis was neither scientist nor theologian. He was a critic. He came back to England to develop an aesthetic that had been only embryonic when he went abroad, to seek for new criteria against which to test literature, and to make the first important distinction in English literary criticism between the Sublime and the Beautiful.[9] His idea of Beauty had not changed, and indeed to the end of his critical life, Dennis reiterated old criteria which he had drawn from the classics and the medieval Fathers—to which he added Newton.[10] "Nature," he wrote in

[9] One of the few modern historians to emphasize English priority in the development of the Sublime was P. Hamelius, *Die Kritik in der englischen Litterautur des 17. und 18. Jahrhunderts* (Leipzig, 1897). Hamelius' treatment of Dennis in this connection is superior to that of any critic before the publication of Hooker's definitive edition of Dennis' *Critical Works*.

[10] Like most of his contemporaries Dennis was a great admirer of Newton, "whose Merit is above what the Muses themselves can Com-

one of his fullest treatments of the subject,[11] "is nothing but that Rule and Order and Harmony, which we find in the visible Creation. The Universe owes its admirable Beauty to the Proportion, Situation, and Dependence of Parts." As in the macrocosm, so in the microscosm: "As Nature is Order and Rule, and Harmony in the visible World, so Reason is the very same throughout the invisible Creation. For Reason is Order, and the Result of Order. And nothing that is Irregular, as far as it is Irregular, ever was, or ever can be either Natural or Reasonable." [12]

Upon such presuppositions of Beauty as reflecting the rationality and regularity of the universe, Dennis based his adherence to the "Rules," which seems to modern critics inconsistent with his critical and aesthetic doctrine as a whole. Dennis' theory of beauty, with his insistence upon the rules, would never have disturbed his neoclassical contemporaries, since it was their own. It was his "Enthusiasm" that brought him into critical disrepute. There were other reasons, of course, than Dennis' peculiar vocabulary for the attack of the Scriblerians, yet it was both his rhetoric and his persistent emphasis upon the "Great" that led Pope and Gay to dub him "Sir Tremendous Longinus," a sobriquet that unfortunately came to replace Dennis' own term, "The Critic," and sent him down the ages as a debased Longinian.

The Longinian Sublime played some part in Dennis' criticism, but it was a minor part. Dennis knew Longinus before he went abroad, but, as we have seen, when he encountered the natural Sublime, Longinus was not enough. Nor was Longinus ever enough for Dennis. He frequently pointed out the limitations he

---

mend," who has "oblig'd and astonish'd the Learned World by his Immortal and unparallel's Treatises; those Treatises that have made him an Honour to his Country, and an Advancer of the noblest Learning, and an Enlarger of the Empire of the Mind" (*Characters and Conduct of Sir John Edgar,*" Letter IV, in *Critical Works,* II, 208.)

[11] *The Advancement and Reformation of Poetry,* in *Critical Works,* I, 202.

[12] *The Grounds of Criticism in Poetry,* in *Critical Works,* I, 335.

felt in the Greek rhetorician. Longinus, he granted, knew the Sublime, but he did not understand its true nature clearly enough to explain it to others. Most of all, Longinus had been concerned only with the effects of the Sublime. Son of a psychological age, Dennis was more concerned with its causes.[13] "Take the Cause and the Effects together," Dennis wrote, "and you have the Sublime." Dennis' contribution to the development of the Sublime was threefold: he analyzed, as had no previous writer, the causes of sublimity; he developed its effects upon psychological grounds unknown to Longinus; he based his conception not upon rhetorical theories but upon his own experience and upon attitudes native to the English, almost unknown to the French. If we can appreciate his position in these matters (in spite of the difficult vocabulary that puzzles modern critics, as it repelled his contemporaries), we shall better understand his position in the history of English aesthetics.

On one occasion Dennis said that the "first hint" of his theory of sublimity came from Halifax' lines, "Rapture and Fury carried me thus far, Transported and amazed." [14] A "hint" he may have had from Halifax, but there is little question that what he himself would have called the "extraordinary hint" came from his experience with the vast, the overwhelming in a Nature that reflected the vastness, the power, the terror of Deity. The true source of the Sublime, for Dennis, was in religion.[15] Beauty might

[13] *Grounds of Criticism*, I, 359; *Advancement and Reformation*, I, 223.
[14] Preface to *Remarks on "Prince Arthur,"* in *Critical Works*, I, 46–47. Dennis' vocabulary was peculiarly his own, as contemporary satirists show. The words "hints" and "extraordinary" were constantly associated with him. Mr. Hooker quotes (I, 452) an anonymous *Battle of the Poets*, in which Dennis was satirized as "a punning Cobler! . . . Yonder he stands without, talking to his gaping Brethren, of the Strength of Genius! the great Hints! the supernatural Emotions! the Soaraethereal Conceptions!"
[15] Understanding of this point of view is essential for any true interpretation of Dennis' ideas of the sublime. Here Clarence Thorpe encounters his greatest difficulty in his interpretation of Dennis in *The Aesthetic Theory of Thomas Hobbes* (London, 1940). Although he

be found in the works of man. The source of sublimity was in God and in the manifestations of His greatness and power in Nature.

The "extraordinary hints" that were the sources of his Sublime were listed by Dennis in three categories. First he named "God, Angels, and other Creatures of the immaterial World." The second group comprised "the great Phaenomena of the Material World; because they too lead the Soul to its Maker." These are such manifestations of Deity in the cosmic universe as "the Heavens and Heavenly Bodies, the Sun, the Moon, the Stars, and the Immensity of the Universe, and the Motions of Heaven and Earth." To these Dennis added a third group, "Ideas of Sublunary Things; as of the four Elements . . . Winds and Meteors of all sorts, Seas, Rivers, Mountains." All these were the same in kind, if different in the degree to which they aroused the "Enthusiastick Passions," Admiration, Terror, Horror, Joy, Sadness, Desire. Man cannot think of God without "Enthusiastick Terrour," compounded of awe and rapture. The manifestations of God's majesty and power in Nature must evoke in sensitive minds some degree of the awe they feel for God Himself, which is the essence of the Sublime experience. In another passage, Dennis was still more specific in listing the "hints" of "Enthusiastick Terrour," which "express'd in Poetry make that Spirit, that Pas-

mentions Dennis' religious ideas, he makes them secondary, rather than primary. Starting out with his thesis that Dennis was a follower of Hobbes, he finds himself in difficulty when he comes to the problem of religion. He says, pp. 230–231: "The psychology upon which Dennis constructs his theory seems generally to be derived from Hobbes. It is an adaptation not a direct borrowing, however, with some important modifications." Mr. Thorpe is, I think, wrong in the whole passage that follows. Dennis was far from being a follower of Hobbes. Mr. Thorpe has tried to orient him in traditions of thought foreign to Dennis. Dennis was much closer to the Cambridge Platonists in every way. Indeed, his theory of "enthusiasm" goes back ultimately to Henry More, and the psychological attitudes which Mr. Thorpe finds inconsistent with Hobbes—and therefore inconsistent in Dennis—may be much more readily understood if read against the background of Cambridge Platonism.

sion, and that Fire, which so wonderfully please." These sources are: "Gods, Daemons, Hell, Spirits and Souls of Men, Miracles, . . . Thunder, Tempests, raging Seas, Inundations, Torrents, Earthquakes, Volcanos, Monsters, Serpents, Lions, Tygers, Fire, War, Pestilence, Famine." Such ideas, he said, "will be found to be the more terrible, as they have more of religion in them." Meditating upon such "Wonders of the Universe" as exhibit the attributes of the Creator in varying degrees, the soul experiences expansion in some degree as when it meditates upon God Himself.[16]

In these lists is implied an outline of the threefold "Aesthetics of the Infinite" as well as an anticipation of the themes of a new descriptive poetry of the eighteenth century, with the "Terror" and "Horror" of earthquakes, volcanoes, thunder, tempests, raging seas, and mountains. Whatever their descendants in the orgies of Gothic romance, these were noble ideas to Dennis. God and the angels, the glory and immensity of the heavenly bodies, the vastness of the seas and mountains on earth—these were the "extraordinary hints," the causes of the Sublime.[17]

[16] *Grounds of Criticism*, I, 339, 348–351, 361.

[17] Among the many illustrations Dennis offered for what I call the "Aesthetics of the Infinite," I pause over his analysis of *Paradise Lost*, I, 344 ff. He uses the poem to prove that Milton's sublimity came first from "Thoughts and Ideas of God, that are worthy of the Creator," in order to show "that a Poet, who intends to give that Elevation and that Gravity to his Poem, which compose Majesty, can fetch his Ideas from no Object so proper as God." Milton served him well, too, for illustration of his second group of ideas arising from meditation upon the cosmic universe, "the Great Phaenomena of the Material World," which "lead the Soul to its Maker, and shew . . . his eternal Power and Godhead." Here he quoted Milton's descriptions of the Sun and Moon and some passages from the scenes of Creation, adding his own paraphrase of the "Te Deum" to illustrate emotions caused by "the Stars, and the Immensity of the Universe." The third group of ideas—dealing with "the World's Immensity"—Dennis illustrated by one passage from Tasso and two from Milton, contrasting "Heaven's wide Circuit" with "this goodly Frame, this World." Dennis added: "I could here bring Examples of the same kind of Spirit, deriv'd in due Proportion from Ideas of Sublunary

From the time he wrote his *Remarks on "Prince Arthur,"*
Dennis tested the supposed sublimity of contemporary literature
against his own standards and found it wanting. His feeling for
the Ancients was quite different from the position of Sir William
Temple and others in the Battle of the Books. Dennis did not
believe that modern literature was inevitably inferior to ancient
because its authors were living in the old age of the world, incapable of the genius and vigor of youth. The Moderns, he insisted,
had the talent and genius necessary for the highest poetry. Their
trouble was that they had departed from the true wellspring of
great poetry, religion.[18] In his critique of Milton he proved that
modern poetry, if its origin is in religion, can be even greater
than ancient, because Christianity is "higher" than paganism.
As he said in his criticism of Longinus, contemporary poets were
attempting the results of the Sublime without experiencing the
causes. Their lips were moved to a language of "Fury, Rapture,
Transport, Ravishment." But their souls had not been affected.
The passions that moved them—if, indeed, passion moved them

Things; as of the four Elements, Water, Earth, Air, Fire; Winds and
Meteors of all sorts, Seas, Rivers, Mountains; but I am afraid of running
into length, and heaping too many Citations one upon another."

[18] This position, reiterated throughout his critical works, is clearly
expressed in *The Grounds of Criticism in Poetry*, I, 365: "And I have
reason to believe, that one of the principal Reasons that has made the
modern Poetry so contemptible, is, That by divesting it self of Religion,
it is fallen from its Dignity, and its original Nature and Excellence; and
from the greatest Production of the Mind of Man, is dwindled to an
extravagant and a vain Amusement. For the modern Poetry being for
the most part profane, has either very little Spirit; or if it has a great one,
that Spirit is out of Nature, because it bears no manner of Proportion to
the Ideas from which it is forcibly deriv'd, nor the Ideas very often to
the Objects from which they are taken: for as Mr. Waller says,

> "In boundless Verse the Fancy soars too high
> For any Object but the Deity:
> What Mortal can with Heav'n pretend to share
> In the Superlatives of Wise and Fair?
> A meaner Object when with these we grace,
> A Giant Habit on a Dwarf we place."

at all—were "ordinary" Passions. Religious ideas, the true
sources of the Sublime, were "extraordinary Ideas" arousing
"extraordinary Passions," expanding the faculties of man to
their highest pitch, exalting the soul until the poet both thought
and felt beyond the limitations of man.

The word "Soul" was often on Dennis' lips and central to
his theories.[19] It is curious that the seventeenth century, which
invented so many new words for new ideas, did not happen
upon the word *psychology*. With its combination of Greek roots,
it is the very sort of word they liked, and they needed it to
describe the "study of the soul" that had been growing throughout the century, leading men to conceptions of the soul that
would have seemed strange to Aristotle and the Fathers, strange
even to the Elizabethans. Dennis was heir to a new psychology
that had gone farther than that of any preceding age in making
men self-conscious in their attempts to analyze the bases of their
own emotional experiences. The Cartesian shears that had separated "the world out there" from "the mind in here" had laid
upon thoughtful men a burden of discovering how nature affected the mind and how mind knew nature. There are reminiscences in Dennis of all the various founders of the "new
psychology," though his ideas go back less to Bacon, Descartes,
and Locke than to the Cambridge Platonists.

In the psychology Dennis developed in order to explain the
effect of "extraordinary Causes" on the soul, he departed more
than he realized from the neoclassical emphasis upon Reason as
the supreme faculty of man. His contemporaries, he felt, were

---

[19] Cf. *Grounds of Criticism*, I, 340–345: "The more the Soul is mov'd
by its greatest ideas, the greater Opinion it must have of its own Capacities.
. . . From whence it follows, that the greater the Soul is, and the larger
the Capacity, the more will it be mov'd by religious Ideas. . . . Now all
the Ideas of God are such, that the more large and comprehensive the
Soul of a Poet is, and the more it is capable of receiving those Ideas,
the more is it sure to be raised, and filled, and lifted to the Skies with
Wonder."

too much concerned with the exposition of "clear ideas." Nothing was true that was not clear, and the clearer the idea, the more nearly true. If that was all there was to poetry, declared Dennis, the subjects of the poets need be only "Logick and Mathematicks." The appeal of great poetry could not be limited to any one faculty. It must be to all the faculties of the soul. "So that must be the best and noblest Art," he wrote, "that makes the best provision at the same Time for the satisfaction of *all* the Faculties, the Reason, the Passions, the Senses. . . . for the Satisfaction of the whole Man together." [20] Under the stimulus of "extraordinary Ideas," Reason and Passion rise together to new heights, one affecting the other, until the Soul reaches that state of exaltation in which it both thinks more clearly and feels more vehemently than before, responding to stimuli so powerful that they can be comprehended neither by ordinary Reason nor ordinary Passion. The effect of the highest poetry upon the soul, then, is one with that of true religion.

In his early *Remarks on "Prince Arthur"* Dennis made a distinction among three groups of poets: "Cold writers," who lacked "a degree of Fire sufficient to give their animal spirits a sudden and swift agitation"; "Fustian-writers," men who had "Fire" but had not "excellent Organs"; truly great poets who combined "greatness of Mind," "reach of Soul," and "extent of Capacity." In *The Grounds of Criticism in Poetry* he developed the idea in his own terms:

Men are mov'd for two Reasons, either because they have weak Minds and Souls, that are capable of being mov'd by little Objects,

[20] *Advancement and Reformation,* I, 263. Some arts, said Dennis, appeal to only one faculty: "In some of them only Reason finds its Account, as in Logick and Mathematicks. In some of them only Reason and Passion, as in the Ancient Eloquence. . . . In others [e.g., music] the Passions and the Senses are charm'd, while Reason finds little Contentment in them." Only poetry, he insists, "provides in such a sovereign Manner . . . for the Satisfaction of the whole Man together."

and consequently by little and ordinary Ideas; or because they have Greatness of Soul and Capacity, to discern and feel the great ones; for the Enthusiastick Passions being caus'd by the Ideas, it follows, that the more the Soul is capable of receiving Ideas whose Objects are truly great and wonderful, the greater will the enthusiasm be that is caus'd by those Ideas. From whence it follows, that the greater the Soul is, and the larger the Capacity, the more will it be mov'd by religious Ideas.[21]

Using his own peculiar vocabulary and following an earlier psychology, Dennis was saying much that Ruskin said in his chapter "The Pathetic Fallacy." Ruskin had his own three groups: men who perceive truly, because they do not feel; men who perceive wrongly, because they feel too much; and men who perceive rightly in spite of their feelings, "the men who are not poets at all, and the poets of the second order, and the poets of the first." Like Dennis, Ruskin felt it "a sign of higher capacity and stand in the ranks of being, that the emotions should be strong enough to vanquish, partly, the intellect"; but there is "a still grander condition" when the intellect rises with the feeling. He too went a step farther: "However great a man may be, there are always some subjects which *ought* to throw him off his balance; some by which his poor human capacity of thought should be conquered, and brought into the inaccurate and vague state of perception, so that the language of the highest inspiration becomes broken, obscure, and wild in metaphor." Ruskin's Prophets are Dennis' "great" poets, who, looking upon the Heavenly City, approaching near to God Himself, speak a language that seems to their contemporaries broken, obscure, wild in metaphor—a language of hyperbole, "Extravagancy," "Enthusiasm."

The distinction Dennis made throughout his critical works between the Beautiful and the Sublime continued to be the distinction he had felt on his Alpine travels. Beauty was equated

[21] *Grounds of Criticism*, I, 340.

with proportion, with order, with regularity, with the rules. "For Reason is Order, and the Result of Order. And nothing that is Irregular, as far as it is Irregular, ever was, or ever can be either Natural or Reasonable." So on his travels he had found Beauty in Nature: "The prospect of Hills and Valleys, or flowry Meads, and murmuring Streams" produced "a delight that is consistent with Reason." In sharp contrast was the unprecedented emotion of the Alpine pass, "unusual Transports that were mingled with horrour, and sometimes with despair." To Dennis the Sublime was not a "higher Beauty"; it was completely antithetic to Beauty [22] and could be expressed only in "Extravagancies";

[22] On this problem there is disagreement among modern scholars. Mr. Monk says in *The Sublime* (New York, 1935), p. 54: "His interest in the sublime, with its powerful emotions and overwhelming effects, left him no time to consider the beautiful, or to make the inevitable separation of the two categories. As a matter of fact, his sublime is simply the highest beauty, not a separate experience, different from one's perception of the beautiful. The distinction of first establishing the sublime as a separate category, is due to Addison, although he may not have realized the significance of what he had done." Mr. Hooker, after consideration of this passage of Mr. Monk's, writes in the introduction to the second volume of Dennis' *Critical Essays* (II, xcv–xcvi): "It is true that in a few passages, Dennis seems to suggest that the enthusiastic passion is distinguished from ordinary passions rather by intensity than by quality. And although he clearly recognized the object of enthusiastic passion as the sublime, he did not explicitly define the object of ordinary passion in art as the beautiful. Yet he carefully distinguished the different sources of the two kinds of passion, and he tried to define the peculiar quality, contributed by reflection, which made the enthusiastic unlike the ordinary esthetic emotions. By implication at least he acknowledged two separate categories. And in a letter written in 1717, he attached names to the categories: the *pulchrum* describes the experience in which enthusiastic passion (or passion colored by reflection) is involved, and the *dulce* describes that in which ordinary passion is involved. The categories existed in Dennis' critical thought before Addison designated them as the sublime and beautiful." Mr. Hooker further discusses the distinction in I, 508, 516, II, 524.

Mr. Hooker seems to me closer to the truth than Mr. Monk. In my treatment of Dennis' conception of beauty in this study, I have necessarily had to limit myself to only a few aspects of that difficult problem, but I believe that Dennis throughout his life felt a sharp distinction between what he called Beauty and what we call the Sublime.

in it Dennis found the appeal of the highest poetry, because its basis was in religion, in God Himself.

III

Anthony Ashley Cooper, third Earl of Shaftesbury, was born in the year during which Burnet made his Alpine journey. In 1686, two years earlier than Dennis, he himself made the Grand Tour. The *Sacred Theory* had appeared in 1681 and 1684. Although Shaftesbury's mountain rhapsody in *The Moralists* was not published until 1709, the reminiscences are such that he might have set them down in 1686 in a journal-letter such as Dennis wrote:

But behold! through a vast tract of sky before us, the mighty Atlas rears his lofty head covered with snow above the clouds. Beneath the mountain's foot the rocky country rises into hills, a proper basis of the ponderous mass above, where huge embodied rocks lie piled on one another, and seem to prop the high arch of heaven. . . . See! with what trembling steps poor mankind tread the narrow brink of the deep precipices, from whence with giddy horror they look down, mistrusting even the ground which bears them, whilst they hear the hollow sound of torrents underneath, and see the ruin of the impending rock, with falling trees which hang with their roots upwards and seem to draw more ruin after them. Here thoughtless men, seized with the newness of such objects, become thoughtful, and willingly contemplate the incessant changes of this earth's surface. They see, as in one instant, the revolutions of past ages, the fleeting forms of things, and the decay even of this our globe, whose youth and first formation they consider, whilst the apparent spoil and irreparable breaches of the wasted mountain show them the world itself only as a noble ruin, and make them think of its approaching period.[23]

[23] *The Moralists: A Philosophical Rhapsody* appeared in 1709 and was republished in 1711 as Treatise V of *Characteristicks of Men, Manners, Opinions, Times, etc.* I have used the edition of *Characteristics* edited by John M. Robertson (London, 1900), II, 122 ff.

"Mighty Atlas" takes the place of the Alpine summit of Burnet and of Dennis. The scene is otherwise identical, with its huge embodied rocks and hollow sound of torrents. So is the reaction of the travelers, seized with giddy horror, mistrusting the ground they walk on, led by new experience with vast and wild Nature to meditate upon the ruins of a world.

"Mid-way the mountain" the travelers found themselves in a thick wood of evergreen "whose towering heads seem endless in the sky." In a gloom almost as dark as night, Shaftesbury's pagan travelers meditated:

And here a different horror seizes our sheltered travellers when they see the day diminished by the deep shades of the vast wood, which, closing thick above, spreads darkness and eternal night below. The faint and gloomy light looks horrid as the shade itself; and the profound stillness of these places imposes silence upon men, struck with the hoarse echoings of every sound within the spacious caverns of the wood. Here space astonishes; silence itself seems pregnant, whilst an unknown force works on the mind, and dubious objects move the wakeful sense. Mysterious voices are either heard or fancied, and various forms of deity seem to present themselves and appear more manifest in these sacred silvan scenes, such as of old gave rise to temples and favoured the religion of the ancient world. Even we ourselves, who in plain characters may read divinity from so many bright parts of earth, choose rather these obscurer places to spell out that mysterious being, which to our weak eyes at best appears under a veil of cloud.

"Space astonishes," but it did not terrify Theocles as it had terrified Pascal. Rather it led to thoughts of God. Shaftesbury's characters were pagans, but whether among pagans or Christians, Shaftesbury implies, human imagination rises from the vast in terrestrial Nature to conceptions of Deity, each man in his own way seeking to "spell out the mysterious being" when he feels himself in the shadow of Infinity.

The mountain scene in *The Moralists* is an episode in an imaginary tour of the universe on which Theocles conducted his pupil, Philocles. Like Young's later mentor in the *Night Thoughts*, Theocles had found his student unconvinced by intellectual arguments of the existence of God. Classical and Christian apologetics made little appeal to intellect, none to the emotions. As Young's Lorenzo found through a series of cosmic voyages the "Consolation" that canceled the "Complaint," so Philocles' conversion came about through stimulation of the imagination as he gradually realized the vastness of nature in the cosmic and terrestrial worlds. In the most familiar section of *The Moralists* we find again the threefold "Aesthetics of the Infinite." Shaftesbury begins with God:

Thy being is boundless, unsearchable, impenetrable. In thy immensity all thought is lost, fancy gives over its flight, and wearied imagination spends itself in vain, finding no coast nor limit of this ocean, nor, in the widest tract through which it soars, one point yet nearer the circumference than the first centre whence it parted. Thus having oft essayed, thus sallied forth into the wide expanse, when I return again within myself, struck with the sense of this so narrow being and of the fulness of that immense one, I dare no more behold the amazing depths nor sound the abyss of Deity.[24]

The second stimulus to the imagination comes from the cosmic universe, as master and pupil take their imaginary way through interstellar space, discovering worlds beyond worlds. Not even the heavens of the telescope were vast enough for a superabundant Deity, never satisfied to limit creation in either time or space:

Besides the neighboring planets what multitudes of fixed stars did we see sparkle not an hour ago in the clear night, which yet had hardly yielded to the day? How many others are discovered by the help of art! Crowded as they seem, their distance from each other is as unmeasurable by art as is the distance between them and us. Whence we are naturally taught the immensity of that being who, through these immense spaces, has disposed such an infinity of bodies, belonging each (as we may well presume) to systems as complete as our own world, since even the smallest spark of this bright galaxy may vie with this our sun, which shining now full out, gives us new life, exalts our spirits, and makes us feel divinity more present.[25]

By means of an apostrophe to the sun, Theocles returns his pupil from the heavens to "this man-container" earth, which at first seems to have shrunk into insignificance in comparison with the greater planets of our own system, the vaster planets of an indefinite universe:

Yet is this mansion-globe, this man-container, of a much narrower compass even than other its fellow-wanderers of our system. How narrow then must it appear compared with the capacious system of its own sun? And how narrow, or as nothing, in respect of those innumerable systems of other suns? [26]

But as we turn the glass and see the geocosm from another point of view, "how immense a body it seems compared with ours of human form, a borrowed remnant of its varible and oft-converted surface." The new lessons he had learned from Space, the shadow of God, Philocles found repeated in the terrestrial earth which, tiny in comparison with the heavens, was becoming vaster than ever before in the imaginations of eighteenth-century men. As master and student turn from their cosmic voyage to a Grand Tour of the world, they discover that "a globe far off" now seems indeed "a boundless continent." Upon wings of fancy the travelers fly "through different climates, from pole to pole, and from the frigid to the torrid zone." First they visit "the darkest and most imperfect parts of our map," where they find "horrors" of the day and night, a sea "immured in walls of crystal," freezing winds that never weary, sea monsters as awesome as Kepler's fantastic denizens of the lunar world. From

[25] *Ibid.*, pp. 112–113.   [26] *Ibid.*, p. 114.

the Arctic they fly to the tropics, where they are astonished at the extreme light and heat of the sun that "confounds weak-sighted mortals, pierced by his scorching beams." Everywhere they find a Nature superabundant, diverse, various, evidence of a God of Plenitude who creates all possible varieties of existence, creates indeed every possible thing except the "ugly" and the "evil." The arctic monster, the dubious species that drink the slimy stream are no more evil than the deserts Lucretius had called waste places in the world:

All ghastly and hideous as they appear, they want not their peculiar beauties. The wildness pleases. We seem to live alone with Nature. We view her in her inmost recesses, and contemplate her with more delight in these original wilds than in the artificial labyrinths and feigned wildernesses of the palace. The objects of the place, the scaly serpents, the savage beasts, and poisonous insects, how terrible soever, or how contrary to human nature, are beauteous in themselves, and fit to raise our thoughts in admiration of that divine wisdom, so far superior to our short views. Unable to declare the use or service of all things in this universe, we are yet assured of the perfection of all, and of the justice of that economy to which all things are subservient, and in respect of which things seemingly deformed are amiable, disorder becomes regular, corruption whole-some, and poisons (such as these we have seen) prove healing and beneficial.[27]

We have come a long way from Sir Thomas Browne with his simple defense of monstrosity.

Shaftesbury's journey in *The Moralists* follows the structure of the "cosmic voyage" he had inherited from the seventeenth century and anticipates the "terrestrial excursion" of poets like David Mallet and James Thomson. The vastness of God, earlier read over into the vastness of cosmic Space, is now reflected in the vastness of a world, filled with all possible variety, a world as engrossing to human imagination as the cosmic heavens had

[27] *Ibid.*, p. 122.

been. Theocles had accomplished his purpose. "Philocles, the cold indifferent Philocles, is become a pursuer of the same mysterious beauty." "Beauty . . . and good with you, Theocles," confessed Philocles, "I perceive are still one and the same."

As Theocles concluded his ecstatic description of the cosmic and terrestrial worlds, his vocabulary changed. Philocles remarked: "I could easily find that we were come to an end of our descriptions, and that whether I would or no, Theocles was now resolved to take his leave of the sublime." [28] The word *sublime* was so seldom on Shaftesbury's lips that it surprises. When he used it at all, it was usually with disparagement. His careful avoidance of the term to describe either the grandness of Nature, the emotions it evoked, or the style in which those

---

[28] Except on this one occasion Shaftesbury did not use the word *sublime* about the style of the lyrical passage in *The Moralists*. When he had occasion to refer to it he called it *enthusiastic*. Distinction between this style and the more conversational tone of the rest of the dialogue is usually implied by contrast, as when Philocles says (II, 124), "Methinks, said he (*changing to a more familiar voice*)." Shaftesbury, as I have said, used the term *sublime* so infrequently that Robertson in his edition entered it only twice in the Index. With the exception of the one quoted from *The Moralists* all the uses of the term I have noticed occur in discussion of early styles. In a passage in *Advice to an Author*, it has a general meaning (I, 157): "So that to deny *the common and natural sense of a sublime and beautiful*, will seem an affectation merely, to any one who considers duly of this affair." Elsewhere he uses the word with some contempt. Referring to Marcus Aurelius, he said (I, 165): "He shows us that this first-formed comedy and scheme of ludicrous wit was introduced upon the neck of the Sublime." Again he wrote (I, 168): "Though every other style and genuine matter of composition has its order and method . . . the sublime can no way condescend thus, or bear to be suspended in its impetuous course." The *sublime style*, he implies, was in primitive times almost as lacking in order and method as the "comic and derisory manner." Again he noted (I, 169): "As for the Sublime, though it be often the subject of criticism, it can never be the manner or afford the means. The way of form and method, the didactic or perceptive manner, as it has been usually practised amongst us, and as our ears have been long accustomed, has so little force towards the winning our attention, that it is apter to tire us than the metre of an old ballad."

emotions were expressed was, I think, deliberate. With "the Sublime" (when he used the term, Shaftesbury usually wrote it so) of contemporary rhetoric Shaftesbury had no sympathy. *Sublime*, he insisted, was a rhetorical term used in early times to describe a primitive form of literature, a form appealing only to children or barbarians. Discussing various literary types, he wrote:

'Tis easy to imagine that, amidst the several styles and manners of discourse or writing, *the easiest attained and earliest practised was the miraculous, the pompous, or what we generally call the sublime.* Astonishment is of all other passions the easiest raised in raw and unexperienced mankind. Children in their earliest infancy are entertained in this manner; and the known way of pleasing such as these is to make them wonder, and lead the way for them in this passion by a feigned surprise at the miraculous objects we set before them. The best music of barbarians is hideous and astonishing sounds. And the fine sights of Indians are enormous figures, various odd and glaring colours, and whatever of that sort is amazingly beheld with a kind of horror and consternation.[29]

Shaftesbury's "Sublime" was not Longinian. Indeed Longinus' name appears in his works so infrequently that a modern editor did not find it necessary to include it in his index. To Shaftesbury the true "Sublime" was not a rhetorical principle. Its source was not in style, but in God and in the manifestations of Deity in the superabundance and diversity of His cosmic and terrestrial works. Rebelling against a word that was coming to cast a hypnotic spell upon his contemporaries, Shaftesbury like Dennis deliberately chose terms that were even more dangerous: "enthusiasm" and "enthusiastic."

The term *enthusiasm* had suffered degeneration throughout the seventeenth century as it became associated with the religious melancholy of fanaticism. It had grown apace among various sects, particularly among lower-class preachers who boasted of

[29] *Advice to an Author*, in *Characteristics*, I, 157. Italics are mine.

being inspired by "the God within." In 1656 Henry More had published his *Enthusiasmus Triumphatus*. His subtitle, *A Brief Discourse of the Nature, Causes, Kinds, and Cure of Enthusiasm*, reminded his generation, as More intended, of the long title of Burton's *Anatomy of Melancholy*.[30] More was writing an anatomy of religious melancholy. "Enthusiasm," More said at the beginning of his work, "is nothing else but a misconceit of being *inspired*. Now to be inspired is, *to be moved in an extraordinary manner of the power or spirit of God to act, speak, or think what is holy, just and true*. From hence it will be easily understood what *Enthusiasm* is, viz., *A full, but false persuasion in a Man that he is inspir'd*." Yet as we have seen, Henry More was a natural "enthusiast" who knew that "Enthusiasm" could be a noble word. He ended his account with tribute to the true and exalted state:

There has not one word all this while been spoken against that *true* and *warrantable Enthusiasm* of devout and holy Souls, who are so strangely transported in that vehement *Love* they bear towards God, and that unexpressible *Joy* and *Peace* they find in him. For they are modest enough and sober enough in all this, they witnessing no other thing to the world, than what others may experience in themselves, and what is plainly set down in the holy Scriptures, That *the Kingdom of God is Righteousness, and Peace and Joy in the Holy Ghost*. . . .

What I have said in behalf of Christians, is in its measure due to those diviner sort of Philosophers, such as Plato and Plotinus, whom you shall find, upon the more than ordinary sensible visits of the divine Love and Beauty descending into their enravished Souls profess themselves no less moved. . . . To such Enthusiasm as this, which is but the triumph of the Soul of man inebriated, as

[30] Burton's title in the first edition of 1621 was *The Anatomy of Melancholy: What It Is, with All the Kindes, Causes, Symptomes, Prognostickes, and Severall Cures of It*. My references to More's work are to the edition published at London in 1712, when it appeared bound with More's *Immortality of the Soul*. The quotation is from p. 2. Italics are More's.

it were, with the delicious sense of the divine life, that blessed Root and Original of all holy wisdom and virtue, I must declare my self as much a friend, as I am to the vulgar fanatical Enthusiasm a professed Enemy.[31]

Dennis had used the terms *enthusiasm* and *enthusiastic* in their literal sense without apology. But the words had come to be even more suspect in 1709, when Shaftesbury published *The Moralists*, because of Swift's *Tale of a Tub* in which he had turned invective against all the enthusiasms of his day. In the *Letter concerning Enthusiasm*, which Shaftesbury wrote in 1708, his mood of wit against false enthusiasms reflected Swift. But, like More, Shaftesbury ended his essay by considering true inspiration:

Nor can divine inspiration, by its outward marks, be readily distinguished from it. For inspiration is a real feeling of the Divine Presence, and enthusiasm a false one. But the passion they raise is much alike. For when the mind is taken up in vision, and fixes its view either on any real object, or mere spectre of divinity; when it sees, or thinks it sees, anything prodigious, and more than human; its horror, delight, confusion, fear, admiration, or whatever passion belongs to it, or is uppermost on this occasion, will have something vast, *immane*, and (as painters say) beyond life.[32]

He continued in words with which both More and Dennis would have agreed: "Something there will be of extravagance and fury, when the ideas or images are too big for the narrow human vessel to contain. So that inspiration may be justly called divine enthusiasm." His *Letter* concluded with a statement that "having, after all, in some measure justified enthusiasm," he "owned" the word. As a Christian Platonist, he henceforth used the term which had fallen into disrepute but which in itself "signifies divine presence, and was made use of by the philosopher whom the earliest Chris-

[31] *Enthusiasmus Triumphatus*, pp. 45, 54.
[32] *A Letter concerning Enthusiasm*, in *Characteristics*, I, 37-38.

tian Fathers called divine, to express whatever was sublime in human passions."

In the last sections of *The Moralists*, Shaftesbury used the word "to express whatever was sublime in human passions," carrying it over from religion to describe the emotions evoked by Nature in the universe and in the world. Words indeed govern understanding, as Shaftesbury's youthful Philocles discovered when he realized that he had been responding to the temper of the times in refusing to acknowledge his own response to Nature because of contemporary connotations of disparagement attached to the word *enthusiasm*. "All those who are deep in this romantic way," he said to Theocles, "are looked upon, you know, as a people either plainly out of their wits, or overrun with melancholy and enthusiasm. . . . And I must own that often when I have found my fancy run this way, I have checked myself, not knowing what it was possessed me, when I was passionately struck with objects of this kind." "Tell me, I entreat you," he continued, "how comes it that, excepting a few philosophers of your sort, the only people who are enamoured in this way, and seek the woods, the rivers, or seashores, are your poor vulgar lovers?" This Theocles denied. "Enthusiasm" had been the inspiration of true religion and of true philosophy. Is it not the same with poets and with all those other students in Nature and the arts which copy after her? In short, is not this the real case of all "who are lovers of the Muses or the Graces?" Poets, philosophers, virtuosi, and the truly religious—all share true "Enthusiasm." The last of his neoclassical scruples satisfied, Philocles gladly adopted the only word that could describe emotions he had long felt but repressed. He made his confession of faith:

You have indeed made good your part of the condition, and may now claim me for a proselyte. If there be any seeming extravagance in the case I must comfort myself the best I can, and consider that all sound love and admiration is enthusiasm. "The Transports of poets, the sublime of orators, the rapture of musicians, the high strains of the virtuosi—all mere enthusiasm! Even learning itself, the love of arts and curiosities, the spirit of travellers and adventurers, gallantry, war, heroism—all, all enthusiasm!" 'Tis enough; I am content to be this new enthusiast in a way unknown to me before.[33]

Theocles replied: "And I am content you should call this love of ours enthusiasm, allowing it the privilege of its fellow-passions."

Enthusiasm and *enthusiastic* were words Shaftesbury shared with Dennis. Shaftesbury did not use them to excess, as did Dennis, in part because he was a more graceful stylist, deftly choosing synonyms and antonyms, in part because the "vast" did not overwhelm him, as it did Dennis. There are similarities between these two first apostles of the non-Longinian Sublime in England, and there are great differences. To both, Infinite God was the true source of the Sublime. Dennis' God, however, was a God of Power, in the presence of whose works man felt exultation and fear. There is almost no terror in Shaftesbury's universe, and no more than natural awe in his attitude toward Deity. His was a God of benignity and goodness, delighting in creation, pouring out before his children more than they could ever need.

In the works and wonders of Almighty Power, as on the mountain pass, Dennis felt "delightful Horrour," "terrible Joy," "Transports that were mingled with Horrour, and sometimes with despair." His imagination was roused and stirred and stimulated. The Sublime did not astound and overwhelm Shaftesbury; it stilled and quieted; in a word used by one of the contemporary poets it "serened." To Dennis the categories of Sublime and Beautiful remained as distinct as they had been to Burnet. But in Shaftesbury's experience the Beautiful and the Sublime had not been antipathetic, nor were they in his aesthetic system. Irregularity was as natural to Nature as regularity:

'Tis true, said I, Theocles, I own it. Your genius, the genius of the place, and the Great Genius have at last prevailed. I shall no longer

33 *The Moralists*, II, 129.

resist the passion growing in me for things of a natural kind, where neither art nor the conceit or caprice of man has spoiled their genuine order by breaking in upon the primitive state. Even the rude rocks, the mossy caverns, the irregular unwrought grottos and broken falls of waters, with all the horrid graces of the wilderness itself, as representing Nature more, will be the more engaging, and appear with a magnificence beyond the mockery of princely gardens.[34]

Insofar as Shaftesbury distinguished between the Beautiful and the Sublime, the Sublime was a higher, a more majestic Beauty. It was a power "which naturally captivates the heart, and raises the imagination to an opinion or conceit of something majestic and divine. . . . We cannot help being transported with the thought of it. It inspires us with something more than ordinary, and raises us above ourselves." All Beauty calls forth admiration, but the more majestic Beauty evokes a deeper feeling. As "we can admire nothing profoundly without a certain religious veneration," we feel the most profound admiration in the presence of objects that lead us closer to the First Good and First Beauty, God. Different in various ways, Dennis and Shaftesbury agreed that the true source of the Sublime is in God and in great ideas which raise the soul of man to thoughts of infinity.

IV

Three years after the first edition of *The Moralists* and a year after it had been reprinted with *Characteristicks*, Addison published in the *Spectator* his *Pleasures of the Imagination*. Addison knew the Longinian tradition well and recognized its importance more sympathetically than either Dennis or Shaftesbury, but even more clearly than they he distinguished between the "rhetorical" and the "natural" Sublime. He showed that the "natural Sublime" afforded what he called the "primary pleasure of the

---

[34] *Ibid.*, II, 125. Edward Niles Hooker discusses *enthusiasm* as an integral part of the Sublime in his edition of Dennis, *Critical Works*, II, 515–516.

imagination" while the pleasures of the "rhetorical Sublime" were "secondary." For the first time he made into a coherent system the two Sublimes that had been developing in parallel.

It would be interesting to determine the date of the earliest draft of the *Pleasures of the Imagination* [35] and compare it with the finished version in the *Spectator* of 1712. Were Addison's ideas of "the great" in his mind even during his university days? To what extent did they change or develop as a result of his foreign travel? Even without that knowledge, however, I think it is possible to show that in his interpretation of the psychological

[35] In 1864 J. Dykes Campbell published a manuscript version of the *Pleasures of the Imagination: Some Portions of Essays Contributed to the Spectator by Mr. Joseph Addison;* privately printed in Glasgow. The manuscript is now in the Houghton Library of Harvard University (MS Eng. 772). Since I have not examined it myself, I quote from a Master's essay written at Columbia University in 1954 by Mark Halpern: "Three distinct hands are visible in the MS. The bulk of the text is in very legible print-like hand which at first caused some speculation that it might be Pope's (see the *Publisher's Circular* XXVII, 1 Sept. 1864, pp. 471–2); the second is in what is generally regarded as Addison's normal writing hand, and the third has not yet been satisfactorily identified." Mr. Halpern points out that the most authoritative statement about the manuscript is still that made by Sir Frederic Madden, head of the Manuscript Department of the British Museum from 1837, whose opinion was quoted by J. Dykes Campbell in a letter published in the *Athenaeum,* November 19, 1864. On the problem of the third hand, Sir Frederic reached only negative conclusions. He said, "The latter is certainly not Steele's (as suggested in the *Publisher's Circular*), nor Tickell's, nor Charles Montagu's." So far as the printed hand is concerned, Sir Frederic wrote: "The further suggestion that the print-like hand is Pope's appeared at first probable; but after a careful comparison of this writing with Pope's printing hand among the papers of his translation of the Iliad, I feel obliged to decide in the negative. On the other hand, the notion that these print-like pages contain the Essays in their first state from the hand of Addison himself is entitled to much consideration." Sir Frederic based his conclusion not only upon similarities between the manuscript and Addison's printing hand but also upon the paper, which as he pointed out was a kind contemporaneous with Addison, usually found in official books, a kind of paper Addison might have used after his appointment as Commissioner of Appeals in 1704.

effect of "greatness" on the imagination Addison was carrying on the philosophical and scientific heritage of the seventeenth century into which he was born and in which he lived out more than half his brief life.

His earliest printed work shows his interest in the new philosophy. Among his compositions was a student exercise, delivered at the Sheldonian Theatre at Oxford when Addison was twenty-one years old. His *Oration in Praise of the New Philosophy* [36] was a minor skirmish in the war between Ancient and Modern, a little sally in the Battle of the Books, in which the youthful Addison took his stand with the Moderns, defending "new philosophy" in general and Descartes in particular. "How long, gentlemen of the University," asked the youthful disputant, "shall we slavishly tread in the steps of the ancients, and be afraid of being wiser than our ancestors?" Then with a bow to "the great ornament of the present age," Newton,[37] who had tran-

[36] The original Latin text is given by A. C. Guthkelch in Joseph Addison, *Miscellaneous Works* (London, 1914), II, 466–469, with a note that the text is from *Theatri Oxoniensis Encaenia, Sive Comitia Philologica, Julii 7, Anno 1693, Celebrata Oxonii, E Theatro Sheldoniano, An. Dom. MDCXCIII*. Richard Hurd published it in the *Works of the Right Honourable Joseph Addison* (London, 1856), VI, 607–612. He added a translation by Richard Rawlinson. It also appeared in translation appended to the second edition of Fontenelle's *Plurality of Worlds*, translated by W. Gardiner (London, 1728). My references are to the Hurd edition.

I suspect that the young author "lifted" a good deal of his oration from the *Plurality of Worlds*, which remained a favorite of his as frequent references in the *Spectator* show. If in the passage quoted (Hurd ed., VI, 607) we read "Copernicus" with Fontenelle, rather than "Descartes" with Addison, we will find a neat student paraphrase of the French author.

[37] This reference to "praeclarum aetatis hujusce specimen" was to produce a curious result. An early editor added a footnote that the reference was to Newton, as it undoubtedly was, since the *Principia*, published in 1687, immediately made Newton "the great ornament of the present age." A later editor gave the English translation the title "An Oration in Defence of the New (or Newtonian) Philosophy," which is entirely misleading, as, except for the one passing reference to Newton, Addison is talking of the Cartesian world scheme.

scended all the Ancients, Addison launched into his defense of modern scientific philosophy:

At length arose Cartesius, a happier genius, who has bravely asserted the truth against the united force of all opposers. . . . A great man indeed he was, and the only one we envy France. He solved the difficulties of the universe, almost as well as if he had been its architect. He destroyed those orbs of glass which the whims of antiquity had fixed above, brought to light that troop of forms till then unknown, and has almost extinguished the element of fire. . . . This philosopher scorned to be any longer bounded within the straits and crystalline walls of an Aristotelic world; no, his delight is to search the regions beyond, to discover new suns, and new worlds, which lay hid among the stars. . . .

Here we have not only new heavens opened to us, but we look down on our earth; this philosophy affords us several kinds of animals; where, by the help of the microscope, our eyes are so far assisted, that we may discern the productions of the smallest creatures while we consider with a curious eye the animated particles of matter, and behold with astonishment the reptile mountains of living atoms.[38]

Here we find Addison, like so many of his contemporaries, showing the impact upon literary imagination of new universes discovered by telescope and microscope, enthralled by the new "Nature" that had emerged from new science. Addison's feeling for the vastness of space is clear. No matter that he attributed the idea of infinity to Descartes—it was his heritage from the tradition of the seventeenth century which had "scorned to be any longer bounded within the straits and crystalline walls of an Aristotelic world." Addison's temperament in youth placed him among the "soaring souls" who found liberation for the imagination in the "vast."

[38] In associating microscopial discoveries with Descartes, Addison was thinking of the *Dioptrics* and of Descartes's other important work on optics that lay behind the rapid development of lenses. Addison's continued interest in the "philosophy" of the microscope is shown in many essays in both the *Tatler* and the *Spectator*.

When Addison set out on the Grand Tour in 1699, he was better prepared for experience with grand Nature than Burnet had been. He had been a student at the Charterhouse, of which Burnet was Master. He was familiar with the *Sacred Theory* and had been impressed by it, as we know from the fact that he had recently published his Latin ode in honor of Burnet.[39] Nevertheless, Addison was as much conditioned by his classical training and his literary heritage as earlier travelers like Evelyn. Like many later tourists, he started on his travels self-consciously, armed with an anthology of the "best selections" from authors who had described the scenes he expected to see. Addison had made his own collection, chiefly from the Latin poets, many of whom he quoted in his *Remarks on Several Parts of Italy*, which he published in 1705.[40]

The three categories he developed in the *Pleasures of the Im-*

[39] This ode was published during the year in which Addison set out on the Grand Tour: "Ad D. Tho. Burnettum" in *Musarum Anglicanarum Analecta* (Oxford, 1699), a volume which also contained two other Latin poems by Addison written on scientific subjects. According to Guthkelch (Addison, *Miscellaneous Works*, I, 282) it had first been printed in *Examen Poeticum Duplex* in 1698. The later version differs in several lines, particularly in the first and last stanzas. Both Latin and English versions were printed with the edition of Burnet's *Sacred Theory of the Earth* that appeared in 1715; the English version is to be found also in some of the later editions of Burnet.

[40] In the preface to his *Remarks on Several Parts of Italy* Addison said: "I have taken care to consider the passages of the ancient poets which have any relation to the places or curiosities that I met with; for before I entered on my voyage, I took care to refresh my memory among classical authors, and to make such collections out of them as I might afterwards have occasion for." He frequently illustrated his "remarks" by quotations from the Latin Poets and sometimes diverted himself by translating them into English verse. See, for instance, his translation from Lucan describing the Apennines, in the edition of the *Remarks on Several Parts of Italy* in *Works*, edited by George Washington Green (New York, 1854), II, 330–331. Although Addison could find satisfactory quotations from the Romans for most of the scenery he saw, he apparently could find few for mountain districts. Several he used are from Silius Italicus.

agination were already at least vaguely in his mind, for he had much to say of the "beautiful," the "great" and the "uncommon." The familiar principles of "variety" and "diversity" appear frequently in the *Remarks*. The "broken and interrupted scene" near the Roman Campagna was "an infinite variety of hills, groves and valleys." He was charmed by the "variety of beautiful mountains near Geneva" and considered "the pleasantest voyage in the world" one that followed the windings of a river "through such a variety of pleasing scenes as the course of it naturally led us." [41]

Casual references to mountains are abundant in the *Remarks*. Addison's vocabulary is usually the conventional one of the period: "the rude prospect of rocks rising one above another"; "vast heaps of mountains . . . thrown together with so much irregularity and confusion"; "a confusion of mountains and hollows." Like other travelers, he had had his moments of vertigo. He wrote to Edward Wortley from Geneva on December 9, 1701:

I am just now arriv'd at Geneva by a very troublesome Journey over the Alps, where I have bin for some days together shivering among the Eternal Snows. My head is still Giddy with mountains and precipices, and you can't Imagine how much I am pleas'd with the sight of a Plain that is as agreeable to me at present as a Shore was about a year ago after our Tempest at Genoa. [42]

A "near prospect of the Alps" at Geneva led him momentarily to a vocabulary reminiscent of Burnet: "The Alps . . . are broken into so many steps and precipices, that they fill the mind with an agreeable kind of horror, and form one of the most irregular, mis-shapen scenes in the world." [43]

Like many contemporary travelers, he was particularly pleased with "prospects." Ill at ease when mountains pressed too close,

[41] *Remarks*, ed. by Greene, pp. 217, 269, 305, 339, 274.
[42] Addison, *Letters*, ed. by Walter Graham (Oxford, 1941), p. 30.
[43] *Remarks*, pp. 339–340.

naturally fearful of immediate danger, he felt imagination expand when he reached a summit. He left no comment written, as was Dennis' journal-letter, immediately after the experience. His *Remarks*, like his reminiscences in the *Pleasures of the Imagination*, were emotions recollected in tranquillity.[44] But that Addison, like Dennis and Shaftesbury, was led to thoughts of Infinity by grand Nature was shown in reflections upon that "Tempest at Genoa," about which he wrote Wortley. "Of all objects that I have ever seen," he wrote in *Spectator* 489, "there is none which affects my imagination so much as the sea or ocean." Even when it was calm, "the heavings of this prodigious bulk of waters" caused "a very pleasing astonishment," but

when it is worked up in a tempest, so that the horizon on every side is nothing but foaming billows and floating mountains, it is impossible to describe the agreeable horror that rises from such a prospect. A troubled ocean, to a man who sails upon it, is, I think, the biggest object that he can see in motion, and consequently gives his imagination one of the highest kinds of pleasure that can arise from greatness. I must confess, it is impossible for me to survey this world of fluid matter, without thinking on the hand that first poured it out, and made a proper channel for its reception. Such an object naturally raises in my thoughts the idea of an Almighty Being, and convinces me of his existence as much as a metaphysical demonstration. The imagination prompts the under-

---

[44] In *Tatler* 161 Addison described a vivid dream in which were many reminiscences of his mountain experiences: "I fancied myself among the Alps, and, as it is natural in a dream, seemed every moment to bound from one summit to another, till at last, after having made this airy progress over the tops of several mountains, I arrived at the very centre of those broken rocks and precipices. I here, methought, saw a prodigious circuit of hills, that reached above the clouds, and encompassed a large space of ground, which I had a great curiosity to look into. I thereupon continued my former way of travelling through a great variety of winter scenes, till I had gained the top of these white mountains, which seemed another Alps of snow. I looked down from hence into a spacious plain, which was surrounded on all sides by this mound of hills, and which presented me with the most agreeable prospect I had ever seen."

standing and by the greatness of the sensible objects, produces in it the idea of a Being who is neither circumscribed by time nor space.

Here, as in his Genevan experience, Addison felt "an agreeable kind of horror," but Dennis' "terrible Joy" is lacking, as is Dennis' language of "extravagancy." Perhaps Addison had been better prepared than Dennis for his Alpine experience by what had already become a "Burnet tradition." Perhaps the difference lay in Addison's cooler temperament that led him to eschew both excessive emotion and a vocabulary of excess. So far as we can judge by the *Remarks*, the "vast" never overwhelmed Addison as it did Dennis. The "pathetic" plays little or no part in his "Sublime," which caused serenity rather than suffering. The majestic aspects of nature, the mountains and ocean, "filled" his imagination—but not to overflowing. But we shall better understand Addison's differences from Dennis when we have considered the system he developed.

Like Burnet and Dennis, Addison attempted to explain his impressions to himself. Although his manuscript notebook cannot be dated with certainty, there is reason to believe that he was working on one version of the *Pleasures of the Imagination* as early as 1704. Comparison of the two manuscripts and the published version [45] show that it was a project on which Addison

[45] My references to the *Spectator* are to be found in Joseph Addison, *Works*, edited by G. W. Greene (New York, 1857), vol. VI. As published, the essays are equally divided between the two kinds of pleasure. There are five on the "primary" pleasures (411–415 inclusive) and five on the "secondary" pleasures (416–420 inclusive). Essay 421 serves as conclusion to both sets. Addison's manuscript version lacks the first three and one-half paragraphs of Essay 411. It begins with the words "Prospect delights ye Soul as much as a Demonstration." The fifth and sixth paragraphs and the first part of the seventh do not appear, nor does the eighth paragraph. Comparison of the two versions shows that the essays on the "primary" pleasures, as published, remained close to the originals though there are some suggestive later additions (and a few omissions, none of them significant). But the essays on the "secondary" pleasures in the manuscript

worked carefully, deleting, adding, changing the text as his ideas developed. Originally he had not intended such an extensive series of essays as he published, in which he devoted almost equal space to the "primary" and the "secondary" pleasures of imagination. His concern in the earlier version had been with the "primary pleasures"—those "which arise from the actual view and survey of outward objects." The "secondary pleasures" (which do not come directly from sense impressions, but are called up by literary descriptions, pictures, or other means) he dismissed much more briefly, saying: "We have already consider'd the first part of this division, & shall therefore *have no occasion to stay long upon ye Second, which ha's, as we shall see, so great a dependence on ye former*." [46] The second group of essays was evidently "secondary" to Addison in more senses than one. His reason for including them would seem to have been to show the dependence of critical ideas upon the "primary" pleasures which man receives directly from Nature.

"By the pleasures of imagination," Addison said in the first essay, *Spectator* 411, "I here mean such as arise from visible objects. . . . We cannot, indeed, have a single image in the fancy that did not make its first entrance through the sight." Addison considered that he was doing something "entirely new"

---

are sketchy; in Dykes Campbell's printed book they occupy five and one-half pages, in contrast to at least a dozen pages that would have been needed were the first essay not incomplete. In the original version of the "primary" pleasures, Addison did not discuss architecture at all, mentioned statuary and painting only in a sentence, and entered into no real discussion of gardens, foreign or English, or of Chinese principles of art. The other significant development we find in the printed version is that in the *Spectator* Addison developed, on at least two occasions, the idea of pleasure in pain which he mentioned only in passing earlier and had more to say of "terror" than in his earlier versions.

[46] *Some Portions of Essays Contributed to the Spectator by Mr. Joseph Addison*, ed. by J. Dykes Campbell (Glasgow, 1864), p. 10. The italics indicate that these words are interlineated, showing that they were added in the second manuscript version.

when he published the *Pleasures of the Imagination;* he was undoubtedly correct in feeling that part of the "novelty" arose
from his association of "imagination" with the "sense of sight."
Classical writers had said that vision was the most important
organ of knowledge, and various theories of sight had been suggested by the Pythagoreans and by the Platonists, by Ptolemy
and by the Arabians. But it was natural that, in the period immediately following the invention of the telescope and other
important optical instruments, emphasis upon sight should have
become even more important that it had been in the past. Kepler
and Descartes had raised important physical and metaphysical
theories; the publication of Newton's *Opticks* in 1704 not only
marked an epoch in the history of science, but proved to be
the prelude to a period of great enthusiasm among poets and
other laymen, as I have attempted to show elsewhere.[47] Addison
had Newton in mind when he wrote the *Pleasures of the Imagination;* he was also remembering Locke, to whom sight was
"the most comprehensive of all our senses," and Berkeley, who
held that sight was "the most noble, pleasant, and comprehensive
of all the senses." But Addison was original in his stress upon
the relation of sight, not to the intellect or mind, but to the
imagination. In the Introduction I suggested that an interregnum
was necessary between neoclassicism and Romanticism, a period
when the imagination was learning to feel through the eyes.
Later poets like Thomson, who went back to Addison as to a
master, learned many things from him, but perhaps none more
important than the necessity of developing the imagination by
looking at and seeing those objects in the natural world that
most stimulated the imagination. Addison's distinction between

[47] I have discussed these matters in detail in *Newton Demands the
Muse,* particularly in chapter iv, "Optics and Vision." There I have given
a brief history of theories of sight and vision in the period before Kepler,
Descartes, and Newton and have suggested the contributions of these
men to the general problems. References to the quotations from Locke
and Berkeley will be found on p. 82.

the "primary" and the "secondary" pleasures of the imagination was, as he knew, a most important one: in the past, a chief stimulus had come from books—from reading about Nature or, as we have seen, looking at Nature with eyes clouded by such reading. Addison was urging upon his contemporaries the necessity of man's looking directly upon Nature and realizing that the stimulus that came from painting or poetry was "secondary."

Addison's essays upon the "secondary" pleasures are somewhat in the Longinian tradition; those on the "primary" pleasures are not at all so and constitute Addison's greatest contribution to the history of criticism. Addison's familiarity with Longinus is shown in various early works. We need only turn to his series of papers on Milton to see his interest in the Greek rhetorician.[48] Against standards of sublimity established by Longinus and Boileau, Addison tested *Paradise Lost* on every possible point of fable, characters, language, sentiment, to prove that in spite of some blemishes—"sun-spots," as he called them —Milton is the most sublime modern poet. The words *sublime* and *sublimity* are frequent in Addison's essays, but they are always associated with literary values and effects.

As early as 1704, Addison realized that as stimuli to the imagination such rhetorical ideas were secondary and that they had a "great dependence" upon primary ideas coming to man direct from Nature. In the introductory essay to the *Pleasures of the Imagination* he made that point even more clearly than in the earlier manuscript. He called attention to various papers on criticism that he had published in earlier numbers of the *Spectator*[49] and went on to say: "I shall next Saturday enter

[48] Addison's interest in Longinus has been discussed in detail by Alfred Rosenberg in *Longinus in England bis zur Ende des 18. Jahrhunderts* (Weimar and Berlin, 1917), pp. 40–54. See also Samuel Monk, *The Sublime*, p. 56.

[49] He mentioned particularly the papers on "Wit" and the essays on Milton: "I entertained the town, for a week together, with an essay upon wit . . . to shew wherein the nature of true wit consists. I after-

upon an essay on 'the pleasures of the imagination,' which, though it shall consider the subject at large, will perhaps suggest what it is that gives a beauty to many passages of the finest writers both in verse and prose."

The vocabulary used by Addison in the essays on the "primary" pleasures shows his careful avoidance of the term *sublime*. On no occasion does he use that word to describe either the "great" in Nature or the effects of "greatness" on the imagination. Instead we find a series of qualitative adjectives which he deftly varied: *great, stupendous, unlimited, spacious, unbounded*. One adjective that the modern reader would expect to find Addison used sparingly. *Vast* appears only twice, in each case associated with a desert. Perhaps Addison remembered Saint-Evremond's dissertation on that word, or perhaps, influenced as he was by French taste, he too felt *vast* a word of excess. At all events, in his vocabulary and in his aesthetic system, he made a careful distinction between the "rhetorical" and the "natural" sublime.

The three categories on which Addison based the pleasures of the imagination were not original with him, though he does not mention his source. He might have picked them up from Longinus,[50] who made the same distinction, though the fragmentary *Peri Hupsous* was so concerned with the "great" that later Longinians did not develop the passing reference to the other two categories. Addison might have adapted them from Burnet's *Sacred Theory* in which, as we have seen, they were

wards gave an instance of the great force which lies in a natural simplicity of thought to affect the mind of the reader, from such vulgar pieces as have little else besides this single qualification to recommend them. I have likewise examined the works of the greatest poet which our nation or perhaps any other has produced, and particularized most of those rational and manly beauties which give a value to that divine work."

[50] *Longinus on the Sublime*, trans. by A. O. Prickard (Oxford, 1906), p. 65: "If one were to look upon life all round, and see how in all things *the extraordinary, the great, the beautiful* stand supreme, he will at once know for what ends we have been made."

all implied. Whatever the source, Addison made them so peculiarly his own that "the great, the uncommon, the beautiful"
were associated with his name throughout the century.

Addison's treatment of Beauty remained on the whole as conventional as that of his predecessors. It implied "elegancy" and
"decorum." It was found in the small and the limited and was
shown in the "symmetry and proportion of parts, in the arrangement and disposition of bodies, or in a just mixture and concurrence of all together." "A beautiful prospect," he wrote in
Spectator 411, "delights the soul, as much as a demonstration.
We are struck, we know not how, with the symmetry of anything we see, and immediately assent to the beauty of an object."
The recognition of Beauty is immediate, and its effect is quiet
happiness and content. "There is nothing that makes its way
more directly to the soul than beauty," he said in *Spectator* 412,
"which immediately diffuses a secret satisfaction and compla-
cency through the imagination."

Addison's second category, "the new or uncommon," need
not detain us. Perhaps because it was never clearly defined and
distinguished by Addison himself, it was capable of leading in
different directions. Sometimes Addison associated it with the
simpler sense of "variety." Sometimes it was the result of "novelty," as he felt when he found himself impressed by various
antiquities in Rome and Naples and made a distinction that he
developed in the *Pleasures of the Imagination*. "I cannot but
think," he wrote, "that our admiration of them does not so
much arise out of their greatness as uncommonness. There are
indeed many extraordinary ruins, but I believe a traveller would
not be so much astonished at them did he find any works of
the same kind in his own country." [51] Basically, Addison suggested in *Spectator* 413, interest in the new, strange, or uncom-

[51] *Remarks on Several Parts of Italy*, II, 244. Clarence Thorpe has
studied this particular category of Addison in "Addison and Some of
His Predecessors on 'Novelty,'" *P.M.L.A.*, LII (1937), 1114-1129.

mon is the result of human curiosity. Such interest "bestows charms on a monster, and makes even the imperfections of nature please us." As a stimulus to imagination, however, the new or uncommon is found less often alone than serving as an enhancement to either the beautiful or the great. There was nothing particularly original in Addison's development of the categories of the beautiful and the novel. It was his analysis of the *great* that led to the important distinction developed in England between the "Sublime" and the "Beautiful." Versified by Akenside in *The Pleasures of Imagination* in 1744, Addison's ideas of the "Beautiful" and the "Great" were made into a system by Edmund Burke who published in 1756 his *Philosophical Enquiry into the Origin of Our Ideas of the Sublime and Beautiful*. They were the basis, too, of the distinction made by Kant in his *Kritik der Urtheilskraft*.[52]

"By greatness," Addison wrote in *Spectator* 412, "I do not mean only the bulk of any single object, but the largeness of a whole view, considered as one entire piece. Such are the prospects of an open champaign country, a vast uncultivated desert, of huge heaps of mountains, high rocks and precipices, or a wide expanse of waters, where we are not struck with the novelty or beauty of the sight, but with that rude kind of magnificence which appears in many of these stupendous works of nature." Addison's illustrations of the great "outward objects" that affect the imagination were drawn from those he had actually seen on his travels.[53] Like Burnet and Dennis, he attempted in this essay

[52] See E. F. Carritt, "The Sources and Effects in England of Kant's Philosophy of Beauty," *Monist*, XXXV (1925), 315–328. In this study I have not entered into several aspects of Addison's aesthetics (including his emphasis upon "sight") which I have discussed in *Newton Demands the Muse*.

[53] My statement here has sometimes been challenged on the ground that Addison did not see deserts on his travels. To be sure he had not seen the Sahara, but he had been much impressed by what he and other travelers called a desert. Indeed, it was one of the first objects he mentioned in his *Remarks*. After speaking of his arrival "at a little port called

to explain the "pleasure" his own imagination had evidently found in the "great":

Our imagination loves to be filled with an object, or to grasp at any thing that is too big for its capacity. We are flung into a pleasing astonishment at such unbounded views, and feel a delightful stillness and amazement in the soul at the apprehension of them. The mind of man naturally hates every thing that looks like a restraint upon it, and is apt to fancy itself under a sort of confinement, when the sight is pent up in a narrow compass, and shortened on every side by the neighbourhood of walls or mountains. On the contrary, a spacious horizon is an image of liberty, where the eye has room to range abroad, to expatiate at large on the immensity of its views, and to lose itself amidst the variety of objects that offer themselves to its observation. Such wide and undetermined prospects are as pleasing to the fancy, as the speculations of eternity or infinitude are to the understanding.

Here, more clearly articulated than before, is an attempt at a psychological explanation of the effect of "greatness" upon the "soul," an attitude of mind for the extremes of which modern psychologists use such terms as "claustrophobia" and "agoraphobia." Bacon had called the unquiet desire of man to escape from limits an "Idol of the Tribe"—the understanding, he said, "still presses onward, but in vain." But to Addison, the human desire to escape from limits is natural and right; "the mind of man naturally hates every thing that looks like a restraint upon it. . . . a spacious horizon is an image of liberty." To *fancy*— a word that Addison used in these essays interchangeably with *imagination*—undetermined prospects are as pleasing as "speculations of eternity or infinitude" to the understanding.

In *Spectator* 413 Addison went farther in his attempt to ex-

Cassis," he wrote: "We were here shown at a distance the Deserts, which have been rendered so famous by the presence of Mary Magdalene, who . . . is said to have wept away the rest of her life among these solitary rocks and mountains. It is so romantic a scene, that it has always probably given occasion to such chimerical relations."

plain the psychological basis of man's feeling for the "great." It is an instinct implanted in man by God to lead man's thoughts back from Nature to the Author of Nature:

One of the final causes of our delight in any thing that is great, may be this. The Supreme Author of our being has so formed the soul of man, that nothing but himself can be its last, adequate, and proper happiness. Because, therefore, a great part of our happiness must arise from the contemplation of this Being, that he might give our souls a just relish of such a contemplation, he has made them naturally delight in the apprehension of what is great or unlimited. Our admiration, which is a very pleasing motion of the mind, immediately rises at the consideration of any object that takes up a great deal of room in the fancy, and, by consequence, will improve into the highest pitch of astonishment and devotion when we contemplate his nature, that is neither circumscribed by time or place, nor to be comprehended by the largest capacity of a created being.

From Infinite God through vast Nature to the soul of man; from the soul of man through vast Nature back to Infinite God—here is the process that was becoming characteristic of "The Aesthetics of the Infinite."

Addison developed the idea of greatness as a "primary" pleasure of the imagination in *Spectator* 414, the theme of which is "The works of nature more pleasing to the imagination than those of art." Works of art may be "beautiful"; they cannot rise to "greatness." "If we consider the works of nature and art, as they are qualified to entertain the imagination," he wrote, "we shall find the last very defective in comparison of the former; for though they may sometimes appear beautiful or strange, they can have nothing in them of vastness and immensity." Art is "polite and delicate"; it cannot be "august and magnificent." This led Addison in certain directions which we shall find of great importance in the new descriptive poetry that was to develop during the eighteenth century. The practitioners of that genre, who frequently went back to Addison as their master, probably read into his words more than he meant—as, indeed, have modern critics. "There is something," he wrote, "more bold and masterly in the rough careless strokes of nature, than in the nice touches and embellishments of art. The beauties of the most stately garden or palace lie in a narrow compass, the imagination immediately runs them over, and requires something else to gratify her; but in the wide fields of nature, the sight wanders up and down without confinement, and is fed with an infinite variety of images, without any stint or number."

Further consideration of this idea, which had been in his mind when he wrote the original version of the *Pleasures of the Imagination*, led Addison to consider here—and also in later essays —the difference between the "regular" gardens of England and those he had seen on the continent:

We have before observed, that there is generally in nature something more grand and august, than what we meet with in the curiosities of art. When, therefore, we see this imitated in any measure, it gives us a nobler and more exalted kind of pleasure than what we receive from the nicer and more accurate productions of art. On this account our English gardens are not so entertaining to the fancy as those in France and Italy, where we see a large extent of ground covered over with an agreeable mixture of garden and forest, which represent every where an artificial rudeness, much more charming than that neatness and elegancy which we meet with in those of our own country.

In the following paragraph—added in the printed version—he spoke of Chinese gardens as excelling the English.[54] The Chinese,

[54] *Spectator* 414. This section on English gardens and the following paragraph on the Chinese were, as I have indicated in note 45 above, added in the printed version. Addison does not use the term "irregularity"; I use it because his contrasts throughout the passage are with regularity. *Spectator* 477 should really be considered as a part of the *Pleasures of the Imagination*, since in the supposed letter from a reader Addison picks up the subject again. I shall not rehearse the various critical discussions

he declared, laugh at English gardens "which are laid out by the rule and line." The English, pruning and clipping their trees and hedges into "cones, globes, and pyramids," deviate from Nature, whereas the Chinese, with their principle of *sharawagi*, follow Nature as closely as possible.

Addison's defense of irregularity over regularity may have been little more than that "grace beyond the reach of art" on which even the strictest neoclassicists agreed. But something in these passages seems to place Addison in this respect part way between Dennis and Shaftesbury. Dennis, we remember, had condemned irregularity as antithetic to beauty: "Nothing that is Irregular, as far as it is Irregular, ever was, or even can be either Natural or Reasonable." Shaftesbury's Philocles, on the contrary, found that irregularity was as natural as regularity and "the irregular inwrought grottos and broken falls of water" were more "engaging and magnificient than the formal mockery of princely gardens." Addison's "irregularity"—he did not use the term—seems less a deviation from the norm of Beauty than a lesser Sublime. Although he indicated on occasion that irregularity enhances Beauty, he introduced the subject by adjectives he reserved for the "Great": "something more grand and august."

One art alone Addison exempted from his stricture that the works of art are "defective" in comparison with those of Nature and their "pleasure" only "secondary." In the published version of the *Pleasures of the Imagination* Addison added an essay—

---

of Addison's interpretation of Chinese gardens. Professor Lovejoy discussed some of the predecessors and followers in "The Chinese Origin of a Romanticism," republished in his *Essays in the History of Ideas* (Baltimore, 1948). I may add to the controversy by saying that two of my Chinese graduate students at Columbia who have reworked the material to which Professor Lovejoy and his student refer can find no evidence that such a principle was recognized in China in the period preceding Addison and that some of my colleagues in the Department of Chinese and Japanese are not convinced of the interpretation made of *sharawagi* by Professor Lovejoy's student.

Spectator 415—of which there is no hint in the manuscript, on
"that particular art, which has a more immediate tendency, than
any other, to produce those primary pleasures of the imagination. . . . The art I mean is that of architecture." Addison's own
interest in architecture is shown in his many comments in the
Remarks and in his "Letter from Italy," though with the usual
prejudice of his times and religion he had little sympathy for the
Gothic. He was greatly disappointed in the "vast Gothic Pile" of
the Milan cathedral, not half-finished on the outside and on the
inside smutted with dust and lamp smoke. He recognized the
cathedral at Siena as "one of the masterpieces of Gothic Architecture," but lamented the prodigious pains and expense of our forefathers which might have produced miracles of architecture had
they been used in the right way. Like nearly every English
traveler he was greatly impressed by Rome. "There are Buildings the most magnificent in the world," he wrote to Dr. John
Hough, "and Ruins more magnificent than they." [55] The Coliseum moved him to Longinian rhetoric of a sort he seldom used:

> When Rome's exalted Beauties I descry
> Magnificent in Piles of Ruins lye:
> An Amphitheater's amazing height
> Here fills my Eye with Terror and Delight.[56]

If in his essays on gardens, Addison was defending a principle
of "irregularity," he shows little sign of it in the essay on architecture. "Let any one reflect on the disposition of mind he finds
in himself, at his first entrance into the Pantheon at Rome," he
wrote, "and how his imagination is filled with something great
and amazing; and at the same time, consider how little, in proportion, he is affected with the inside of a Gothic cathedral, though
it be five times larger than the other; which can arise from noth-

[55] Addison, *Letters*, p. 27.
[56] "A Letter from Italy to the Right Hon. Charles Lord Halifax in the
Year MDCCI" (London, 1709). The letter is reprinted in *Miscellaneous
Works*, edited by Guthkelch, I, 49–61.

ing else, but the greatness of the manner in the one, and the meanness in the other." The effect of "greatness," so far as architecture is concerned, must arise from something other than mere size, and indeed, because Addison was not yet ready to appreciate the Gothic, he was forced to make a distinction, which he does not make elsewhere. "Greatness," so far as architecture is concerned, may be the result of bulk or it may be an effect of "the manner in which it is built." The majestic structures that affected imagination primarily because of their size Addison could find only among buildings he had never seen—the Wonders of the World, renowned "among the eastern nations of the world, infinitely superior to the moderns." There were the Tower of Babel, even the foundations of which "looked like a spacious mountain," Babylon with its walls and temple "that rose a mile high," and the huge rock cut into the figure of Semiramis. These are gone, but modern man might still see with his own eyes the Egyptian pyramids and the Great Wall of China.

The architecture Addison admired in Italy impressed less because of mere bulk than because of the "manner" of building. The appeal of the Pantheon to "imagination" was the result of the fact that, like mountains and ocean and the wide expanses of earth, it led man to thoughts of God:

We are obliged to devotion for the noblest buildings that have adorned the several countries of the world. It is this which has set men at work on temples and public places of worship, not only that they might, by the magnificence of the building, invite the Deity to reside within it, but that such stupendous works might, at the same time, open the mind to vast conceptions, and fit it to converse with the divinity of the place. For every thing that is majestic, imprints an awfulness and reverence on the mind of the beholder, and strikes in with the natural greatness of the soul.

In the *Pleasures of the Imagination* we find again the threefold "Aesthetics of the Infinite." Addison has been concerned so far with the "great" in external nature—or in architecture—as leading the soul of man to God, but he did not forget those vast regions where the stars inhabit. He was still as responsive as he had been in youth to the "new philosophy." When he was discussing the secondary pleasures of the imagination in *Spectator* 420, he placed highest among the kinds of literature that enlarge imagination "the authors of the new philosophy":

There are none who more gratify and enlarge the imagination, than the authors of the new philosophy, whether we consider their theories of the earth or heavens, the discoveries they have made by glasses, or any other of their contemplations on nature. We are not a little pleased to find every green leaf swarm with millions of animals, that at their largest growth are not visible to the naked eye. There is something very engaging to the fancy, as well as to our reason, in the treatises of metals, minerals, plants, and meteors. But when we survey the whole earth at once, and the several planets that lie within its neighbourhood, we are filled with a pleasing astonishment, to see so many worlds hanging one above another, and sliding round their axles in such an amazing pomp and solemnity. If, after this, we contemplate those wide fields of aether, that reach in height almost to an infinitude, our imagination finds its capacity filled with so immense a prospect, as puts it upon the stretch to comprehend it. But if we rise yet higher, and consider the fixed stars as so many vast oceans of flame, that are each of them attended with a different set of planets, and still discover new firmaments and new lights, that are sunk farther in those unfathomable depths of aether, so as not to be seen by the strongest of our telescope, we are lost in such a labyrinth of suns and worlds, and confounded with the immensity and magnificence of nature.

Like his predecessors in the seventeenth century, Addison stressed particularly astronomy and microbiology, with their discovery of new universes of the infinitely great and the infinitely small, but he added, as they did not, a passing reference to geology, which the Burnet controversy had made much more familiar to laymen than it had been in the preceding century.

Throughout the *Spectator* papers, we find the response of Addison's own imagination to the new astronomy, never more movingly expressed by him than in *Spectator* 565, a meditation upon the night skies. As he considered "the heavens, the works of thy finger, the moon and stars which thou hast ordained," he wondered with the Psalmist, "what is man that thou art mindful of him?"

When I considered that infinite host of stars or, to speak more philosophically, of suns, which were then shining upon me, with those innumerable sets of planets or worlds, which were moving round their respective suns; when I still enlarged the idea, and supposed another heaven of suns and worlds rising still above this which we discovered, and these still enlightened by a superior firmament of luminaries . . . I could not but reflect on that little insignificant figure which I myself bore admist the immensity of God's works.

Were the sun, which enlightens this part of the creation, with all the host of planetary worlds that move about him, utterly extinguished and annihilated, they would not be missed more than a grain of sand upon the sea-shore. The space they possess is so exceedingly little, in comparison of the whole, that it would scarce make a blank in the creation. . . . There is no question but the universe has certain bounds set to it: but when we consider that it is the work of infinite power, prompted by infinite goodness, with an infinite space to exert itself in, how can the imagination set any bounds to it?

From Infinite God to Infinite Space to vast objects in the world and back again from the "great" in external Nature through Space and infinite or indefinite worlds to Infinite God— such is the threefold process of the "pleasures of the imagination." The "pleasure" man felt in mountains and ocean, in stars and space, lay in the enlargement of the soul to experience more completely the powers, desires, and aspirations given by its great Original, the true Infinite.

Like Dennis, Addison took for granted the religious origin of man's feeling for sublimity and was groping for a psychological explanation of the effect of "greatness" on the "soul." But there are important differences. To Dennis the important "faculty" of the soul was Passion; to Addison it was Imagination. We find nothing in Addison to correspond to Dennis' description of his emotions in the Alps, "at the same time, that I was infinitely pleas'd, I *trembled*." Addison used no physiological terms. Neither in the *Remarks* nor in the *Pleasures of the Imagination* does "suffering" play an important part.[57] Indeed, the evidence of the manuscripts is that originally Addison paid no real attention to "pain" as a part of the Sublime experience; the two sections he later added in the printed version are mild and restrained in comparison with almost any section of Dennis. The Sublime did not astound, appall, overwhelm—and certainly did not "ravish" Addison. "Admiration," "pleasing astonishment," "delight," "devotion"—this is his characteristic vocabulary. It was natural "awe" rather than "terror" that he felt in contemplation of Deity. The effect of the Sublime upon Addison is closer to that which we have found in Shaftesbury, though Shaftesbury is more emotional, more lyrical. And there is one very important difference. To Shaftesbury the Sublime is the highest Beauty. To Addison the categories of the Sublime and Beautiful are separate and distinct, as are the emotions aroused by each, though the line of demarcation is not so sharp and abrupt

[57] One of the few instances of Addison's use of a vocabulary of excess occurs in the concluding essay of the series, *Spectator* 421. Discussing "the influence that one man has over the fancy of another," Addison said: "[God] can transport the imagination with such beautiful and glorious visions . . . or haunt it with such ghastly spectres and apparitions, as would make us hope for annihilation, and think existence no better than a curse. In short, he can so exquisitely ravish or torture the soul through this single faculty, as might suffice to make up the whole heaven or hell of any finite being." The passage reads as in the first manuscript version with the exception of the fact that in the second version Addison changed the word "please" to "ravish."

as in Dennis, since in Addison one category may enhance the others.

As we read Dennis and Addison, it is clear that we stand at a turning point in the history of these aesthetic concepts. To both the source of the Sublime is in Deity. But Dennis' was a God of Power, and the emotions evoked when one contemplated Him— or the grand Nature He had made—involved dread and terror: "at the same time, that I was infinitely pleas'd, I trembled." The essence of Addison's Sublime lay in vastness rather than in power. From this time forth, we shall find men following one or the other of the three critics who were responsible for the developing concept of the Sublime: some will differentiate sharply between the Sublime and the Beautiful; some will feel the Sublime a higher Beauty; some will emphasize the vastness of size in the objects God—or man—has made; some will emphasize power shown in the most vehement and violent aspects of Nature. In time the rhetorical and natural Sublimes will become parts of a single whole. But to Dennis, Shaftesbury, and Addison, differ though they might in other respects, the "primary" stimulus to the Sublime lay in vast objects in Nature— mountains and ocean, stars and cosmic space—all reflecting the glory of Deity. The "rhetorical" Sublime was only secondary.

Chapter Eight

A New Descriptive Poetry

"A Globe Far Off Now Seems a Boundless Continent"

I

"DIFF'RENT minds," wrote Akenside in *The Pleasures of Imagination*, "incline to diff'rent objects,"

> one pursues
> The vast alone, the wonderful, the wild,
> Another sighs for harmony, and grace,
> And gentlest beauty.

The eighteenth-century poets were not so sharply divided as Akenside's distinction implies, many of them responding to both beauty and sublimity. Among neoclassicists Beauty continued to be associated with the small, the limited, the proportioned, and its appeal was still to Reason. But as the age went on, its province widened. Irregularity that had once repelled began to attract. As imagination responded to the appeal of the grand and vast in Nature—and in architecture—the Sublime and Beautiful were more and more closely merged. Sometimes the Sublime was a "dreadful" Beauty—the creation of a God of Power; sometimes it was a "higher" Beauty—the reflection of a God of Benignity.

Among neoclassical poets who described landscape, older literary traditions continued, perhaps in part because the Greek spirit had all but disappeared and the neoclassical temper was predominantly Latin. Although the "warts and wens" were gone, a stereotyped vocabulary remained. Didactic poets repeated old truisms:

> Oh, sons of earth! attempt ye still to rise
> By mountains piled on mountains to the skies?

Pelion and Ossa were still more familiar in poetry than Helvellyn. Indeed, as late as 1801 Wordsworth, who had done so much to break down old conventions, wrote:

> Pelion and Ossa flourish side by side,
> Together in immortal books enrolled:
> His ancient dower Olympus hath not sold;
> And that inspiring Hill, which "did divide
> Into two ample horns his forehead wide,"
> Shines with poetic radiance as of old;
> While not an English Mountain we behold
> By the celestial Muses glorified.
> Yet round our sea-girt shore they rise in crowds.

Virgilian example ruled the pastoral; the influence of Milton was second only to that of the master. On "hill and dale and plain," landscape tended to be stylized, with shallow brooks and rivers wide, towers and battlements bosomed high in tufted trees, their origin less in Nature than in "L'Allegro." The "softly-swelling hill," "the gilded mountain and the herbaged vale"— such "delicious regions" remained as artificial as they had been for years. Although hills are much more common in eighteenth-century poetry than they had been a century earlier, that fact by itself would be no proof that the later poets were more interested in grand Nature. Some of them were merely following another literary convention established by "Cooper's Hill." [1] "Windsor Forest" and "Grongar Hill" were only the most famous of Denham's literary progeny. As William Pultney, Earl of Bath, suggested:

> Since Denham sang of Cooper's
> There's scarce a hill around,
> But what in song or ditty
> Is turned to fairy ground. . . .
> On lofty hills like Windsor,
> Such heroes ought to dwell,
> But the little folk of Strawberry-hill
> Like Strawberry-hill as well.[2]

It is amusing to consider what might have happened in the development of neoclassical landscape poetry if the young Pope had been physically able to follow the advice of George Berkeley,[3] who urged him to travel to the continent "in order

[1] Robert Arnold Aubin, who collected an extensive bibliography of hill poems in his *Topographical Poetry in XVIII-England* (New York, 1936), writes (pp. 35–36): "Appearing naturally in the nineteen collected editions of its author's poems between 1668 and 1857, *Cooper's Hill* was besides reprinted as a whole or in large part fourteen times between 1642 and 1794, and in 1676 was honored with a Latin translation. Between 1666 and 1808 fifteen topographical poems (including *Windsor Forest*) were published that are either direct and obvious imitations of Denham's chief poem or are very greatly indebted to it; between 1650 and 1841 more than two hundred works in verse or prose either referred to . . . or borrowed slightly from it."

[2] *Shorter Poems of the Eighteenth Century*, ed. by Iolo Williams (London, 1923), pp. 111–112.

[3] The earlier letter was written from Leghorn, May 1, 1714, the second from Naples, October 22 (N.S.), 1717. Both are reprinted in Alexander Pope, *Correspondence*, edited by George Sherburn (Oxford 1956), I, 221–222, 445–446.

James Thomson set out on his travels for much the reason Berkeley suggested. He wrote in October, 1730, to Budd Doddington (Douglas Grant, *James Thomson: Poet of the Seasons* [London, 1951], p. 117): "Travelling has long been my fondest wish for the very purpose you recommend. The storing one's imagination with ideas of all-beautiful,

to store his mind with strong Images of Nature." English fields, meadows, and streams were well enough in their way, declared the philosopher, but they were not the stuff of the finest poetry. "To enable a man to describe rocks and precipices," Berkeley wrote, "it is absolutely necessary that he pass the Alps." He particularly recommended to Pope the unspoiled island of Inarime, its "barren Spots and naked Rocks . . . and that which crowns the Scene, is a large Mountain rising out of the middle of the Island (once a horrible Volcano)." This island, he felt, "is an Epitome of the whole Earth, containing within the compass of eighteen Miles, a wonderful variety of Hills, Vales, ragged Rocks, fruitful Plains, and barren Mountains, all thrown together in a most romantic Confusion." Berkeley might have been writing a prescription for the "new poets," though he seemed to feel that Pope could best describe this "romantic Confusion"; "this noble Landscape . . . would demand an Imagination as warm, and numbers as flowing as your own." Perhaps Berkeley knew the young Pope's potentialities better than we know them. Certainly Pope's essay in the *Guardian* was as influential as Addison's *Spectator* papers on the growing English taste for "natural" gardens. And at about the time that Berkeley first wrote, Pope was sharing the enthusiasm of his contemporaries for the "discoveries made by glasses" of the "authors of the new astronomy" whom Addison considered so important for the development of the imagination. Returning from one of Whiston's astronomical lectures, Pope wrote:

You cannot wonder my thoughts are scarce consistent, when I tell you how they are distracted. Every hour of my life my mind is strangely divided. This minute, perhaps, I am above the stars, with a thousand systems round about me, looking forward into the vast abyss of eternity, and losing my whole comprehension in the bound-

---

and all-perfect Nature; these are the pure *Materia Poetica*, the light and colours, with which fancy kindles up her whole creation, paints a sentiment, and even embodies an abstracted thought."

less spaces of the extended creation, in dialogues with Whiston and
the astronomers; the next moment I am below all trifles, even
grovelling with Tidcombe in the very centre of nonsense. . . .
Good God! what an incongruous animal is man! [4]

It is useless to wonder whether Pope would have shared the
enthrallment of Burnet and Dennis had he seen the Alps or
whether, like Evelyn, he would have swept aside the rubbish of
the world in a brilliant metaphor. Pope did not follow Berkeley's
advice, nor did he continue his enthusiasm for those aspects of
the new science that were breaking down world barriers and the
basis of neoclassical ethics and aesthetics. Before and after this
time, however, other poets were discovering the shadow of
divinity in a new earth, as their seventeenth-century predecessors had found it in the expanded heavens.

In spite of inherited tradition and convention, a new descriptive poetry was emerging for which there had been no parallel
in the past. In its broad outlines, it was a georgic poetry, though
there were many passages, themes, and moods which Virgil
would not have recognized. Its creators did not claim the highest
peak on Parnassus, but in an age that could not—at least did not
—produce epics, the long leisurely descriptive poem established
a genre of its own. If it was not a tale of heroes half-divine, it
had its own protagonist, Nature, a character greater and infinitely more complex to the authors than any Odysseus or
Aeneas. "I know no subject," James Thomson wrote in the
Preface to the second edition of "Winter," "more elevating
. . . more ready to awake the poetical enthusiasm, the philosophical reflection, and the moral sentiment, than the works of

---

[4] *Works*, ed. by Whitwell Elwin and W. J. Courthope (London, 1871–
1889), VI, 190–191. According to Professor Sherburn the letter was written to John Caryll, though it was printed as having been written to
Addison. I have quoted it from Professor Sherburn's "Pope and the Great
Shew of Nature," in *The Seventeenth Century: Studies in the History of
English Thought and Literature* by Richard Foster Jones and others (Stan-
ford, 1951), pp. 306 ff.

Nature. Where can we meet with such variety, such beauty, such magnificence? All that enlarges and transports the soul!" The Nature of the eighteenth-century descriptive poets included landscape of the sort Berkeley recommended to Pope. But their Nature was much more than landscape. "Is it not evident," Dryden had written, "in these last hundred years (when the study of philosophy has been the business of all the Virtuosi in Christendom) that almost a new Nature has been revealed to us?" [5]

As they looked through Nature up to Nature's God, the poets were conscious that both had grown immeasurably. *Natura naturata* was "a gay profusion of luxurious bliss . . . unbounded beauty . . . this pomp of nature . . . a complex stupendous scheme of things." *Natura naturans* was "Nature exuberant . . . universal Bounty . . . restless Goodness." Her "ample lap" was filled with limitless treasures from which her "liberal" or even "careless" hand flung "lavish stores." "Creative Bounty burns with warmest beams. . . . Full Nature swarms with life." She is the word, the wisdom, the effectual might of a Deity who has become "Immense Creator . . . Deity Immense . . . God most bounteous . . . Infinite of Goodness and of Love. . . . Nature's God, First source of all things lovely, all things good." [6] In the new God and the new Nature, the pre-Romantic poets found the source of a new Sublime, which makes the descriptive poetry of the eighteenth century very different in structure, style, and emphasis from the poetry of the English Renaissance.

II

The most characteristic descriptive poem of the eighteenth century was the "excursion," a natural development of the "cos-

[5] John Dryden, *Essays*, ed. by W. P. Ker (Oxford, 1900), I, 36–37.
[6] The quotations are from Thomson's *Seasons*. All quotations from Thomson are from the *Complete Poetical Works*, edited by J. L. Robertson (Oxford, 1908).

mic voyage" [7] that the seventeenth century had adapted in part from old themes of trance and ecstasy, in part from the voyages to the moon and planets that became increasingly popular after Galileo's discoveries. The pattern had become so well established that no specific source for the "excursion poem" need be determined, though to some extent Thomson, Mallet, Savage, and others looked back to the imaginary voyage of Theocles and Philocles in Shaftesbury's *Characteristicks,* as Shaftesbury in turn looked back to Burton's "long winged hawk" and other imaginary voyages of the seventeenth century. The "excursion" was a peculiarly fitting vehicle for a generation of poets even more conscious of science than their predecessors, a philosophical and scientific device that permitted them to wander through space and around the earth and to ponder the nature and causes of things.

To earlier cosmic voyagers earth had been chiefly a point of departure for flight to the empyrean. The attitude of the poets had been somewhat similar to that of a modern air traveler, as he watches objects on earth becoming smaller and smaller until they disappear from sight. The only interest in earth shown by John Hughes in "Ecstasy" was the single comment, "What lofty mountains downward fly!" Cowley in his "Exstasie," as he left "Mortality and things below" watched England disappear from sight:

> Where shall I find the noble British Land?
> Lo, I at last a Northern Spec espie,
>   Which in the Sea does lie,
>   And seems a Grain o' th' Sand!

John Hughes's "Ode to the Creator of the World" reflects the older techniques, yet anticipates the newer. Winging through space, the poet watches the earth and sea, observes storms that

---

[7] I have discussed the origin and development of the cosmic voyage in *Voyages to the Moon* (New York, 1948).

shake the globe, and allows his fancy to wander to different lands in different seasons.

The "excursion" poets of the eighteenth century rose upon "wings sublime," soared into the Newtonian heavens, then descended to earth where they flew to different lands, plumbed the depths of ocean, and dived "beneath the darksome caverns" into the secret places, constantly reiterating their "delight," "wonder," "awe," and "astonishment" at the variety and profusion of a Nature made in the image of an exuberant Deity. As they flew or swooped or dived, they philosophized, seeking natural rather than supernatural explanations for fossils and gems, meteors, storms, earthquake, thunder and lightning, volcanic eruptions. Richard Bentley ironically suggested the prerequisites for the "new poetry":

> Who strives to mount Parnassus hill,
> And thence poetic laurels bring,
> Must first acquire due force ånd skill,
> Must fly with swan or eagle's wing. . . .
>
> Who nature's treasures would explore,
> Her mysteries and arcana know,
> Must high as lofty Newton soar,
> Must stoop, as searching Woodward, low.[8]

Though the interest of the "excursion" poets came to be more and more upon earth—they were "geology conscious" as no writers before them—they did not forget the vastness of Space or the vastness of Deity. The greatness of God, reflected in "the sightless realms of space" and "the planetary way," they found again in "the mighty prospects . . . the mountain's brow, the long-extended wood, Or the rude rock that threatens o'er the flood."

As we descend to earth with the Muse of the new poetry, our

[8] Richard Bentley, "Verses in Reply to Mr. Titley," in *Shorter Poems of the Eighteenth Century*, p. 3.

immediate impression is that it has grown immensely in magnitude and in the size of natural objects—ironically enough, in view of the extent to which our planet had shrunk into comparative insignificance as a result of the new astronomy. As Young said in the *Night Thoughts*:

> Is is not this home-creation, in the map
> Of universal Nature, as a speck,
> Like fair Britannia in our little ball;
> Exceeding fair, and glorious, for its size,
> But, elsewhere, far out-measur'd, far outshone? [9]

But both Britannia and the terrestrial globe of which it was a part had grown extensively in the minds of the physicotheologists. The eighteenth-century earth has become a wide, wide world indeed, with extraordinarily extensive panoramas and prospects, in which mountains, plains, rivers, and seas are on a majestic scale and caverns seem actually measureless to man. The Muse refuses to be bounded by England. Mere passing mention of a river stirs her to flight over the "prolific streams" of "vast regions near the rising sun" where flow "Indus, Ganges, and Hydaspes," then to another distant continent where, "swelled by a thousand streams . . . huge descends the mighty Orellana." From such "dread expanses" as the "sea-like Plata," excursive Fancy speeds on "where the Northern Ocean in vast whirls" boils around "the naked melancholy isles of farthest Thule," until she has circumnavigated the globe, with its "mighty continents out-stretch'd immense." The climates of the far-off lands are as extreme as their canvases are extensive. "On the Northern blast, Bleak horrors rise . . . dire Winter rules . . . and rides in whirlwinds." Above the equator "still Horror reigns," even at the height of noon, when "incessant vapors roll" and clouds are "whirl'd tempestuous by the gusty wind." In the burning zones of the equator, on the frozen ice fields of the north, in all the distant re-

[9] Young, *Night Thoughts*, IX, 1595–1599.

gions of earth still accessible only to Fancy, the Muse discovers "unbounded wilds . . . plains immense . . . forests huge . . . vast enbowering shades. . . . Great are the scenes with dreadful beauty crowned."

None of the excursive—and exclamatory—poets exaggerated horrors, wonders, and vastness more than did the untraveled Richard Savage, sitting in a London room and writing according to a recipe established by others.[10] His "wild Fancy" strode over Norwegian hills, strained up steep mountains, paused on "yon Zemblan rocks," and was off again to frozen seas. Samuel Johnson, torn between his own aesthetic judgment and his loyalty to his friend, spoke of the "irregular" disposition of parts, the "obscure" design and the "perplexed" plan of *The Wanderer,* but concluded that the poem as a whole was "a heap of shining materials thrown together by accident, which strikes rather with the solemn magnificence of a stupenduous ruin than the elegant grandeur of a finished pile." *Magnificence, vastness, ruin*—no three words could better sum up the effects for which the "excursion" poets were striving. In most of them a theory of the "natural Sublime" was implied. In Mallet and Thomson it was both implicit and explicit.

These two poets worked together on their major poems, sending each other sections for criticism. "Sublimity," Thomson wrote to Mallet, "must be the characteristic of your piece." He continued, setting down a program for the new poetry:

My idea of your Poem is a description of the grand works of Nature raised and animated by moral and sublime reflections; therefore before you quit this earth you ought to leave no great scene unvisited. Eruptions, earthquakes, the sea wrought into a horrible tempest, the abyss amidst whose amazing prospects, how pleasing

[10] Samuel Johnson in his *Life* said that Savage "had no knowledge but from pastorals and songs." Savage listed his sources, in the first canto of *The Wanderer* (Johnson, *The Works of the English Poets* [London, 1790], XLI, 132–135), as Young, Mallet, Hill, and Thomson.

must be that of a deep valley covered with all the tender profusion of Spring.[11]

Mallet was willing to follow the program. He had recently returned from foreign travel, his mind filled with "sublime" scenes. He had read extensively in the Burnet controversy and in the physicotheologists. *The Excursion* shows that he was much interested in science, particularly geology and meteorology. As Thomson ordered, he left no great scene unvisited: eruptions, volcanoes, earthquakes, violent storms, the Deluge—all are there. Reading over some of the passages, Thomson exclaimed: "This is Poetry; this is arousing fancy—enthusiasm—rapturous terror."

In its structure Mallet's *Excursion* looks before and after, one book a cosmic voyage through the universe, the other an excursion over the terrestrial globe. Thomson's *Seasons* marks the beginning of an era in which the attention of poets was devoted to Nature in this world even more than to Nature in the cosmos. Thomson always acknowledged the origin of the Sublime in God and Space; but as an artist he made no such self-conscious distinction between geocosm and macrocosm as did Mallet. "Philosophy," involving reason and imagination, leads from heaven to earth, from earth to heaven:

> Nor to this evanescent speck of earth
> Poorly confined: the radiant tracks on high
> Are her exalted range; intent to gaze
> Creation through, and, from the full complex
> Of never-ending wonders, to conceive
> Of the sole Being right, who spoke the word,
> And Nature moved complete.[12]

To "Philosophy" our world may have become "this evanescent speck of earth," but to Thomson earth was as engrossing to

---

[11] As quoted in Peter Cunningham, "James Thomson and David Mallet," *Miscellanies of the Philobiblon Society*, IV (1857–1858), 30. Alan Dugald McKillop has discussed the letter in *The Background of Thomson's Seasons* (Minneapolis, 1942), p. 129.

[12] "Summer," ll. 1782–1788.

the imagination as the heavens had been to earlier poets. The vastness and majesty of cosmic Nature he found equally in the terrestrial world. "Spring" alone, in which the poet emphasized Beauty rather than the Sublime, is limited in its canvas. In the other books, "Air, earth and ocean smile immense"; "Earth's universal face is one wild dazzling waste." The "far horizon wide-diffused" is a "boundless deep immensity of shade." "Solemn and slow the shadows blacker fall And all is awful listening gloom around." As his Fancy traveled over all the world, known and unknown, Thomson found immensity everywhere. The desert is "a wide expanse of lifeless sand and sky."

> Plains immense
> Lie stretched below, interminable meads
> And vast savannas, where the wandering eye,
> Unfixt, is in a verdant ocean lost.[13]

"The circling deep that awes the world" stretches out as indefinitely as the horizon. Rivers, particularly those remote from England, are on the grand scale. "With annual pomp, Rich king of floods! o'erflows the Nile." "His brother Niger too" flows on in majesty. "Retired from little scenes of Art, great Nature swells in awful solitude." The extent to which terrestrial phenomena were growing in size during the first half of the century can be seen by comparing the different versions of *The Seasons*.[14] Thomson's panoramas become more spacious, his mountains more majestic, Nature increasingly more rich, more diversified, more bounteous, more sublime:

> Nature! great parent! whose unceasing hand
> Rolls round the Seasons of the changeful year,
> How mighty, how majestic are thy works!

[13] *Ibid.*, ll. 690–693.

[14] Thomson's development in these respects may be seen in the Robertson edition, which lists the variant readings of *The Seasons*. Alan Dugald McKillop has discussed various aspects of the changes in *The Background of Thomson's Seasons*.

> With what a pleasing dread they swell the soul,
> That sees astonish'd, and astonish'd, sings! [15]

III

The neoclassical enthusiasm for ruins—at first sight inconsistent with their principle of regularity—is familiar to all readers. In their literature, as in their gardens and their landscape paintings, we stumble upon ruins on every side—Ruins of Art, Ruins of Time, Ruins of Nature. Burnet had said, in answer to Erasmus Warren's defense of irregularities as a part of the beauty of mountains and clouds: "These make a great noise, but they might all be apply'd to the ruins of an old Bridge fallen into the Water." Fifty years after the *Sacred Theory* one of the chief appeals of ruins lay in the very asymmetry that had "appalled" Burnet's Reason. In addition to irregularity, the eighteenth-century poets felt before Ruins of Time a sense of mystery and awe.

John Dyer's *Ruins of Rome*, the most popular poem on this persistent theme, was a deliberate attempt to describe the pleasure Addison said imagination might find in architecture.[16] "Vastness, magnificence, ruin" were his themes as he saw the great city, like Milton's Satan, "majestic though in ruin":

> Fall'n, fall'n, a silent heap; her heroes all
> Sunk in their urns; behold the pride of pomp,

---

[15] "Winter," ll. 106–110.

[16] Addison said in *Spectator* 415: "Let one reflect on the disposition of mind he finds himself in, at his first entrance into the Pantheon at Rome, and how his imagination is filled with something great and amazing." On the same subject Dyer said in *The Ruins of Rome* (in Alexander Chalmers, *Works of the English Poets* [London, 1810], XIII, 224–225):

> Amid the towery ruins, huge, supreme,
> Th' enormous amphitheatre behold,
> Mountains pile! o'er whose capacious womb
> Pours the broad firmament its varied light;
> While from the central floor the seats ascend
> Round above round, slow-widening to the verge,
> A circuit vast and high.

> The throne of nations fall'n; obscur'd in dust;
> Ev'n yet majestical: the solemn scene
> Elates the soul.

The "solitary, silent, solemn scene" is on the grand scale: "globose and huge, Grey-mould'ring temples swell, and wide o'er cast The solitary landskip." Everywhere in Rome the poet is conscious of a solemn vastness—in "yon fabrick huge . . . huge inscriptive stones . . . columns huge, innumerous as cedars." "Latium's wide champain, forlorn and waste," is a "solemn wilderness." The Coliseum, the Pantheon, the Theban obelisk are like the "Etruscan mountains . . . with ruins crown'd." [17]

Conscious of their insularity, English travelers carried home "many-figur'd sculptures . . . half-beauteous, half-effac'd," ancient "heroes and gods" with which to "deck their long galleries and winding groves," as Dyer said. They carried with them, too, a sense of strangeness and romance evoked by the Ruins of Time, leading them with mingled pride and humility to meditate upon their own past, ruder than that of Rome, but hardly less grand and moving. When Shenstone in "The Ruined Abbey" saw "betwixt the grove's extended arms An Abbey's rude remains," his

[17] The extent to which Dyer could find the "natural Sublime" in unexpected places is shown by his meditation upon the sewers of Rome (*The Ruins of Rome*, in Chalmers, XIII, 225):

> The sunk ground startles me with dreadful chasm,
> Breathing forth darkness from the vast profound
> Of aisles and halls, within the mountain's womb.
> Nor these the nether works; all these beneath,
> And all beneath the vales and hills around,
> Extend the cavern'd sewers, massy, firm,
> As the Sibylline grot beside the dead
> Lake of Avernus; such the sewers huge.

Dyer was equally interested in the aqueducts (*ibid.*, p. 16). Savage, who had never seen them, also described them "awful in decay" (*The Wanderer*, p. 55).

mind went back to the early history of Britain.[18] John Cunningham, meditating upon the "vestige of an ancient abbey . . . close by a ruin'd castle's rude remains," recalled the days when "rev'rend shrines in Gothic grandeur stood." [19] Dyer felt some of the emotions he had experienced in Rome when he returned to England and saw

> the spacious plain
> Of Sarum, spread like Ocean's boundless round,
> Where solitary Stonehenge, gray with moss,
> Ruin of ages, nods.[20]

"Lost in the Circle of devouring days," Stonehenge, the "noblest monument of Albion's isle," became a symbol of a remote, though virile past, a memorial to a heroic period when the "huge frame of giant-hands" was raised as an "unknown shrine" to victory. Ruins were the stock in trade of the Gothic novelist and equally of the poets of melancholy, with their "ruin'd seats . . . yon abbey's moss-grown piles . . . mouldering caverns dark and deep." Their irregularity charmed; memorials to antiquity, they evoked dim memories of indefinite time. They became to their devotees "a little Sublime."

"You paint ruins with a masterly hand," Thomson wrote to Mallet. Thomson was thinking less of Mallet's passages on the Ruins of Time than of the long sections on the Ruins of Nature.[21] The Burnet controversy was in large part responsible for

[18] William Shenstone, "The Ruined Abbey," in Chalmers, XIII, 321–324.

[19] John Cunningham, "Elegy on a Pile of Ruins," in *The Cabinet of Poetry* (London, 1808), V, 184 ff.

[20] "The Fleece," bk. I, in Chalmers, XIII, 229.

[21] In *The Background of Thomson's Seasons*, p. 70, Alan Dugald McKillop, discussing the Thomson-Mallet correspondence, quotes "Summer" ll. 732–735:

> Much of the Force of foreign Summer's still,
> Of growling Hills, that shoot the pillar'd Flame
> Of Earthquake, and pale Famine, could I sing:
> But equal Scenes of Horror call Me Home.

the widespread interest of the descriptive poets in volcanic eruptions, earthquakes, and tempests. Storms and other violences of
Nature were nothing new in poetry, but no generation before
this had treated in such detail:

> The infuriate hill that shoots the pillared flame;
> And, roused within the subterranean world,
> The expanding earthquake, that resistless shakes
> Aspiring cities from their solid base,
> And buried mountains in their flaming gulf.[22]

After the Lisbon earthquake of 1755 shocked the civilized
world, there was naturally a great outpouring of verse upon the
subject, yet well before that the violence of Nature had become

---

He comments: "I hope this was a graceful intimation that at this point he
was willing to concede the volcano, the earthquake, and the famine to
Mallet."

[22] James Thomson, "Summer," ll. 1096–1100. I cannot discuss here the
great interest shown by all these poets in scientific theory, but shall reserve
that for a paper in which the "new geology" and eighteenth-century
poetry will be treated. There is no greater contrast in "nature poetry"
than we find in the treatment of storms, earthquakes, and so on. For centuries, like the plague or comets, earthquakes and volcanoes had been
associated in the popular mind with the punishment of sinful men by a
God of Vengeance. Classical authorities had offered no clearer explanation for such hypogene forces than that they were caused by commingling
of moist and dry within the earth. This was in general the position of
medieval Fathers, combined frequently with a theory of a central fire,
which supplied heat and flames to both Hell and volcanoes. In the
earlier seventeenth century, if writers sought other than supernatural
explanations, they vaguely associated earthquakes with comets and meteorological phenomena. The followers and adversaries of Burnet spoke
of an accumulation of exhalations, sulphurous or bituminous, and therefore inflammable. The majority held a notion of a central fire, though
some suggested beds of combustible matter near the surface of the earth.
They differed in their theories of the immediate cause of earthquakes and
volcanic eruptions, some accepting Descartes's notion of a "spark," others
the mixture of salts with nitrous exhalations. The most complete account
of these phenomena was John Beaumont's *Considerations on a Book,
Entituled The Theory of the Earth.* Keill and Whiston both discussed
earthquakes and volcanoes at length in their examination of Burnet.

an integral part of descriptive poetry. Blackmore and Young, Thomson, Smart, and Brooke, with many others, introduced long descriptions of thunderstorms, earthquakes, and volcanoes. Some were more interested in scientific causes, others in justifying the ways of God toward earth. All felt such themes an essential element in the "natural Sublime," manifestations as they were of God's Might and Power. There was general agreement that Mallet was the master of the new combination of science and sublimity. In *The Excursion* we see "yonder clouds, pregnant with fate," and watch the fiery tempest as it "swells Sulphureous steam and nitrous, late exhal'd From mine or unctuous soil." [23] The thunderstorm is a forerunner of more deadly horrors. Within the bosom of the globe, where sulphur and niter had slept peacefully for many ages, ferment begins:

> Vapory steams . . .
> Their deadly breath apply. Th' enkindled mass,
> Mine fir'd by mine in train, with boundless rage,
> With horror unconceiv'd, disploded bursts
> Its central prison. . . .
>   Half the globe
> Her frame convulsive rocking to and fro
> Trembles with second agony.

"Here, if you could insert a sketch of the Deluge, what more affecting and noble?" Thomson had suggested. Mallet complied

[23] *The Excursion*, in Chalmers, XIV, 20–21. Although Mallet was interested in various scientific theories, he did not go as far as Henry Brooke, the most "scientific" of the poets. See *Universal Beauty*, bk. II, ll. 161 ff., in Chalmers, XVII, 353–355. The treatment of earthquakes and volcanoes, as I have briefly suggested, varies greatly. Samuel Boyse in "Deity" (Chalmers, XIV, 544–552) was primarily concerned with the vindication of the ways of God to man, as was Isaac Watts in "Divine Judgment" (Chalmers, XIII, 21–22). John Hughes introduced into his otherwise placid "Ecstasy" (Chalmers, X, 60–62) a very conventional earthquake observed by the celestial Muse. Thomas Yalden in his "conquest of Namur" (Chalmers, XI, 85–87) described Etna's raging, its flaming entrails hurling great rocks into the air. William Broome in "A Poem on the Seat of War in Flanders" (Chalmers, XII, 21) added a tidal wave to his earthquake.

with a long passage in which he adapted Burnet's scenes of the bursting of the shell of the Mundane Egg. And then, as if humanity had not borne enough, earthquake and flood are made still more horrible by volcanic eruption. The mountain bursts into flame, and man with all his works lies buried in the Ruins of Nature.

IV

With her unslaked thirst for new descriptive worlds to conquer, the "adventurous Muse" who had so often ascended to the empyrean descended into the secret places of Nature, dived "beneath the darksome Caves," flew to "Northern Albion's tinembowel'd fields," pried into Nature's recesses to

> search, undismay'd, the dark profound
> Where nature works in secret; view the beds
> Of mineral treasure, and th' eternal vault
> That bounds the hoary ocean; . . . behold the seeds
> Of being, and the energy of life
> Kindling the mass with ever-active flame.[24]

Poetic interest in caves, caverns, and grottoes was of course nothing new in poetry. Imported from warmer lands, the "cool grot," which had served a practical purpose, settled into an English literary commonplace in the sixteenth and seventeenth centuries. Lovelace's "black cave or grot" was no more realistic than Milton's "Stygian cave forlorn" or William Browne's "uncouth place, Where hags and goblins might retire a space," which was ultimately Spenser's, though the "beloved caves" of Charles Cotton were actual features of the "Peak." In the "grotto fad" that peppered English estates with artificial retreats, the new geology merged with old literary conventions to produce something that distinguishes eighteenth-century caves and caverns from those of their predecessors. Responding to Nature,

---

[24] Mark Akenside, *The Pleasures of Imagination* (London, 1744), I, 512–519.

they yearned for Art: responding to Art, they realized that Nature's caverns put their own to shame. If a "grot" were natural, it must be improved by Art; if artificial, it must seem to follow Nature.[25] Since, as Henry Brooke said,

> The Maker! ample in his bounty, spread
> The various strata of Earth's genial bed,[26]

it was the duty and the privilege of His servant, the eighteenth-century poet, to seek further evidence of His Power and Glory in the hidden places of the earth.

Thomas Yalden had more reason than most poets to claim that his "useful verse" dealt with a novel theme, "What spacious veins enrich the British soil." [27] Earlier poets like Drayton had described barren, gloomy mining districts, but they had done so for topographical reasons, or half-apologetically, and had limited their descriptions to superficial aspects, feeling that such ugly places were not fitting subjects for poetry. To Yalden mining districts were ugly only as a woman in labor: "Earth, distorted with her pregnant womb." Yalden was no poet, even though he was one of the five that Samuel Johnson added to the

[25] It is interesting to watch this combination of Nature and Art in verses celebrating or describing grottoes. Cf. "Oakley: To Sir John Chetwode" in *Poems on Several Occasions* (Manchester, 1733), p. 109, in which Sir John Chetwode is praised for having on his estate "two pleasing Grottoes . . . One form'd by Art, and one by Nature's hand." In the longest single episode in *The Wanderer*, the traveler visits a hermit's cave, which, originally the product of wild Nature, has been so improved by Art that it seems like a "grot, delightful seat." Considering the fact that the hermit lives in one of the most remote regions of earth, he is remarkably up to date in his discussion of the "natural" crystals, which seem to have been developed into telescopic lenses.

[26] *Universal Beauty*, bk. III, ll. 21-22, in Chalmers, XVII, 346.

[27] "To Sir Humphry Mackworth," in Chalmers, XI, 74-75. The poem was written about 1698. The only seventeenth-century poem that resembles Yalden's is John Cleveland's "News from Newcastle; or, Newcastle Coal-Pits," published in 1659, but Cleveland's realism is so overshadowed by metaphysical conceits that the impression is entirely different.

list designed by his booksellers for *The Lives of the Poets*. Yet in "To Sir Humphry Mackworth" he was a pioneer in a fashion that caught popular fancy:

> Downward, my Muse, direct thy steepy flight,
> Where smiling shades and beauteous realms invite; . . .
> Through dark retreats pursue the winding ore,
> Seek Nature's depth, and view her boundless store;
> The secret cause in tuneful measures sing,
> How metals first were fram'd, and whence they spring.

He turned the old cosmic voyage to new uses; he capitalized upon the popular interest in geology, and he insisted that the mining regions of England were as legitimate themes for poetry as upland pastures or quiet hills. The extent to which realistic description of mining districts become a part of descriptive poetry may be seen in Richard Jago's description in the longest hill poem of the century, *Edge-Hill*, in which we are taken on a subterranean tour even more extensive and realistic than Yalden's.

Before Jago published his poem in 1767, however, popular interest in geology had grown to such an extent that tours to the earth's entrails were common. In 1755, Dr. John Dalton addressed verses to "two Ladies at their Return from Viewing the Mines near Whitehaven." [28] Led by "Prospero" (the colliery superintendent) the ladies made the Grand Tour of the subterranean world, emerging to see through new eyes the beauties of Cumberland. The "craggy cliff, impendent woods," "Rocky torrents," and "rough rocks of dread Lodore" emphasize the beauties of Keswick. The aesthetic reaction of the ladies, both to the bowels of the earth and to the ruggedness of the Cumberland landscape, is expressed in phrases which had been conventional ever since eighteenth-century men and women had begun to appreciate the irregularities of Nature:

[28] John Dalton, "A Descriptive Poem Addressed to Two Ladies," in *A Collection of Poems*, ed. by Pearch (London, 1770), I, 36–41.

> Horrors like these at first alarm
> But soon with savage grandeur charm,
> And raise to noblest thoughts the mind.

Jago concluded his long description of the mining districts of Warwickshire with a patriotic passage, urging Englishmen to be proud of their own mines and feel no envy for fabulous, far-off Potosí, Golconda, and Peru. But other poets who dealt with "rocks rich with mines, and mountains big with gems" let their fancies range to far-flung regions of the world to find "beds of glitt'ring ore and glowing gems," to imagine

> The miny caverns blazing on the deep
> Of Abyssinia's cloud-compelling cliffs.

When poets like Thomson sought "fatal treasures hid Deep in the bowels of the pitying earth," they found not English ore, but

> Golconda's gems, and sad Potosi's mines
> Where dwelt the gentlest children of the Sun.[29]

These exotic regions and others as remote summoned Christopher Smart's imagination from the beds of ocean:

> Hence, thro' the genial bowels of the Earth
> Easy my fancy pass; till at thy mines,
> Gani, or Raolconda, she arrive,
> And from the Adamant's imperial blaze
> Form weak ideas of her maker's glory.
> Next to Pegu, or Ceylon let me rove,
> Where the rich ruby (deem'd by sages old
> Of sovereign virtue) sparkles ev'n like Sirius
> And blushes into flames. Thence will I go
> To undermine the treasure-fertile womb
> Of the huge Pyrenean.[30]

[29] "Summer," ll. 869–870.
[30] Christopher Smart, "On the Immensity of the Supreme Being," in Chalmers, XVI, 30.

There is no more charming illustration of the combination of "new astronomy" and "new geology" than that of the eighteenth-century poets when they discovered Newton's prism in "rocks rich with gems." Nor is there a better example of their ability to find the Beautiful and the Sublime everywhere in Nature. In Thomson's "Summer," which begins with the light of the sun "in whom best seen shines out thy Maker," light, after playing "on rocks, and hills, and towers, and wandering streams," darts deep "into the embowelled caverns," where it wakens the precious stones. The white light of the diamond is resolved into the prismatic colors, running the gamut from the ruby of morning to the amethyst of evening. The colors come together in the "whitening opal," which reflects each one and again returns them to the white light from which they came. There is Beauty in the colors of the gems; light, the bright effluence of Deity, is sublime.[31]

V

If the "Mountain Glory" did not shine full splendor in the earlier eighteenth century, the "Mountain Gloom" was gone. We find nothing to parallel Marvell's "unjust" and "hook-shouldered" mountains that deformed earth, nothing (except in conventional hymns) of the early Christian strain of abasing the hills in order to exalt the valleys. Mountains had ceased to be monstrosities and had become an integral part of varied and diversified Nature. One of the most striking changes that has come about is the extensiveness of the mountain descriptions in both the "excursion" and the "physicotheological" poets.

Poets like Richard Blackmore and Henry Needler, to be sure, were still conventional in their treatment of mountains, still in-

[31] "Summer," ll. 142–152. In *Newton Demands the Muse*, pp. 26 ff., I have discussed various passages in which the eighteenth-century poets interpret precious stones in connection with Newton's prism. As I have suggested there, Thomson and many of these other poets associate color with Beauty and light with Sublimity.

clined to justify them intellectually rather than enjoy them emotionally. Their position was largely that of Ray and Derham, whom they were evidently reading. Blackmore devoted a long passage of over one hundred and fifty lines [32] in the first book of the *Creation* to the "amazing skill" shown in the structure of the earth:

> See how the hills, which high in air ascend,
> From pole to pole their lofty lines ascend.

Since Blackmore's poem was intended as a reply to Lucretius, however, it is natural that his desire was chiefly to prove that mountains were not waste places, but that they performed an important function in the structures of earth. This is true even of the passage that has frequently been quoted as suggesting that Blackmore found aesthetic gratification in mountains:

> See how sublime th' uplifted Mountains rise,
> And with their pointed Heads invade the Skies. . . .
> The hollow Vales their smiling Pride unfold,
> What rich abundance do their bosoms hold?

Although Blackmore was chiefly concerned with the old utilitarian argument, he showed a stirring of the new consciousness of geology that marks all these poets. He raised three of the chief problems that writers in the Burnet controversy had debated: the relation of mountains to the production of minerals and gems; the problem of the stratification of the earth; and the question of the relationship of mountains to the origin of rivers and springs. Henry Brooke, most scientific of these poets, de-

---

[32] Blackmore, *Creation*, I, 338–470, in Johnson's *Works of the English Poets*, vol. XXIV. Ray's *Wisdom of God* was still widely read. Even more popular was William Derham's *Physico-Theology*, published in 1713, which went through many editions and was one of the most popular "scientific" handbooks for two generations of poets. Derham's mountain passages were largely based on Ray, from whom he picked up the many utilitarian "justifications." Blackmore parallels him so closely in the *Creation*, which appeared in the same year, that he might have been writing with a copy of the *Physico-Theology* before him.

veloped all these themes *in extenso*, but each theme is suggested by a majority of the poets when they come to their mountain passages. Various ideas suggested among the followers and antagonists of Burnet appear and reappear. If minerals and metals were not created on the Third Day, have they been concocted by the action of the sun upon subterraneous matter? Are they "petrific seeds"? Did they grow like vegetables, as a result of sap circulating in the body of the earth? Are they perhaps not mineral at all, but vegetable or animal? We have already seen the interest of the Burnet writers in theories of stratification, which made the Mundane Egg quite different from what it had been before. And the problem of the circulation of waters still remained.

Blackmore's mountain passages suggest the danger shared by all these "physicotheological" poets of allowing their intellectual interests to obscure emotional feeling. In spite of a vocabulary that included "sublime," "astonished," "amazing," and various other clichés that were being popularized by Longinians, there is no indication that Blackmore took any pleasure in mountains, or indeed that he ever looked at them. His passages are filled with generalizations. This is not true of Mallet or Jago, not true even of Brooke, who for all his scientific terminology and even more scientific footnotes had his occasional poetic moments. It was certainly not true of James Thomson.

Thomson was as scientific in his description of mountains as any poet except Henry Brooke. The different versions of *The Seasons* show the extent to which he reworked his passages on the relationship of mountains to rivers and streams, turning now to this authority, now to that. "Attraction," "distillation," "percolation"—all the theories are here, drawn from authorities Thomson had been reading. One need only compare his long passage on the origin of waters with that immediately preceding to see the danger faced by these poets who had become over conscious of geology—too careful reading and pondering upon scientific problems might obscure real art. But if scientific interest had an adverse effect upon eighteenth-century art, in another way it was performing an important service in teaching eyes to see more exactly and helping offset the widespread tendency of the day to think in terms of general Nature. Earlier poets had thought about mountains generically. Thomson had actually looked at them and seen them. He had watched the fog settle over a mountain such as he was describing in the passage that led to his long digression upon distillation and percolation:

> No more the mountain, horrid, vast, sublime,
> Who pours a sweep of waters from his sides,
> And high between contending kingdoms rears
> The rocky long division, fills the view
> With great variety; but in a night
> Of gathering vapour, from the baffled sense,
> Sinks dark and dreary. Thence expanding far,
> The huge dusk gradual swallows up the plain;
> Vanish the woods: the dim-seen river seems,
> Sullen and slow, to roll the misty wave. . . .
> The huge dusk, gradual, swallows up the plain.
> Vanish the woods. . . .
>   Indistinct on earth,
> Seen thro' the turbid air, beyond the life,
> Objects appear; and, wilder'd, o'er the waste
> The shepherd stalks gigantick; till at last,
> Wreath'd around, in deeper circles still
> Successive, sits the general fog
> Unbounded o'er the world, and mingling thick,
> A formless grey confusion covers all.[33]

Thomson had an important prerequisite for his appreciation of the mighty and majestic works of God which he emphasized

[33] "Autumn," ll. 711–731. Alan Dugald McKillop has discussed the variant versions of this passage, together with authorities whom Thomson followed or consulted during the composition of the poem (*The Background of Thomson's Seasons*, pp. 77 ff.).

in his apostrophe to Nature: he was a Scot. Like Thomson's own
Laplanders, many Scots

> ask no more than simple Nature gives;
> They love their mountains, and enjoy their storms.[34]

As Wordsworth in Cumberland, Thomson grew up among hills
in Roxburghshire. Wordsworth's university years were spent
in the fen country, Thomson's corresponding period among the
grand irregularities of Edinburgh. When Thomson made the
Grand Tour, he experienced no such shock as had writers of
the earlier century. There is no horror or repulsion in the lines
describing his memory of the Alps—only personal reminiscences:

> their shaggy mountains charm
> More than or Gallic or Italian plains;
> And sickening fancy oft, when absent long,
> Pines to behold their Alpine views again—
> The hollow-winding stream: the vale, fair-spread
> Amid an amphitheatre of hills,
> Whence, vapour-winged, the sudden tempest springs,
> From steep to steep ascending, the gay train
> Of fogs thick-rolled into romantic shapes;
> The flitting cloud, against the summit dashed;
> And, by the sun illumined, pouring bright
> A gemmy shower—hung o'er amazing rocks,
> The mountain ash, and solemn sounding pine;
> The snow-fed torrent, in white mazes tossed
> Down to the clear ethereal lake below;
> And, high o'ertopping all the broken scene,
> The mountain fading into sky.[35]

[34] "Winter," ll. 845–846. Thomson knew Burnet's work well. The lines
in "Spring" (309–316) about Burnet's theory of the Deluge have already
been quoted in chapter Six. There are other passing references to spots
left by Nature in her rage (e.g., *Liberty*, IV, 283–284), as well as the
correspondence with Mallet.

[35] *Liberty*, IV, 344–360.

"Although Thomson occasionally climbed a hill," writes Alan Dugald McKillop, "[his mountain] landscapes are for the most part imaginary." This is true, of course, of many passages in Thomson's vast, expansive canvas that included mountains as remote and exotic as his rivers and deserts. When his Muse scaled "the Nubian mountains, and the secret bounds Of jealous Abyssinia," or sped to "Tornea's lake, And Hecla flaming through a waste of snow," the poet was certainly writing with his eye not on the object but on books.[36] The most majestic of his extended mountain passages is naturally imaginary—the roll call of the greatest mountains in the world, in which he remembered, as did many others, Burnet's obituary spoken over the mountains which were the last vestiges of creation to be dissolved by the Conflagration:

> Oh! lay the mountains bare, and wide display
> Their hidden structure to the astonished view;
> Strip from the branching Alps their piny load,
> The hugh incumbrance of horrific woods
> From Asian Taurus, from Imaus stretched
> Athwart the roving Tartar's sullen bounds;
> Give opening Hemus to my searching eye,
> And high Olympus pouring many a stream!
> Oh, from the sounding summits of the north,
> The Dofrine Hills, through Scandinavia rolled
> To farthest Lapland and the frozen main;
> From lofty Caucasus, far seen by those
> Who in the Caspian and black Euxine toil;
> From cold Riphaean rocks, which the wild Russ
> Believes the stony girdle of the world;
> And all the dreadful mountains wrapt in storm

[36] Professor McKillop has shown the sources of these passages, as well as the Lapland scenes and others. Although he is undoubtedly correct in the parallels he finds between Thomson's catalogue of the mountains and sources in Varenius and Abbé Pluche, the mood of the catalogue seems to me reminiscent of the *Sacred Theory*.

Whence wide Siberia draws her lonely floods;
Oh, sweep the eternal snows! Hung o'er the deep,
That ever works beneath his sounding base,
Bid Atlas, propping heaven, as poets feign,
His subterranean wonders spread! Unveil
The miny caverns, blazing on the day,
Of Abyssinia's cloud-compelling cliffs,
And of the bending Mountains of the Moon!
O'ertopping all these giant-sons of earth,
Let the dire Andes, from the radiant Line
Stretched to the stormy seas that thunder round
The Southern Pole, their hideous deeps unfold!
Amazing scene! [37]

To disparage Thomson as a mountain poet—a persistent tendency even among critics who admire other aspects of his nature poetry [38]—is to misread him. Perhaps because so much scholarship has been devoted to his sources, he is made to appear more derivative and "literary" than he was. Thomson drew from books, to be sure—as did Wordsworth.[39] He followed estab-

[37] "Autumn," ll. 779–807.

[38] This tendency has been curiously persistent. As I mentioned in the Introduction, Myra Reynolds, who was far ahead of her contemporaries in her appreciation of some aspects of Thomson, declared: "Towards mountains Thomson held almost the traditional attitude." Even Mr. McKillop, like Miss Manwaring and Mr. Hussey, seems to dismiss his more rugged landscape as largely in the "picturesque" tradition. After quoting two passages from *Liberty*, Mr. McKillop says (*The Background of Thomson's Seasons*, pp. 73–75): "All this illustrates the cult of the varied prospect rather than any profound feeling for the bleak, the austere, or the awful. Mountain regions afforded sweeping and varied views. Precipices and storms are part of the 'softer Canvas.' The picturesque thus becomes a sentimental, decorative mode, and falls in with Thomson's idyllic vein. Although Thomson occasionally climbed a hill, such landscapes are for the most part imaginary."

[39] In no. VI of Wordsworth's "Descriptive Sketches," notes for which were "taken during a pedestrian tour among the Alps," the author added: "For most of the images in the next sixteen lines, I am indebted to M. Raymond's interesting observations, annexed to his translation of Coxe's Tour in Switzerland." His editors and critics have added many more.

lished literary traditions—as again did Wordsworth. When he wrote, "Thus up the mount, in airy vision rapt, I stray, regardless whither," he was probably, like many another poet, sitting in his study. Yet his waterfall was recollected in tranquillity. He knew "thy hill, delightful Shene," and had seen the prospects he described. Even though his "raptured eye" sweeps over the "goodly prospect" in the manner of Denhan, Dyer, and other hill poets, he enjoyed those evening walks as sincerely as Wordsworth enjoyed his:

> Now the soft hour
> Of walking comes to him who lonely loves
> To seek the distant hills, and there converse
> With nature.[40]

In 1743, when he was visiting the Lyttletons at Hagley Park and working on the revisions of *The Seasons*, he added passages that came from his own experience. His description of a favorite walk at Hagley may be "picturesque," but it is not less sincere. At this time, too, he localized a thunderstorm, which in earlier versions had been generalized, and brought it home to Wales, "amid Carnarvon's mountain . . . the rude rocks of Pennmanmaur . . . and Snowdon's peak." [41] In early versions of "Summer," Thomson had briefly mentioned his native Scottish hills, but in later editions he transferred the passage to "Autumn," expanding it greatly to include Caledonia's mountains, forests, lakes, and rivers. The most austere, the most dour, and in some ways the most realistic of all his mountains are those in "Winter." The "loose disjointed cliffs and fractured mountains wild" need no specific location, but when the "father of tempests . . . wrapt in glooms" descends upon the north and "joyless rains . . . dash up the mountain's brow and shake the woods," [42] we feel ourselves in the Scotland that Thomson knew in youth.

Thomson is the finest English mountain poet before Words-

[40] "Summer," ll. 1379–1382.   [41] *Ibid.*, ll. 1161–1168.
[42] "Autumn," ll. 880–893; "Winter," ll. 69 ff.

worth. As we look back over the many earlier writers who had described hills and mountains, we appreciate his range, his virtuosity, his affection for hills, his admiration for mountains. The canvas of *The Seasons* is so extensive that it includes, as Thomson intended, nearly all the phenomena of Nature at various seasons, at various times of day and night. Among them what were still called "rugosities" held a high place. Sometimes his hills are generalized like those of the seventeenth century—"swelling mounds Thrown graceful round by Nature's careless hand," "graceful with hills and dales." Hills that he had climbed—Shene, Hagley Park, Dodington, and the "pure Dorsetian downs"—are real to us, as they were to him. In common with his generation, Thomson preferred the "broken scene." *The Seasons* abounds in rocks, cliffs, precipices. The "pointed promontory's top" sparkles in the sun or is dreary and desolate with "amazing frown," "Abrupt, projecting horror on the blackened flood." The mountains may be "romantic, forest-crowned"; they may be "horrid, vast, sublime." Waterfalls and cataracts sometimes enhance beauty, sometimes add terror, "broad brown cataracts of snow-fed torrents," rushing on to destruction.

Mountains and promontories, caves, caverns, and mines, exotic lands and rivers never seen by English eyes, the Ruins of Nature and the Ruins of Time—all are integral parts of the new Nature, filled with variety and diversity, majestic, magnificent, vast:

> O Nature! all-sufficient! over all
> Enrich me with the knowledge of thy works;
> Snatch me to heaven; thy rolling wonders there,
> World beyond world, in infinite extent
> Profusely scattered o'er the blue immense,
> Show me; their motions, periods, and their laws
> Give me to scan; through the disclosing deep
> Light my blind way: the mineral strata there;
> Thrust blooming thence the vegetable world;
> O'er that the rising system, more complex,

Of animals; and, higher still, the mind,
The varied scene of quick-compounded thought,
And where the mixing passions endless shift;
These ever open to my ravished eye—
A search, the flight of time can ne'er exhaust.[43]

VI

After the long "excursion" that has led us from the reaches of
the new cosmic space to the expanded earth of the eighteenth
century, we return to a point from which we started: the belief
of nineteenth-century literary historians that the change in mountain attitudes could be explained by the fact that Thomas Gray
crossed the Alps, kept a journal, and wrote letters in which he
expressed emotions presumably never felt before. Familiar though
the passages are, they may bear repetition against the background established here. To a greater extent than we realize, we
carry with us on our travels what we find. Gray was self-
consciously prepared for his Alpine experience, as Burnet and
Dennis could not have been. As he himself wrote to Richard
West when he was visiting the ruins of Rome: "Mr. Walpole
says our memory sees more than our eyes in this country." [44] It
is comparatively easy to reconstruct many of the "memories"
Gray carried with him when he crossed the Alps.

In 1739 Horace Walpole and Thomas Gray set out on the
Grand Tour, respectively twenty-two and twenty-three years
of age. When they were born, Burnet's Alpine experiences were
already ancient history, though the *Sacred Theory* was still
widely known. Dennis, Shaftesbury, and Addison had been read

[43] "Autumn," ll. 1352–1366.
[44] Thomas Gray, *Works*, ed. by Edmund Gosse (New York, 1885),
II, 79. The extent to which Gray was self-consciously prepared for various
experiences is suggested in a letter to West from Turin, November 16,
1739 (*ibid.*, II, 44–45): "I own I have not, as yet, anywhere met with
those grand and simple works of Art, that are to amaze one, and whose
sight one is to be the better for." He added: "But those of Nature have
astonished me beyond expression."

by their fathers before them. The early books of *The Seasons* had been published when they were children, the first collected edition of it, Mallet's *Excursion*, Savage's *Wanderer*, and other "excursion" poems when they were entering adolescence. Classically trained (Gray was to be one of the best classical scholars of his generation), they had nevertheless grown up in a period when "the picturesque" was familiar, Italian landscape admired, the cult of "the Sublime" in full flower, when poets, critics, aestheticians praised the vast, the grand, the wild. Indeed, a work published by a minor writer shortly before Gray and Walpole left England implies that there was an established recipe for the "sublime" experience. In an essay, "How the mind is rais'd to the Sublime," Hildebrand Jacob said: "A Mind truly disposed for the Perceptions of that, which is great and marvelous, whether in nature or in art, is a product of nature and cannot be attained through study. All the vast and wonderful Scenes . . . which the Universe affords, have this Effect upon the Imagination." [45] Among the "Scenes" are ocean in calm or storm, the rising and setting sun, dreadful precipices, caverns, and great ruins. Burnet and Dennis had been shocked because the Alps violated their theories of Beauty. Gray and Walpole went abroad fully expecting to experience the Sublime.

In the Alps, as later in the Apennines, the young travelers encountered "indifferent weather," which obscured the "beauties" they had anticipated and emphasized the savageness of the landscape. They were fully conscious of the dangers they encountered. "Mount Cenis, I confess," Walpole wrote to Richard West, "carries the permission mountains have of being frightful too far; and its horrors were accompanied with too much danger to give one time to reflect upon their beauties." [46] A day or two

[45] The essay was published in Hildebrand Jacob, *Works* (London, 1735), pp. 421–426. I have borrowed the reference from Samuel Monk, *The Sublime* (New York, 1935), pp. 60–61.

[46] Horace Walpole, *Letters*, ed. by Mrs. Paget Toynbee (Oxford, 1903), I, 38. The letter is dated from Aix in Savoy, September 30, 1793 (N.S.).

before the ascent of Mont Cenis, Walpole's dog had been killed by a wolf. Gray wrote to his mother: "We were at that time in a very rough road, not two yards broad at most; on one side was a great wood of pines, and on the other a vast precipice. . . . If [the dog] had not been there, and the creature had thought fit to lay hold of one of the horses; chaise, and we, and all must inevitably have tumbled above fifty fathoms perpendicular down the precipice." Arrived at the foot of Mont Cenis, they discovered to their consternation that it "is so situated as to allow no room for any way but over the top of it. Here the chaise was forced to be pulled to pieces, and the baggage and that carried by mules. We ourselves were wrapped up in our furs, and seated upon a sort of matted chair without legs, which is carried upon poles in the manner of a bier, and so begun to ascend by the help of eight men." [47] Alpine travel was exactly as dangerous in Gray's time as it had been in Coryat's. But though fear remained, it was transmuted by Gray's time into the "Terror" that was an integral part of the Sublime experience.

The ascent to the Grande Chartreuse remained in Gray's mind as the high point of his Alpine experience. Even here he was fully aware of danger, for, as he wrote to West, "You have Death perpetually before your eyes, only so far removed as to compose the mind without frighting it." [48] Mingled with fear but transcending it was an exaltation such as he had never before experienced. He set down his first impressions briefly in his journal: "Magnificent rudeness, and steep precipices. . . . You here meet with all the beauties so savage and horrid a place can present you with; Rocks of various and uncouth figures, Cascades pouring down from an immense height out of hanging Groves of Pine-Trees, & the solemn Sound of the Stream, that roars below, all concur to form one of the most poetical scenes imaginable." [49] As time went on, the scene became increasingly "poeti-

[47] Gray, *Works*, II, 41–42.   [48] *Ibid.*, II, 45.
[49] "Journal in France, 1739," in *Works*, I, 244.

cal." He described it to his mother, using several phrases from the journal, declaring that it was "one of the most solemn, the most romantic, and the most astonishing views I ever beheld." To West he wrote: "In our little journey up to the Grande Chartreuse, I do not remember to have gone ten paces without an exclamation, that there was no restraining. Not a precipice, not a torrent, not a cliff, but is pregnant with religion and poetry. There are certain scenes that would awe an atheist into belief, without the help of other arguments." [50] At about the same time, Walpole wrote to their friend:

But the road, West, the road! winding round a prodigious mountain, and surrounded with others, all shagged with hanging woods, obscured with pines, or lost in clouds! Below, a torrent breaking through cliffs, and tumbling thick fragments of rocks! Sheets of cascades forcing their silver speed down channeled precipices, and hasting into the roughened river at the bottom! Now and then an old foot-bridge, with a broken rail, a leaning cross, a cottage, or the ruins of an hermitage! This sounds too bombast and too romantic to one that has not seen it, too cold for one that has. If I could send you my letter post between two lovely tempests that echoed each other's wrath, you might have some idea of this noble roaring scene, as you were reading it. [51]

The "grand works of Art," which Gray had expected to "improve" his taste and "amaze" him, fell short of his expectations, but, although he went abroad as fully prepared for the "Sublime" experience as anyone can be, he found that the works of Nature "have astonished me beyond expression." Throughout his life he continued to feel the enthrallment of the vast, the wild, the irregular, as his experiments in poetry and his letters and later journals show. Nearly thirty years after he had crossed the Alps, he wrote to William Mason:

I am returned from Scotland, charmed with my expedition; it is of the Highlands I speak; the Lowlands are worth seeing once, but the mountains are ecstatic, and ought to be visited in pilgrimage once a year. None but those monstrous creatures of God know how to join so much beauty with so much horror. A fig for your poets, painters, gardeners, and clergymen, that have not been among them; their imagination can be made up of nothing but bowling-greens, flowering shrubs, horseponds, Fleet ditches, shell grottoes, and Chinese rails. Then I had so beautiful an autumn, Italy could hardly produce a nobler scene.[52]

VII

In 1744, five years after Gray's Grand Tour, Thomson published the revised *Seasons*, Young the complete *Night Thoughts*, Akenside *The Pleasures of Imagination*. In their various ways, they brought together the strands of the rhetorical and the natural Sublime, which had been developing in parallel, and made them into a pattern which the youthful Burke employed when in the mid-century he wrote his *Philosophical Inquiry into the Origin of Our Ideas of the Sublime and Beautiful*.[53]

Thomson was on the whole content to draw and paint the new, expansive, diversified Nature, rather than to psychologize upon her effect upon the soul of man. Aware of Beauty though he was, particularly in "Spring," he was still more conscious of the sublimity of Nature, as both his descriptions and his vocabulary show, though he went to no such extremes of language as did many of his contemporaries and made less attempt at a self-conscious analysis of his own emotions. When he used the Longinian vocabulary, it was not lip service, but an attempt to

[52] Gray, *Works*, III, 223.

[53] Burke's essay was published in 1756 or 1757, but the original draft, read before the club Burke had founded at Trinity College, Dublin, may well have been written about 1748, when Burke was nineteen years old. I have discussed Burke's possible debt to the earlier poets in *Newton Demands the Muse*, pp. 123 ff. In that book I have developed a number of points which I raise here only in passing.

express sincere emotion. In the tender mood of "Spring" he felt "all various Nature pressing on the heart," but in "Summer," when "great are the scenes with dreadful Beauty crowned," [54]

> Deep-roused, I feel
> *A sacred terror, a severe delight.*

"Devotion" rises to "rapture and astonishment" in "Autumn":

> With swift wing
> O'er land and sea imagination roams,
> Or truth, divinely breaking on his mind,
> *Elates his being,* and *unfolds his powers.*

"Summer" and "Winter" are the most "sublime" books of *The Seasons*, because their subjects led to those extremes which Burke later stressed: heat and cold, light and darkness, calm and violence. In "Winter" Thomson apostrophized his Muse and his goddess:

> Nature! great parent! whose unceasing hand
> Rolls round the Seasons of the changeful year.
> How mighty, how majestic are thy works!
> *With what a pleasing dread they swell the soul,*
> *That sees astonished,* and *astonished sings.*

Beauty and Sublimity are everywhere in Thomson's Nature, "to reason's and to fancy's eye displayed." Reason may comprehend Nature, but it is Fancy that "receives"

> The whole magnificence of heaven and earth,
> And every beauty, delicate or bold.

Although Fancy still "receives" rather than "creates," [55] we have come a long way from the nature poetry of the seventeenth century.

[54] In the following passages I have purposely italicized the phrases which by this time were current in the Longinian vocabulary.

[55] This I have discussed in *Newton Demands the Muse,* particularly pp. 167 ff.

In the 1744 edition of *The Pleasures of Imagination*, Akenside was in part versifying Addison's essays, in part adapting to his own period the categories of the vast, the wonderful, the fair.[56] Akenside was not a landscape poet. Though he introduced scenery, it was always generic. He thought of himself as a philosophical poet, drawing upon many systems of philosophy, welding them into a system which he considered his own. Unlike Thomson, who was as concrete as Akenside was abstract, he was not concerned with the Beautiful and the Sublime as they appear in Nature, but with the effect upon man of

> The uncreated images of things;
> The radiant sun, the moon's nocturnal lamp,
> The mountains, woods and streams, the rolling globe.[57]

Elsewhere I have discussed his equation of color with Beauty and of light with Sublimity and the extensive passage in which, combining Addison, Shaftesbury, and various Neoplatonic predecessors, he traced the "rising lustre" of Nature's charms, from the simple beauty of color to the sublime "meridian splendor" of light.[58]

Akenside made every attempt to be just both to Beauty and to the Sublime:

> We hasten to recount the various springs
> Of adventitious pleasure, which adjoin
> Their grateful influence to the prime effect
> Of objects grand or beauteous, and inlarge
> Their complicated joy.[59]

But, like his generation, he was most concerned with the effect of the Sublime, to him the highest Beauty:

[56] The 1744 version develops each of the three categories; in the later version published in 1772 Akenside omitted the "wonderful" and stressed only the Sublime and the Beautiful.

[57] Akenside, *The Pleasures of Imagination*, I, 66–68.

[58] *Newton Demands the Muse*, pp. 117 ff.

[59] *The Pleasures of Imagination*, II, 69–73.

> Or shall I mention, where coelestial truth
> Her awful light discloses, to effuse
> A more majestic pomp on beauty's frame? [60]

He was interested in the effect of Sublimity upon the soul of man:

> Wherefore darts the mind,
> With such resistless ardor to embrace
> Majestic forms? [61]

He pondered, as did Longinus, "what high capacious powers lie folded up in man?" rousing him to aspire to an Infinite beyond his powers of comprehension but never beyond his imagination or his desires.

Akenside leads us back to the seventeenth-century empyrean of Burton's hawk and More's "enlargèd arms." For a time the eighteenth-century poets have seemed more interested in the expanded earth than in the extended heavens. Akenside's "high-born soul" sets off on another cosmic voyage, the companion of those storms and whirlwinds that had become the stuff of "Sublime" poetry:

> The high-born soul
> Disdains to rest her heav'n-aspiring wing
> Beneath its native quarry. Tir'd of earth
> And this diurnal scene, she springs aloft
> Thro' fields of air; pursues the flying storm;
> Rides on the volley'd lightning thro' the heav'ns,
> Or yolk'd with whirlwinds, and the northern blast
> Sweeps the long tract of day. Then high she soars
> The blue profound.[62]

Sublunary meteorological disturbances outdistanced, the soul rises through the new universe of the new astronomy, through "the redundant streams of light," past the "reluctant planets";

[60] *Ibid.*, II, 97–99.   [61] *Ibid.*, I, 169–171.
[62] *Ibid.*, I, 183–191.

then "up the long career of devious comets," she "looks back on all the starrs whose blended light, as with a milky zone, invests the orient," until

> amaz'd she views
> Th' empyreal waste, where happy spirits hold,
> Beyond this concave heav'n, their calm abode; . . .
> Ev'n on the barriers of the world untir'd
> She meditates th' eternal depth below;
> Till, half recoiling, down the headlong steep
> She plunges; soon o'erwhelm'd and swallow'd up
> In that immense of being.[63]

The climax of the conception of the "vast Sublime" is found in the "Ninth Night" of the *Night Thoughts*. No poet was ever more "space intoxicated" than Edward Young, nor did any other eighteenth-century poet or aesthetician equal him in his obsession with the "psychology of infinity"—the effect of vastness and the vast upon the soul of man. He is par excellence the poet of the Sublime. There is no Beauty in the "Ninth Night," no landscape, no color, only passing feeling for the small and exquisite, though, to be sure, he acknowledged the minute in Nature as evidence of God's power:

> True; all things speak a God; but in the small,
> Men trace out him; in great, he seizes Man;
> Seizes, and elevates, and raps, and fills.[64]

As I have said elsewhere: "There is no color in the world of the *Night Thoughts;* there is only light, the 'confluence of ethereal fires From urns unnumber'd,' streaming from the steep of heaven. Young's external nature is dark and void of color. His was, indeed, the kind of world which the telescope had shown the moon to be, a world shining only by reflected light, white and dead." [65] Young had no desire to emulate the "excursion" poets

[63] *Ibid.*, I, 201–211   [64] Young, *Night Thoughts*, IX, 772–774.
[65] *Newton Demands the Muse*, p. 150.

in describing Nature on this earth. His song "shot, ambitious of unbounded scenes, Beyond the flaming limits of the world." His canvas is interstellar space, his technique that of the cosmic voyagers, the "soaring souls that sail among the spheres." Like Shaftesbury's Philocles, Young's Lorenzo, who had remained obstinately unconvinced throughout eight long, tedious books of the *Night Thoughts,* was converted by the "mathematic glories of the skies," after his mentor led him on a series of cosmic voyages, to approach, as closely as human imagination can ever approach, the Source of Vastness, the true Infinite:

> Loose me from earth's inclosure, from the sun's
> Contracted circle set my heart at large;
> Eliminate my spirit, give it range
> Through provinces of thought yet unexplor'd. . . .
> Thy travels dost thou boast o'er foreign realms:
> Thou stranger to the world! thy tour begin.[66]

"The soul of man was made to walk the skies." From prison released, imagination, spirit, and soul rise to freedom in an infinity native to them, as finite earth had never been. Here for the first time

> she can rove at large;
> There, freely can respire, dilate, extend,
> In full proportion let loose all her pow'rs;
> And, undeluded, grasp at something great.[67]

In space, "the noble pasture of the mind," the soul "expatiates, strengthens, and exults," realizing to the full potentialities which had long lain dormant:

> How great,
> How glorious, then, appears the mind of man,
> When in it all the stars, and planets, roll!
> And what it seems, it is; Great objects make

[66] *Night Thoughts*, IX, 586–606.   [67] *Ibid.*, IX, 1016–1023.

> Great minds, enlarging as their views enlarge;
> Those still more godlike, as these more divine.[68]

Greatness and vastness are the keynotes of the "Ninth Night," as they were the basis of Young's belief. His is the Romantic insatiability that refuses to be content with the present or with the finite in any form. It is the mood of Henry Power's "elastical souls of the universe," who recognized no "Non Plus Ultra," of Henry More and of Thomas Traherne, whose souls would not be satisfied with less than the all they could never attain. There is no frustration here—only an exultant awareness that there are worlds beyond, that the more man knows, the more there is to know, that the true greatness of man lies in his ability to aspire far beyond his potentialities. Happiness lies in aspiration, in discontent with limitations:

> The mind that would be happy, must be great,
> Great in its wishes; great in its surveys.
> Extended views a narrow mind extend;
> Push out its corrugate, expansive make.[69]

The discontent is "divine," implanted by God in man, who has a "previous sense of objects great." This is God's way of leading man on from limitation to infinite perfection:

> Nature delights in progress; in advance
> From worse to better: But when minds ascend,
> Progress, in part, depends upon themselves.[70]

Here for the first time Young uses the word "progress" in the sense in which it has been understood down to our own time. If "progress" is not yet as inevitable in Nature as it became in the Darwinian period, nevertheless Young has gone far beyond the simple idea of "progress" of the Baconian generation. Man can, if he will, proceed farther and farther in perfectibility through

[68] *Ibid.*, IX, 1059–1064.   [69] *Ibid.*, IX, 1379–1382.
[70] *Ibid.*, IX, 1957–1959.

the full range of powers native to him, by refusing to be content
with the limitations which the finite would impose upon him, by
giving free rein to that "soul," which is not finite but infinite:

> The soul of man, His face design'd to see,
> Who gave these wonders to be seen by Man,
> Has here a previous sense of objects great,
> On which to dwell; to stretch to that expanse
> Of thought, to rise to that exalted height
> Of admiration, to contract that awe,
> And give her whole capacities that strength,
> Which best may qualify for final joy.
> The more our spirits are enlarg'd on earth,
> The deeper draughts shall they receive of Heav'n.[71]

Whether Infinite Space or Infinite God—in Young's vocabulary
they seem to be much the same, though his emphasis is even more
upon Space than upon God—

> Nothing can satisfy, but what confounds;
> Nothing, but what astonishes, is true.[72]

In spite of Young's obsession with infinite space, he did not
forget that other concept which had dawned upon his generation—infinite time. "Eternity," he said, "is written in the stars."
As he led his pupil on the journeys through the universe of stars
and planets, he mused:

> The boundless space, through which these rovers take
> Their restless roam, suggests the sister thought
> Of boundless time.[73]

The old limitations of time and space are gone. The long-winged
hawk of human imagination has not only world enough, but cosmic universe beyond cosmic universe, stretching perhaps to
infinity. Time, which had long been limited by the Six Days'
works—even by six millennia—has become Eternity. The dread

[71] *Ibid.*, IX, 568–577.   [72] *Ibid.*, IX, 836–837.
[73] *Ibid.*, IX, 1172–1174.

of the end of the world that had hovered so possessively over the earlier seventeenth century has vanished before a sense of space and time more intoxicating than it has ever been since the mid-eighteenth century. The Millennium has come—and has come on earth.

In a single passage in the "Ninth Night," [74] Young indicated the basic shift in taste that makes the new aesthetics of the eighteenth and nineteenth centuries different from all that went before. For centuries aestheticians had been more interested in Art than in external Nature. The "great," the "amazing," the "marvellous" had been found in the Seven Wonders of the World—the pyramids, the hanging gardens of Babylon, the Temple of Diana at Ephesus, the Colossus, the Olympian Zeus of Phidias, the Pharos. All these were the works of man, the works of Art. With one exception Young dismissed such "childish toys":

> Thy watery columns squirted to the clouds!
> Thy bason'd rivers and imprison'd seas!
> Thy mountains moulded into forms of men!
> Thy hundred-gated capitals. . .
> Arches triumphal, theatres immense
> Or nodding gardens pendent in mid-air!

These are the work of "Vain Art! thou pigmy pow'r," that seems to swell and strut with pride, only to show its own littleness. In one work of Art alone he found greatness. Like Addison before him, Byron later, and his own contemporary Dyer, he said: "Enter a temple. It will strike an awe." Even the pagan temples might be "proud to meet their gods half-way"; in Christian cathedrals men felt the shadow of divinity.

Far greater than the works of man were the works of Nature in the geocosm, reflecting as they did the vastness of Space and Deity:

[74] *Ibid.*, IX, 905–931. I have purposely reversed Young's order.

Seas, rivers, mountains, forests, deserts, rocks,
The promontory's height, the depth profound
Of subterranean, excavated grots,
Black-brow'd, and vaulted high, and yawning wide,
From Nature's structure, or the scoop of Time:
If ample of dimension, vast of size,
Ev'n these an aggrandizing impulse give;
Of solemn thought enthusiastic heights
Ev'n these infuse.

"But what of vast in these?" Young asks. He replies, "Nothing:
—or we must own the skies forgot." Yet great objects make
great minds, and even the lesser majesties of earth discovered by
Young's contemporaries had enlarged their thoughts and led
them to greater awe for the true Vast from whom their own
potentialities were drawn.

From Art—far less important now than it had been for centuries—through grand Nature in this world, through cosmic
Space, eighteenth-century imagination rose to the true Vast, the
Infinite. From that Infinite, through the reaches of space discovered by the new astronomy, sublimity descended to exalt
and ennoble "the wide Sea and the Mountains of the Earth."
Such was the process of "The Aesthetics of the Infinite."

VIII

We have reached the end of our journey, a far longer journey
than we had anticipated. It is time to stop and look back, to
remember the lines in which Drummond and Pope—and a half-
dozen other English poets—paraphrased Lucretius. At the beginning of the journey it seemed easy to take "short views . . .
nor see the lengths behind":

But more advanced, [we] behold with strange surprise
New distant scenes of endless science rise.

"New distant scenes of science," we have learned, were discovered by our ancestors, "Scientia" leading at one time to

philosophy, at another to what we today call "science." Radical changes have taken place in both. These changes and many others have put an end to certain theological presuppositions that long colored the vision of men when they looked at Nature "And God saw everything that he had made, and behold, it was very good. And there was evening and there was morning, the sixth day." So it was in the beginning. But we have also heard the ominous words, "Cursèd is the earth." As time has gone on both these conceptions have gradually disappeared. The miracle of the Six Days' work has been replaced by ideas of long and leisurely earth processes. For a long time we have heard no echo of the dread phrase about the cursing of the earth. Genesis has given way to geology which in turn has led scientists and laymen to look at a new earth with different eyes. Even the poetic vocabulary has changed. Well down into the seventeenth century, as we have seen, men who wrote of mountains described them in conventional, generic, or allegorical terms, inherited from the classics or the Bible. In the eighteenth century, poets have been drawing their mountain imagery less from books more from actual observation. They are looking at mountains and seeing them, attempting to describe them with the eye on the object. *Sight* has become important to an extent not recognized before. Philosophers, scientists, poets, and novelists spoke their sympathy for "a man born blind" because he was deprived of the pleasures of sight.[75] Secondary "pleasures of the imagination" have become much less important than primary pleasures arising from the actual observation of grand objects in Nature. Age-old assumptions and unconscious presuppositions that had made for "Mountain Gloom" have all but disappeared. In their place have arisen other fundamental assumptions and precon-

[75] In *Newton Demands the Muse*, pp. 82–85, I have discussed the interest of Locke, Molyneux, and Berkeley in this theme and have briefly indicated that it may be found also in Steele, Fielding, Watts, Johnson, and others. Wordsworth was still interested in it in *The Prelude*.

ceptions, which we accept today and which, three hundred years from now, may seem as strange to our descendants as the "warts and wens" of the seventeenth century seem to us. Whether time will find them right or wrong, they have banished the gloom and made it possible for us to lift up our eyes to the "Mountain Glory." Pope's imagery of a long journey over a mountain range looked back to the past, and its language was the derivative one we have almost forgotten. Wordsworth's tribute to the imagination in the last book of *The Prelude* may better serve as conclusion and as transition:

> This faculty hath been the feeding source
> Of our long labour; we have traced the stream
> From the blind cavern whence is faintly heard
> Its natal murmur; followed it to light
> And open day; accompanied its course
> Among the ways of Nature, for a time
> Lost sight of it bewildered and engulphed;
> Then given it greeting as it rose once more
> In strength, reflecting from the placid breast
> The works of man and face of human life;
> And lastly, from its progress have we drawn
> Faith in life endless, the sustaining thought
> Of human Being, Eternity, and God.[76]

[76] *The Prelude*, XIV, 193–205.

Epilogue

All hail, Sublimity! thou lofty one,
    For thou dost walk upon the blast, and gird
Thy majesty with terrors, and thy throne
    Is on the whirlwind, and thy voice is heard
In thunders and in shakings; thy delight
    Is in the secret wood, the blasted heath,
The ruin'd fortress, and the dizzy height,
    The grave, the ghastly charnel-house of death,
In vaults, in cloisters, and in gloomy piles,
Long corridors and towers and solitary aisles!

SO Alfred Tennyson wrote about 1825. ("I was between 15 and 17," [1] he noted in a later Preface to *Poems by Two Brothers*.) Taking his point of departure from a sentence in Burke's *Essay on the Sublime and Beautiful*, which he quoted as epigraph— "The sublime always dwells on great objects and terrible"—the youthful poet stirred together the ingredients prescribed in recipes of the eighteenth century to make "the mixture as be-

---

[1] "On Sublimity," in *Poems by Two Brothers* (New York, 1893), pp. vi, 103–108.

fore." In Tennyson's "On Sublimity" we find all the familiar themes, settings, and adjectives: rugged mountains, familiar and remote, Teneriffe's peak, Kilda's giant height; the mighty deep, the wild cascade, Niagara's flood of matchless might, immense, sublime, magnificent, profound; elemental forces of Nature, echoing winds, forked bolts of lightning, loud Stromboli and the quaking isles; august cathedrals, with bones of prelates beneath the pavements, tombs that gape and yawn, the pillared cave of Morven's giant king (side by side with Kentucky's chamber of eternal gloom [2]); black night, lurid light, shadows but half-distinguished:

> These, these are sights and sounds that freeze the blood,
> Yet charm the awe-struck soul which doats on solitude.

An adolescent poet, born when the cult of sublimity was at its peak, may be forgiven such a pastiche of the obvious, particularly when most of the Romantic poets he admired had lingered over emotions experienced when crossing the Alps. The English traveler of the early nineteenth century now went abroad conditioned by attitudes diametrically opposed to those of Burnet and Dennis. Like Gray and Walpole he self-consciously anticipated the "sublime" experience. Indeed, as Wordsworth noted in his *Guide to the Lakes*, "A stranger to mountain imagery naturally on his first arrival looks out for sublimity in every object that admits of it." [3] As the century went on, the traveler, armed with his "guides" and with the poems of Wordsworth, Byron, and Shelley, gazed at the Alps or the lesser sublimities

---

[2] Niagara became a part of "sublime" poetry in England at least as early as James Ralph's *Night* (1728). I have not found an earlier reference to the supposed sublimity of the Kentucky caverns, which Tennyson says he picked up from an article in the *Monthly Magazine* for October, 1816.

[3] Wordsworth, *Guide to the Lakes* (London, 1835), p. 99. The *Guide* was first published anonymously in 1810 as an introduction to Joseph Wilkinson's *Select Views of Cumberland*.

of the Lake District and felt, or thought he felt—or pretended to feel—as Burnet or Dennis or Wordsworth actually had felt.

At the end of the nineteenth century, Samuel Butler (himself a sincere admirer of grand Nature, as his *Alps and Sanctuaries of Piedmont and Ticino* shows) had his fun with the type of English tourist who traveled to the Alps to "emote." "Mr. George Pontifex," Butler wrote in *The Way of All Flesh*, "went abroad more than once." Like all well-taught travelers he kept a diary. "The author before starting had made up his mind to admire only what he thought it would be creditable to admire, *to look at nature and art only through the spectacles that had been handed down to him by generation after generation of prigs and impostors*":

The first glimpse of Mont Blanc threw Mr. Pontifex into a conventional ecstasy. "My feelings I cannot express. I gasped, yet hardly dared to breathe, as I viewed for the first time the monarch of the mountains. I seemed to fancy the genius seated on his stupendous throne far above his aspiring brethren and in his solitary might defying the universe. I was so overcome by my feelings that I was almost bereft of my faculties, and would not for worlds have spoken after my first exclamation till I found some relief in a gush of tears. With pain I tore myself from contemplating for the first time 'at distance dimly seen' (though I felt as if I had sent my soul and eyes after it) this sublime spectacle." [4]

Later, on a Sunday, he visited the Mer de Glace and inscribed in the visitors' book lines he considered "suitable to the day and scene," a neat parody on some of the eighteenth-century poets:

> Lord, while these wonders of thy hand I see,
> My soul in holy reverence bends to thee.
> These awful solitudes, this dread repose,
> Yon pyramid sublime of spotless snows,
> These spiry pinnacles, those smiling plains,

[4] Samuel Butler, *The Way of All Flesh* (New York, 1950), ch. iv. The italics are mine.

> This sea, where one eternal winter reigns,
> These are thy works, and while on them I gaze
> I hear a silent tongue that speaks thy praise.

"Taking the verses all round," said Butler, "I should say that Mr. Pontifex was right in considering them suitable to the day; I don't like being too hard even on the Mer de Glace, so will give no opinion as to whether they are suitable to the scene also." Mr. Pontifex went on to the Great St. Bernard where he again contributed some verses, this time in Latin. "He also took good care to be properly impressed by the Hospice and its situation." He wrote in his diary:

The whole of this most extraordinary journey seemed like a dream, its conclusion especially, in gentlemanly society, with every comfort and accommodation amidst the rudest rocks and in the region of perpetual snow. The thought that I was sleeping . . . in the highest inhabited spot in the old world and in a place celebrated in every part of it, kept me awake some time.

"As a contrast to this," wrote Overton-Butler, "I may quote here an extract from a letter written to me last year by his grandson Ernest. . . . The passage runs: 'I went up to the Great St. Bernard and saw the dogs.' "

Butler dated the Alpine travels of Mr. George Pontifex shortly after the Battle of Waterloo, but his satire was leveled not at the contemporaries of Wordsworth who were really feeling the emotions Mr. Pontifex pretended, but at travelers of his own time, who no longer had the experience of Burnet, Dennis, or Gray, for a reason that Wordsworth himself made clear in 1844 when he protested the building of a Kendal and Windermere Railway through the Lake District. In his letter to the editor of the *Morning Post*, Wordsworth quoted his own lines on the Simplon Pass. He went on to say:

Thirty years afterwards, I crossed the Alps by the same Pass; and what had become of the forms and powers to which I had been indebted for those emotions: Many of them remained of course undestroyed and indestructible. But, though the road and torrent continued to run parallel to each other, their fellowship was put an end to. The stream had dwindled into comparative insignificance, so much had Art interfered with and taken the lead of Nature. . . . The oratories heretofore not infrequently met with, on a road still somewhat perilous, were gone; the simple and rude bridges, swept away; and instead of travellers proceeding, with leisure to observe and feel, were pilgrims of fashion hurried along in their carriages, not a few of them perhaps discussing the merits of "the last new novel," or poring over their Guide-books, or fast asleep.[5]

Mountain travel had become safe and rapid and comfortable; the old "Sublime," involving "Horror" and "Terror," was gone. But it had still been an integral part of the traveler's experience when the young Romantics brought to an artistic climax the new descriptive poetry that had been developing throughout the eighteenth century.

There is no sharp line of demarcation between the "excursion poems" and such descriptive poems as *The Excursion* and *The Prelude*, *Alastor*, and *Childe Harold's Pilgrimage*. Even though elements have entered that were not present in the earlier period, the broader settings, the smaller details, the themes, even the moods, are similar. The Burnet controversy was a thing of the remote past, though Shelley, Wordsworth, and Coleridge remembered the *Sacred Theory*. In "The Pass of Kirkstone" Wordsworth saw in "stone or rock" a "model roughly hewn, And left as if by earthquake strewn, Or from the Flood escaped." The Wanderer in *The Excursion* [6] looked down from an eminence on a smooth green valley:

> In rugged arms how softly does it lie,
> How tenderly protected! Far and near
> We have an image of the pristine earth,
> The planet in its nakedness.

[5] *Guide to the Lakes*, pp. 163–164. [6] *The Excursion*, II, 358–361.

In the light passages in *Prometheus Unbound* [7] Shelley, like earlier poets who had followed the Burnet controversy, was conscious of "the melancholy ruins of cancelled cycles" in fossils and petrification of "anchors, beaks of ships, Planks turned to marble,"

> The anatomies of unknown winged things,
> And fishes which were isles of living scale.

All these were "sepulchred emblems Of dead destruction, ruin within ruin!" From such ruins of a broken world, his mind turned to old theories of the destruction of that world by a comet,

> till the blue globe
> Wrapped deluge round it like a cloak, and they
> Yelled, gasped, and were abolished; or some God
> Whose throne was in a comet, passed, and cried,
> Be not! and like my words they were no more.

Most of all, as we have seen, Coleridge had felt the spell of Burnet's mountains and his graphic pictures of the Conflagration. In *The Road to Xanadu*, we feel, as did Professor Lowes when he discovered the *Sacred Theory*, "the electric contact of one mind with another," and share the illumination of imagination in lines based on Burnet in "The Ancient Mariner" on "the bloody Sun, at noon," or "the central fires through nether seas upthundering" in the "Ode to the Departing Year." "Burnet's titanic conception of a dark illimitable ocean, lurking between the unmeasured gulfs and chasms of the world," Professor Lowes wrote of "Kubla Khan," "was present (I think we may safely assume) somewhere in the background of the dream." [8] But except in the case of Coleridge, Burnet reminiscences among the Romantic poets are incidental. They are not self-consciously knitted into the pattern of their poetry, as had been the case

[7] *Prometheus Unbound*, IV, 270–318.

[8] John Livingston Lowes, *The Road to Xanadu* (Boston and New York, 1927), pp. 159–160, 502–503, 393–394.

among the "excursion" poets who were discovering a "new geology" for the first time. The Romantic poets experienced neither the shock nor the enthrallment of the seventeenth-century poets at the birth of a new cosmos or that of the eighteenth-century poets when a new world rose from the ashes of the old (even though Wordsworth at least lived into a period self-conscious about a "new geology"). Wordsworth, Coleridge, Byron, and Shelley grew up with conceptions of time and space that had once startled or captivated their ancestors. Yet they were as responsive as earlier poets had been to themes that had become basic to eighteenth-century poetry.

Ruskin's visitor to the art gallery, whom we met in the Introduction, had been as much surprised at the ruins as at the mountains he saw everywhere on the gallery walls. His contemporary "intelligent reader," whom we introduced to Romantic descriptive poetry, would have found ruins almost as persistent a motif as they had been among the "excursion" poets. Wordsworth alone, among the three poets we considered earlier, seldom paused to describe them.[9] Such subjects as Tintern Abbey and Peele Castle led him rather to meditation than to description. But Byron, like the eighteenth-century poets, stumbled on ruins wherever he went. Steeped in the Gothic tradition as he was, he could outdo the Gothic novelists with his "seven pillars of Gothic mould In Chillon's dungeons deep and old." "Wandering in youth," like Childe Harold, he had seen the ruins of Aegina, Piraeus, and Corinth. He was intensely conscious of the Ruins of Time, symbolized in "hillocks heap'd On what were chambers, arch crush'd, column strown In fragments." The sense of time particularly affected him when, like so many of his predecessors, he remembered his emotions among the ruins of the Coliseum:

[9] There are occasional glimpses of ruins in Wordsworth's longer descriptive poems. On his travels he wrote sonnets on the ruins of a convent in the Apennines, on Furness Abbey, and on the ruins of a castle in North Wales.

> There is given
> Unto the things of earth, which Time hath bent,
> A spirit's feeling; and where he hath leant
> His hand, but broke his scythe, there is a power
> And magic in the ruin'd battlement. . . .
> Oh, Time! the beautifier of the dead,
> Adorner of the ruin . . .
> Time the avenger.[10]

Byron's dirge was not confined to Rome. As he pondered "the crush'd relics of the vanquished might" of Italy, he thought of Dante's tomb and Petrarch's, of "Machiavelli's earth return'd to whence it rose."

> But my soul wanders; I demand it back
> To meditate amongst decay, and stand
> A ruin amidst ruins; there to track
> Fall'n states and buried greatness, o'er a land
> Which *was* the mightiest in its old command,
> And *is* the loveliest.[11]

Since Shelley's Poet in *Alastor* was "a youth of uncorrupted feelings" who desired "familiarity with all that is excellent and majestic," he inevitably sought the Ruins of Time that had exalted the thoughts of his predecessors; he found them in Athens and Tyre "and the waste where stood Jerusalem," among "the fallen towers Of Babylon, the eternal pyramids"

> till meaning on his vacant mind
> Flash'd like strong inspiration, and he saw
> The thrilling secrets of the birth of time.[12]

The experiences of Shelley's Poet among ruins are as traditional as those of the "excursion" poets among whom the ruin motif

[10] *Childe Harold's Pilgrimage*, canto IV, stanzas lxxix–lxxx, cvii, cxviii–cxxx. There is another extensive description of the Coliseum in *Manfred*, III, iv, 8–32.

[11] *Manfred*, IV, xxv   [12] *Alastor*, ll. 126–128.

had settled into a literary convention. But no one before Shelley
had caught the vast sweep of indefinite time or the irony that
mingled the Ruins of Art with the Ruins of Time as he did in
"Ozymandias," the literary climax of the long ruin tradition:

> Round the decay
> Of that colossal wreck, boundless and bare
> The lone and level sands stretch far away.

The "secret places of the earth" still charmed the Romantic
poets,[13] most of all Shelley. Mont Blanc's "vast caves shine in
the rushing torrent's restless gloom." Her caverns echo to "a
loud, lone sound no other sound can make." Caves, chasms, and
"the tongueless Caverns of the craggy hills" are everywhere in
Prometheus Unbound. The mysterious "little boat" in which the
Poet in *Alastor* "fled before the storm" pursued "the windings
of the cavern" and "huge caves Scoop'd in the dark base of their
aery rocks." There are moments when Shelley's caves and
caverns vividly recall Thomson's "Summer"[14] and Thomas
Heyrick's "Submarine Voyage," though there are many more
when Shelley's levels of meaning are far removed from either of
those predecessors. The caves that were Ruins of Nature to the
eighteenth-century poets have been touched by Neoplatonic
mysticism to become symbols of secret places in the soul of man.
Coleridge, including but transcending the conventions estab-

[13] Byron, except for an occasional passing reference to mountain caves
in *Manfred*, paid little attention to this theme. Wordsworth wrote four
sonnets about the caves of Staffa. An odd example of the survival of a
tradition is the fairly extensive—and really unnecessary—passage in *The
Prelude* (VIII, 559–589) on

> The curious traveller, who, from open day,
> Hath passed with torches into some huge cave,
> The grotto of Antiparus, or the Den
> In old time haunted by the Danish witch . . .

[14] This is particularly true in Panthea's long speech on light (*Prometheus
Unbound*, II, ii, 10 ff.) which in its whole structure is strongly reminiscent
of the corresponding passage on light in "Summer."

lished by the eighteenth-century poets, gave supreme expression to the description of "the secret places of Nature,"

> Where Alph, the sacred river, ran
> Through caverns measureless to man
> > Down to a sunless sea. . . .
> But oh! that deep romantic chasm which slanted
> Down the green hill athwart a cedarn cover!

Byron and Shelley, at least, shared the relish of earlier poets for thunderstorm and tempest, earthquake and volcanic eruption, though they no longer needed to weigh and balance scientific theories of the origin of such phenomena to such an extent as Brooke and Mallet and even Thomson. In *Manfred* are voices of slumbering earthquake, of hurricane and lightning, of volcanoes and toppling crags of ice, of the "avalanche, whom a breath draws down In mountainous o'erwhelming." Childe Harold exulted in mountain storms:

> > > Far along,
> From peak to peak, the rattling crags among
> Leaps the live thunder! Nor from one lone cloud
> But every mountain now hath found a tongue,
> And Jura answers, through her misty shroud,
> Back to the joyous Alps, who call to her aloud! [15]

In *Prometheus Unbound*, too, we hear through the voices of spirits, of elements or Furies, the cry of earthquake and of thunderbolt, the whirlwind-peopled mountain, the white fire that has cloven the snow-laden cedar, the volcano's meteor-breathing chasm:

> > The sound is of whirlwind underground,
> > Earthquake, and fire, and mountains cloven;
> > The shape is awful, like the sound. [16]

[15] *Childe Harold's Pilgrimage*, III, xcii.
[16] *Prometheus Unbound*, I, 231-233.

Byron is not at all "scientific" in his use of these phenomena. *Prometheus Unbound* may be, as it has been interpreted, "a drama of the chemical elements"; Shelley's volcanoes, as a recent critic has pointed out,[17] may have been based upon his scientific knowledge, but the science does not intrude—as in some of the eighteenth-century poets—into the poetry. It is an integral part of it. This is not only because Byron and Shelley were greater poets than Mallet and Brooke, important though that is. It is in part because many disparate elements that were still in flux during the eighteenth century have been brought into equilibrium, so that the Romantic poets, conscious though they are of geology, have ceased to be self-conscious and need no longer intellectualize their emotions. If this is true of such lesser matters as the poetic treatment of the violent phenomena of Nature, it is far more profoundly true in the feeling of nearly all the Romantic poets for two major concepts which underlie their descriptive poetry: eternity and infinity.

"Shakespeare lived in a world of time, Milton in a universe of space." The souls of Henry More and Thomas Traherne soared not only into a universe but into an infinity of universes, as did Young's voyagers in the "Ninth Night." Philosophy and science had broken down the barriers that for so long "cabin'd, cribb'd, confin'd" man, who had felt himself "pester'd in this pin-fold here." Many seventeenth-century poets had been self-conscious about space, many eighteenth-century writers self-conscious about time. The Romantic poets no longer needed to argue and debate philosophical theories of either space or time. They were natural heirs to their great tradition of infinity and eternity. The sense of the vastness of Nature that once appalled has become a part of their goodly heritage, as has the feeling for an irregu-

---

[17] In "A Volcano's Voice in Shelley" (*E.L.H.*, XXIV [Sept., 1957], 191–228), G. M. Matthews has studied Shelley's many references to volcanoes and earthquakes and suggested possible sources in Shelley's reading and personal experience.

larity that need not be either justified or condemned. Nature *is* vast; Nature *is* irregular. The poets—no longer victims of the "abhorred shears" that had once cut man from Nature and Nature from man—are involved in Nature. Mountains and ocean, like the sweep of indefinite time or the sense of infinite space, are shadows of divinity. In their presence or in memories of them, poets experience even more fully than in the past an expansion of imagination, a stretching spirit of "elastical souls of the Universe." Mountains and ocean are overwhelming in themselves, but even more in their adumbration of the power or benignity of the God who made them. "Among the more awful scenes of the Alps," Wordsworth wrote to his sister a few days after he first crossed the Simplon Pass, "I had not a thought of man, or a single created being, my whole soul was turned to him who produced the terrible majesty before us." [18]

Byron alone among the major Romantic poets seems to have experienced—or at least expressed—the response to the vast in architecture that we have found in Addison and other writers of the preceding century. Manfred's memory, like Childe Harold's, turned back to the Coliseum when the moon

> cast a wide and tender light,
> Which soften'd down the hoar austerity
> Of rugged desolation, and fill'd up,
> As 'twere anew, the gaps of centuries;
> Leaving that beautiful that still was so,
> And making that which was not, till the place
> Became religion.[19]

Most of all, Byron's "elastical soul" expanded in St. Peter's, which moved him to language he used elsewhere only in connection with mountains and other grand aspects of Nature:

[18] This is in the Keswil letter written by Wordsworth to his sister in September, 1790. I quote here from *The Prelude* edited from the manuscripts by Ernest de Selincourt (London, 1936), pp. 279–280.

[19] *Manfred*, III, iv, 292–298.

But lo, the dome, the vast and wondrous dome
To which Diana's marvel was a cell,
Christ's mighty shrine above his martyr's tomb! . . .

Enter: its grandeur overwhelms thee not;
And why? it is not lessen'd; but thy mind,
Expanded by the genius of the spot,
Has grown colossal.[20]

A mountain analogy immediately came to Byron's mind:

Thou movest—but increasing with the advance,
Like climbing some great Alp, which still doth rise,
Deceived by its gigantic elegance;
Vastness which grows, but grows to harmonize—
All musical in its immensities.

As with grand Nature, "thou seest not all" upon a glance; the whole is more than the sum of the parts. Again we find an analogy with Nature, this time with ocean that "many bays will make." Let man control his thoughts "until thy mind hath got by heart Its eloquent proportions." Then he will feel his imagination expanding with the vastness it contemplates,

Till, growing with its growth, we thus dilate
Our spirits to the size of that they contemplate.

Byron's stanzas, describing the emotions of Childe Harold in St. Peter's, are the finest expression of man's growing feeling for "The Aesthetics of the Infinite" in the presence of that lesser vast, architecture:

The fountain of sublimity displays
Its depth, and thence may draw the mind of man
Its golden sands, and learn what great conceptions are.

Upon a mountain pass in 1671 Thomas Burnet had experienced emotions in the presence of mountains which he had formerly felt in Nature only when he considered the heavens, the work

[20] *Childe Harold's Pilgrimage*, IV, cliii–clix.

of God's fingers. He had been led to make a sharp distinction between what he had always called Beauty and what he did not yet recognize as Sublimity. Mountains, ocean, and "those boundless regions where the Stars inhabit" shared "the Shadow and Appearance of INFINITE, as all Things have that are too big for our Comprehension," so that "they fill and overbear the Mind with their Excess, and cast it into a pleasing kind of Stupor and Admiration." [21] The conceptions of beauty and sublimity, which had seemed so "truly Paralel" that they could never meet, have merged, so that the Romantic poets no longer feel the sharp distinction of Burnet or Dennis or Addison.

Byron, who often shows his eighteenth-century heritage, seemed to emphasize the old distinction more than did the others. His "night thoughts" frequently led him—or his characters—to peace and serenity, to beauty, as we have seen in Manfred's memories of the Coliseum by moonlight. At the beginning of the soliloquy, Manfred says:

> The stars are forth, the moon above the tops
> Of the snow-shining mountains,—Beautiful!
> I linger yet with Nature, for the Night
> Hath been to me a more familiar face
> Than that of man; and in her starry shade
> Of dim and solitary loveliness
> I learn'd the language of another world.[22]

On the shores of "clear placid Leman," Childe Harold also felt the eternal calm and the beauty and mystery of "Ye stars! which are the poetry of heaven":

> All heaven and earth are still—though not in sleep,
> But breathless, as we grow when feeling most;
> And silent as we stand in thoughts too deep;—
> All heaven and earth are still: From the high host

[21] Thomas Burnet, *Sacred Theory*, I, 188–189.
[22] *Manfred*, III, iv, 1–7.

> Of stars, to the lull'd lake and mountain-coast,
> All is concenter'd in a life intense . . .
> Then stirs the feeling infinite, so felt
> In solitude, when we are *least* alone.[23]

But this is not Byron's customary mood, nor are these quiet scenes the most recurrent in either *Manfred* or *Childe Harold's Pilgrimage*. Across the peace and beauty of the night on Lake Leman came a storm:

> The sky is changed!—and such a change! Oh night,
> And storm, and blackness, yet are wondrous strong,
> Yet lovely in your strength.[24]

"Most glorious night!" Childe Harold exults as the storm gathers fury, "Let me be A sharer in thy fierce and far delight, A portion of the tempest and of thee!" The phrases that came most often to Byron's lips in descriptions of grand Nature were such words and epithets as, "rapture," "horribly beautiful," "charming the eye with dread," "rocks that shock, yet please the soul." To Childe Harold and to Manfred, Nature was more often in motion than at rest:

> Ye Elements, in whose ennobling stir,
> I feel myself exalted.

Sound and motion and elemental energy—even elemental fury—led Byron to exultation, even more than to exaltation:

> The roar of waters!—from the headlong height
> Velino cleaves the wave-worn precipice;
> The fall of waters! rapid as the light
> The flashing mass foams skirting the abyss;
> The hell of waters! where they howl and hiss,
> And boil in endless torture; . . .
>   how profound
> The gulf! and how the giant element

---

[23] *Childe Harold's Pilgrimage*, III, lxxxv.   [24] *Ibid.*, xcii–xciii.

> From rock to rock leaps with delirious bound,
> Crushing the cliffs, which, downward worn and rent,
> With his fierce footsteps, yield in chasms a fearful vent! . . .
> Lo! where it comes like an eternity,
> As if to sweep down all things in its track,
> Charming the eye with dread, a matchless cataract,
> Horribly beautiful! [25]

Byron's most characteristic Sublime in external Nature was less a higher Beauty than—like that of Burnet and Dennis—something distinct from Beauty, involving violence, terror, exultation. In every mood he was immensely responsive to mountains: "Are not the mountains, waves and skies a part Of me and of my soul, as I of them?" The Alps, those "palaces of Nature" that "throned Eternity in icy walls Of cold sublimity," were the greatest manifestations on earth of the Power that had created them. "All that expands the spirit, yet appals Gather around these summits." In all their moods—and in all his moods—high mountains were indeed a feeling to Byron.

Shelley's characteristic epithets for grand Nature were often similar to Byron's: "terrible, strange, sublime, and beauteous shapes"; "dizzy Ravine"; "dizzy distances"; "awful scene"—the adjective "awful" is often on his lips. He, too, was conscious of elemental Nature in motion:

> dark, deep Ravine—
> Thou many-coloured, many voiced vale,
> Over whose pines, and crags, and caverns sail
> Fast cloud-shadows, and sunbeams! awful scene,
> Where Power in likeness of the Arve comes down
> From the ice-gulfs that gird his secret throne,
> Bursting through these dark mountains like the flame
> Of lightning through the tempest! [26]

But the total effect of Shelley's description of grand Nature is very different from that of Byron. Movement and change, of

[25] *Ibid.*, IV, lxix–lxxii. [26] "Mont Blanc," ll. 12–19.

which he too was ever-conscious, were not, as they often seem in Byron, the rapidly shifting scenes of a kaleidoscopic Nature, which swings exultantly from one extreme to another. Since to Shelley earth is but a shadow, "the shadow of some spirit lovelier still,"

> The everlasting universe of things
> Flows through the mind, and rolls its rapid waves,
> Now dark—now glittering—now reflecting gloom—
> Now lending splendour, where from secret springs
> The source of human thought its tribute brings.[27]

Shelley was as conscious as Byron of the "joy, and exultation" inspired by "the majesty of Earth." But Shelley added, as Byron did not, "mystery" to "majesty."

Shelley's clouds change, but cannot die. His autumn leaves are driven over the universe to quicken a new birth. The waterfalls around Mont Blanc "leap for ever"; "the chainless winds still come and ever come"; the "dizzy Ravine" is in constant restless motion:

> Thy caverns echoing to the Arve's commotion—
> A loud lone sound no other sound can tame.
> Thou art pervaded with that ceaseless motion,
> Thou art the path of that unresting sound.[28]

Yet for all the movement, all the change, all the apparent restlessness, "the strange sleep . . . Wraps all in its own deep eternity," and, in spite of earlier ruin by fire or earthquake, "all seems eternal now." Always surmounting change,

> Far, far above, piercing the infinite sky,
> Mont Blanc appears,—still, snowy and serene.

"This poem," Shelley said of "Mont Blanc," [29] "was composed under the immediate impression of the deep and powerful feel-

[27] *Ibid.*, ll. 1–5.   [28] *Ibid.*, ll. 30–33.
[29] Preface to *History of a Six Weeks Tour*, 1817; quoted in *Complete Poetical Works* (Boston and New York, 1901), p. 347.

ings excited by the objects which it attempts to describe; and, as an undisciplined overflowing of the soul, rests its claim to approbation on an attempt to imitate the untamable wildness and inaccessible solemnity from whence these feelings sprang." The cataracts, the gulfs of ice, the winds, and the ravine are wild and untamable but Mont Blanc remains, an earthly symbol of the eternal and the infinite, abiding evidence that One remains though many change and pass:

> All things that move and breathe with toil and sound
> Are born and die, revolve, subside and swell;
> Power dwells apart in its tranquillity,
> Remote, serene, and inaccessible;—
> And *this*, the naked countenance of earth
> On which I gaze, even these primeval mountains,
> Teach the adverting mind. . . .
> Mont Blanc yet gleams on high; the power is there,
> The still and solemn power of many sights
> And many sounds, and much of love and death. . . .
>   The secret strength of things,
> Which governs thought, and to the infinite dome
> Of heaven is as a law, inhabits thee! [30]

There is no mountain mood or attitude we have found since the dawn of the Mountain Glory that is not reflected in Wordsworth. In youth, as every reader of *The Prelude* or "Tintern Abbey" knows, he vacillated between moods of terror and exultation, with fear often predominant, "more like a man flying from something that he dreads than one Who sought the thing he loved," when he "heard among the solitary hills Low breathings coming after me" or when, alone in his boat at night, he felt only the terror of a mountain, familiar enough by day:

> the foundations of his mind were laid,
> In such communion, not from terror free,
> While yet a child, and long before his time,

---

[30] "Mont Blanc," ll. 94–100, 127–141.

> Had he perceived the presence and the power
> Of greatness; and deep feelings had impressed
> So vividly great objects that they lay
> Upon his mind like substances.[31]

Like many other children, even in "the morn of childhood" he had become vaguely aware of abstract ideas through familiar objects. Mountains first introduced him to concepts of eternity and infinity:

> a disappearing line
> One daily present to my eyes, that crossed
> The naked summit of a far-off hill
> Beyond the limits that my feet had trod,
> Was like an invitation into space
> Boundless, or guide into eternity.[32]

More fully than any other poet, Wordsworth recognized the great heritage of infinity and eternity, of which mountains remained throughout his life the great exemplars. "Compassed about by mountain solitudes" in youth, Wordsworth throughout his life found in mountains the supreme example in the natural world of the greatness which is the essence of sublimity. Like his Wanderer:

> Early had he learned
> To reverence the volume that displays
> The mystery, the life which cannot die;
> But in the mountains did he *feel* his faith.
> All things responsive to the writing, there
> Breathed immortality, revolving life,
> And greatness still revolving; infinite:
> There littleness was not; the least of things
> Seemed infinite; and there his spirit shaped
> Her prospects, nor did he believe—he *saw*.

---

[31] *The Excursion*, I, 132–138.   [32] *The Prelude*, XIII, 147–152.

> What wonder if his being thus became
> Sublime and comprehensive? [33]

In the *Guide to the Lakes* Wordsworth compared the emotional effect of the Alps with the sensations a visitor might expect in the English Lake District:

If a traveller be among the Alps, let him surrender up his mind to the fury of the gigantic torrents, and take delight in the contemplation of their almost irresistible violence. . . . Among the Alps are few places that do not preclude [the] feeling of tranquil sublimity. Havoc, and ruin, and desolation, and encroachment, are everywhere more or less obtruded; and it is difficult, nothwithstanding the naked loftiness of the *pikes,* and the snow-capped summits of the *mounts,* to escape from the depressing sensation that the whole are in a rapid process of dissolution; and, were it not that the destructive agency must abate as the heights diminish, would, in time to come, be levelled with the plains.

The prophecy of Isaiah still lingered, even if no longer theologically, in the minds of men who thought of mountains. Wordsworth went on to compare with the vehemence and violence and destructive havoc of the Alps the impression made by English mountains:

With respect to the mountains, though these are comparatively of diminutive size, and no voice of summer-avalanches is heard among them; and though traces left by the ravages of the elements are here comparatively rare and unimpressive, yet out of this very deficiency proceeds a sense of stability and permanence that is, to many minds, more grateful.[34]

The fury of the gigantic torrents, the irresistible violence, the perpetual change of encroachment and dissolution among the Alps gives way, in most of the mature descriptive poetry of

[33] *The Excursion,* I, 223–334.
[34] *Guide to the Lakes,* pp. 98–99. I have purposely reversed Wordsworth's order and combined two passages on the Alps.

the English Lake District, to a sense of stability and permanence, "the calm that Nature breathes among the hills and groves":

> the brook itself,
> Old as the hills that feed it from afar,
> Doth rather deepen than disturb the calm
> Where all things else are still and motionless.[35]

Among English mountains, the English poet found what he called "tranquil sublimity." As he stood on the top of Black Comb, his eye returned from ruggedness and wildness to the serenity of an English prospect:

> In depth, in height, in circuit, how serene,
> The spectacle how pure!—Of Nature's works
> In earth, and air, and earth-embracing sea
> A revelation infinite it seems;
> Display august of man's inheritance.[36]

Remembering both the dread and the rapture, the turmoil and "happy stillness" he had experienced among great natural objects, Wordsworth wrote toward the end of *The Prelude*:

> From Nature doth emotion come, and moods
> Of calmness equally are Nature's gifts;
> This is her glory; these two attributes
> Are sister horns that constitute her strength.[37]

In the "solemn temples" of mountains, Wordsworth had experienced the "earliest visitations" of emotions that remained with him all his life, whether among the Alps or when in England he lifted up his eyes to the peace of the everlasting hills.

In the lines on the Simplon Pass, perhaps written on the first visit to the Alps,[38] later incorporated into *The Prelude* and again

[35] "Airey-Force Valley."
[36] "View from the Top of Black Comb."
[37] *The Prelude*, XIII, 1–4.
[38] In all published versions "The Simplon Pass" is dated 1799, not 1790, the date of Wordsworth's first Italian journey. I am using the poem as if,

repeated in the letter to the editor of the *Morning Post,* Wordsworth brought to an artistic climax all the moods and themes poets had been trying to express since the Mountain Glory dawned in England. Old familiar motifs of the savagery and terror of Nature echo through his description of his early experience in the Alps: "winds thwarting winds, bewildered and forlorn"; "rocks that muttered close upon our ears"; "black drizzling crags"; "the sick sight and giddy prospect of the raging stream." Originally he added lines,[39] written presumably shortly after the ascent, that were omitted from later versions:

> And ever as we halted, or crept on,
> Huge fragments of primeval mountain spread
> In powerless ruin, blocks as huge aloft
> Impending, nor permitted yet to fall,
> The sacred Death-cross, monument forlorn
> Though frequent, of the perished travellers.

But this is not the final mood of the whole. If at times Wordsworth, like many poets before him, felt the antithesis of Beauty and Sublimity, his most characteristic Sublime included both beauty and terror as inevitable parts of the experience. Change and decay, which earlier poets had lamented, are in Nature, but they are an inevitable part of the "enormous permanences of Nature":

> The immeasureable height
> Of woods decaying, never to be decayed,
> The stationary blasts of waterfalls,
> And in the narrow rent at every turn
> Winds thwarting winds, bewildered and forlorn,
> The rocks that muttered close upon our ears,
> Black drizzling crags that spake by the way-side

---

as Wordsworth implied when he incorporated it into *The Prelude,* it had been composed at the time of his first Alpine experience.

[39] Quoted by Raymond Dexter Havens in *The Mind of a Poet* (Baltimore, 1941), p. 45.

> As if a voice were in them, the sick sight
> And giddy prospect of the raving stream,
> The unfettered clouds and regions of the Heavens,
> Tumult and peace, the darkness and the light—
> Were all like workings of one mind, the features
> Of the same face, blossoms upon one tree;
> Characters of the great Apocalypse,
> The types and symbols of Eternity,
> Of first, and last, and midst, and without end.[40]

Here is the perfect expression of "The Aesthetics of the Infinite," the transfer of Infinity and Eternity from a God of Power and a God of Benignity to Space, then to the grandeur and majesty of earth. From mountains, the mind and soul of man rises again, through Space, to Eternity and Infinity, with awe and reverence for the power of God, to the serene and tranquil peace that passes all understanding.

As in youth, so in maturity, among the Cumberland hills or among the Alps, mountains remained symbols to Wordsworth and to his generation of that "more beyond" to which imagination persistently aspires, of the eternity and infinity that are the unattainable goals of the imagination. In Wordsworth's ears continued to echo words he had heard—or thought he heard—in youth. "That voice was Nature's, uttered from her Alpine throne," reminding man of the power of the eternal hills and the power of all grand natural objects,

> that imaginative impulse sent
> From those majestic floods, yon shining cliffs,
> The untransmuted shapes of many worlds,
> Cerulean ether's pure inhabitants,
> Those forests unapproachable by death,
> That shall endure as long as man endures,
> To think, to hope, to worship, and to feel.[41]

[40] *The Prelude*, VI, 624–640. [41] *Ibid.*, VI, 462–468.

The Messenger Lectures

In their original form the first five chapters of this book consisted of six lectures delivered at Cornell University in April and May of 1948, namely, the Messenger Lectures on the Evolution of Civilization. That series was founded and its title prescribed by Hiram J. Messenger, B.Litt., Ph.D., of Hartford, Connecticut, who directed in his will that a portion of his estate be given to Cornell University and used to provide annually a "course or courses of lectures on the evolution of civilization, for the special purpose of raising the moral standard of our political, business, and social life." The lectureship was established in 1923.

Index

Mazonis, Jacobus, 149

Mede, Joseph, 126-127, 146, 186, 218, 239

Mercer, John, 99

"Metaphysical Society," 146 n, 185

Millennium, theories of, 125-127, 142, 366

Milton, John, 1, 8, 30, 31, 36, 40, 42, 51, 74, 79-80, 85, 86-87, 98, 100-107, 127, 150, 152, 160, 177, 185, 193, 206, 208, 232, 250-251, 273-276, 283 n, 284, 310, 325, 336, 341, 381

Mohler, Nora, 249 n

Molyneux, William, 245 n, 368

Monk, Samuel, 29-31, 276 n, 288 n, 310 n, 355 n

Montagu, Lady Mary Wortley, 21

Montesquieu, Charles Louis de Secondat, 32, 43 n

Moore, Cecil, vii, 21, 97 n, 191 n

More, Henry, 114-140, 146, 158, 167-168, 186, 218-220, 239, 242, 252, 254, 274, 297, 364, 381; *Antidote against Atheism*, 115-120; *Divine Dialogues*, 119-120, 135, 138-140; *Philosophical Poems*, 130-137; *Enchiridion Metaphysicum*, 135-136; *Enthusiasmus Triumphatus*, 219, 221, 296-299; mountains, 116-120, 138; Hobbes, 117-119; Lucretius, 118-121; aesthetics, 121-125, 138-139; apocalyptical interpretations, 125-130; Platonism, 130 ff.; new astronomy, 130-138; infinity, 132-137; Burnet, 218-220; enthusiasm, 219, 221, 296-299

Morgan, B. Q., 46 n

Mornet, D., 234 n

Mountains:
attitudes toward: classical, 7, 38-42, 220-222, 325-326; Scriptural, 42-45, 68-69; medieval, 46-52, 72-112; Renaissance, 8, 50-59; early trav-

elers, 55-56, 59-67; eighteenth century, 345-358; Romantic poets, viii, 1-17, 371-393; nineteenth-century critics, 17-27; Calvin, 99-100; Luther, 102-103; Hakewill, 108-111; More, 116-120, 138; Burnet, 184-224; Milton, 273-276; Dennis, 276-289; Shaftesbury, 289-291; Addison, 304-307; Thomson, 347-354; Gray, 354-358; Byron, 1, 9-11, 13, 16-17, 383-386; Ruskin, 4-7; Shelley, 8-9, 14-15, 379, 386-388; Wordsworth, 2-3, 12-14, 18, 174-175, 388-393

literary conventions, 35-71, 325-326; theological presuppositions, 72-112; theories of origin, 82-92, 196-200, 240-245; pragmatic defense, 109-111, 116-117, 121, 255-262, 345; effect of astronomy, 131-133, 140-143; mountains in the moon, 131-133, 140-143; geological theories, 144-183; altitude, 148-154; catalogues of, 223-224, 232, 350; effect of "Burnet controversy" on theories of, 253-270

"Mundane Egg," theories of, 78-81, 92, 100 n, 177, 183, 201, 203, 228, 245, 341, 347

Murray, Gilbert, 38

Nathan, Rabbi, 83

Needler, Henry, 345

Newton, Isaac, ix, x, 114, 126, 129, 135, 136, 158, 176, 187, 188, 234, 235, 245, 272, 279, 302, 309, 331

Nichols, William, 118

Ocean, xii, 7, 10, 14, 230, 270, 306-307, 382, 384

Ogden, H. S. V., xi, 209 n

Ogilvie, John, 229